Town and Country Planning Act 1990

CHAPTER 8

[A Table showing the derivation of the provisions of this consolidation Act will be found at the end of the Act. The Table has no official status.]

ARRANGEMENT OF SECTIONS

PART I

PLANNING AUTHORITIES

Local plans

Conformity between plans

Supplementary

PART III

CONTROL OVER DEVELOPMENT

Meaning of development

Requirement for planning permission

Development orders

Applications for planning permission

PART V

COMPENSATION FOR RESTRICTIONS ON NEW DEVELOPMENT IN LIMITED CASES

Preliminary

PART VI

RIGHTS OF OWNERS ETC. TO REQUIRE PURCHASE OF INTERESTS

CHAPTER I

INTERESTS AFFECTED BY PLANNING DECISIONS OR ORDERS

Service of purchase notices

PART VIII

SPECIAL CONTROLS

CHAPTER I

TREES

General duty of planning authorities as respects trees

Tree preservation orders

Compensation for loss or damage caused by orders, etc.

Consequences of tree removal, etc.

Trees in conservation areas

CHAPTER II

LAND ADVERSELY AFFECTING AMENITY OF NEIGHBOURHOOD

Application of Act as respects Crown land

Provisions relating to anticipated disposal of Crown land

Enforcement in respect of war-time breaches of planning control by the Crown

PART XIV

FINANCIAL PROVISIONS

PART XV

MISCELLANEOUS AND GENERAL PROVISIONS

Application of Act in special cases

Town and Country Planning Act 1990

1990 CHAPTER 8

An Act to consolidate certain enactments relating to town and country planning (excluding special controls in respect of buildings and areas of special architectural or historic interest and in respect of hazardous substances) with amendments to give effect to recommendations of the Law Commission.

[24th May 1990]

BE IT ENACTED by the Queen's most Excellent Majesty, by and with the advice and consent of the Lords Spiritual and Temporal, and Commons, in this present Parliament assembled, and by the authority of the same, as follows:—

PART I

PLANNING AUTHORITIES

Local planning authorities: general.

1.—(1) In a non-metropolitan county—

(a) the council of a county is the county planning authority for the county, and

(b) the council of a district is the district planning authority for the district,

and references in the planning Acts to a local planning authority in relation to a non-metropolitan county shall be construed, subject to any express provision to the contrary, as references to both the county planning authority and the district planning authorities.

(2) The council of a metropolitan district is the local planning authority for the district and the council of a London borough is the local planning authority for the borough.

PART I

(3) In England (exclusive of the metropolitan counties, Greater London and the Isles of Scilly) and in Wales all functions conferred on local planning authorities by or under the planning Acts shall be exercisable both by county planning authorities and district planning authorities.

(4) In this Act "mineral planning authority" means—

(a) in respect of a site in a non-metropolitan county, the county planning authority; and

(b) in respect of a site in a metropolitan district or London borough, the local planning authority.

(5) This section has effect subject to any express provision to the contrary in the planning Acts and, in particular—

1972 c. 70.

(a) subsections (1) to (4) have effect subject to sections 5 to 8 of this Act and Part I of Schedule 17 to the Local Government Act 1972 (National Parks);

(b) subsections (1) and (2) have effect subject to sections 2 and 9; and

(c) subsection (3) has effect subject to section 4 and Schedule 1 (which contains provisions as to the exercise of certain functions under this Act by particular authorities and liaison between them).

Joint planning boards.

2.—(1) If it appears to the Secretary of State that it is expedient that a joint board should be established as the county planning authority for the areas or parts of the areas of any two or more county councils or as the district planning authority for the areas or parts of the areas of any two or more district councils, he may by order—

(a) constitute those areas or parts as a united district for the purposes of this Act; and

(b) constitute a joint board (in this Act referred to as a "joint planning board") as the county planning authority or, as the case may be, the district planning authority for that united district.

(2) The Secretary of State shall not make such an order except after holding a local inquiry unless all the councils concerned have consented to the making of the order.

(3) Where a joint planning board is constituted for a united district, references in the planning Acts to the area of a local planning authority—

(a) in relation to the board, shall be construed as references to that district; and

(b) in relation to any local planning authority being the council of a county or district of which part (but not the whole) is included in the united district, shall be construed as references to so much of the county or district as is not so included.

(4) A joint planning board constituted by an order under subsection (1) shall consist of such number of members as may be determined by the order, to be appointed by the constituent councils.

(5) A joint planning board so constituted shall be a body corporate, with perpetual succession and a common seal.

(6) An order constituting a joint planning board and any order amending or revoking any order constituting a joint planning board— PART I

(a) may, without prejudice to the provisions of section 241 of the Local Government Act 1972 (which authorises the application of the provisions of that Act to joint boards), provide for regulating the appointment, tenure of office and vacation of office of members of the board, for regulating the meetings and proceedings of the board, and for the payment of the expenses of the board by the constituent councils; 1972 c. 70.

(b) may provide for the transfer and compensation of officers, the transfer of property and liabilities, and the adjustment of accounts and apportionment of liabilities;

(c) may contain such other provisions as appear to the Secretary of State to be expedient for enabling the board to exercise their functions; and

(d) may apply to the board, with any necessary modifications and adaptations, any of the provisions of sections 102 and 103 of the Local Government Act 1972.

(7) This section shall have effect subject to sections 5 to 9 of this Act and Part I of Schedule 17 to the Local Government Act 1972 (joint planning boards and special planning boards for National Parks).

Joint planning committee for Greater London. 1985 c. 51.

3.—(1) The joint planning committee for Greater London established under section 5 of the Local Government Act 1985 shall continue to discharge the functions mentioned in subsection (2).

(2) The joint planning committee shall—

(a) consider and advise the local planning authorities in Greater London on matters of common interest relating to the planning and development of Greater London;

(b) inform the Secretary of State of the views of those authorities concerning such matters including any such matters as to which he has requested their advice;

(c) inform the local planning authorities for areas in the vicinity of Greater London, or any body on which those authorities and the local planning authorities in Greater London are represented, of the views of the local planning authorities in Greater London concerning any matters of common interest relating to the planning and development of Greater London and those areas;

and the committee may, if it thinks fit, contribute towards the expenses of any such body as is mentioned in paragraph (c).

(3) The expenses of the joint planning committee which have been incurred with the approval of at least two-thirds of the local planning authorities in Greater London shall be defrayed by those authorities in such proportions as they may decide or, in default of a decision by them, as the Secretary of State may determine.

(4) References in this section to the local planning authorities in Greater London are to the authorities which are local planning authorities for the purposes of Part II.

PART I

National Parks.

4.—(1) As respects an area in a National Park outside a metropolitan county all functions conferred by or under the planning Acts on a local planning authority or district planning authority shall, subject to subsections (2) and (3), be functions of the county planning authority and no other authority, and references in those Acts in their application to a National Park outside a metropolitan county to a local planning authority or district planning authority shall be construed accordingly.

(2) The functions conferred on a local planning authority by sections 198 to 201, 206 to 209 and 211 to 215 shall as respects any part of a National Park outside a metropolitan county be exercisable concurrently with the county planning authority by the district planning authority whose area includes that part of the Park.

1949 c. 97.

(3) Where an order is made under section 7 of the National Parks and Access to the Countryside Act 1949 designating or extending the area of a National Park, the functions exercisable by a local planning authority immediately before the coming into force of the order for any area which under the order becomes part of the Park shall continue to be exercisable by that authority as respects that area unless and until a joint planning board is constituted under section 2 or a National Park Committee is appointed under Part I of Schedule 17 to the Local Government Act 1972 for an area co-terminous with or including that area or, as the case may be, is authorised to exercise those functions.

1972 c. 70.

(4) Where a joint planning board for a National Park situated partly in one or more metropolitan counties is the local planning authority as respects the part of the Park situated in that county or those counties, it shall continue to be so.

The Broads.

5.—(1) For the purposes of Chapter I of Part VIII and sections 249, 250, 300 and 324(1)(b) and (c) and (7) and any other provision of this Act so far as it has effect for the purposes of those provisions, "local planning authority", in relation to land in the Broads, includes the Broads Authority.

(2) For the purposes of the provisions mentioned in subsection (3) the Broads Authority shall be the sole district planning authority for the Broads.

(3) The provisions referred to in subsection (2) are sections 36 to 49, 50(6) to (9), 51, 62, 64 to 72, 76 to 81, 91 to 95, 97 to 99, 102, 103, 106, 172, 173, 178, 183, 184, 188, 191 to 197, 211 to 215, 219 to 221, 224, 294, 295, 297, 299, 301, 316(1) to (3) and 324(1)(a).

Enterprise zones.
1980 c. 65.

6.—(1) An order under paragraph 5 of Schedule 32 to the Local Government, Planning and Land Act 1980 (designation of enterprise zone) may provide that the enterprise zone authority shall be the local planning authority for the zone for such purposes of the planning Acts and in relation to such kinds of development as may be specified in the order.

(2) Without prejudice to the generality of paragraph 15(1) of that Schedule (modification of orders by the Secretary of State), an order under that paragraph may provide that the enterprise zone authority shall be the local planning authority for the zone for different purposes of the planning Acts or in relation to different kinds of development.

(3) Where such provision as is mentioned in subsection (1) or (2) is made by an order designating an enterprise zone or, as the case may be, an order modifying such an order, while the zone subsists the enterprise zone authority shall be, to the extent mentioned in the order (as it has effect subject to any such modifications) and to the extent that it is not already, the local planning authority for the zone in place of any authority who would otherwise be the local planning authority for the zone.

(4) The Secretary of State may by regulations make transitional and supplementary provision in relation to a provision of an order under paragraph 5 of that Schedule made by virtue of subsection (1).

(5) Such regulations may modify any provision of the planning Acts or any instrument made under any of them or may apply any such enactment or instrument (with or without modification) in making such transitional or supplementary provision.

Urban development areas. 1980 c. 65.

7.—(1) Where an order is made under subsection (1) of section 149 of the Local Government, Planning and Land Act 1980 (urban development corporation as planning authority), the urban development corporation specified in the order shall be the local planning authority for such area as may be so specified in place of any authority who would otherwise be the local planning authority for that area for such purposes and in relation to such kinds of development as may be so specified.

(2) Where an order under subsection (3)(a) of that section confers any functions on an urban development corporation in relation to any area the corporation shall have those functions in place of any authority (except the Secretary of State) who would otherwise have them in that area.

Housing action areas. 1988 c. 50.

8.—(1) Where an order is made under subsection (1) of section 67 of the Housing Act 1988 (housing action trust as planning authority), the housing action trust specified in the order shall be the local planning authority for such area as may be so specified in place of any authority who would otherwise be the local planning authority for that area for such purposes and in relation to such kinds of development as may be so specified.

(2) Where an order under subsection (3)(a) of that section confers any functions on a housing action trust in relation to any area the trust shall have those functions in place of any authority (except the Secretary of State) who would otherwise have them in that area.

Power to make consequential and supplementary provision about authorities.

9. Regulations under this Act may make such provision consequential upon or supplementary to the provisions of sections 1 and 2 as appears to the Secretary of State to be necessary or expedient.

PART II

DEVELOPMENT PLANS

CHAPTER I

UNITARY DEVELOPMENT PLANS: METROPOLITAN AREAS INCLUDING LONDON

Preliminary

Application of Chapter I to Greater London and metropolitan counties.

10. This Chapter applies, subject to section 28, to the area of any local planning authority in Greater London or a metropolitan county (other than any area in such a county which is part of a National Park).

Surveys etc.

Survey of planning areas.

11.—(1) The local planning authority—

(a) shall keep under review the matters which may be expected to affect the development of their area or the planning of its development; and

(b) may, if they think fit, institute a survey or surveys of their area or any part of their area for examining those matters.

(2) Without prejudice to the generality of subsection (1), the matters to be kept under review or examined under that subsection shall include—

(a) the principal physical and economic characteristics of the area of the authority (including the principal purposes for which land is used) and, so far as they may be expected to affect that area, of any neighbouring areas;

(b) the size, composition and distribution of the population of that area (whether resident or otherwise);

(c) without prejudice to paragraph (a), the communications, transport system and traffic of that area and, so far as they may be expected to affect that area, of any neighbouring areas;

(d) any considerations not mentioned in paragraphs (a), (b) and (c) which may be expected to affect any matters mentioned in them;

(e) such other matters as may be prescribed or as the Secretary of State may in a particular case direct;

(f) any changes already projected in any of the matters mentioned in any of paragraphs (a) to (e) and the effect which those changes are likely to have on the development of that area or the planning of such development.

(3) A local planning authority shall, for the purpose of discharging their functions under this section of keeping under review and examining any matters relating to the area of another such authority, consult with that other authority about those matters.

Preparation and adoption of unitary development plans

Preparation of unitary development plan.

12.—(1) The local planning authority shall, within such period (if any) as the Secretary of State may direct, prepare for their area a plan to be known as a unitary development plan.

(2) A unitary development plan shall comprise two parts.

(3) Part I of a unitary development plan shall consist of a written statement formulating the authority's general policies in respect of the development and other use of land in their area (including measures for the improvement of the physical environment and the management of traffic).

(4) Part II of a unitary development plan shall consist of—

(a) a written statement formulating in such detail as the authority think appropriate (and so as to be readily distinguishable from the other contents of the plan) their proposals for the development and other use of land in their area or for any description of development or other use of such land;

(b) a map showing those proposals on a geographical basis;

(c) a reasoned justification of the general policies in Part I of the plan and of the proposals in Part II of it; and

(d) such diagrams, illustrations or other descriptive or explanatory matter in respect of the general policies in Part I of the plan or the proposals in Part II of it as the authority think appropriate or as may be prescribed.

(5) A unitary development plan shall also contain such other matters as may be prescribed or as the Secretary of State may in any particular case direct.

(6) In formulating the general policies in Part I of a unitary development plan the authority shall have regard—

(a) to any strategic guidance given by the Secretary of State to assist them in the preparation of the plan;

(b) to current national and regional policies;

(c) to the resources likely to be available; and

(d) to such other matters as the Secretary of State may direct the authority to take into account.

(7) The proposals in Part II of a unitary development plan shall be in general conformity with Part I.

(8) Part II of a unitary development plan may designate any part of the authority's area as an action area, that is to say, an area which they have selected for the commencement during a prescribed period of comprehensive treatment by development, redevelopment or improvement (or partly by one and partly by another method) and if an area is so designated that Part of the plan shall contain a description of the treatment proposed by the authority.

(9) In preparing a unitary development plan the authority shall take into account the provisions of any scheme under paragraph 3 of Schedule 32 to the Local Government, Planning and Land Act 1980 relating to land in their area which has been designated under that Schedule as an enterprise zone. 1980 c. 65.

Publicity in connection with preparation of unitary development plan.

13.—(1) When preparing a unitary development plan for their area and before finally determining its contents the local planning authority shall take such steps as will in their opinion secure—

(a) that adequate publicity is given in their area to the matters which they propose to include in the plan;

PART II

(b) that persons who may be expected to desire an opportunity of making representations to the authority with respect to those matters are made aware that they are entitled to an opportunity of doing so; and

(c) that such persons are given an adequate opportunity of making such representations.

(2) The authority shall consider any representations made to them within the prescribed period.

(3) Where the local planning authority have prepared a unitary development plan, before adopting it they shall—

(a) make copies of it available for inspection at their office and at such other places as may be prescribed; and

(b) send a copy to the Secretary of State.

(4) Each copy made available for inspection under subsection (3) shall be accompanied by a statement of the time within which objections to the plan may be made to the authority.

(5) The copy of a unitary development plan sent to the Secretary of State under subsection (3) shall be accompanied by a statement—

(a) of the steps which the authority have taken to comply with subsections (1) and (2); and

(b) of the authority's consultations with, and their consideration of the views of, other persons.

(6) If, on considering the statement submitted with and the matters contained in a unitary development plan and any other information provided by the local planning authority, the Secretary of State is not satisfied that the purposes of paragraphs (a) to (c) of subsection (1) have been adequately achieved by the steps taken by the authority in compliance with that subsection, he may, within 21 days of the receipt of the statement, direct the authority not to take further steps for the adoption of the plan without taking such further action as he may specify in order better to achieve those purposes and satisfying him that they have done so.

(7) A local planning authority who are given directions by the Secretary of State under subsection (6) shall—

(a) immediately withdraw the copies of the unitary development plan made available for inspection as required by subsection (3); and

(b) notify any person by whom objections to the plan have been made to the authority that the Secretary of State has given such directions.

Withdrawal of unitary development plan.

14.—(1) A unitary development plan may be withdrawn by the local planning authority at any time before it is adopted by the authority or approved by the Secretary of State and shall be withdrawn by the authority if the Secretary of State so directs.

(2) Where a unitary development plan is withdrawn the authority shall—

(a) withdraw the copies made available for inspection and sent to the Secretary of State under section 13(3); and

(b) give notice that the plan has been withdrawn to every person who has made an objection to it.

(3) In determining the steps to be taken by a local planning authority to secure the purposes of paragraphs (a) to (c) of subsection (1) of section 13, the authority and the Secretary of State may take into account any steps taken to secure those purposes in connection with any unitary development plan which the authority have previously withdrawn.

(4) Where a unitary development plan is withdrawn the copies of the plan shall be treated as never having been made available under section 13(3).

Adoption of unitary development plan by local planning authority.

15.—(1) After the expiry of the period given for making objections to a unitary development plan or, if such objections have been duly made during that period, after considering those objections, the local planning authority may, subject to the following provisions of this section and to sections 17 and 18, by resolution adopt the plan either as originally prepared or as modified to take account—

(a) of those objections;

(b) of any other objections made to the plan;

(c) of any other considerations which appear to the authority to be material.

(2) A unitary development plan shall not be adopted unless Part II of the plan is in general conformity with Part I.

(3) Where an objection to a unitary development plan has been made by the Minister of Agriculture, Fisheries and Food and the local planning authority do not propose to modify the plan to take account of the objection, the authority—

(a) shall send the Secretary of State particulars of the objection and a statement of their reasons for not modifying the plan to take account of it; and

(b) shall not adopt the plan unless the Secretary of State authorises them to do so.

(4) Subject to the following provisions of this Chapter and to section 287, a unitary development plan shall become operative on the date on which it is adopted.

Local inquiries.

16.—(1) For the purpose of considering objections to a unitary development plan the local planning authority may, and shall in the case of objections made in accordance with regulations under this Chapter, cause a local inquiry or other hearing to be held by a person appointed by the Secretary of State or, in such cases as may be prescribed by regulations under this Chapter, by the authority themselves.

(2) Subsections (2) and (3) of section 250 of the Local Government Act 1972 (power to summon and examine witnesses) shall apply to an inquiry held under this section as they apply to an inquiry under that section. 1972 c. 70.

PART II

1971 c. 62.

(3) The Tribunals and Inquiries Act 1971 shall apply to a local inquiry or other hearing held under this section as it applies to a statutory inquiry held by the Secretary of State, but as if in section 12(1) of that Act (statement of reasons for decisions) the reference to any decision taken by the Secretary of State were a reference to a decision taken by a local planning authority.

(4) Regulations made for the purposes of this section may—

(a) make provision with respect to the appointment and qualifications for appointment of persons to hold a local inquiry or other hearing under this section, including provision enabling the Secretary of State to direct a local planning authority to appoint a particular person or one of a specified list or class of persons;

(b) make provision with respect to the remuneration and allowances of a person appointed for that purpose.

(5) No local inquiry or other hearing need be held under this section if all persons who have made objections have indicated in writing that they do not wish to appear.

Secretary of State's powers concerning plans

Direction to reconsider proposals.

17.—(1) After a copy of a unitary development plan has been sent to the Secretary of State under section 13(3) and before it is adopted by the local planning authority, the Secretary of State may, if it appears to him that the plan is unsatisfactory, direct the authority to consider modifying the proposals in such respects as are indicated in the direction.

(2) An authority to whom a direction is given shall not adopt the plan unless they satisfy the Secretary of State that they have made the modifications necessary to conform with the direction or the direction is withdrawn.

Calling in of unitary development plan for approval by Secretary of State.

18.—(1) After a copy of a unitary development plan has been sent to the Secretary of State under section 13(3) and before it is adopted by the local planning authority, the Secretary of State may direct that the whole or part of the plan shall be submitted to him for his approval.

(2) If such a direction is given—

(a) the authority shall not take any further steps for the adoption of the plan until the Secretary of State has given his decision on the plan or the relevant part of it; and

(b) the plan or the relevant part of it shall not have effect unless approved by him and shall not require adoption under the previous provisions of this Chapter.

(3) Where particulars of an objection to a unitary development plan have been sent to the Secretary of State under section 15(3), then, unless he is satisfied that the Minister of Agriculture, Fisheries and Food no longer objects to the plan, the Secretary of State must give a direction in respect of it under subsection (1).

(4) Subsection (2)(a) applies in particular to holding or proceeding with a local inquiry or other hearing in respect of the plan under section 16; and at any such inquiry or hearing which is subsequently held or resumed a local planning authority need not give any person an opportunity of being heard in respect of any objection which has been

heard at an examination, local inquiry or other hearing under section 20 or which the Secretary of State states that he has considered in making his decision.

Approval of unitary development plan by Secretary of State.

19.—(1) Subject to section 20, the Secretary of State may after considering a plan or part of a plan submitted to him under section 18(1) either approve it (in whole or in part and with or without modifications or reservations) or reject it.

(2) In considering a plan or part of a plan submitted to him under that section the Secretary of State may take into account any matters which he thinks relevant, whether or not they were taken into account in the plan or that part of it.

(3) The Secretary of State shall give a local planning authority such statement as he considers appropriate of the reasons governing his decision on any plan or part of a plan submitted to him.

(4) Where the whole or part of Part I of a unitary development plan is approved by the Secretary of State with modifications, the local planning authority shall, before adopting the remainder of the plan, make such modifications in Part II as may be directed by the Secretary of State for bringing it into general conformity with Part I and, in the absence of any such direction, shall make such modifications for that purpose in Part II as appear to the authority to be required.

(5) Subject to section 287, a plan or part of a plan which is approved by the Secretary of State under this section shall become operative on such day as he may appoint.

Local inquiry, public examination and consultation by Secretary of State.

20.—(1) Before deciding whether or not to approve a plan or part of a plan submitted to him under section 18(1), the Secretary of State shall consider any objection to it so far as made in accordance with regulations under this Chapter.

(2) Where the whole or part of Part II of a unitary development plan is submitted to the Secretary of State under section 18(1) (whether or not the whole or part of Part I is also submitted), then, if any objections have been made to the plan or the relevant part of it as mentioned in subsection (1), before deciding whether to approve it he shall cause a local inquiry or other hearing to be held for the purpose of considering those objections.

(3) The Secretary of State need not under subsection (1) consider any objections which have already been considered by the local planning authority and need not cause a local inquiry or other hearing to be held under subsection (2) if that authority have already held a local inquiry or other hearing into the objections under section 16 or the Secretary of State, on taking the plan or the relevant part of it into consideration, decides to reject it.

(4) Where the whole or part of Part I of a unitary development plan (but not the whole or any part of Part II) is submitted to the Secretary of State under section 18(1) he may cause a person or persons appointed by him for the purpose to hold an examination in public of such matters affecting the Secretary of State's consideration of the part of the plan submitted to him as he considers ought to be so examined.

(5) The Secretary of State may, after consultation with the Lord Chancellor, make regulations with respect to the procedure to be followed at any examination under subsection (4).

PART II

(6) The Secretary of State shall not be required to secure to any local planning authority or other person a right to be heard at an examination under subsection (4), and the bodies and persons who may take part shall be such only as he may, whether before or during the course of the examination, in his discretion invite to do so; but the person or persons holding the examination shall have power, exercisable either before or during the course of the examination, to invite additional bodies or persons to take part if it appears to him or them desirable to do so.

1971 c. 62.

(7) An examination under subsection (4) shall constitute a statutory inquiry for the purposes of section 1(1)(c) of the Tribunals and Inquiries Act 1971 but shall not constitute such an inquiry for any other purpose of that Act.

(8) On considering a plan or part of a plan submitted to him under section 18(1) the Secretary of State may consult with or consider the views of any local planning authority or other person but he need not do so except as provided by this section.

Alteration of plans

Alteration or replacement of unitary development plan.

21.—(1) A local planning authority may at any time, and shall if so directed by the Secretary of State, make proposals for the alteration or replacement of a unitary development plan adopted or approved for their area under the previous provisions of this Chapter but, except in pursuance of such a direction, a local planning authority shall not without the consent of the Secretary of State make proposals under this section in respect of any plan or part of a plan if that plan or any part of it has been approved by him under those provisions.

(2) Subject to section 22, sections 12 to 20 (other than subsection (1) of section 12) shall apply in relation to the making of proposals under this section and to any alteration or replacement so proposed as they apply to the preparation of a unitary development plan under section 12 and to a plan prepared under that section.

(3) As soon as practicable after—

1980 c. 65.

(a) an order has been made under paragraph 5 of Schedule 32 to the Local Government, Planning and Land Act 1980 (designation of enterprise zone); or

(b) a notification has been given under paragraph 11(1) of that Schedule (approval of modification of enterprise zone scheme),

the local planning authority for an area in which the zone is wholly or partly situated shall review any unitary development plan for that area in the light of the provisions of the scheme or modified scheme under that Schedule and prepare proposals under this section for any consequential alterations to the plan which they consider necessary.

Short procedure for certain alterations and replacements.

22.—(1) Where a local planning authority propose to alter or replace a unitary development plan and it appears to them that the issues involved are not of sufficient importance to warrant the full procedure set out in section 13(1) to (4), they may proceed instead in accordance with this section.

(2) They shall—

(a) prepare the relevant documents (that is, the proposed alterations or replacement plan),

(b) make a copy of them available for inspection at their office and at such other places as may be prescribed, and

(c) send a copy to the Secretary of State.

(3) Each copy of the documents made available for inspection shall be accompanied by a statement of the time within which representations or objections may be made.

(4) They shall then take such steps as may be prescribed for the purpose of—

(a) advertising the fact that the documents are available for inspection and the places and times at which and period during which they may be inspected, and

(b) inviting the making of representations or objections in accordance with regulations;

and they shall consider any representations made to them within the prescribed period.

(5) The documents sent by the local planning authority to the Secretary of State under subsection (2) shall be accompanied by a statement of the steps which the authority are taking to comply with subsection (4).

(6) If, on considering the statement submitted with and the matters contained in the documents sent to him under subsection (2) and any other information provided by the local planning authority, the Secretary of State is not satisfied with the steps taken by the authority he may, within 21 days of the receipt of the statement, direct the authority not to take further steps for the adoption of their proposals without—

(a) proceeding in accordance with section 13(1) to (4), or

(b) taking such further action as he may specify,

and satisfying him that they have done so.

(7) A local planning authority who are given directions by the Secretary of State under subsection (6) shall—

(a) immediately withdraw the copies of documents made available for inspection as required by subsection (2); and

(b) notify any person by whom objections to the proposals have been made to the authority that the Secretary of State has given such directions.

(8) Where a local planning authority proceed in accordance with this section, the references in sections 14(2)(a) and (4) and 18(1) to copies made available or sent to the Secretary of State under section 13(3) shall be construed as references to copies made available or sent to the Secretary of State under subsection (2).

Joint plans

Joint unitary development plans.

23.—(1) A joint unitary development plan or joint proposals for the alteration or replacement of such a plan may be prepared by two or more local planning authorities in Greater London or by two or more local planning authorities in a metropolitan county; and the previous provisions of this Chapter shall, in relation to any such joint plan or proposals, have effect subject to the following provisions of this section.

PART II

(2) Subsections (3) and (4) shall apply in relation to a joint unitary development plan instead of subsections (1) and (2) of section 13, and references in subsections (5) and (6) of that section and in section 14(3) to subsections (1) and (2) of section 13 and the purposes of paragraphs (a) to (c) of subsection (1) of that section shall include references to subsections (3) and (4) of this section and the purposes of paragraphs (a) to (c) of subsection (3) respectively.

(3) The local planning authorities shall jointly take such steps as will in their opinion secure—

(a) that adequate publicity is given in their areas to the matters proposed to be included in the plan;

(b) that persons who may be expected to desire an opportunity of making representations to any of the authorities are made aware that they are entitled to such an opportunity; and

(c) that such persons are given an adequate opportunity of making such representations.

(4) The local planning authorities shall consider any representations made to them within the prescribed period.

(5) Each of the local planning authorities by whom a joint unitary development plan is prepared shall have the duty imposed by subsection (3) of section 13 of making copies of the plan available for inspection.

(6) Objections to such a plan may be made to any of those authorities and the statement required by subsection (4) of section 13 to accompany copies of the plan shall state that objections may be so made.

(7) It shall be for each of the local planning authorities by whom a joint unitary development plan is prepared to adopt the plan under section 15(1) and they may do so as respects any part of their area to which the plan relates, but any modifications subject to which the plan is adopted must have the agreement of all those authorities.

(8) Where a unitary development plan has been prepared jointly, the power of making proposals in respect of the plan under section 21 may be exercised as respects their respective areas by any of the authorities by whom it was prepared and the Secretary of State may under that section direct any of them to make proposals as respects their respective areas.

(9) In relation to any proposals made jointly under section 21, the reference in subsection (2) of that section to sections 12 to 20 shall include a reference to subsections (3) and (4) of this section.

(10) In relation to any such joint proposals—

(a) the reference in section 22(1) to section 13(1) to (4) shall include a reference to subsections (3) and (4) of this section; and

(b) the references in section 22 to the local planning authority shall be construed as references to the authorities acting jointly, except that—

(a) each of the authorities shall have the duty under subsection (2) of making copies of the relevant documents available for inspection, and

(b) representations or objections may be made to any of the authorities, and the statement required by subsection (3) of that section shall state that objections may be so made.

(11) The date of the coming into operation of a unitary development plan prepared jointly by two or more local planning authorities or for the alteration or replacement of such a plan in pursuance of proposals so prepared shall be a date jointly agreed by those authorities.

Supplementary

Disregard of certain representations.

24. Notwithstanding anything in the previous provisions of this Chapter, neither the Secretary of State nor a local planning authority shall be required to consider representations or objections with respect to a unitary development plan or any proposals for the alteration or replacement of such a plan if it appears to the Secretary of State or, as the case may be, the authority that those representations or objections are in substance representations or objections with respect to things done or proposed to be done in pursuance of—

(a) an order or scheme under section 10, 14, 16, 18, 106(1) or (3) or 108(1) of the Highways Act 1980; 1980 c. 66.

(b) an order or scheme under any provision replaced by the provisions mentioned in paragraph (a), namely, an order or scheme under section 7, 9, 11, 13 or 20 of the Highways Act 1959, section 3 of the Highways (Miscellaneous Provisions) Act 1961 or section 1 or 10 of the Highways Act 1971; or 1959 c. 25. 1961 c. 63. 1971 c. 41.

(c) an order under section 1 of the New Towns Act 1981. 1981 c. 64.

Default powers.

25.—(1) Where, by virtue of any of the previous provisions of this Chapter, any unitary development plan or proposals for the alteration or replacement of such a plan are required to be prepared, or steps are required to be taken for the adoption of any such plan or proposals, then—

(a) if at any time the Secretary of State is satisfied, after holding a local inquiry or other hearing, that the local planning authority are not taking the steps necessary to enable them to prepare or adopt such a plan or proposals within a reasonable period; or

(b) in a case where a period is specified for the preparation or adoption of any such plan or proposals, if no such plan or proposals have been prepared or adopted by the local planning authority within that period,

the Secretary of State may prepare and make the plan or any part of it or, as the case may be, alter or replace it, as he thinks fit.

(2) The previous provisions of this Chapter shall, so far as practicable, apply with any necessary modifications in relation to the doing of anything under this section by the Secretary of State and the thing so done.

(3) The authority mentioned in subsection (1) shall on demand repay to the Secretary of State so much of any expenses incurred by him in connection with the doing of anything which should have been done by them as he certifies to have been incurred in the performance of their functions.

PART II

Regulations and directions.

26.—(1) Without prejudice to the previous provisions of this Chapter, the Secretary of State may make regulations with respect to the form and content of unitary development plans and the procedure to be followed in connection with their preparation, withdrawal, adoption, submission, approval, making, alteration or replacement.

(2) Such regulations may in particular—

(a) provide for publicity to be given to the results of any review or survey carried out under section 11;

(b) provide for the notice to be given of or the publicity to be given to—

(i) matters included or proposed to be included in any unitary development plan,

(ii) the approval, adoption or making of any such plan or any alteration or replacement of it, or

(iii) any other prescribed procedural step,

and for publicity to be given to the procedure to be followed as mentioned in subsection (1);

(c) make provision with respect to the making and consideration of representations with respect to matters to be included in, or objections to, any such plan or proposals for its alteration or replacement;

(d) without prejudice to paragraph (b), provide for notice to be given to particular persons of the approval, adoption, alteration or replacement of any plan if they have objected to the plan and have notified the local planning authority of their wish to receive notice, subject (if the regulations so provide) to the payment of a reasonable charge;

(e) require or authorise a local planning authority to consult with, or consider the views of, other persons before taking any prescribed procedural step;

(f) require a local planning authority, in such cases as may be prescribed or in such particular cases as the Secretary of State may direct, to provide persons making a request in that behalf with copies of any plan or document which has been made public for the purpose mentioned in section 13(1)(a) or 23(3)(a) or has been made available for inspection under section 13(3)(a) or 22(2)(b), subject (if the regulations so provide) to the payment of a reasonable charge;

(g) provide for the publication and inspection of any unitary development plan which has been adopted, approved or made or any document approved, adopted or made altering or replacing any such plan, and for copies of any such plan or document to be made available on sale.

(3) Regulations under this section may make different provision for different cases.

(4) Subject to the previous provisions of this Chapter and to any regulations under this section, the Secretary of State may give directions to any local planning authority or to local planning authorities generally—

(a) for formulating the procedure for the carrying out of their functions under this Chapter;

PART II

(b) for requiring them to give him such information as he may require for carrying out any of his functions under this Chapter.

Meaning of "development plan" in Greater London and metropolitan counties.

27. For the purposes of this Act and any other enactment relating to town and country planning, the Land Compensation Act 1961 and the Highways Act 1980, the development plan for any district in Greater London or a metropolitan county (whether the whole or part of the area of a local planning authority) shall be taken as consisting of—

1961 c. 33.
1980 c. 66.

(a) the provisions of the unitary development plan for the time being in force for that area or the relevant part of it, together with a copy of the local planning authority's resolution of adoption or the Secretary of State's notice of approval or, where part of the plan has been adopted and the remainder approved, copies of the resolution and the notice; and

(b) any alteration to that plan, together with a copy of the authority's resolution of adoption, or the Secretary of State's notice of approval, of the alteration or, where part of the alteration has been adopted and the remainder approved, copies of the resolution and the notice.

Commencement of Chapter I: transitional provisions.

28.—(1) Subject to subsection (2), the provisions of this Chapter shall come into force in the area of any local planning authority in Greater London or a metropolitan county (other than any area in that county which is part of a National Park) on such day as may be appointed in relation to that area by an order made by the Secretary of State.

(2) Subsection (1) does not apply in any area in relation to which an order has been made before the commencement of this Act under section 4(1) of the Local Government Act 1985 (commencement of Part I of Schedule 1 to that Act) and in any such area the provisions of this Chapter shall come into force at the commencement of this Act or, if later, on the day appointed by the order.

1985 c. 51.

(3) Until a unitary development plan becomes operative under this Chapter for such an area as is mentioned in subsection (1) (or where parts of such a plan become operative on different dates until every part has become operative)—

(a) if it is the area of a local planning authority in a metropolitan county, Part I of Schedule 2 (which provides for existing plans to continue in force and applies some of the provisions of Chapter II) shall apply in relation to it;

(b) if it is the area of a local planning authority in Greater London, Part II of that Schedule (which makes similar provision) shall apply in relation to it; and

(c) Part III of that Schedule shall apply in relation to it for the purpose of making continuing provision for the transitional matters for which provision was made immediately before the commencement of this Act by Schedule 7 to the 1971 Act (old development plans etc.).

(4) The power to make orders under this section may be exercised so as to make different provision for different cases, including different provision for different areas.

PART II

CHAPTER II

STRUCTURE AND LOCAL PLANS: NON-METROPOLITAN AREAS

Preliminary

Application of Chapter II to non-metropolitan areas.

29. Subject to the transitional provisions in Schedule 2, this Chapter applies only to the area of any local planning authority outside Greater London and the metropolitan counties and to any part of a National Park in such a county.

Surveys, etc.

Survey of planning areas.

30.—(1) The local planning authority—

(a) shall keep under review the matters which may be expected to affect the development of their area or the planning of its development; and

(b) may, if they think fit, at any time institute a fresh survey of their area examining those matters.

(2) Without prejudice to the generality of subsection (1), the matters to be kept under review and examined under that subsection shall include—

(a) the principal physical and economic characteristics of the area of the authority (including the principal purposes for which land is used) and, so far as they may be expected to affect that area, of any neighbouring areas;

(b) the size, composition and distribution of the population of that area (whether resident or otherwise);

(c) without prejudice to paragraph (a), the communications, transport system and traffic of that area and, so far as they may be expected to affect that area, of any neighbouring areas;

(d) any considerations not mentioned in paragraph (a), (b) or (c) which may be expected to affect any matters so mentioned;

(e) such other matters as may be prescribed or as the Secretary of State may in any particular case direct;

(f) any changes already projected in any of the matters mentioned in any of the previous paragraphs and the effect which those changes are likely to have on the development of that area or the planning of such development.

(3) A survey under subsection (1)(b) may relate to only part of the area of an authority; and references in subsection (2) to the area of an authority or any neighbouring areas shall be construed accordingly.

(4) A local planning authority shall, for the purpose of discharging their functions under this section of examining and keeping under review any matters relating to the area of another such authority, consult with that other authority about those matters.

Structure plans

Structure plans: continuity, form and content.

31.—(1) Each structure plan approved by the Secretary of State under the 1971 Act with respect to the area of a local planning authority which is in operation immediately before the commencement of this Act shall continue in force after its commencement (subject to any alterations then in operation and to the following provisions of this Part).

PART II

(2) The structure plan for any area shall be a written statement—

(a) formulating the local planning authority's policy and general proposals in respect of the development and other use of land in that area (including measures for the improvement of the physical environment and the management of traffic); and

(b) containing such other matters as may be prescribed or as the Secretary of State may in any particular case direct.

(3) The written statement shall be illustrated by such diagram or diagrams as may be prescribed, which shall be treated as forming part of the plan.

(4) In formulating their policy and general proposals under subsection (2), the local planning authority shall secure that the policy and proposals are justified by the results of their survey under section 6 of the 1971 Act or any fresh survey instituted by them under section 30 and by any other information which they may obtain and shall have regard—

(a) to current policies with respect to the economic planning and development of the region as a whole;

(b) to the resources likely to be available for the carrying out of the proposals of the structure plan; and

(c) to such other matters as the Secretary of State may direct them to take into account.

(5) Where under section 7(7) of the 1971 Act the Secretary of State gave a consent or direction for the preparation of a structure plan for part of the area of a local planning authority, references in this Part of this Act to the area of the authority shall, in relation to a structure plan, be construed as including references to part of that area.

Alteration and replacement of structure plans.

32.—(1) A local planning authority may at any time submit to the Secretary of State and shall, if so directed by him, submit to him within a period specified in the direction, proposals for such alterations to the structure plan for their area as appear to them to be expedient or, as the case may be, as the Secretary of State may direct.

(2) Such proposals may relate to the whole or part of the area to which the plan relates.

(3) A local planning authority may at any time submit proposals for the repeal and replacement of the structure plan for their area to the Secretary of State.

(4) An authority submitting a proposal under subsection (3) for the repeal and replacement of a structure plan shall at the same time submit to the Secretary of State the structure plan with which they propose that it shall be replaced.

(5) Proposals under subsection (1) or (3) shall be accompanied by an explanatory memorandum summarising—

(a) in the case of proposals under subsection (1), the reasons which in the opinion of the local planning authority justify the alterations which they are proposing; and

(b) in the case of proposals under subsection (3), the reasons which in their opinion justify the repeal and replacement of the structure plan.

PART II

(6) The explanatory memorandum shall also state the relationship of the proposals to general proposals for the development and other use of land in neighbouring areas which may be expected to affect the area to which the proposals relate.

(7) The explanatory memorandum—

(a) shall also contain any information on which the proposals are based; and

(b) may contain such illustrative material as the local planning authority think appropriate.

Publicity in connection with proposals for alteration or replacement of structure plans.

33.—(1) When preparing proposals for the alteration or repeal and replacement of a structure plan for their area and before finally determining their content for submission to the Secretary of State, the local planning authority shall take such steps as will in their opinion secure—

(a) that adequate publicity is given in their area to the matters which they propose to include in the proposals and to the proposed content of the explanatory memorandum relating to each such matter;

(b) that persons who may be expected to desire an opportunity of making representations to the authority with respect to those matters are made aware that they are entitled to an opportunity of doing so; and

(c) that such persons are given an adequate opportunity of making such representations.

(2) The authority shall consider any representations made to them within the prescribed period.

(3) Not later than the submission of proposals to the Secretary of State, the local planning authority shall make copies of the proposals as submitted to the Secretary of State and of the explanatory memorandum available for inspection at their office and at such other places as may be prescribed.

(4) Each copy of the proposals and of the explanatory memorandum shall be accompanied by a statement of the time within which objections to the proposals may be made to the Secretary of State.

(5) Proposals submitted by the local planning authority to the Secretary of State for his approval shall be accompanied by a statement containing such particulars, if any, as may be prescribed—

(a) of the steps which the authority have taken to comply with subsections (1) and (2); and

(b) of the authority's consultations with, and consideration of the views of, other persons with respect to those matters.

(6) If after considering the statement submitted with, and the matters included in, the proposals and any other information provided by the local planning authority, the Secretary of State is satisfied that the purposes of paragraphs (a) to (c) of subsection (1) have been adequately achieved by the steps taken by the authority in compliance with that subsection, he shall proceed to consider whether to approve the proposals.

(7) If the Secretary of State is not satisfied as mentioned in subsection (6), he shall return the proposals to the authority and direct them—

(a) to take such further action as he may specify in order better to achieve those purposes; and

(b) after doing so, to resubmit the proposals with such modifications, if any, as they then consider appropriate and, if so required by the direction, to do so within a specified period.

(8) Where the Secretary of State returns the proposals to the local planning authority under subsection (7), he shall—

(a) inform the authority of his reasons for doing so, and

(b) if any person has made an objection to the proposals to him, also inform that person that he has returned the proposals.

(9) A local planning authority who are given directions under subsection (7) shall immediately withdraw the copies of the proposals made available for inspection as required by subsection (3).

(10) Subsections (3) to (9) shall apply, with the necessary modifications, in relation to proposals resubmitted to the Secretary of State in accordance with directions given under subsection (7) as they apply in relation to the proposals as originally submitted.

Withdrawal of proposals for alteration and replacement of structure plans.

34.—(1) Proposals for the alteration or repeal and replacement of a structure plan submitted to the Secretary of State for his approval may be withdrawn by the local planning authority submitting them by a notice given to the Secretary of State at any time before he has approved them.

(2) Proposals which are so withdrawn shall be treated as never having been submitted.

(3) On the withdrawal of such proposals, the authority preparing them shall also withdraw the copies of the proposals which they have made available for inspection in accordance with section 33(3), and shall give notice that the proposals have been withdrawn to every person who has made an objection to them.

(4) In determining the steps to be taken by them to secure the purposes of paragraphs (a) to (c) of section 33(1), the local planning authority preparing such proposals may take into account any steps taken to secure those purposes in connection with any other such proposals which either were not submitted to the Secretary of State for his approval or were so submitted and then withdrawn.

(5) The authority submitting for approval by the Secretary of State proposals in the case of which they have taken any steps into account by virtue of subsection (4) shall give particulars of those steps in their statement to him under subsection (5) of section 33 and the Secretary of State may treat the steps as having been taken by them in connection with those proposals in determining under subsection (6) of that section whether he is satisfied as there mentioned.

Approval or rejection of proposals for alteration or replacement of structure plans.

35.—(1) The Secretary of State may, after considering proposals for the alteration or repeal and replacement of a structure plan submitted (or resubmitted) to him, either approve them (in whole or in part and with or without modifications or reservations) or reject them.

PART II

(2) In considering any such proposals the Secretary of State may take into account any matters which he thinks are relevant, whether or not they were taken into account in the proposals as submitted to him.

(3) Where on taking any such proposals into consideration the Secretary of State does not determine then to reject them, he shall before determining whether or not to approve them—

(a) consider any objections to the proposals, so far as they are made in accordance with regulations under this Chapter, and

(b) subject to subsection (4), cause a person or persons appointed by him for the purpose to hold an examination in public of such matters affecting his consideration of the proposals as he considers ought to be so examined.

(4) If it appears to the Secretary of State, on consideration of the proposals, that no matters which require an examination in public arise from them or from any structure plan submitted with them under section 32(4), no such examination need be held.

(5) The Secretary of State may, after consultation with the Lord Chancellor, make regulations with respect to the procedure to be followed at any examination under subsection (3)(b).

(6) The Secretary of State need not secure to any local planning authority or other person a right to be heard at any such examination and, subject to subsection (7), only such bodies and persons as he may before or during the course of the examination invite to do so may take part in it.

(7) The person or persons holding the examination may before or during the course of the examination invite additional bodies or persons to take part in it if it appears to him or them desirable to do so.

1971 c. 62.

(8) An examination under subsection (3)(b) shall constitute a statutory inquiry for the purposes of section 1(1)(c) of the Tribunals and Inquiries Act 1971 but shall not constitute such an inquiry for any other purpose of that Act.

(9) On considering any proposals the Secretary of State may (but need not) consult with or consider the views of any local planning authority or other person.

(10) On exercising his powers under subsection (1) in relation to any proposals, the Secretary of State shall give such statement as he considers appropriate of the reasons governing his decision.

Local plans

Local plans.

36.—(1) A local plan shall consist of—

(a) a written statement formulating in such detail as the local planning authority think appropriate their proposals for the development and other use of land in their area, or for any description of development or other use of such land, including such measures as the authority think fit for the improvement of the physical environment and the management of traffic;

(b) a map showing those proposals; and

PART II

(c) such diagrams, illustrations or other descriptive matter as the authority think appropriate to explain or illustrate the proposals in the plan, or as may be prescribed.

(2) Different local plans may be prepared for different purposes for the same area.

(3) In formulating their proposals in a local plan the local planning authority shall have regard to any information and any other considerations which appear to them to be relevant or which may be prescribed or which the Secretary of State may in any particular case direct them to take into account.

(4) A local planning authority may prepare a local plan for a part of their area (an "action area") which they have selected for the commencement during a prescribed period of comprehensive treatment, by development, redevelopment or improvement of the whole or part of the area selected, or partly by one method and partly by another.

(5) A local plan prepared for an action area shall indicate the nature of the treatment selected for the area.

(6) For the purpose of discharging their functions with respect to local plans a district planning authority may, in so far as it appears to them necessary to do so having regard to any survey made by the county planning authority under section 6 of the 1971 Act or section 30, examine the matters mentioned in subsections (1) and (2) of section 30 so far as relevant to their area.

(7) In preparing a local plan a local planning authority shall take into account the provisions of any scheme under paragraph 3 of Schedule 32 to the Local Government, Planning and Land Act 1980 relating to land in their area which has been designated under that Schedule as an enterprise zone.

1980 c.65.

Local plan schemes.

37.—(1) A local plan scheme for each county shall be maintained in accordance with this section setting out a programme for the making, alteration, repeal or replacement of local plans for areas in the county, except any part of the county included in a National Park.

(2) The scheme shall, as regards each local plan for which it provides—

(a) specify the title and nature of the plan and the area to which it is to apply and give an indication of its scope,

(b) indicate where appropriate its relationship with the other local plans provided for by the scheme, and

(c) designate the local planning authority, whether county or district, responsible for the plan;

and may contain any appropriate incidental, consequential, transitional and supplementary provisions.

(3) The district planning authorities shall keep under review the need for, and adequacy of, local plans for their area and may make recommendations to the county planning authority for incorporation into the local plan scheme.

(4) The county planning authority shall, in the light of the recommendations of the district planning authorities and in consultation with those authorities, make and then keep under review and from time to time amend the local plan scheme.

PART II

(5) As soon as practicable after making or amending a local plan scheme the county planning authority shall send a copy of the scheme, or the scheme as amended, to the Secretary of State.

(6) If a district planning authority make representations to the Secretary of State that they are dissatisfied with a local plan scheme, the Secretary of State may amend the scheme.

(7) A local planning authority may prepare proposals for the making, alteration, repeal or replacement of a local plan—

(a) in any case, except in the case of proposals relating only to land in a National Park, only where authorised to do so by the local plan scheme, and

(b) in the case of proposals for the alteration, repeal or replacement of a local plan approved by the Secretary of State, only with the consent of the Secretary of State;

but subject to any direction of the Secretary of State under section 38.

Power of Secretary of State to direct making of local plan, etc.

38.—(1) The Secretary of State may, after consulting a local planning authority, direct them to make, alter, repeal or replace a local plan with respect to their area or part of it.

(2) A direction for the making, alteration or replacement of a local plan shall specify the nature of the plan or, as the case may be, the nature of the alteration required.

(3) The authority shall comply with the direction as soon as possible.

(4) The county planning authority shall make such amendments of the relevant local plan scheme as appear to them appropriate in consequence of the direction.

Publicity and consultation: general.

39.—(1) A local planning authority who propose to make, alter, repeal or replace a local plan shall proceed in accordance with this section, unless section 40 applies.

(2) They shall take such steps as will in their opinion secure—

(a) that adequate publicity is given to the proposals in the area to which the plan relates;

(b) that persons who may be expected to wish to make representations about the proposals are made aware that they are entitled to do so; and

(c) that such persons are given an adequate opportunity of making such representations.

(3) They shall consider any representations made to them within the prescribed period.

(4) They shall—

(a) consult the county planning authority or, as the case may be, the district planning authority with respect to their proposals;

(b) give that authority a reasonable opportunity to express their views; and

(c) take those views into consideration.

(5) They shall then, having prepared the relevant documents, that is, the proposed plan, alterations, instrument of repeal or replacement plan, as the case may be, and having obtained any certificate required by section 46—

(a) make copies of the documents available for inspection at their office,

(b) send a copy of them to the Secretary of State, and

(c) send a copy of them to the district or county planning authority, as the case may require.

(6) Each copy of the documents made available for inspection shall be accompanied by a statement of the time within which objections may be made.

Publicity and consultation: short procedure for certain alterations, etc.

40.—(1) Where a local planning authority propose to alter, repeal or replace a local plan and it appears to them that the issues involved are not of sufficient importance to warrant the full procedure set out in section 39, they may proceed instead in accordance with this section.

(2) They shall prepare the relevant documents, that is, the proposed alterations, instrument of repeal or replacement plan, as the case may be, and, having obtained any certificate required by section 46, shall—

(a) make copies of the documents available for inspection at their office,

(b) send a copy of them to the Secretary of State, and

(c) send a copy of them to the county or district planning authority, as the case may require.

(3) Each copy of the documents made available for inspection shall be accompanied by a statement of the time within which representations or objections may be made.

(4) They shall then take such steps as may be prescribed for the purpose of—

(a) advertising the fact that the documents are available for inspection and the places and times at which, and period during which, they may be inspected, and

(b) inviting the making of representations or objections in accordance with regulations.

(5) They shall consider any representations made to them within the prescribed period.

Powers of Secretary of State to secure adequate publicity and consultation.

41.—(1) The documents sent by the local planning authority to the Secretary of State under section 39 shall be accompanied by a statement—

(a) of the steps which the authority have taken to comply with subsections (2) and (3) of that section, and

(b) of the authority's consultations with other persons and their consideration of the views of those persons.

(2) The documents sent by the local planning authority to the Secretary of State under section 40 shall be accompanied by a statement of the steps which the authority are taking to comply with subsections (4) and (5) of that section.

PART II

(3) If, on considering the statement and the proposals and any other information provided by the local planning authority, the Secretary of State is not satisfied with the steps taken by the authority, he may, within 21 days of the receipt of the statement, direct the authority not to take further steps for the adoption of the proposals without—

(a) if they have proceeded in accordance with section 40, proceeding instead in accordance with section 39, or

(b) in any case, taking such further steps as he may specify,

and satisfying him that they have done so.

(4) A local planning authority who are given directions by the Secretary of State shall—

(a) immediately withdraw the copies of the documents made available for inspection as required by section 39(5) or 40(2), and

(b) notify any person by whom objections to the proposals have been made to the authority that the Secretary of State has given such directions.

Objections: local inquiry or other hearing.

42.—(1) The local planning authority may cause a local inquiry or other hearing to be held for the purpose of considering objections to their proposals for the making, alteration, repeal or replacement of a local plan.

(2) They shall hold such a local inquiry or other hearing in the case of objections made in accordance with regulations unless all the persons who have made such objections have indicated in writing that they do not wish to appear.

(3) A local inquiry or other hearing shall be held by a person appointed by the Secretary of State or, in such cases as may be prescribed, by the authority themselves.

(4) Regulations may—

(a) make provision with respect to the appointment, and qualifications for appointment, of persons to hold a local inquiry or other hearing;

(b) include provision enabling the Secretary of State to direct a local planning authority to appoint a particular person, or one of a specified list or class of persons;

(c) make provision with respect to the remuneration and allowances of the person appointed.

1972 c. 70.

(5) Subsections (2) and (3) of section 250 of the Local Government Act 1972 (power to summon and examine witnesses) apply to an inquiry held under this section.

1971 c. 62.

(6) The Tribunals and Inquiries Act 1971 shall apply to a local inquiry or other hearing held under this section as it applies to a statutory inquiry held by the Secretary of State, but as if in section 12(1) of that Act (statement of reasons for decisions) the reference to any decision taken by the Secretary of State were a reference to a decision taken by a local authority.

Adoption of proposals.

43.—(1) After the expiry of the period given for making objections to proposals for the making, alteration, repeal or replacement of a local plan or, if such objections were duly made within that period, after considering the objections so made, the local planning authority may, subject to this section and to section 44, by resolution adopt the proposals.

(2) They may adopt the proposals as originally prepared or as modified so as to take account of—

(a) any such objections as are mentioned in subsection (1) or any other objections to the proposals, or

(b) any other considerations which appear to the authority to be material.

(3) The authority shall not adopt any proposals which do not conform generally to the structure plan.

(4) After copies of the proposals have been sent to the Secretary of State and before they have been adopted by the local planning authority, the Secretary of State may, if it appears to him that the proposals are unsatisfactory, direct the authority to consider modifying the proposals in such respects as are indicated in the direction.

(5) An authority to whom a direction is given shall not adopt the proposals unless they satisfy the Secretary of State that they have made the modifications necessary to conform with the direction or the direction is withdrawn.

(6) Where an objection to the proposals has been made by the Minister of Agriculture, Fisheries and Food and the local planning authority do not propose to modify their proposals to take account of the objection—

(a) the authority shall send particulars of the objection to the Secretary of State, together with a statement of their reasons for not modifying their proposals to take account of it, and

(b) they shall not adopt the proposals unless the Secretary of State authorises them to do so.

Calling in of proposals for approval by Secretary of State.

44.—(1) After copies of proposals have been sent to the Secretary of State and before they have been adopted by the local planning authority, the Secretary of State may direct that the proposals shall be submitted to him for his approval.

(2) If he does give such a direction—

(a) the authority shall not take any further steps for the adoption of the proposals and in particular shall not hold or proceed with a local inquiry or other hearing in respect of the proposals under section 42; and

(b) the proposals shall not have effect unless approved by the Secretary of State and shall not require adoption by the authority.

(3) Where particulars of an objection made by the Minister of Agriculture, Fisheries and Food have been sent to the Secretary of State under section 43(6), then, unless the Secretary of State is satisfied that that Minister no longer objects to the proposals, he shall give a direction in respect of the proposals under this section.

PART II

Approval of proposals by Secretary of State.

45.—(1) The Secretary of State may after considering proposals submitted to him under section 44 either approve them (in whole or in part and with or without modifications or reservations) or reject them.

(2) In considering the proposals he may take into account any matters he thinks are relevant, whether or not they were taken into account in the proposals as submitted.

(3) Where on taking the proposals into consideration the Secretary of State does not determine then to reject them, he shall before determining whether or not to approve them—

(a) consider any objections to them made in accordance with regulations,

(b) give any person who made such an objection which has not been withdrawn an opportunity of appearing before and being heard by a person appointed by him for the purpose, and

(c) if a local inquiry or other hearing is held, also give such an opportunity to the authority and such other persons as he thinks fit,

except so far as the objections have already been considered, or a local inquiry or other hearing into the objections has already been held, by the authority.

(4) In considering the proposals the Secretary of State may consult with or consider the views of any local planning authority or any other person; but he need not do so, or give an opportunity for the making of representations or objections, or cause a local inquiry or other hearing to be held, except as provided by subsection (3).

Conformity between plans

Certificate of conformity.

46.—(1) The proposals in a local plan shall be in general conformity with the structure plan.

(2) A district planning authority who have prepared proposals for the making, alteration, repeal or replacement of a local plan shall not take the steps mentioned in section 39(5) or 40(2) unless a certificate that the proposals conform generally to the structure plan has been issued in accordance with this section.

(3) The district planning authority shall request the county planning authority to certify that their proposals so conform and that authority shall, within a month of receiving the request, or such longer period as may be agreed between the authorities, consider the matter and, if satisfied that the proposals do so conform, issue a certificate to that effect.

(4) If it appears to the county planning authority that the proposals do not so conform in any respect, they shall, during or as soon as possible after the end of that period, refer the question whether they so conform in that respect to the Secretary of State to be determined by him.

(5) The Secretary of State may in any case by direction to a county planning authority reserve for his own determination the question whether proposals for the making, alteration, repeal or replacement of a local plan conform generally to the structure plan.

(6) On determining a question so referred to or reserved for him, the Secretary of State—

(a) if he is of the opinion that the proposals do so conform, may issue, or direct the county planning authority to issue, a certificate to that effect, and

(b) if he is of the contrary opinion, may direct the district planning authority to revise their proposals in such respects as he thinks appropriate so that they will so conform.

Alteration of structure plan.

47.—(1) Where proposals for the alteration or replacement of a structure plan have been prepared and submitted to the Secretary of State, a local planning authority proposing to make, alter, repeal or replace a local plan may apply to him for a direction under subsection (2).

(2) On such an application the Secretary of State may direct that it shall be assumed for the purpose of the making, alteration, repeal or replacement of the local plan that the structure plan proposals have been approved by him, subject to such modifications as may from time to time be proposed by him and notified to the county planning authority.

(3) Such a direction ceases to have effect if the Secretary of State rejects the proposals for the alteration or replacement of the structure plan.

(4) Before giving such a direction the Secretary of State shall consult—

(a) in the case of an application by a county planning authority, any district planning authority whose area is affected by the relevant local plan proposals;

(b) in the case of an application by a district planning authority, the county planning authority.

(5) A county planning authority shall, on the approval of proposals for the alteration or replacement of a structure plan, consider whether the local plans for areas affected conform generally to the structure plan as altered or, as the case may be, to the new plan.

(6) Within the period of one month from the date on which the county planning authority receive notice of the Secretary of State's approval of the proposals, they shall send—

(a) to the Secretary of State, and

(b) to every district planning authority responsible for such a local plan,

lists of the local plans so affected which, in their opinion, do and do not so conform.

Local plan to prevail in cases of conflict with structure plan.

48.—(1) Where there is a conflict between any of the provisions of a local plan in force for an area and the provisions of the relevant structure plan, the provisions of the local plan shall be taken to prevail for all purposes.

(2) Where the structure plan is altered or replaced and the local plan is specified in a list under section 47(6) as a plan which does not conform to the structure plan as altered or replaced, subsection (1) does not apply until a proposal for the alteration of the local plan, or for its repeal and replacement, has been adopted or approved by the Secretary of State and the alteration, or replacement plan, has come into force.

PART II

Supplementary

Disregarding of representations with respect to development authorised by or under other enactments.

49. Notwithstanding anything in the previous provisions of this Chapter, neither the Secretary of State nor a local planning authority need consider representations or objections with respect to a local plan or any proposal to alter, repeal or replace a structure plan or a local plan if it appears to the Secretary of State or, as the case may be, the authority that those representations or objections are in substance representations or objections with respect to things done or proposed to be done in pursuance of—

1980 c. 66.

(a) an order or scheme under section 10, 14, 16, 18, 106(1) or (3) or 108(1) of the Highways Act 1980;

1959 c. 25. 1961 c. 63. 1971 c. 41.

(b) an order or scheme under any provision replaced by the provisions of the Highways Act 1980 mentioned in paragraph (a) (namely, an order or scheme under section 7, 9, 11, 13 or 20 of the Highways Act 1959, section 3 of the Highways (Miscellaneous Provisions) Act 1961 or section 1 or 10 of the Highways Act 1971);

1981 c. 64.

(c) an order under section 1 of the New Towns Act 1981.

Joint structure and local plans.

50.—(1) Where a structure plan has been prepared by two or more local planning authorities jointly, the power of making proposals under section 32 for the alteration or for the repeal and replacement of the plan may be exercised as respects their respective areas by any of the authorities by whom it was prepared, and the Secretary of State may under that section direct any of them to submit such proposals as respects their respective areas.

(2) Subsection (3) shall apply instead of section 33(1)(b) and (c) in relation to joint proposals to alter or repeal and replace a joint structure plan and references in section 33 to subsection (1) of that section and the purposes of paragraphs (a) to (c) of it shall include references to subsection (3) and the purposes of paragraphs (a) and (b) of that subsection respectively.

(3) The local planning authorities shall take such steps as will in their opinion secure—

(a) that persons who may be expected to desire an opportunity of making representations to any of the authorities are made aware that they are entitled to an opportunity of doing so;

(b) that such persons are given an adequate opportunity of making such representations.

(4) Each of the authorities by whom proposals for the alteration or repeal and replacement of a joint structure plan have been prepared shall have the duty imposed by section 33(3) of making copies of the proposals and explanatory memorandum available for inspection.

(5) Where two or more local planning authorities jointly prepare proposals for the alteration or repeal and replacement of a structure plan under this section, all or any of them may withdraw them under section 34(1) and on their doing so all the authorities shall comply with subsection (3) of that section.

(6) Where two or more local planning authorities jointly prepare proposals for the making, alteration, repeal or replacement of a local plan—

(a) the local planning authorities are jointly responsible for taking the steps required by section 39 or 40, except that they each have the duty imposed by section 39(5)(a) or 40(2)(a) of making copies of the relevant documents available for inspection and objections to the proposals may be made to any of those authorities and the statement required by section 39(6) or 40(3) to accompany the relevant documents shall state that objections may be so made;

(b) it shall be for each of the local planning authorities to adopt the proposals under section 43(1) and they may do so as respects any part of their area to which the proposals relate, but any modifications subject to which the proposals are adopted must have the agreement of all those authorities.

(7) Where—

(a) a structure plan has been jointly prepared by two or more county planning authorities, or

(b) a local plan has been jointly prepared by two or more district planning authorities,

a request for a certificate under section 46 that the local plan conforms generally to the structure plan shall be made by each district planning authority to the county planning authority for the area comprising the district planning authority's area and it shall be for that county planning authority to deal with the request.

(8) Where a local plan has been made jointly, the power of making proposals for its alteration, repeal or replacement may be exercised as respects their respective areas by any of the authorities by whom it was made, in accordance with the provisions of the relevant local plan scheme, and the Secretary of State may under section 38 direct any of them to make proposals as respects their respective areas.

(9) The date appointed under section 53(5) for the coming into operation of a local plan prepared jointly by two or more local planning authorities or for the alteration, repeal or replacement of a local plan in pursuance of proposals so prepared shall be one jointly agreed by those authorities and shall be specified in their respective resolutions adopting the plan or proposals.

Default powers.

51.—(1) Where, by virtue of any of the previous provisions of this Chapter, any survey is required to be carried out, or any local plan or proposals for the alteration, repeal or replacement of such a plan or of a structure plan are required to be prepared or submitted to the Secretary of State, or steps are required to be taken for the adoption of any local plan or any such proposals, then—

(a) if at any time the Secretary of State is satisfied, after holding a local inquiry or other hearing, that the relevant local planning authority are not carrying out the survey or are not taking the steps necessary to enable them to submit or adopt a local plan or such proposals within a reasonable period; or

PART II

(b) in a case where a period is specified for the submission or adoption of a local plan or any such proposals, if no such plan or proposals have been submitted or adopted within that period,

the Secretary of State may carry out the survey or prepare and make a local plan or, as the case may be, alter, repeal or replace such a plan or a structure plan, as he thinks fit.

(2) Where under subsection (1) the Secretary of State may do anything which should have been done by a local planning authority ("the defaulting authority") he may, if he thinks fit, authorise any other local planning authority who appear to him to have an interest in the proper planning of the area of the defaulting authority to do it.

(3) The previous provisions of this Chapter shall, so far as applicable, apply with any necessary modifications in relation to the doing of anything under this section by the Secretary of State or an authority other than the defaulting authority and the thing so done.

(4) The defaulting authority—

(a) shall on demand repay to the Secretary of State so much of any expenses incurred by him in connection with the doing of anything which should have been done by them as he certifies to have been incurred in the performance of their functions; and

(b) shall repay to any other authority who do under this section anything which should have been done by the defaulting authority any expenses certified by the Secretary of State to have been reasonably incurred by that other authority in connection with the doing of that thing.

Reviews of plans in enterprise zones.
1980 c. 65.

52.—(1) As soon as practicable after an order has been made under paragraph 5 of Schedule 32 to the Local Government, Planning and Land Act 1980 (adoption of enterprise zone scheme) or a notification has been given under paragraph 11 of that Schedule (modification of such a scheme)—

(a) any county planning authority for an area in which the enterprise zone is wholly or partly situated shall review any structure plan for their area or for part of it which relates to the whole or part of the zone in the light of the provisions of the scheme or modified scheme; and

(b) any local planning authority for an area in which the enterprise zone is wholly or partly situated shall review any local plan prepared by it which relates to any land in the zone.

(2) A county planning authority shall submit to the Secretary of State proposals for any alterations to a structure plan which they consider necessary to take account of the scheme or the modified scheme.

(3) A local planning authority shall make proposals for any alterations to such a local plan as is mentioned in subsection (1)(b) which they consider necessary to take account of the scheme or the modified scheme, or for the repeal or replacement of any such plan whose repeal or replacement they consider necessary for that purpose.

PART II

Supplementary provisions as to structure and local plans.

53.—(1) Without prejudice to the previous provisions of this Chapter, the Secretary of State may make regulations with respect to the form and content of structure and local plans and the procedure to be followed in connection with their preparation, withdrawal, adoption, submission, approval, making, alteration, repeal and replacement.

(2) In particular any such regulations may—

(a) provide for publicity to be given to the report of any survey carried out by a local planning authority under section 30;

(b) provide for the notice to be given of or the publicity to be given to—

(i) matters included or proposed to be included in any such plan,

(ii) the approval, adoption or making of any such plan or any alteration, repeal or replacement of it, or

(iii) any other prescribed procedural step,

and for publicity to be given to the procedure to be followed as mentioned in subsection (1);

(c) make provision with respect to the making and consideration of representations with respect to matters to be included in, or objections to, any such plan or proposals for its alteration, repeal or replacement;

(d) without prejudice to paragraph (b), provide for notice to be given to particular persons of the approval, adoption or alteration of any plan, if they have objected to the plan and have notified the relevant local planning authority of their wish to receive notice, subject (if the regulations so provide) to the payment of a reasonable charge for receiving it;

(e) require or authorise a local planning authority to consult with, or consider the views of, other persons before taking any prescribed procedural step;

(f) require a local planning authority, in such cases as may be prescribed or in such particular cases as the Secretary of State may direct, to provide persons making a request with copies of any plan or document which has been made public for the purpose mentioned in section 33(1)(a) or 39(2)(a) or has been made available for inspection under section 33(3) or 39(5)(a) or 40(2)(a), subject (if the regulations so provide) to the payment of a reasonable charge;

(g) provide for the publication and inspection of any structure plan or local plan which has been approved, adopted or made, or any document approved, adopted or made altering, repealing or replacing any such plan, and for copies of any such plan or document to be made available on sale.

(3) Regulations under this section may extend throughout England and Wales or to specified areas only and may make different provision for different cases.

(4) Subject to the previous provisions of this Chapter and to any regulations under this section, the Secretary of State may give directions to any local planning authority, or to local planning authorities generally—

PART II

(a) for formulating the procedure for the carrying out of their functions under this Chapter;

(b) for requiring them to give him such information as he may require for carrying out any of his functions under this Chapter.

(5) Subject to the provisions of section 287, a structure plan or local plan or any alteration, repeal or replacement of such a plan shall become operative on a date appointed for the purpose in the relevant notice of approval, resolution of adoption or notice of the making, alteration, repeal or replacement of the plan.

Meaning of "development plan" outside Greater London and the metropolitan counties.

1961 c. 33.

1980 c. 66.

54.—(1) Subject to subsection (4), for the purposes of this Act and any other enactment relating to town and country planning, the Land Compensation Act 1961 and the Highways Act 1980, the development plan for any district outside Greater London and the metropolitan counties (whether the whole or part of the area of a local planning authority) shall be taken as consisting of—

(a) the provisions of the structure plan for the time being in force for that area or the relevant part of that area, together with the Secretary of State's notice of approval of the plan;

(b) any alterations to that plan, together with the Secretary of State's notices of approval of them;

(c) any provisions of a local plan for the time being applicable to the district, together with a copy of the authority's resolution of adoption or, as the case may be, the Secretary of State's notice of approval of the local plan; and

(d) any alterations to that local plan, together with a copy of the authority's resolutions of adoption or, as the case may be, the Secretary of State's notices of approval of them.

(2) References in subsection (1) to the provisions of any plan, notices of approval, alterations and resolutions of adoption shall, in relation to a district forming part of the area to which they are applicable, be respectively construed as references to so much of those provisions, notices, alterations and resolutions as is applicable to the district.

(3) References in subsection (1) to notices of approval shall, in relation to any plan or alteration made by the Secretary of State under section 51, be construed as references to notices of the making of the plan or alteration.

(4) This section has effect subject to Part III of Schedule 2 (old development plans).

(5) Any reference in the Land Compensation Act 1961 to an area defined in the current development plan as an area of comprehensive development shall be construed as a reference to an action area for which a local plan is in force.

PART III

CONTROL OVER DEVELOPMENT

Meaning of development

55.—(1) Subject to the following provisions of this section, in this Act, except where the context otherwise requires, "development," means the carrying out of building, engineering, mining or other operations in, on, over or under land, or the making of any material change in the use of any buildings or other land.

Meaning of "development" and "new development".

(2) The following operations or uses of land shall not be taken for the purposes of this Act to involve development of the land—

(a) the carrying out for the maintenance, improvement or other alteration of any building of works which—

(i) affect only the interior of the building, or

(ii) do not materially affect the external appearance of the building,

and are not works for making good war damage or works begun after 5th December 1968 for the alteration of a building by providing additional space in it underground;

(b) the carrying out on land within the boundaries of a road by a local highway authority of any works required for the maintenance or improvement of the road;

(c) the carrying out by a local authority or statutory undertakers of any works for the purpose of inspecting, repairing or renewing any sewers, mains, pipes, cables or other apparatus, including the breaking open of any street or other land for that purpose;

(d) the use of any buildings or other land within the curtilage of a dwellinghouse for any purpose incidental to the enjoyment of the dwellinghouse as such;

(e) the use of any land for the purposes of agriculture or forestry (including afforestation) and the use for any of those purposes of any building occupied together with land so used;

(f) in the case of buildings or other land which are used for a purpose of any class specified in an order made by the Secretary of State under this section, the use of the buildings or other land or, subject to the provisions of the order, of any part of the buildings or the other land, for any other purpose of the same class.

(3) For the avoidance of doubt it is hereby declared that for the purposes of this section—

(a) the use as two or more separate dwellinghouses of any building previously used as a single dwellinghouse involves a material change in the use of the building and of each part of it which is so used;

(b) the deposit of refuse or waste materials on land involves a material change in its use, notwithstanding that the land is comprised in a site already used for that purpose, if—

(i) the superficial area of the deposit is extended, or

(ii) the height of the deposit is extended and exceeds the level of the land adjoining the site.

PART III

(4) For the purposes of this Act mining operations include—

(a) the removal of material of any description—

(i) from a mineral-working deposit;

(ii) from a deposit of pulverised fuel ash or other furnace ash or clinker; or

(iii) from a deposit of iron, steel or other metallic slags; and

(b) the extraction of minerals from a disused railway embankment.

(5) Without prejudice to any regulations made under the provisions of this Act relating to the control of advertisements, the use for the display of advertisements of any external part of a building which is not normally used for that purpose shall be treated for the purposes of this section as involving a material change in the use of that part of the building.

(6) In this Act "new development" means any development other than development of a class specified in Part I or Part II of Schedule 3; and Part III of that Schedule has effect for the purposes of Parts I and II.

Time when development begun.

56.—(1) Subject to the following provisions of this section, for the purposes of this Act development of land shall be taken to be initiated—

(a) if the development consists of the carrying out of operations, at the time when those operations are begun;

(b) if the development consists of a change in use, at the time when the new use is instituted;

(c) if the development consists both of the carrying out of operations and of a change in use, at the earlier of the times mentioned in paragraphs (a) and (b).

(2) For the purposes of the provisions of this Part mentioned in subsection (3) development shall be taken to be begun on the earliest date on which any material operation comprised in the development begins to be carried out.

(3) The provisions referred to in subsection (2) are sections 85(2), 86(6), 87(4), 91, 92 and 94.

(4) In subsection (2) "material operation" means—

(a) any work of construction in the course of the erection of a building;

(b) the digging of a trench which is to contain the foundations, or part of the foundations, of a building;

(c) the laying of any underground main or pipe to the foundations, or part of the foundations, of a building or to any such trench as is mentioned in paragraph (b);

(d) any operation in the course of laying out or constructing a road or part of a road;

(e) any change in the use of any land which constitutes material development.

PART III

(5) In subsection (4)(e) "material development" means any development other than—

(a) development for which planning permission is granted by a general development order for the time being in force and which is carried out so as to comply with any condition or limitation subject to which planning permission is so granted;

(b) development falling within any of paragraphs 1, 2, 3 and 5 to 8 of Schedule 3 (as read with Part III of that Schedule); and

(c) development of any class prescribed for the purposes of this subsection.

(6) In subsection (5) "general development order" means a development order (within the meaning of section 59) made as a general order applicable (subject to such exceptions as may be specified in it) to all land in England and Wales.

Requirement for planning permission

Planning permission required for development.

57.—(1) Subject to the following provisions of this section, planning permission is required for the carrying out of any development of land.

(2) Where planning permission to develop land has been granted for a limited period, planning permission is not required for the resumption, at the end of that period, of its use for the purpose for which it was normally used before the permission was granted.

(3) Where by a development order planning permission to develop land has been granted subject to limitations, planning permission is not required for the use of that land which (apart from its use in accordance with that permission) is its normal use.

(4) Where an enforcement notice has been issued in respect of any development of land, planning permission is not required for its use for the purpose for which (in accordance with the provisions of this Part of this Act) it could lawfully have been used if that development had not been carried out.

(5) In determining for the purposes of subsections (2) and (3) what is or was the normal use of land, no account shall be taken of any use begun in contravention of this Part or of previous planning control.

(6) For the purposes of this section a use of land shall be taken to have been begun in contravention of previous planning control if it was begun in contravention of Part III of the 1947 Act, Part III of the 1962 Act or Part III of the 1971 Act.

(7) Subsection (1) has effect subject to Schedule 4 (which makes special provision about use of land on 1st July 1948).

Granting of planning permission: general.

58.—(1) Planning permission may be granted—

(a) by a development order;

(b) by the local planning authority (or, in the cases provided in this Part, by the Secretary of State) on application to the authority in accordance with a development order;

(c) on the adoption or approval of a simplified planning zone scheme or alterations to such a scheme in accordance with section 82 or, as the case may be, section 86; or

PART III

1980 c. 65.

(d) on the designation of an enterprise zone or the approval of a modified scheme under Schedule 32 to the Local Government, Planning and Land Act 1980 in accordance with section 88 of this Act.

(2) Planning permission may also be deemed to be granted under section 90 (development with government authorisation).

(3) This section is without prejudice to any other provisions of this Act providing for the granting of permission.

Development orders

Development orders: general.

59.—(1) The Secretary of State shall by order (in this Act referred to as a "development order") provide for the granting of planning permission.

(2) A development order may either—

(a) itself grant planning permission for development specified in the order or for development of any class specified; or

(b) in respect of development for which planning permission is not granted by the order itself, provide for the granting of planning permission by the local planning authority (or, in the cases provided in the following provisions, by the Secretary of State) on application to the authority in accordance with the provisions of the order.

(3) A development order may be made either—

(a) as a general order applicable, except so far as the order otherwise provides, to all land, or

(b) as a special order applicable only to such land or descriptions of land as may be specified in the order.

Permission granted by development order.

60.—(1) Planning permission granted by a development order may be granted either unconditionally or subject to such conditions or limitations as may be specified in the order.

(2) Without prejudice to the generality of subsection (1), where planning permission is granted by a development order for the erection, extension or alteration of any buildings, the order may require the approval of the local planning authority to be obtained with respect to the design or external appearance of the buildings.

(3) Without prejudice to the generality of subsection (1), where planning permission is granted by a development order for development of a specified class, the order may enable the Secretary of State or the local planning authority to direct that the permission shall not apply either—

(a) in relation to development in a particular area, or

(b) in relation to any particular development.

(4) Any provision of a development order by which permission is granted for the use of land for any purpose on a limited number of days in a period specified in that provision shall (without prejudice to the generality of references in this Act to limitations) be taken to be a provision granting permission for the use of land for any purpose subject

to the limitation that the land shall not be used for any one purpose in pursuance of that provision on more than that number of days in that period.

Development orders: supplementary provisions.

61.—(1) A general development order may make different provision with respect to different descriptions of land.

(2) For the purpose of enabling development to be carried out in accordance with planning permission, or otherwise for the purpose of promoting proper development in accordance with the development plan, a development order may direct that any pre 1947 Act enactment, or any regulations, orders or byelaws made at any time under any such enactment—

(a) shall not apply to any development specified in the order, or

(b) shall apply to it subject to such modifications as may be so specified.

(3) In subsection (2) "pre 1947 Act enactment" means—

(a) any enactment passed before 6th August 1947 (the date of the passing of the 1947 Act), and

(b) any enactment contained in the Highways Act 1980 which— 1980 c. 66.

(i) is an enactment derived from the Highways Act 1959, and 1959 c. 25.

(ii) re-enacts (with or without modifications) any such enactment as is mentioned in paragraph (a).

Applications for planning permission

Form and content of applications for planning permission.

62. Any application to a local planning authority for planning permission—

(a) shall be made in such manner as may be prescribed by regulations under this Act; and

(b) shall include such particulars and be verified by such evidence as may be required by the regulations or by directions given by the local planning authority under them.

Applications in connection with existing buildings and uses.

63.—(1) An application for planning permission may relate to buildings or works constructed or carried out, or a use of land instituted, before the date of the application.

(2) Such an application may be—

(a) in respect of buildings or works constructed or carried out, or a use instituted, without planning permission or in accordance with planning permission granted for a limited period; or

(b) for permission to retain buildings or works, or continue the use of land, without complying with some condition subject to which a previous planning permission was granted.

(3) Any power to grant planning permission to develop land under this Act shall include power to grant planning permission for the retention on land of buildings or works constructed or carried out, or for the continuance of a use of land instituted, as mentioned in subsection (2); and references in the planning Acts to planning permission to develop land or to carry out any development of land, and to applications for such permission, shall be construed accordingly.

PART III

(4) Any planning permission granted in accordance with subsection (3) may be granted—

(a) so as to take effect from the date on which the buildings or works were constructed or carried out or the use was instituted, or

(b) in the case of buildings or works constructed or carried out or a use instituted in accordance with planning permission granted for a limited period, so as to take effect from the end of that period.

(5) Subsection (3) shall not affect the construction of section 65, 71(1) or 197 or Part V.

Applications to determine whether planning permission required.

64.—(1) If any person who proposes to carry out any operations on land, or to make any change in the use of land—

(a) wishes to have it determined whether the carrying out of those operations, or the making of that change, would constitute or involve development of the land, and

(b) if so, whether an application for planning permission in respect of it is required under this Part (having regard to the provisions of any development order, enterprise zone scheme or simplified planning zone scheme),

he may apply to the local planning authority to determine that question.

(2) An application under subsection (1) may be made either as part of an application for planning permission or without any such application.

(3) The provisions of sections 59, 69(1), (2) and (5), 70, 74, 77, 78 and 79 shall, subject to any necessary modifications, apply in relation to any application under this section, and to the determination of it, as they apply in relation to applications for planning permission and to the determination of such applications.

Publicity for applications

Publication of notices of applications for planning permission for designated development.

65.—(1) A development order may designate any class of development as development to which this section is to apply; and a class of development which is for the time being so designated is in this section referred to as "development of a designated class".

(2) An application for planning permission for development of a designated class shall not be entertained by the local planning authority unless it is accompanied—

(a) by a copy of a notice of the application, in such form as may be prescribed by a development order, and by such evidence as may be so prescribed that the notice has been published in a local newspaper circulating in the locality in which the land to which the application relates is situated; and

(b) by a certificate signed by or on behalf of the applicant stating—

(i) that he has complied with subsection (3) and when he did so, or

(ii) that he has been unable to comply with it because he has not such rights of access or other rights in respect of the land as would enable him to do so, and that he has taken such reasonable steps as are open to him (specifying them) to acquire those rights but has been unable to acquire them.

(3) In order to comply with this subsection a person must—

(a) post on the land a notice, in such form as may be prescribed by a development order, stating that the application for planning permission is to be made; and

(b) leave the notice in position for not less than seven days in a period of not more than one month immediately preceding the making of the application to the local planning authority.

(4) The notice mentioned in subsection (3)—

(a) must be posted by affixing it firmly to some object on the land, and

(b) must be sited and displayed in such a way as to be easily visible and legible by members of the public without their going on the land.

(5) An applicant shall not be treated as unable to comply with subsection (3) if the notice is, without any fault or intention of his, removed, obscured or defaced before the seven days referred to in subsection (3)(b) have elapsed, if he has taken reasonable steps for its protection and, if need be, replacement.

(6) If an applicant has cause to rely on subsection (5) his certificate under subsection (2)(b) must state the relevant circumstances.

(7) The notice mentioned in subsection (2)(a) or required by subsection (3) shall (in addition to any other matters required to be contained in it) name a place within the locality where a copy of the application for planning permission, and of all plans and other documents submitted with it, will be open to inspection by the public at all reasonable hours during such period as may be specified in the notice.

(8) That period shall not be less than 21 days beginning with the date on which the notice is published or, as the case may be, first posted.

(9) An application for planning permission for development of a designated class shall not be determined by the local planning authority before the end of the period of 21 days beginning with the date of the application.

Notification of applications to owners and agricultural tenants.

66.—(1) Without prejudice to section 65, a local planning authority shall not entertain any application for planning permission unless it is accompanied by one of the following certificates signed by or on behalf of the applicant—

(a) a certificate stating that, at the beginning of the period of 21 days ending with the date of the application, no person (other than the applicant) was the owner of any of the land to which the application relates;

(b) a certificate stating that the applicant has given the requisite notice of the application to all the persons (other than himself) who at the beginning of that period were owners of any of the land to which the application relates, and setting out—

(i) the names of those persons,

(ii) the addresses at which notice of the application was given to them respectively, and

(iii) the date of service of each such notice;

(c) a certificate stating—

(i) that the applicant is unable to issue a certificate in accordance with paragraph (a) or (b),

(ii) that he has given the requisite notice of the application to such one or more of the persons mentioned in paragraph (b) as are specified in the certificate (setting out their names, the addresses at which notice of the application was given to them respectively, and the date of the service of each such notice), and

(iii) that he has taken such steps as are reasonably open to him (specifying them) to ascertain the names and addresses of the remainder of those persons but has been unable to do so;

(d) a certificate stating—

(i) that the applicant is unable to issue a certificate in accordance with paragraph (a), and

(ii) that he has taken such steps as are reasonably open to him (specifying them) to ascertain the names and addresses of the persons mentioned in paragraph (b) but has been unable to do so.

(2) Any such certificate as is mentioned in paragraph (c) or (d) of subsection (1) must also contain a statement that the requisite notice of the application, as set out in the certificate, has on a date specified in the certificate been published in a local newspaper circulating in the locality in which the land in question is situated.

(3) The date specified in a certificate under subsection (2) must not be earlier than the beginning of the period mentioned in subsection (1)(a).

(4) In addition to any other matters required to be contained in a certificate issued for the purposes of this section, every such certificate must contain a statement —

(a) that none of the land to which the application relates constitutes or forms part of an agricultural holding; or

(b) that the applicant has given the requisite notice of the application to every person (other than himself) who, at the beginning of the period mentioned in subsection (1)(a), was a tenant of any agricultural holding any part of which was comprised in the land to which the application relates.

(5) Such a statement as is mentioned in subsection (4)(b) must set out—

(a) the name of each person to whom the applicant has given notice of the application,

(b) the address at which notice was given to him, and

(c) the date of service of that notice.

(6) Where an application for planning permission is accompanied by such a certificate as is mentioned in subsection (1)(b),(c) or (d), or by a certificate containing a statement in accordance with subsections (4)(b) and (5), the local planning authority shall not determine the application before the end of the period of 21 days beginning with the date appearing from the certificate to be the latest of the dates of service of notices as mentioned in the certificate, or, if later, the date of publication of a notice as mentioned in the certificate.

(7) In this section—

"owner", in relation to any land, means a person who for the time being is—

(a) the estate owner in respect of the fee simple in the land, or

(b) entitled to a tenancy of the land granted or extended for a term of years certain of which not less than seven years remain unexpired; and

"agricultural holding" has the same meaning as in the Agricultural Holdings Act 1986. 1986 c. 5.

Notification of applications for planning permission for mineral working.

67.—(1) In the case of applications for planning permission for development consisting of the winning and working of minerals section 66 shall have effect with the following modifications.

(2) Subsection (1) of that section and the following provisions of this section shall have effect as if any person entitled to an interest in a relevant mineral in any of the land to which the application relates were an owner of the land.

(3) In the case of an application for planning permission for development consisting of the winning and working of minerals by underground mining operations, the local planning authority may entertain the application if, instead of being accompanied by any of the certificates mentioned in subsection (1) of that section, it is accompanied by a certificate signed by or on behalf of the applicant—

(a) stating that he has given the requisite notice of the application to such one or more of the persons specified in the certificate who, at the beginning of the period of 21 days ending with the date of the application, were owners (within the meaning of section 66) of any of the land to which the application relates or entitled to an interest in a relevant mineral in that land;

(b) setting out the names of those persons, the addresses at which notice of the application was given to them respectively and the date of service of each such notice;

(c) stating that there is no such person as is mentioned in paragraph (a) whom the applicant knows to be such a person and whose name and address is known to the applicant but to whom he has not given the requisite notice of the application; and

(d) stating that he has complied with subsection (7) and when he did so.

(4) In this section "relevant mineral" means any mineral other than oil, gas, coal, gold or silver.

(5) Any such certificate as is mentioned in subsection (3) must also contain a statement that the requisite notice of the application, as set out in the certificate, has on a date specified in it been published in a local newspaper circulating in the locality in which the land in question is situated.

(6) The date specified under subsection (5) must not be earlier than the beginning of the period mentioned in paragraph (a) of subsection (3).

PART III

(7) In order to comply with this subsection the applicant must—

(a) post the requisite notice of the application, sited and displayed in such a way as to be easily visible and legible by members of the public, in at least one place in every parish or community within which there is situated any part of the land to which the application relates; and

(b) leave the notice in position for not less than seven days in the period of 21 days immediately preceding the making of the application to the local planning authority.

(8) The applicant shall not be treated as unable to comply with subsection (7) if the notice is, without any fault or intention of his, removed, obscured or defaced before the seven days referred to in subsection (7)(b) have elapsed, if he has taken reasonable steps for its protection and, if need be, replacement.

(9) If the applicant has cause to rely on subsection (8), his certificate under subsection (3) shall state the relevant circumstances.

(10) The notice required by subsection (7) shall (in addition to any other matters required to be contained in it) name a place within the area of the local planning authority to whom the application is made where a copy of the application for planning permission, and of all plans and other documents submitted with it, will be open to inspection by the public at all reasonable hours during such period as may be specified in the notice (which must not be less than 21 days beginning with the date on which the notice is first posted).

(11) Subsections (4), (5) and (6) of section 66 shall apply in relation to certificates under subsection (3) as they apply to certificates under subsection (1)(b) of that section but as if at the end of subsection (6) there were added the words "or, if later, the latest of the dates on which a notice was posted as mentioned in subsection (7)(a) of section 67".

Further provisions as to certificates under sections 65 to 67.

68.—(1) If any person—

(a) issues a certificate which purports to comply with the requirements of subsection (2)(b) of section 65 or of section 66 or 67 and contains a statement which he knows to be false or misleading in a material particular, or

(b) recklessly issues a certificate which purports to comply with those requirements and contains a statement which is false or misleading in a material particular,

he shall be guilty of an offence.

(2) A person guilty of an offence under subsection (1) shall be liable on summary conviction to a fine not exceeding level 3 on the standard scale.

(3) Any certificate issued for the purpose of section 65, 66 or 67 shall be in such form as may be prescribed by a development order for a certificate under that section.

(4) Any reference in any provision of section 66 or 67 to the requisite notice, where a form of notice is prescribed by a development order for the purposes of that provision, is a reference to a notice in that form.

PART III

Registers of applications, etc.

69.—(1) Every local planning authority shall keep, in such manner as may be prescribed by a development order, a register containing such information as may be so prescribed with respect to applications for planning permission made to that authority.

(2) The register shall contain—

(a) information as to the manner in which such applications have been dealt with, and

(b) such information as may be prescribed by a development order with respect to simplified planning zone schemes relating to zones in the authority's area.

(3) A development order may make provision for the register to be kept in two or more parts, each part containing such information relating to applications for planning permission made to the authority as may be prescribed by the order.

(4) A development order may also make provision—

(a) for a specified part of the register to contain copies of applications and of any plans or drawings submitted with them; and

(b) for the entry relating to any application, and everything relating to it, to be removed from that part of the register when the application (including any appeal arising out of it) has been finally disposed of (without prejudice to the inclusion of any different entry relating to it in another part of the register).

(5) Every register kept under this section shall be available for inspection by the public at all reasonable hours.

Determination of applications

Determination of applications: general considerations.

70.—(1) Where an application is made to a local planning authority for planning permission—

(a) subject to sections 91 and 92, they may grant planning permission, either unconditionally or subject to such conditions as they think fit; or

(b) they may refuse planning permission.

(2) In dealing with such an application the authority shall have regard to the provisions of the development plan, so far as material to the application, and to any other material considerations.

(3) Subsection (1) has effect subject to sections 65, 66 and 67 and to the following provisions of this Act, to sections 66, 67, 72 and 73 of the Planning (Listed Buildings and Conservation Areas) Act 1990 and to section 15 of the Health Services Act 1976.

1990 c. 9.
1976 c. 83.

Consultations in connection with determinations under s. 70.

71.—(1) In determining any application for planning permission for development of a class designated under section 65, the local planning authority shall take into account any representations relating to that application which are received by them before the end of the period of 21 days beginning with the date of the application.

PART III

(2) Where an application for planning permission is accompanied by such a certificate as is mentioned in subsection (1)(b), (c) or (d) of section 66 or subsection (3) of section 67, or by a certificate containing a statement in accordance with subsection (4)(b) and (5) of section 66, the local planning authority—

(a) in determining the application, shall take into account any representations relating to it which are made to them, before the end of the period mentioned in subsection (6) of section 66, by any person who satisfies them that he is an owner of any land to which the application relates or that he is the tenant of an agricultural holding any part of which is comprised in that land; and

(b) shall give notice of their decision to every person who has made representations which they were required to take into account in accordance with paragraph (a);

and in the case of an application to which section 67 applies the reference in paragraph (a) to section 66(6) is a reference to that section as it applies by virtue of section 67(11).

(3) Before a local planning authority grant planning permission for the use of land as a caravan site, they shall, unless they are also the authority with power to issue a site licence for that land, consult the local authority with that power.

(4) In this section—

"agricultural holding" has the same meaning as in section 66;

"owner" has the same meaning as in section 66 or, as the case may be, section 67; and

1960 c. 62.

"site licence" means a licence under Part 1 of the Caravan Sites and Control of Development Act 1960 authorising the use of land as a caravan site.

Conditional grant of planning permission.

72.—(1) Without prejudice to the generality of section 70(1), conditions may be imposed on the grant of planning permission under that section—

(a) for regulating the development or use of any land under the control of the applicant (whether or not it is land in respect of which the application was made) or requiring the carrying out of works on any such land, so far as appears to the local planning authority to be expedient for the purposes of or in connection with the development authorised by the permission;

(b) for requiring the removal of any buildings or works authorised by the permission, or the discontinuance of any use of land so authorised, at the end of a specified period, and the carrying out of any works required for the reinstatement of land at the end of that period.

(2) A planning permission granted subject to such a condition as is mentioned in subsection (1)(b) is in this Act referred to as "planning permission granted for a limited period".

(3) Where—

(a) planning permission is granted for development consisting of or including the carrying out of building or other operations subject to a condition that the operations shall be commenced not later than a time specified in the condition; and

(b) any building or other operations are commenced after the time so specified,

the commencement and carrying out of those operations do not constitute development for which that permission was granted.

(4) Subsection (3)(a) does not apply to a condition attached to the planning permission by or under section 91 or 92.

(5) Part I of Schedule 5 shall have effect for the purpose of making special provision with respect to the conditions which may be imposed on the grant of planning permission for development consisting of the winning and working of minerals, and subsection (2) has effect subject to paragraph 1(6)(a) of that Schedule.

Determination of applications to develop land without compliance with conditions previously attached.

73.—(1) This section applies, subject to subsection (4), to applications for planning permission for the development of land without complying with conditions subject to which a previous planning permission was granted.

(2) On such an application the local planning authority shall consider only the question of the conditions subject to which planning permission should be granted, and—

(a) if they decide that planning permission should be granted subject to conditions differing from those subject to which the previous permission was granted, or that it should be granted unconditionally, they shall grant planning permission accordingly, and

(b) if they decide that planning permission should be granted subject to the same conditions as those subject to which the previous permission was granted, they shall refuse the application.

(3) Special provision may be made with respect to such applications—

(a) by regulations under section 62 as regards the form and content of the application, and

(b) by a development order as regards the procedure to be followed in connection with the application.

(4) This section does not apply if the previous planning permission was granted subject to a condition as to the time within which the development to which it related was to be begun and that time has expired without the development having been begun.

Directions etc. as to method of dealing with applications.

74.—(1) Provision may be made by a development order for regulating the manner in which applications for planning permission to develop land are to be dealt with by local planning authorities, and in particular—

(a) for enabling the Secretary of State to give directions restricting the grant of planning permission by the local planning authority, either indefinitely or during such period as may be

PART III

specified in the directions, in respect of any such development, or in respect of development of any such class, as may be so specified;

(b) for authorising the local planning authority, in such cases and subject to such conditions as may be prescribed by the order or by directions given by the Secretary of State under it, to grant planning permission for development which does not accord with the provisions of the development plan;

(c) for requiring that, before planning permission for any development is granted or refused, local planning authorities prescribed by the order or by directions given by the Secretary of State under it shall consult with such authorities or persons as may be so prescribed;

(d) for requiring the local planning authority to give to any applicant for planning permission, within such time as may be prescribed by the order, such notice as may be so prescribed as to the manner in which his application has been dealt with;

(e) for requiring the local planning authority to give any applicant for any consent, agreement or approval required by a condition imposed on a grant of planning permission notice of their decision on his application, within such time as may be so prescribed;

(f) for requiring the local planning authority to give to the Secretary of State, and to such other persons as may be prescribed by or under the order, such information as may be so prescribed with respect to applications for planning permission made to the authority, including information as to the manner in which any such application has been dealt with.

1990 c. 9.

(2) Subsection (1) is subject to the provisions of section 71 of this Act and sections 67(7) and 73(1) of the Planning (Listed Buildings and Conservation Areas) Act 1990.

Effect of planning permission.

75.—(1) Without prejudice to the provisions of this Part as to the duration, revocation or modification of planning permission, any grant of planning permission to develop land shall (except in so far as the permission otherwise provides) enure for the benefit of the land and of all persons for the time being interested in it.

(2) Where planning permission is granted for the erection of a building, the grant of permission may specify the purposes for which the building may be used.

(3) If no purpose is so specified, the permission shall be construed as including permission to use the building for the purpose for which it is designed.

Duty to draw attention to certain provisions for benefit of disabled.
1970 c. 44.

76.—(1) This section applies when planning permission is granted for any development which will result in the provision—

(a) of a building or premises to which section 4 of the Chronically Sick and Disabled Persons Act 1970 applies (buildings or premises to which the public are to be admitted whether on payment or otherwise);

(b) of any of the following (being in each case, premises in which persons are employed to work)—

(i) office premises, shop premises and railway premises to which the Offices, Shops and Railway Premises Act 1963 applies; 1963 c. 41.

(ii) premises which are deemed to be such premises for the purposes of that Act; or

(iii) factories as defined by section 175 of the Factories Act 1961; 1961 c. 34.

(c) of a building intended for the purposes of a university, university college or college, or of a school or hall of a university;

(d) of a building intended for the purposes of an institution within the PCFC funding sector; or

(e) of a building intended for the purposes of a school or an institution which provides higher education or further education (or both) and is maintained or assisted by a local education authority.

(2) The local planning authority granting the planning permission shall draw the attention of the person to whom the permission is granted—

(a) in the case of such a building or premises as are mentioned in subsection (1)(a)—

(i) to sections 4 and 7 of the Chronically Sick and Disabled Persons Act 1970; and 1970 c. 44.

(ii) to the Code of Practice for Access of the Disabled to Buildings (British Standards Institution code of practice BS 5810: 1979) or any prescribed document replacing that code;

(b) in the case of such premises as are mentioned in subsection (1)(b), to sections 7 and 8A of that Act and to that code or any such prescribed document replacing it;

(c) in the case of such a building as is mentioned in subsection (1)(c), (d) or (e), to sections 7 and 8 of that Act and to Design Note 18 "Access for Disabled People to Educational Buildings" published in 1984 on behalf of the Secretary of State, or any prescribed document replacing that note.

(3) Expressions used in subsection (1)(d) and (e) and in the Education Act 1944 have the same meanings as in that Act. 1944 c. 31.

Secretary of State's powers as respects planning applications and decisions

77.—(1) The Secretary of State may give directions requiring applications for planning permission, or for the approval of any local planning authority required under a development order, to be referred to him instead of being dealt with by local planning authorities. Reference of applications to Secretary of State.

(2) A direction under this section—

(a) may be given either to a particular local planning authority or to local planning authorities generally; and

(b) may relate either to a particular application or to applications of a class specified in the direction.

PART III

(3) Any application in respect of which a direction under this section has effect shall be referred to the Secretary of State accordingly.

(4) Subject to subsection (5), where an application for planning permission is referred to the Secretary of State under this section, sections 65(2) and (9), 66, 67, 70, 71(1) and (2), 72(1) and (5) and 73 shall apply, with any necessary modifications, as they apply to such an application which falls to be determined by the local planning authority.

(5) Before determining an application referred to him under this section, the Secretary of State shall, if either the applicant or the local planning authority wish, give each of them an opportunity of appearing before, and being heard by, a person appointed by the Secretary of State for the purpose.

(6) Subsection (5) does not apply to an application for planning permission referred to a Planning Inquiry Commission under section 101.

(7) The decision of the Secretary of State on any application referred to him under this section shall be final.

Right to appeal against planning decisions and failure to take such decisions.

78.—(1) Where a local planning authority—

(a) refuse an application for planning permission or grant it subject to conditions;

(b) refuse an application for any consent, agreement or approval of that authority required by a condition imposed on a grant of planning permission or grant it subject to conditions; or

(c) refuse an application for any approval of that authority required under a development order or grant it subject to conditions,

the applicant may by notice appeal to the Secretary of State.

(2) A person who has made such an application may also appeal to the Secretary of State if the local planning authority have neither—

(a) given notice to the applicant of their decision on the application; nor

(b) given notice to him that the application has been referred to the Secretary of State in accordance with directions given under section 77,

within such period as may be prescribed by the development order or within such extended period as may at any time be agreed upon in writing between the applicant and the authority.

(3) Any appeal under this section shall be made by notice served within such time and in such manner as may be prescribed by a development order.

(4) The time prescribed for the service of such a notice must not be less than—

(a) 28 days from the date of notification of the decision; or

(b) in the case of an appeal under subsection (2), 28 days from the end of the period prescribed as mentioned in subsection (2) or, as the case may be, the extended period mentioned in that subsection.

(5) For the purposes of the application of sections 79(1), 253(2)(c), 266(1)(b) and 288(10)(b) in relation to an appeal under subsection (2), it shall be assumed that the authority decided to refuse the application in question.

Determination of appeals.

79.—(1) On an appeal under section 78 the Secretary of State may—

(a) allow or dismiss the appeal, or

(b) reverse or vary any part of the decision of the local planning authority (whether the appeal relates to that part of it or not),

and may deal with the application as if it had been made to him in the first instance.

(2) Before determining an appeal under section 78 the Secretary of State shall, if either the appellant or the local planning authority so wish, give each of them an opportunity of appearing before and being heard by a person appointed by the Secretary of State for the purpose.

(3) Subsection (2) does not apply to an appeal referred to a Planning Inquiry Commission under section 101.

(4) Subject to subsection (2), the provisions of sections 66, 67, 70, 71(2), 72(1) and (5) and 73 and Part I of Schedule 5 shall apply, with any necessary modifications, in relation to an appeal to the Secretary of State under section 78 as they apply in relation to an application for planning permission which falls to be determined by the local planning authority.

(5) The decision of the Secretary of State on such an appeal shall be final.

(6) If, before or during the determination of such an appeal in respect of an application for planning permission to develop land, the Secretary of State forms the opinion that, having regard to the provisions of sections 70 and 72(1), the development order and any directions given under that order, planning permission for that development—

(a) could not have been granted by the local planning authority; or

(b) could not have been granted otherwise than subject to the conditions imposed,

he may decline to determine the appeal or to proceed with the determination.

(7) Schedule 6 applies to appeals under section 78, including appeals under that section as applied by or under any other provision of this Act.

Review of planning decisions where compensation claimed.

80.—(1) This section and section 81 apply where, in accordance with the provisions of Part V, one or more claims for compensation in respect of a planning decision have been transmitted to the Secretary of State and the claim, or (if there is more than one) one or more of the claims, has not been withdrawn.

(2) If, in the case of a planning decision of the local planning authority, it appears to the Secretary of State that, if the application for permission to develop the land in question had been referred to him for determination, he would have made a decision more favourable to the applicant, the Secretary of State may give a direction substituting that decision for the decision of the local planning authority.

PART III

(3) The reference in subsection (2) to a decision more favourable to the applicant shall be construed—

(a) in relation to a refusal of permission, as a reference to a decision granting the permission, either unconditionally or subject to conditions, and either in respect of the whole of the land to which the application for permission related or in respect of part of that land; and

(b) in relation to a grant of permission subject to conditions, as a reference to a decision granting the permission applied for unconditionally or subject to less stringent conditions.

(4) If in any case it appears to the Secretary of State that planning permission could properly be granted (either unconditionally or subject to certain conditions) for some development of the land in question other than the development to which the application for planning permission related, the Secretary of State may give a direction that this Act shall have effect in relation to that application and to the planning decision—

(a) as if the application had included an application for permission for that other development, and the decision had included the grant of planning permission (unconditionally or, as the case may be, subject to those conditions) for that development; or

(b) as if the decision had been made by him and had included an undertaking to grant planning permission (unconditionally or, as the case may be, subject to those conditions) for that development,

as may be specified in the direction.

Provisions supplementary to s. 80.

81.—(1) Before giving a direction under section 80 the Secretary of State shall give notice in writing of his proposed direction—

(a) to the local planning authority to whose decision that direction relates, and

(b) to any person who made, and has not since withdrawn, a claim for compensation in respect of that decision.

(2) If so required by the local planning authority or by any such person, the Secretary of State shall give each of them an opportunity to appear before, and be heard by, a person appointed by the Secretary of State for the purpose.

(3) In giving any direction under section 80, the Secretary of State shall have regard—

(a) to the provisions of the development plan for the area in which the land in question is situated (in so far as those provisions are material to the development of that land); and

(b) to the local circumstances affecting the proposed development, including the use which prevails generally in the case of contiguous or adjacent land; and

(c) to any other material considerations.

(4) Where the Secretary of State gives a direction under section 80, he shall give notice of the direction—

(a) to the local planning authority to whose decision the direction relates; and

(b) to any person who made, and has not since withdrawn, a claim for compensation in respect of that decision.

Simplified planning zones

Simplified planning zones.

82.—(1) A simplified planning zone is an area in respect of which a simplified planning zone scheme is in force.

(2) The adoption or approval of a simplified planning zone scheme has effect to grant in relation to the zone, or any part of it specified in the scheme, planning permission—

(a) for development specified in the scheme, or

(b) for development of any class so specified.

(3) Planning permission under a simplified planning zone scheme may be unconditional or subject to such conditions, limitations or exceptions as may be specified in the scheme.

Making of simplified planning zone schemes.

83.—(1) Every local planning authority shall consider, as soon as practicable after 2nd November 1987, the question for which part or parts of their area a simplified planning zone scheme is desirable, and then shall keep that question under review.

(2) If as a result of their original consideration or of any such review a local planning authority decide that it is desirable to prepare a scheme for any part of their area they shall do so; and a local planning authority may at any time decide—

(a) to make a simplified planning zone scheme, or

(b) to alter a scheme adopted by them, or

(c) with the consent of the Secretary of State, to alter a scheme approved by him.

(3) Schedule 7 has effect with respect to the making and alteration of simplified planning zone schemes and other related matters.

Simplified planning zone schemes: conditions and limitations on planning permission.

84.—(1) The conditions and limitations on planning permission which may be specified in a simplified planning zone scheme may include—

(a) conditions or limitations in respect of all development permitted by the scheme or in respect of particular descriptions of development so permitted, and

(b) conditions or limitations requiring the consent, agreement or approval of the local planning authority in relation to particular descriptions of permitted development.

(2) Different conditions or limitations may be specified in a simplified planning zone scheme for different cases or classes of case.

(3) Nothing in a simplified planning zone scheme shall affect the right of any person—

(a) to do anything not amounting to development, or

(b) to carry out development for which planning permission is not required or for which permission has been granted otherwise than by the scheme.

PART III

(4) No limitation or restriction subject to which permission has been granted otherwise than under the scheme shall affect the right of any person to carry out development for which permission has been granted under the scheme.

Duration of simplified planning zone scheme.

85.—(1) A simplified planning zone scheme shall take effect on the date of its adoption or approval and shall cease to have effect at the end of the period of 10 years beginning with that date.

(2) When the scheme ceases to have effect planning permission under it shall also cease to have effect except in a case where the development authorised by it has been begun.

Alteration of simplified planning zone scheme.

86.—(1) This section applies where alterations to a simplified planning zone scheme are adopted or approved.

(2) The adoption or approval of alterations providing for the inclusion of land in the simplified planning zone has effect to grant in relation to that land, or such part of it as is specified in the scheme, planning permission for development so specified or of any class so specified.

(3) The adoption or approval of alterations providing for the grant of planning permission has effect to grant such permission in relation to the simplified planning zone, or such part of it as is specified in the scheme, for development so specified or development of any class so specified.

(4) The adoption or approval of alterations providing for the withdrawal or relaxation of conditions, limitations or restrictions to which planning permission under the scheme is subject has effect to withdraw or relax the conditions, limitations or restrictions immediately.

(5) The adoption or approval of alterations providing for—

(a) the exclusion of land from the simplified planning zone,

(b) the withdrawal of planning permission, or

(c) the imposition of new or more stringent conditions, limitations or restrictions to which planning permission under the scheme is subject,

has effect to withdraw permission, or to impose the conditions, limitations or restrictions, with effect from the end of the period of 12 months beginning with the date of the adoption or approval.

(6) The adoption or approval of alterations to a scheme does not affect planning permission under the scheme in any case where the development authorised by it has been begun.

Exclusion of certain descriptions of land or development.

87.—(1) The following descriptions of land may not be included in a simplified planning zone—

(a) land in a National Park;

(b) land in a conservation area;

(c) land within the Broads;

1949 c. 97.

(d) land in an area designated under section 87 of the National Parks and Access to the Countryside Act 1949 as an area of outstanding natural beauty;

(e) land identified in the development plan for the district as part of a green belt;

PART III

(f) land in respect of which a notification or order is in force under section 28 or 29 of the Wildlife and Countryside Act 1981 (areas of special scientific interest). 1981 c. 69.

(2) Where land included in a simplified planning zone becomes land of a description mentioned in subsection (1), that subsection does not operate to exclude it from the zone.

(3) The Secretary of State may by order provide that no simplified planning zone scheme shall have effect to grant planning permission—

(a) in relation to an area of land specified in the order or to areas of land of a description so specified, or

(b) for development of a description specified in the order.

(4) An order under subsection (3) has effect to withdraw such planning permission under a simplified planning zone scheme already in force with effect from the date on which the order comes into force, except in a case where the development authorised by the permission has been begun.

Enterprise zone schemes

Planning permission for development in enterprise zones.

88.—(1) An order designating an enterprise zone under Schedule 32 to the Local Government, Planning and Land Act 1980 shall (without more) have effect on the date on which the order designating the zone takes effect to grant planning permission for development specified in the scheme or for development of any class so specified. 1980 c.65.

(2) The approval of a modified scheme under paragraph 11 of that Schedule shall (without more) have effect on the date on which the modifications take effect to grant planning permission for development specified in the modified scheme or for development of any class so specified.

(3) Planning permission so granted shall be subject to such conditions or limitations as may be specified in the scheme or modified scheme or, if none is specified, shall be unconditional.

(4) Subject to subsection (5), where planning permission is so granted for any development or class of development the enterprise zone authority may direct that the permission shall not apply in relation—

(a) to a specified development; or

(b) to a specified class of development; or

(c) to a specified class of development in a specified area within the enterprise zone.

(5) An enterprise zone authority shall not give a direction under subsection (4) unless—

(a) they have submitted it to the Secretary of State, and

(b) he has notified them that he approves of their giving it.

(6) If the scheme or the modified scheme specifies, in relation to any development it permits, matters which will require approval by the enterprise zone authority, the permission shall have effect accordingly.

(7) The Secretary of State may by regulations make provision as to—

(a) the procedure for giving a direction under subsection (4); and

PART III

(b) the method and procedure relating to the approval of matters specified in a scheme or modified scheme as mentioned in subsection (6).

(8) Such regulations may modify any provision of the planning Acts or any instrument made under them or may apply any such provision or instrument (with or without modification) in making any such provision as is mentioned in subsection (7).

(9) Nothing in this section prevents planning permission being granted in relation to land in an enterprise zone otherwise than by virtue of this section (whether the permission is granted in pursuance of an application made under this Part or by a development order).

(10) Nothing in this section prejudices the right of any person to carry out development apart from this section.

Effect on planning permission of modification or termination of scheme.

89.—(1) Modifications to an enterprise zone scheme do not affect planning permission under the scheme in any case where the development authorised by it has been begun before the modifications take effect.

(2) When an area ceases to be an enterprise zone, planning permission under the scheme shall cease to have effect except in a case where the development authorised by it has been begun.

Deemed planning permission

Development with government authorisation.

90.—(1) Where the authorisation of a government department is required by virtue of an enactment in respect of development to be carried out by a local authority, or by statutory undertakers who are not a local authority, that department may, on granting that authorisation, direct that planning permission for that development shall be deemed to be granted, subject to such conditions (if any) as may be specified in the direction.

1989 c. 29.

(2) On granting a consent under section 36 or 37 of the Electricity Act 1989 in respect of any operation or change of use that constitutes development, the Secretary of State may direct that planning permission for that development and any ancillary development shall be deemed to be granted, subject to such conditions (if any) as may be specified in the direction.

(3) The provisions of this Act (except Parts V and XII) shall apply in relation to any planning permission deemed to be granted by virtue of a direction under this section as if it had been granted by the Secretary of State on an application referred to him under section 77.

(4) For the purposes of this section development is authorised by a government department if—

(a) any consent, authority or approval to or for the development is granted by the department in pursuance of an enactment;

(b) a compulsory purchase order is confirmed by the department authorising the purchase of land for the purpose of the development;

(c) consent is granted by the department to the appropriation of land for the purpose of the development or the acquisition of land by agreement for that purpose;

(d) authority is given by the department—

(i) for the borrowing of money for the purpose of the development, or

(ii) for the application for that purpose of any money not otherwise so applicable; or

(e) any undertaking is given by the department to pay a grant in respect of the development in accordance with an enactment authorising the payment of such grants;

and references in this section to the authorisation of a government department shall be construed accordingly.

(5) In subsection (2) "ancillary development", in relation to development consisting of the extension of a generating station, does not include any development which is not directly related to the generation of electricity by that station; and in this subsection "extension" and "generating station" have the same meanings as in Part I of the Electricity Act 1989. 1989 c. 29.

Duration of planning permission

General condition limiting duration of planning permission.

91.—(1) Subject to the provisions of this section, every planning permission granted or deemed to be granted shall be granted or, as the case may be, be deemed to be granted, subject to the condition that the development to which it relates must be begun not later than the expiration of—

(a) five years beginning with the date on which the permission is granted or, as the case may be, deemed to be granted; or

(b) such other period (whether longer or shorter) beginning with that date as the authority concerned with the terms of planning permission may direct.

(2) The period mentioned in subsection (1)(b) shall be a period which the authority consider appropriate having regard to the provisions of the development plan and to any other material considerations.

(3) If planning permission is granted without the condition required by subsection (1), it shall be deemed to have been granted subject to the condition that the development to which it relates must be begun not later than the expiration of five years beginning with the date of the grant.

(4) Nothing in this section applies—

(a) to any planning permission granted by a development order;

(b) to any planning permission granted under section 63 on an application relating to buildings or works completed, or a use of land instituted, before the date of the application;

(c) to any planning permission granted for a limited period;

(d) to any planning permission for development consisting of the winning and working of minerals which is granted (or deemed to be granted) subject to a condition that the development to which it relates must be begun before the expiration of a specified period after the completion of other development consisting of the winning and working of minerals which is already being carried out by the applicant for the planning permission;

(e) to any planning permission granted by an enterprise zone scheme;

PART III

(f) to any planning permission granted by a simplified planning zone scheme; or

(g) to any outline planning permission, as defined by section 92.

Outline planning permission.

92.—(1) In this section and section 91 "outline planning permission" means planning permission granted, in accordance with the provisions of a development order, with the reservation for subsequent approval by the local planning authority or the Secretary of State of matters not particularised in the application ("reserved matters").

(2) Subject to the following provisions of this section, where outline planning permission is granted for development consisting in or including the carrying out of building or other operations, it shall be granted subject to conditions to the effect—

(a) that, in the case of any reserved matter, application for approval must be made not later than the expiration of three years beginning with the date of the grant of outline planning permission; and

(b) that the development to which the permission relates must be begun not later than—

(i) the expiration of five years from the date of the grant of outline planning permission; or

(ii) if later, the expiration of two years from the final approval of the reserved matters or, in the case of approval on different dates, the final approval of the last such matter to be approved.

(3) If outline planning permission is granted without the conditions required by subsection (2), it shall be deemed to have been granted subject to those conditions.

(4) The authority concerned with the terms of an outline planning permission may, in applying subsection (2), substitute, or direct that there be substituted, for the periods of three years, five years or two years referred to in that subsection such other periods respectively (whether longer or shorter) as they consider appropriate.

(5) They may also specify, or direct that there be specified, separate periods under paragraph (a) of subsection (2) in relation to separate parts of the development to which the planning permission relates; and, if they do so, the condition required by paragraph (b) of that subsection shall then be framed correspondingly by reference to those parts, instead of by reference to the development as a whole.

(6) In considering whether to exercise their powers under subsections (4) and (5), the authority shall have regard to the provisions of the development plan and to any other material considerations.

Provisions supplementary to ss. 91 and 92.

93.—(1) The authority referred to in section 91(1)(b) or 92(4) is—

(a) the local planning authority or the Secretary of State, in the case of planning permission granted by them,

(b) in the case of planning permission deemed to be granted under section 90(1), the department on whose direction planning permission is deemed to be granted, and

(c) in the case of planning permission deemed to be granted under section 90(2), the Secretary of State.

(2) For the purposes of section 92, a reserved matter shall be treated as finally approved—

(a) when an application for approval is granted, or

(b) in a case where the application is made to the local planning authority and on an appeal to the Secretary of State against the authority's decision on the application the Secretary of State grants the approval, when the appeal is determined.

(3) Where a local planning authority grant planning permission, the fact that any of the conditions of the permission are required by the provisions of section 91 or 92 to be imposed, or are deemed by those provisions to be imposed, shall not prevent the conditions being the subject of an appeal under section 78 against the decision of the authority.

(4) In the case of planning permission (whether outline or other) which has conditions attached to it by or under section 91 or 92—

(a) development carried out after the date by which the conditions require it to be carried out shall be treated as not authorised by the permission; and

(b) an application for approval of a reserved matter, if it is made after the date by which the conditions require it to be made, shall be treated as not made in accordance with the terms of the permission.

Termination of planning permission by reference to time limit: completion notices.

94.—(1) This section applies where—

(a) by virtue of section 91 or 92, a planning permission is subject to a condition that the development to which the permission relates must be begun before the expiration of a particular period, that development has been begun within that period, but that period has elapsed without the development having been completed; or

(b) development has been begun in accordance with planning permission under a simplified planning zone scheme but has not been completed by the time the area ceases to be a simplified planning zone; or

(c) development has been begun in accordance with planning permission under an enterprise zone scheme but has not been completed by the time the area ceases to be an enterprise zone.

(2) If the local planning authority are of the opinion that the development will not be completed within a reasonable period, they may serve a notice ("a completion notice") stating that the planning permission will cease to have effect at the expiration of a further period specified in the notice.

(3) The period so specified must not be less than 12 months after the notice takes effect.

(4) A completion notice shall be served—

(a) on the owner of the land,

(b) on the occupier of the land, and

(c) on any other person who in the opinion of the local planning authority will be affected by the notice.

PART III

(5) The local planning authority may withdraw a completion notice at any time before the expiration of the period specified in it as the period at the expiration of which the planning permission is to cease to have effect.

(6) If they do so they shall immediately give notice of the withdrawal to every person who was served with the completion notice.

Effect of completion notice.

95.—(1) A completion notice shall not take effect unless and until it is confirmed by the Secretary of State.

(2) In confirming a completion notice the Secretary of State may substitute some longer period for that specified in the notice as the period at the expiration of which the planning permission is to cease to have effect.

(3) If, within such period as may be specified in a completion notice (which must not be less than 28 days from its service) any person on whom the notice is served so requires, the Secretary of State, before confirming the notice, shall give him and the local planning authority an opportunity of appearing before and being heard by a person appointed by the Secretary of State for the purpose.

(4) If a completion notice takes effect, the planning permission referred to in it shall become invalid at the expiration of the period specified in the notice (whether the original period specified under section 94(2) or a longer period substituted by the Secretary of State under subsection (2)).

(5) Subsection (4) shall not affect any permission so far as development carried out under it before the end of the period mentioned in that subsection is concerned.

Power of Secretary of State to serve completion notices.

96.—(1) If it appears to the Secretary of State to be expedient that a completion notice should be served in respect of any land, he may himself serve such a notice.

(2) A completion notice served by the Secretary of State shall have the same effect as if it had been served by the local planning authority.

(3) The Secretary of State shall not serve such a notice without consulting the local planning authority.

Revocation and modification of planning permission

Power to revoke or modify planning permission.

97.—(1) If it appears to the local planning authority that it is expedient to revoke or modify any permission to develop land granted on an application made under this Part, the authority may by order revoke or modify the permission to such extent as they consider expedient.

(2) In exercising their functions under subsection (1) the authority shall have regard to the development plan and to any other material considerations.

(3) The power conferred by this section may be exercised—

(a) where the permission relates to the carrying out of building or other operations, at any time before those operations have been completed;

(b) where the permission relates to a change of the use of any land, at any time before the change has taken place.

(4) The revocation or modification of permission for the carrying out of building or other operations shall not affect so much of those operations as has been previously carried out.

(5) References in this section to the local planning authority are to be construed in relation to development consisting of the winning and working of minerals as references to the mineral planning authority, and Part II of Schedule 5 shall have effect for the purpose of making special provision with respect to the conditions which may be imposed by an order under this section revoking or modifying permission for such development.

Procedure for s. 97 orders: opposed cases.

98.—(1) Except as provided in section 99, an order under section 97 shall not take effect unless it is confirmed by the Secretary of State.

(2) Where a local planning authority submit such an order to the Secretary of State for confirmation, they shall serve notice on—

(a) the owner of the land affected,

(b) the occupier of the land affected, and

(c) any other person who in their opinion will be affected by the order.

(3) The notice shall specify the period within which any person on whom it is served may require the Secretary of State to give him an opportunity of appearing before, and being heard by, a person appointed by the Secretary of State for the purpose.

(4) If within that period such a person so requires, before the Secretary of State confirms the order he shall give such an opportunity both to him and to the local planning authority.

(5) The period referred to in subsection (3) must not be less than 28 days from the service of the notice.

(6) The Secretary of State may confirm an order submitted to him under this section either without modification or subject to such modifications as he considers expedient.

Procedure for s. 97 orders: unopposed cases.

99.—(1) This section applies where—

(a) the local planning authority have made an order under section 97; and

(b) the owner and the occupier of the land and all persons who in the authority's opinion will be affected by the order have notified the authority in writing that they do not object to it.

(2) Where this section applies, instead of submitting the order to the Secretary of State for confirmation the authority shall advertise in the prescribed manner the fact that the order has been made, and the advertisement must specify—

(a) the period within which persons affected by the order may give notice to the Secretary of State that they wish for an opportunity of appearing before, and being heard by, a person appointed by the Secretary of State for the purpose; and

(b) the period at the expiration of which, if no such notice is given to the Secretary of State, the order may take effect by virtue of this section without being confirmed by the Secretary of State.

PART III

(3) The authority shall also serve notice to the same effect on the persons mentioned in subsection (1)(b).

(4) The period referred to in subsection (2)(a) must not be less than 28 days from the date the advertisement first appears.

(5) The period referred to in subsection (2)(b) must not be less than 14 days from the expiration of the period referred to in subsection (2)(a).

(6) The authority shall send a copy of any advertisement published under subsection (2) to the Secretary of State not more than three days after the publication.

(7) If—

(a) no person claiming to be affected by the order has given notice to the Secretary of State under subsection (2)(a) within the period referred to in that subsection, and

(b) the Secretary of State has not directed within that period that the order be submitted to him for confirmation,

the order shall take effect at the expiry of the period referred to in subsection (2)(b), without being confirmed by the Secretary of State as required by section 98(1).

(8) This section does not apply—

(a) to an order revoking or modifying a planning permission granted or deemed to have been granted by the Secretary of State under this Part or Part VII, or

(b) to an order modifying any conditions to which a planning permission is subject by virtue of section 91 or 92.

Revocation and modification of planning permission by the Secretary of State.

100.—(1) If it appears to the Secretary of State that it is expedient that an order should be made under section 97, he may himself make such an order.

(2) Such an order which is made by the Secretary of State shall have the same effect as if it had been made by the local planning authority and confirmed by the Secretary of State.

(3) The Secretary of State shall not make such an order without consulting the local planning authority.

(4) Where the Secretary of State proposes to make such an order he shall serve notice on the local planning authority.

(5) The notice shall specify the period (which must not be less than 28 days from the date of its service) within which the authority may require an opportunity of appearing before and being heard by a person appointed by the Secretary of State for the purpose.

(6) If within that period the authority so require, before the Secretary of State makes the order he shall give the authority such an opportunity.

(7) The provisions of this Part and of any regulations made under this Act with respect to the procedure to be followed in connection with the submission by the local planning authority of any order under section 97 and its confirmation by the Secretary of State shall have effect, subject to any necessary modifications, in relation to any proposal by the Secretary of State to make such an order and its making by him.

(8) Subsection (5) of section 97 applies for the purposes of this section as it applies for the purposes of that section.

References to Planning Inquiry Commission

Power to refer certain planning questions to Planning Inquiry Commission.

101.—(1) The Secretary of State may constitute a Planning Inquiry Commission to inquire into and report on any matter referred to them under subsection (2) in the circumstances mentioned in subsection (3).

(2) The matters that may be referred to a Planning Inquiry Commission are—

(a) an application for planning permission which the Secretary of State has under section 77 directed to be referred to him instead of being dealt with by a local planning authority;

(b) an appeal under section 78 (including that section as applied by or under any other provision of this Act);

(c) a proposal that a government department should give a direction under section 90(1) that planning permission shall be deemed to be granted for development by a local authority or by statutory undertakers which is required by any enactment to be authorised by that department;

(d) a proposal that development should be carried out by or on behalf of a government department.

(3) Any of those matters may be referred to any such commission under this section if it appears expedient to the responsible Minister or Ministers that the question whether the proposed development should be permitted to be carried out should be the subject of a special inquiry on either or both of the following grounds—

(a) that there are considerations of national or regional importance which are relevant to the determination of that question and require evaluation, but a proper evaluation of them cannot be made unless there is a special inquiry for the purpose;

(b) that the technical or scientific aspects of the proposed development are of so unfamiliar a character as to jeopardise a proper determination of that question unless there is a special inquiry for the purpose.

(4) Part I of Schedule 8 shall have effect as respects the constitution of any such commission and its functions and procedure on references to it under this section, and the references in subsection (3) and in that Schedule to "the responsible Minister or Ministers" shall be construed in accordance with Part II of that Schedule.

(5) In relation to any matter affecting both England and Wales, the functions of the Secretary of State under subsection (1) shall be exercised by the Secretaries of State for the time being having general responsibility in planning matters in relation to England and in relation to Wales acting jointly.

Other controls over development

Orders requiring discontinuance of use or alteration or removal of buildings or works.

102.—(1) If, having regard to the development plan and to any other material considerations, it appears to a local planning authority that it is expedient in the interests of the proper planning of their area (including the interests of amenity)—

PART III

(a) that any use of land should be discontinued or that any conditions should be imposed on the continuance of a use of land; or

(b) that any buildings or works should be altered or removed,

they may by order—

(i) require the discontinuance of that use, or

(ii) impose such conditions as may be specified in the order on the continuance of it, or

(iii) require such steps as may be so specified to be taken for the alteration or removal of the buildings or works,

as the case may be.

(2) An order under this section may grant planning permission for any development of the land to which the order relates, subject to such conditions as may be specified in the order.

(3) Section 97 shall apply in relation to any planning permission granted by an order under this section as it applies in relation to planning permission granted by the local planning authority on an application made under this Part.

(4) The power conferred by subsection (2) includes power, by an order under this section, to grant planning permission, subject to such conditions as may be specified in the order—

(a) for the retention, on the land to which the order relates, of buildings or works constructed or carried out before the date on which the order was submitted to the Secretary of State under section 103; or

(b) for the continuance of a use of that land instituted before that date.

(5) Any planning permission granted in accordance with subsection (4) may be granted—

(a) so as to take effect from the date on which the buildings or works were constructed or carried out, or the use was instituted, or

(b) in the case of buildings or works constructed or a use instituted in accordance with planning permission granted for a limited period, so as to take effect from the end of that period.

(6) Where the requirements of an order under this section will involve the displacement of persons residing in any premises, it shall be the duty of the local planning authority, in so far as there is no other residential accommodation suitable to the reasonable requirements of those persons available on reasonable terms, to secure the provision of such accommodation in advance of the displacement.

(7) Subject to section 103(8), in the case of planning permission granted by an order under this section, the authority referred to in sections 91(1)(b) and 92(4) is the local planning authority making the order.

(8) The previous provisions of this section do not apply to the use of any land for development consisting in the winning or working of minerals except as provided in Schedule 9, and that Schedule shall have effect for the purpose of making provision as respects land which is or has been so used.

PART III

Confirmation by Secretary of State of s. 102 orders.

103.—(1) An order under section 102 shall not take effect unless it is confirmed by the Secretary of State, either without modification or subject to such modifications as he considers expedient.

(2) The power of the Secretary of State under this section to confirm an order subject to modifications includes power—

(a) to modify any provision of the order granting planning permission, as mentioned in subsections (2) to (5) of section 102;

(b) to include in the order any grant of planning permission which might have been included in the order as submitted to him.

(3) Where a local planning authority submit an order to the Secretary of State for his confirmation under this section, they shall serve notice—

(a) on the owner of the land affected,

(b) on the occupier of that land, and

(c) on any other person who in their opinion will be affected by the order.

(4) The notice shall specify the period within which any person on whom it is served may require the Secretary of State to give him an opportunity of appearing before, and being heard by, a person appointed by the Secretary of State for the purpose.

(5) If within that period such a person so requires, before the Secretary of State confirms the order, he shall give such an opportunity both to him and to the local planning authority.

(6) The period referred to in subsection (4) must not be less than 28 days from the service of the notice.

(7) Where an order under section 102 has been confirmed by the Secretary of State, the local planning authority shall serve a copy of the order on the owner and occupier of the land to which the order relates.

(8) Where the Secretary of State exercises his powers under subsection (2) in confirming an order granting planning permission, he is the authority referred to in sections 91(1)(b) and 92(4).

Power of the Secretary of State to make s. 102 orders.

104.—(1) If it appears to the Secretary of State that it is expedient that an order should be made under section 102, he may himself make such an order.

(2) Such an order made by the Secretary of State shall have the same effect as if it had been made by the local planning authority and confirmed by the Secretary of State.

(3) The Secretary of State shall not make such an order without consulting the local planning authority.

(4) Where the Secretary of State proposes to make such an order he shall serve notice on the local planning authority.

(5) The notice shall specify the period within which the authority may require an opportunity of appearing before and being heard by a person appointed by the Secretary of State for the purpose.

(6) If within that period the authority so require, before the Secretary of State makes the order he shall give the authority such an opportunity.

PART III

(7) The period referred to in subsection (5) must not be less than 28 days from the date of the service of the notice.

(8) The provisions of this Part and of any regulations made under this Act with respect to the procedure to be followed in connection with the submission by the local planning authority of any order under section 102, its confirmation by the Secretary of State and the service of copies of it as confirmed shall have effect, subject to any necessary modifications, in relation to any proposal by the Secretary of State to make such an order, its making by him and the service of copies of it.

Duty of mineral planning authorities to review mineral workings.

105.—(1) It shall be the duty of every mineral planning authority—

(a) to undertake at such intervals as they consider fit reviews of every site in their area in, on or under which operations for the winning and working of minerals—

(i) are being carried out; or

(ii) have been carried out at any time during the relevant period; or

(iii) are authorised by planning permission but have not been begun; and

(b) to make in respect of any such site any order under section 97 or under paragraph 1, 3, 5 or 6 of Schedule 9 that they consider appropriate.

(2) In subsection (1) "the relevant period", in relation to a review, means the period of five years preceding the date of the beginning of the review or such other period as may be prescribed.

Agreements regulating development or use of land.

106.—(1) A local planning authority may enter into an agreement with any person interested in land in their area for the purpose of restricting or regulating the development or use of the land, either permanently or during such period as may be prescribed by the agreement.

(2) Any such agreement may contain such incidental and consequential provisions (including financial ones) as appear to the local planning authority to be necessary or expedient for the purposes of the agreement.

(3) An agreement made under this section with any person interested in land may be enforced by the local planning authority against persons deriving title under that person in respect of that land as if the local planning authority were possessed of adjacent land and as if the agreement had been expressed to be made for the benefit of such land.

(4) Nothing in this section or in any agreement made under it shall be construed—

(a) as restricting the exercise, in relation to land which is the subject of any such agreement, of any powers exercisable by any Minister or authority under this Act so long as those powers are exercised in accordance with the provisions of the development plan, or in accordance with any directions which may have been given by the Secretary of State as to the provisions to be included in such a plan; or

(b) as requiring the exercise of any such powers otherwise than as mentioned in paragraph (a).

PART IV

COMPENSATION FOR EFFECTS OF CERTAIN ORDERS, NOTICES, ETC.

Compensation for revocation of planning permission, etc.

Compensation where planning permission revoked or modified.

107.—(1) Subject to section 116, where planning permission is revoked or modified by an order under section 97, then if, on a claim made to the local planning authority within the prescribed time and in the prescribed manner, it is shown that a person interested in the land or in minerals in, on or under it—

(a) has incurred expenditure in carrying out work which is rendered abortive by the revocation or modification; or

(b) has otherwise sustained loss or damage which is directly attributable to the revocation or modification,

the local planning authority shall pay that person compensation in respect of that expenditure, loss or damage.

(2) For the purposes of this section, any expenditure incurred in the preparation of plans for the purposes of any work, or upon other similar matters preparatory to it, shall be taken to be included in the expenditure incurred in carrying out that work.

(3) Subject to subsection (2), no compensation shall be paid under this section in respect—

(a) of any work carried out before the grant of the permission which is revoked or modified, or

(b) of any other loss or damage arising out of anything done or omitted to be done before the grant of that permission (other than loss or damage consisting of depreciation of the value of an interest in land).

(4) In calculating for the purposes of this section the amount of any loss or damage consisting of depreciation of the value of an interest in land, it shall be assumed that planning permission would be granted for development of the land of any class specified in Schedule 3.

(5) In this Part any reference to an order under section 97 includes a reference to an order under the provisions of that section as applied by section 102(3) (or, subject to section 116, by paragraph 1(2) of Schedule 9).

Compensation for refusal or conditional grant of planning permission formerly granted by development order.

108.—(1) Where—

(a) planning permission granted by a development order is withdrawn (whether by the revocation or amendment of the order or by the issue of directions under powers conferred by the order); and

(b) on an application made under Part III planning permission for development formerly permitted by that order is refused or is granted subject to conditions other than those imposed by that order,

section 107 shall apply as if the planning permission granted by the development order—

PART IV

(i) had been granted by the local planning authority under Part III; and

(ii) had been revoked or modified by an order under section 97.

(2) Where planning permission granted by a development order is withdrawn by revocation or amendment of the order, this section applies only if the application referred to in subsection (1)(b) is made before the end of the period of 12 months beginning with the date on which the revocation or amendment came into operation.

(3) This section shall not apply in relation to planning permission for the development of operational land of statutory undertakers.

Apportionment of compensation for depreciation.

109.—(1) Where compensation becomes payable under section 107 which includes compensation for depreciation of an amount exceeding £20, the local planning authority—

(a) if it appears to them to be practicable to do so, shall apportion the amount of the compensation for depreciation between different parts of the land to which the claim for that compensation relates; and

(b) shall give particulars of any such apportionment to the claimant and to any other person entitled to an interest in land which appears to the authority to be substantially affected by the apportionment.

(2) In carrying out an apportionment under subsection (1)(a), the local planning authority shall divide the land into parts and shall distribute the compensation for depreciation between those parts, according to the way in which different parts of the land appear to the authority to be differently affected by the order or, in a case falling within section 108, the relevant planning decision, in consequence of which the compensation is payable.

(3) Regulations under this section shall make provision, subject to subsection (4)—

(a) for enabling the claimant and any other person to whom particulars of an apportionment have been given under subsection (1), or who establishes that he is entitled to an interest in land which is substantially affected by such an apportionment, if he wishes to dispute the apportionment, to require it to be referred to the Lands Tribunal;

(b) for enabling the claimant and every other person to whom particulars of any such apportionment have been so given to be heard by the Tribunal on any reference under this section of that apportionment; and

(c) for requiring the Tribunal, on any such reference, either to confirm or to vary the apportionment and to notify the parties of the decision of the Tribunal.

(4) Where on a reference to the Lands Tribunal under this section it is shown that an apportionment—

(a) relates wholly or partly to the same matters as a previous apportionment, and

PART IV

(b) is consistent with that previous apportionment in so far as it relates to those matters,

the Tribunal shall not vary the apportionment in such a way as to be inconsistent with the previous apportionment in so far as it relates to those matters.

(5) On a reference to the Lands Tribunal by virtue of subsection (3), subsections (1) and (2), so far as they relate to the making of an apportionment, shall apply with the substitution, for references to the local planning authority, of references to the Lands Tribunal.

(6) In this section and in sections 110 and 113—

"compensation for depreciation" means so much of any compensation payable under section 107 as is payable in respect of loss or damage consisting of depreciation of the value of an interest in land,

"interest" (where the reference is to an interest in land) means the fee simple or a tenancy of the land and does not include any other interest in it, and

"relevant planning decision" means the planning decision by which planning permission is refused, or is granted subject to conditions other than those previously imposed by the development order.

Registration of compensation for depreciation.

110.—(1) Where compensation becomes payable under section 107 which includes compensation for depreciation of an amount exceeding £20, the local planning authority shall give notice to the Secretary of State that such compensation has become payable, specifying the amount of the compensation for depreciation and any apportionment of it under section 109.

(2) Where the Secretary of State is given such notice he shall cause notice of that fact to be deposited—

(a) with the council of the district or London borough in which the land is situated, and

(b) if that council is not the local planning authority, with the local planning authority.

(3) Notices deposited under this section must specify—

(a) the order, or in a case falling within section 108 the relevant planning decision, and the land to which the claim for compensation relates; and

(b) the amount of compensation and any apportionment of it under section 109.

(4) Notices deposited under this section shall be local land charges, and for the purposes of the Local Land Charges Act 1975 the council with whom any such notice is deposited shall be treated as the originating authority as respects the charge constituted by it. 1975 c. 76.

(5) In relation to compensation specified in a notice registered under this section, references in this Part to so much of the compensation as is attributable to a part of the land to which the notice relates shall be construed as follows—

PART IV

(a) if the notice does not include an apportionment under section 109, the amount of the compensation shall be treated as distributed rateably according to area over the land to which the notice relates;

(b) if the notice includes such an apportionment—

(i) the compensation shall be treated as distributed in accordance with that apportionment as between the different parts of the land by reference to which the apportionment is made; and

(ii) so much of the compensation as, in accordance with the apportionment, is attributed to a part of the land shall be treated as distributed rateably according to area over that part.

Recovery of compensation under s. 107 on subsequent development.

111.—(1) No person shall carry out any new development to which this section applies on land in respect of which a notice ("a compensation notice") is registered under section 110 until any amount which is recoverable under this section in accordance with section 112 in respect of the compensation specified in the notice has been paid or secured to the satisfaction of the Secretary of State.

(2) Subject to subsections (3) and (4), this section applies to any new development—

(a) which is development of a residential, commercial or industrial character and consists wholly or mainly of the construction of houses, flats, shop or office premises, or industrial buildings (including warehouses), or any combination of them; or

(b) which consists in the winning and working of minerals; or

(c) to which, having regard to the probable value of the development, it is in the opinion of the Secretary of State reasonable that this section should apply.

(3) This section shall not apply to any development by virtue of subsection (2)(c) if, on an application made to him for the purpose, the Secretary of State has certified that, having regard to the probable value of the development, it is not in his opinion reasonable that this section should apply to it.

(4) Where the compensation under section 107 specified in the notice registered under section 110 became payable in respect of an order modifying planning permission or, in a case falling within section 108, of a relevant planning decision (within the meaning of section 109) granting conditional planning permission, this section shall not apply to development in accordance with that permission as modified by the order or, as the case may be, in accordance with those conditions.

(5) For the purposes of this section and section 112 "new development" includes—

(a) any development of a class specified in paragraph 1 or 3 of Schedule 3 which is carried out otherwise than subject to the condition set out in Schedule 10; and

(b) any development excluded by paragraph 14 of Schedule 3 from that Schedule in its application to any determination to which section 326(1) applies.

Part IV

Amount recoverable under s. 111 and provisions for payment or remission of it.

112.—(1) Subject to the following provisions of this section, the amount recoverable under section 111 in respect of the compensation specified in a notice registered under section 110—

(a) if the land on which the development is to be carried out ("the development area") is identical with, or includes (with other land) the whole of, the land comprised in the notice, shall be the amount of compensation specified in the notice;

(b) if the development area forms part of the land comprised in the notice, or includes part of that land together with other land not comprised in the notice, shall be so much of the amount of the compensation specified in the notice as is attributable to land comprised in the notice and falling within the development area.

(2) Where, in the case of any land in respect of which such a notice has been so registered, the Secretary of State is satisfied, having regard to the probable value of any proper development of that land, that no such development is likely to be carried out unless he exercises his powers under this subsection, he may, in the case of any particular development, remit the whole or part of any amount otherwise recoverable under section 111.

(3) Where part only of any such amount has been remitted in respect of any land, the Secretary of State shall cause the notice registered under section 110 to be amended by substituting in it, for the statement of the amount of the compensation, in so far as it is attributable to that land, a statement of the amount which has been remitted under subsection (2).

(4) Where, in connection with the development of any land, an amount becomes recoverable under section 111 in respect of the compensation specified in such a notice, then, except where, and to the extent that, payment of that amount has been remitted under subsection (2), no amount shall be recoverable under that section in respect of that compensation, in so far as it is attributable to that land, in connection with any subsequent development of it.

(5) No amount shall be recoverable under section 111 in respect of any compensation by reference to which a sum has become recoverable by the Secretary of State under section 308.

(6) An amount recoverable under section 111 in respect of any compensation shall be payable to the Secretary of State either—

(a) as a single capital payment, or

(b) as a series of instalments of capital and interest combined, or

(c) as a series of other annual or periodical payments, of such amounts, and payable at such times, as the Secretary of State may direct.

(7) Before giving a direction under subsection (6)(c) the Secretary of State shall take into account any representations made by the person by whom the development is to be carried out.

(8) Except where the amount payable under subsection (6) is payable as a single capital payment, it shall be secured by the person by whom the development is to be carried out in such manner (whether by mortgage, covenant or otherwise) as the Secretary of State may direct.

PART IV

(9) If any person initiates any new development to which section 111 applies in contravention of subsection (1) of that section, the Secretary of State may serve a notice on him—

(a) specifying the amount appearing to the Secretary of State to be the amount recoverable under that section in respect of the compensation in question, and

(b) requiring him to pay that amount to the Secretary of State within such period as may be specified in the notice.

(10) The period specified under subsection (9)(b) must not be less than three months after the service of the notice.

(11) Subject to subsection (12), any sum recovered by the Secretary of State under section 111 shall be paid to the local planning authority who paid the compensation to which that sum relates.

(12) Subject to subsection (13), in paying any such sum to the local planning authority, the Secretary of State shall deduct from it—

(a) the amount of any contribution paid by him under section 113 in respect of the compensation to which the sum relates;

(b) the amount of any grant paid by him under Part XIV in respect of that compensation.

(13) If the sum recovered by the Secretary of State under section 111—

(a) is an instalment of the total sum recoverable, or

(b) is recovered by reference to development of part of the land in respect of which the compensation was payable,

any deduction to be made under paragraph (a) or paragraph (b) of subsection (12) shall be a deduction of such amount as the Secretary of State may determine to be the proper proportion of the amount referred to in that paragraph.

Contribution by Secretary of State towards compensation in certain cases.

113.—(1) Where—

(a) a notice under section 110 is given to the Secretary of State in consequence of the making of an order under section 97 revoking or modifying planning permission or, in a case falling within section 108, of a relevant planning decision refusing planning permission or granting it conditionally, and

(b) if that permission had been refused, or, as the case may be, had been granted as so modified or subject to those conditions, at the time when it was granted, compensation under Part V could have been claimed and would have been payable by the Secretary of State,

the Secretary of State may pay to the local planning authority a contribution of the amount appearing to him to be the amount of compensation which would have been so payable by him under Part V.

(2) The amount of any such contribution shall not exceed—

(a) the amount of the compensation for depreciation paid by the local planning authority; or

(b) the unexpended balance of established development value of the land in respect of which that compensation was paid at the date of the making of the order or, in a case falling within section 108, of the relevant planning decision.

(3) Regulations made under this section shall make provision, in relation to cases where the Secretary of State proposes to pay a contribution under this section—

(a) for requiring the Secretary of State to give notice of his proposal—

(i) to persons entitled to such interests in the land to which the proposal relates as may be prescribed, and

(ii) to such other persons (if any) as may be determined in accordance with the regulations to be affected by the proposal;

(b) for enabling persons to whom notice of the proposal is given to object to the proposal on the grounds—

(i) that compensation would not have been payable as mentioned in subsection (1), or

(ii) that the amount of the compensation so payable would have been less than the amount of the proposed contribution;

(c) for enabling any person making such an objection to require the matter in dispute to be referred to the Lands Tribunal for determination; and

(d) where a contribution under this section is paid, for applying (with any necessary modifications) the provisions of Part V as to the reduction or extinguishment of the unexpended balance of established development value of land as if the contribution had been a payment of compensation under that Part.

Compensation for other planning decisions

Compensation for planning decisions restricting development other than new development.

114.—(1) This section applies where, on an application for planning permission to carry out development of any class specified in Part II of Schedule 3, the Secretary of State, either on appeal or on the reference of the application to him for determination, refuses the permission or grants it subject to conditions.

(2) If, on a claim made to the local planning authority within the prescribed time and in the prescribed manner, it is shown that the value of the interest of any person in the land is less than it would have been if the permission had been granted or, as the case may be, had been granted unconditionally, the local planning authority shall pay that person compensation of an amount equal to the difference.

(3) In determining, for the purposes of subsection (2), whether or to what extent the value of an interest in land is less than it would have been if the permission had been granted, or had been granted unconditionally—

(a) it shall be assumed that any subsequent application for similar planning permission would be determined in the same way; but

(b) if, in the case of a refusal of planning permission, the Secretary of State, on refusing that permission, undertook to grant planning permission for some other development of the land if an application were made for it, regard must be had to that undertaking; and

(c) no account shall be taken of any prospective use which would contravene the condition set out in Schedule 10.

PART IV

(4) Where, on such an application as is mentioned in subsection (1), planning permission is granted by the Secretary of State subject to conditions for regulating the design or external appearance or the size or height of buildings, the Secretary of State may direct that those conditions shall be disregarded, either altogether or to such extent as may be specified in the direction, in assessing the compensation (if any) payable under this section.

(5) The Secretary of State shall only give a direction under subsection (4) if it appears to him to be reasonable to do so having regard to the local circumstances.

(6) For the purposes of subsection (1)—

(a) paragraph 3 of Schedule 3 shall be construed as not extending to the enlargement of a building which was in existence on 1st July 1948 if—

(i) the building contains two or more separate dwellings divided horizontally from each other or from some other part of the building; and

(ii) the enlargement would result in either an increase in the number of such dwellings contained in the building or an increase of more than one-tenth in the cubic content of any such dwelling contained in the building;

(b) that paragraph shall be construed as not extending to works involving any increase in the cubic content of a building erected after that date (including any building resulting from the carrying out of such works as are described in paragraph 1 of Schedule 3); and

(c) paragraph 7 of that Schedule shall not apply to any such building as mentioned in paragraph (b).

(7) For the purposes of this section the conditions referred to in sections 91 and 92 shall be disregarded.

(8) No compensation shall be payable under this section in respect of an interest in land in respect of which a purchase notice is served.

Compensation in respect of orders under s. 102, etc.

115.—(1) This section shall have effect where an order is made under section 102—

(a) requiring a use of land to be discontinued,

(b) imposing conditions on the continuance of it, or

(c) requiring any buildings or works on land to be altered or removed.

(2) If, on a claim made to the local planning authority within the prescribed time and in the prescribed manner, it is shown that any person has suffered damage in consequence of the order—

(a) by depreciation of the value of an interest to which he is entitled in the land or in minerals in, on or under it, or

(b) by being disturbed in his enjoyment of the land or of such minerals,

that authority shall pay to that person compensation in respect of that damage.

(3) Without prejudice to subsection (2), any person who carries out any works in compliance with the order shall be entitled, on a claim made as mentioned in that subsection, to recover from the local planning authority compensation in respect of any expenses reasonably incurred by him in that behalf.

(4) Any compensation payable to a person under this section by virtue of such an order as is mentioned in subsection (1) shall be reduced by the value to him of any timber, apparatus or other materials removed for the purpose of complying with the order.

(5) Subject to section 116, this section applies where such an order as is mentioned in subsection (6) is made as it applies where an order is made under section 102.

(6) The orders referred to in subsection (5) are an order under paragraph 1 of Schedule 9—

(a) requiring a use of land to be discontinued, or

(b) imposing conditions on the continuance of it, or

(c) requiring any buildings or works or plant or machinery on land to be altered or removed,

or an order under paragraph 3, 5 or 6 of that Schedule.

Special basis for compensation in respect of certain orders affecting mineral working.

116. Schedule 11 shall have effect for the purpose of making special provision as respects the payment of compensation in certain circumstances where an order under section 97 modifies planning permission for development consisting of the winning and working of minerals or an order is made under paragraph 1, 3, 5 or 6 of Schedule 9.

General and supplemental provisions

General provisions as to compensation for depreciation under Part IV.
1961 c.33.

117.—(1) For the purpose of assessing any compensation to which this section applies, the rules set out in section 5 of the Land Compensation Act 1961 shall, so far as applicable and subject to any necessary modifications, have effect as they have effect for the purpose of assessing compensation for the compulsory acquisition of an interest in land.

(2) Subject to regulations under paragraph 1 of Schedule 11, this section applies to any compensation which under the provisions of this Part is payable in respect of depreciation of the value of an interest in land.

(3) Where an interest in land is subject to a mortgage—

(a) any compensation to which this section applies, which is payable in respect of depreciation of the value of that interest, shall be assessed as if the interest were not subject to the mortgage;

(b) a claim for any such compensation may be made by any mortgagee of the interest, but without prejudice to the making of a claim by the person entitled to the interest;

(c) no compensation to which this section applies shall be payable in respect of the interest of the mortgagee (as distinct from the interest which is subject to the mortgage); and

PART IV

(d) any compensation to which this section applies which is payable in respect of the interest which is subject to the mortgage shall be paid to the mortgagee, or, if there is more than one mortgagee, to the first mortgagee, and shall in either case be applied by him as if it were proceeds of sale.

Determination of claims for compensation.

118.—(1) Except in so far as may be otherwise provided by any regulations made under this Act, any question of disputed compensation under this Part shall be referred to and determined by the Lands Tribunal.

1961 c.33.

(2) In relation to the determination of any such question, the provisions of sections 2 and 4 of the Land Compensation Act 1961 shall apply subject to any necessary modifications and to the provisions of any regulations made under this Act.

PART V

COMPENSATION FOR RESTRICTIONS ON NEW DEVELOPMENT IN LIMITED CASES

Preliminary

Scope of Part V.

119.—(1) This Part shall have effect for enabling compensation to be claimed in respect of planning decisions by which permission for the carrying out of new development of land is refused or is granted subject to conditions, in cases where at the time of the decision the land, or part of the land, has an unexpended balance of established development value.

(2) Schedule 12 shall have effect for the purpose of determining whether land has an unexpended balance of established development value for the purposes of this Part and, if so, what the amount of that balance is and for making further provision with respect to those questions.

(3) In accordance with subsection (5) of section 63, subsection (3) of that section does not apply for the purposes of this Part.

(4) In this Part—

(a) "interest" (where the reference is to an interest in land) means the fee simple or a tenancy of the land and does not include any other interest in it; and

(b) "local planning authority", in relation to a planning decision, means the authority who made the decision.

Right to compensation

Right to compensation: general principles.

120. Subject to the provisions of this Part, a person shall be entitled to compensation under this Part in respect of a planning decision by which planning permission for the carrying out of new development of land is refused, or is granted subject to conditions, if—

(a) at the time of the decision he is entitled to an interest in any land to which the decision relates which has an unexpended balance of established development value; and

(b) the value of that interest or, in the case of an interest extending to other land, the value of that interest in so far as it subsists in the land referred to in paragraph (a) is depreciated by the decision.

Planning decisions not ranking for compensation.

121.—(1) Compensation under this Part shall not be payable—

(a) in respect of the refusal of planning permission for any development which consists of or includes the making of any material change in the use of any buildings or other land; or

(b) in respect of any decision made on an application in pursuance of regulations under section 220 for consent to the display of advertisements.

(2) Compensation under this Part shall not be payable in respect of the imposition, on the granting of planning permission to develop land, of any condition relating to—

(a) the number or disposition of buildings on any land;

(b) the dimensions, design, structure or external appearance of any building, or the materials to be used in its construction;

(c) the manner in which any land is to be laid out for the purposes of the development, including the provision of facilities for the parking, loading, unloading or fuelling of vehicles on the land;

(d) the use of any buildings or other land; or

(e) the location or design of any means of access to a highway or the materials to be used in the construction of any such means of access,

or in respect of any condition subject to which permission is granted for the winning and working of minerals.

(3) In subsection (2) "means of access to a highway" does not include a service road.

(4) Compensation under this Part shall not be payable in respect of the application to any planning permission of any of the conditions referred to in sections 91 and 92.

(5) Subject to subsection (6), compensation under this Part shall not be payable in respect of the refusal of permission to develop land, if the reason or one of the reasons stated for the refusal is that development of the kind proposed would be premature by reference to either or both of the following matters, that is to say—

(a) the order of priority (if any) indicated in the development plan for the area in which the land is situated for development in that area;

(b) any existing deficiency in the provision of water supplies or sewerage services, and the period within which any such deficiency may reasonably be expected to be made good.

(6) Subsection (5) shall not apply if—

(a) the reason or one of the reasons stated as mentioned in that subsection is that the development would be premature by reference to the matters mentioned in paragraph (a) of that subsection, and

(b) the planning decision refusing the permission is made on an application made more than seven years after the date of a previous planning decision by which permission to develop the same land was refused for the same reason, or for reasons which included the same reason.

PART V

(7) Compensation under this Part shall not be payable in respect of the refusal of permission to develop land if the reason or one of the reasons stated for the refusal is that the land is unsuitable for the proposed development on account of its liability to flooding or to subsidence.

(8) For the purposes of this section, a planning decision by which permission to develop land is granted subject to a condition prohibiting development on a specified part of that land shall be treated as a decision refusing the permission with respect to that part.

No compensation if certain other development permitted.

122.—(1) Subject to subsection (2), compensation under this Part shall not be payable in respect of a planning decision by which permission is refused for the development of land if, notwithstanding that refusal, there is available with respect to that land planning permission for development to which this section applies.

(2) Where such permission is available with respect to part only of the land, this section shall have effect only in so far as the interest subsists in that part.

(3) Where a claim for compensation under this Part is made in respect of an interest in any land, planning permission for development to which this section applies shall be taken for the purposes of this section to be available with respect to that land or a part of it if, immediately before the Secretary of State gives notice of his findings in respect of that claim, there is in force with respect to that land, or that part of it, a grant of, or an undertaking by the Secretary of State to grant, planning permission for some such development, subject to no conditions other than such as are mentioned in section 121(2).

(4) This section applies to any development which—

(a) is of a residential, commercial or industrial character, and

(b) consists wholly or mainly of the construction of houses, flats, shop or office premises, or industrial buildings (including warehouses), or any combination of them.

Further exclusions from compensation.

123.—(1) Where an interest in any land has (whether before or after the commencement of this Act) been compulsorily acquired by, or sold to, an authority possessing compulsory purchase powers (other than statutory undertakers or the British Coal Corporation), that authority, and any person deriving title from that authority under a disposition made by that authority on or at any time after 1st July 1948, shall not be entitled to compensation under this Part in respect of a planning decision made after the service of the notice to treat or, as the case may be, after the making of the contract of sale by reason that the value of that interest, or of any interest created (whether immediately or derivatively) out of that interest, is depreciated by the decision.

(2) Subsection (1) shall apply to land which has at any time on or after 1st July 1948 (whether before or after the commencement of this Act) been appropriated by a local authority for a purpose for which the authority could have been authorised to acquire the land compulsorily as it applies to land in which an interest has been acquired as mentioned in that subsection, with the substitution for the reference to the service of the notice to treat of a reference to the appropriation.

(3) Where at the relevant date any land was or is operational land of statutory undertakers, or land of the British Coal Corporation of a class specified in regulations made under section 90 of the 1947 Act or under section 273 of the 1971 Act or under section 317 of this Act, the statutory undertakers or, as the case may be, the British Coal Corporation and any person deriving title from those undertakers or that Corporation shall not be entitled to compensation under this Part, in respect of a planning decision made after the relevant date, by reason that the value of any interest in that land is depreciated by that decision. PART V

(4) In subsection (3) "the relevant date"—

(a) in relation to land which was such operational land or land of the British Coal Corporation as is mentioned in that subsection on 1st January 1955, means that day, and

(b) in relation to land which (whether before or after the commencement of this Act) became or becomes such operational land or land of the British Coal Corporation on a date subsequent to 1st January 1955, means that subsequent date.

(5) A person shall not be entitled to compensation under this Part in respect of depreciation of the value of an interest in land by a planning decision if he is entitled to compensation by virtue of section 108 in respect of depreciation of the value of that interest by that decision.

Grant of planning permission treated as subject to notional condition.

124.—(1) This section shall have effect where—

(a) on an application for planning permission for the carrying out of new development of land, a planning decision is made by which the permission is granted, whether unconditionally or subject to conditions; and

(b) the Secretary of State certifies that he is satisfied that particular buildings or works to which the application related were only included in it because the applicant had reason to believe that permission for the other development to which the application related (in this section referred to as "the principal development") would not have been granted except subject to a condition requiring the erection or construction of those buildings or works.

(2) Where subsection (1) applies, then for the purposes of this Part—

(a) the application shall be deemed to have included, in the place of those buildings or works, such other development of the land on which the buildings or works were to be erected or constructed as might reasonably have been expected to have been included having regard to the principal development; and

(b) the permission shall be deemed to have been granted for the principal development subject to a condition requiring the erection or construction of those buildings or works.

Amount of compensation

General provisions as to amount of compensation.

125.—(1) Where a person is entitled to compensation under this Part in respect of depreciation by a planning decision of the value of an interest in land, the amount of the compensation, subject to the following provisions of this section, shall be—

PART V

(a) the amount by which the value of that interest, in so far as it subsists in land to which this section applies, is depreciated by the decision; or

(b) if less, the amount of the unexpended balance of established development value, immediately before the decision, of so much of the land in which the interest subsists as is land to which this section applies.

(2) Land to which this section applies, in relation to a planning decision, is land which—

(a) constitutes or forms part of the decision area; and

(b) at the time of the decision has an unexpended balance of established development value.

(3) If, in the case of any land to which this section applies—

(a) compensation is payable under this Part in respect of two or more interests in that land by reason of the same planning decision, and

(b) the aggregate amount of compensation payable apart from this subsection in respect of those interests would exceed the amount mentioned in paragraph (b) of subsection (1),

the amount mentioned in that paragraph shall be allocated between those interests in proportion to the depreciation of the value of each of them respectively, and the amount of the compensation payable in respect of any of those interests shall be the sum so allocated to that interest.

(4) Where the land constituting the decision area, taken as a whole, does not satisfy both of the following conditions, that is to say—

(a) that at the time of the decision it has an unexpended balance of established development value; and

(b) that every interest subsisting in it, the value of which is depreciated by the decision, subsists in the whole of that land,

subsection (5) has effect for the purpose of assessing the compensation payable under this Part in respect of any interest subsisting in that land or any part of it.

(5) Where this subsection applies in relation to an interest in land—

(a) the depreciation of the value of the interest by the planning decision shall first be ascertained with reference to the whole of the land which constitutes or forms part of the decision area and is land in which that interest subsists;

(b) the land referred to in paragraph (a) shall then be treated as divided into as many parts as may be requisite to ensure that each such part consists of land which either—

(i) satisfies both of the conditions mentioned in subsection (4); or

(ii) is not land which, at the time of the decision, has an unexpended balance of established development value; and

(c) the depreciation of the value of the interest, ascertained in accordance with paragraph (a), shall then be apportioned between those parts, according to the nature of those parts and the effect of the planning decision in relation to each of them; and

(d) the amount of the compensation shall be the aggregate of the amounts which would be payable by virtue of the previous provisions of this section if the planning decision had been made separately with respect to each of those parts.

(6) In this section "the decision area" in relation to a planning decision means the aggregate of the land to which the decision relates.

Assessment of depreciation.

126.—(1) For the purposes of this Part, the value of an interest in land, or of an interest in so far as it subsists in particular land, shall be taken to be depreciated by a planning decision (in this section referred to as "the relevant decision") if, and to the extent to which, that value, calculated in accordance with this section, falls short of what that value so calculated would have been if the relevant decision had been a decision to the contrary effect.

(2) Subject to the following provisions of this section, any such value shall for the purposes of this section be calculated—

(a) as at the time of the relevant decision; but

(b) as affected by that decision, by any grant of planning permission made after that decision and in force immediately before the Secretary of State gives notice of his findings on the claim for compensation in respect of that decision, and by any undertaking to grant planning permission so in force; and

(c) on the assumption that, after the relevant decision and apart from any such permission or undertaking as is mentioned in paragraph (b), planning permission would not be granted for any new development of the land in question, but would be granted for any development of it other than new development.

(3) If in consequence of another planning decision or of an order, being a decision or order made—

(a) before the relevant decision; and

(b) either in respect of the whole or part of the land to which the relevant decision relates or in respect of land which includes the whole or part of that land,

compensation to which this subsection applies has become or becomes payable in respect of that other planning decision or that order, the calculation to be made under this section shall be made as if that other planning decision had been a decision to the contrary effect or, as the case may be, that order had not been made.

(4) Subsection (3) applies—

(a) to any compensation payable under this Part or under Part II or Part V of the 1954 Act or Part VI of the 1962 Act or Part VII of the 1971 Act; and

(b) to so much of any compensation payable under section 107 of this Act, or section 164 of the 1971 Act, or section 118 of the 1962 Act, or under the provisions of those sections as applied by section 108 of this Act, or section 165 of the 1971 Act or section 119 of the 1962 Act respectively, and so much of any compensation to which Part IV of the 1954 Act applied, as is or was payable in respect of loss or damage consisting of depreciation of the value of an interest in land.

PART V

(5) In this section "a decision to the contrary effect"—

(a) in relation to a decision refusing permission, means a decision granting the permission subject to such condition (if any) of a description falling within section 121(2) as the authority making the decision might reasonably have been expected to impose if the permission had not been refused; and

(b) in relation to a decision granting the permission subject to conditions, means a decision granting the permission applied for subject only to such of those conditions (if any) as fall within that section.

Claims for and payment of compensation

General provisions as to claims for compensation.

127.—(1) Compensation under this Part shall not be payable unless a claim for it is duly made in accordance with this section.

(2) Subject to subsection (3), a claim for compensation under this Part shall not have effect unless it is made before the end of the period of six months beginning with the date of the planning decision to which it relates.

(3) The Secretary of State may in any particular case (either before, on or after the date on which the time for claiming would otherwise have expired) allow an extended, or further extended, period for making such a claim.

(4) Regulations made under this section may—

(a) require claims for compensation under this Part to be made in a form prescribed by the regulations;

(b) require a claimant to provide such evidence in support of the claim, and such information as to the interest of the claimant in the land to which the claim relates and as to the interests of other persons in it which are known to the claimant, as may be so prescribed.

(5) Any claim for such compensation in respect of a planning decision shall be sent to the local planning authority.

(6) That authority shall transmit the claim to the Secretary of State as soon as possible after receiving it and furnish him with—

(a) any evidence or other information provided by the claimant in accordance with regulations made under this section; and

(b) such other information (if any) as may be required by or under regulations made under this section, being information appearing to the Secretary of State to be relevant to the exercise of his powers under the provisions of Part III relating to the review of planning decisions where compensation is claimed.

(7) Where a claim is transmitted to the Secretary of State under subsection (6) and it appears to the Secretary of State—

(a) that the development to which the planning decision related was not new development, or

(b) that at the time of the planning decision no part of the land to which the claim relates had an unexpended balance of established development value, or

(c) that compensation is excluded by section 121 or 122,

he shall notify the claimant accordingly, stating on which of those grounds it appears to him that compensation is not payable, and inviting the claimant to withdraw the claim.

(8) Unless a claim transmitted to the Secretary of State under subsection (6) is withdrawn, the Secretary of State shall give notice of the claim to every other person (if any) appearing to him to have an interest in the land to which the planning decision related.

Effect on claims of direction under s. 80.

128.—(1) Where, in accordance with section 81(4), the Secretary of State gives notice of a direction under section 80 to a person who has made a claim for compensation in respect of the planning decision to which that direction relates, that person, if he does not withdraw the claim, may, at any time within 30 days after the service on him of the Secretary of State's notice, give notice to the Secretary of State modifying the claim.

(2) Subject to any such modification, where the Secretary of State gives a direction under section 80 in respect of a decision of a local planning authority, any claim made in respect of that decision shall have effect as if it had been made in respect of the decision which, by virtue of the direction, is substituted for the decision of the authority or, as the case may be, as if it had been made in respect of the decision of the authority as modified by the direction.

Determination of claims.

129.—(1) Regulations under this section shall make provision—

(a) for requiring claims for compensation under this Part to be determined by the Secretary of State in such manner as may be prescribed;

(b) for regulating the practice and procedure to be followed in connection with the determination of such claims;

(c) for requiring the Secretary of State on determining any such claim—

(i) to give notice of his findings to the claimant and to any other person who has made a claim for compensation under this Part in respect of the same planning decision, and

(ii) if his findings include an apportionment, to give particulars of the apportionment to any other person entitled to an interest in land appearing to the Secretary of State to be an interest substantially affected by the apportionment.

(2) Subject to subsection (3), provision shall be made by such regulations—

(a) for enabling the claimant or any other person to whom notice of the Secretary of State's findings has been given in accordance with subsection (1), if he wishes to dispute the findings, to require them to be referred to the Lands Tribunal;

(b) for enabling the claimant and any other person to whom particulars of an apportionment included in those findings have been so given, or who establishes that he is entitled to an interest in land which is substantially affected by such an apportionment, if he wishes to dispute the apportionment, to require it to be referred to the Lands Tribunal;

PART V

(c) for enabling the claimant and every other person to whom notice of any findings or apportionment has been given as mentioned in paragraph (a) or (b) to be heard by the Tribunal on any reference under this section of those findings or, as the case may be, of that apportionment; and

(d) for requiring the Tribunal, on any such reference, either to confirm or to vary the Secretary of State's findings or the apportionment, as the case may be, and to notify the parties of the decision of the Tribunal.

(3) Where on a reference to the Lands Tribunal under this section it is shown that an apportionment—

(a) relates wholly or partly to the same matters as a previous apportionment, and

(b) is consistent with that previous apportionment in so far as it relates to those matters,

the Tribunal shall not vary the apportionment in such a way as to be inconsistent with the previous apportionment in so far as it relates to those matters.

Payment of compensation.

130. Where compensation is determined under section 129 to be payable, the Secretary of State shall pay the compensation to the person entitled to it in accordance with the previous provisions of this Part.

Recovery of compensation

Apportionment of compensation.

131.—(1) Where, on a claim for compensation under this Part in respect of a planning decision, the Secretary of State determines that compensation is payable and that the amount of the compensation exceeds £20, the Secretary of State shall—

(a) if it appears to him to be practicable to do so, apportion the amount of the compensation between different parts of the land to which the claim for compensation relates, and

(b) include particulars of the apportionment in the notice of his findings under section 129.

(2) In carrying out such an apportionment the Secretary of State shall divide the land into parts and distribute the compensation between them according to the way in which the different parts appear to him to be differently affected by the planning decision.

(3) Subsections (1) and (2) shall apply on a reference to the Lands Tribunal under section 129 with the substitution for references to the Secretary of State of references to the Lands Tribunal (unless the decision of the Tribunal will not affect the amount of the compensation or any apportionment of it by the Secretary of State).

Registration of compensation.

132.—(1) Where, on a claim for compensation under this Part in respect of a planning decision, compensation of an amount exceeding £20 has become payable, the Secretary of State shall cause notice of that fact to be deposited—

(a) with the council of the district or London borough in which the land is situated, and

(b) if that council is not the local planning authority, with the local planning authority.

PART V

(2) Notices deposited under this section must specify—

(a) the planning decision and the land to which the claim for compensation relates,

(b) the amount of compensation, and

(c) any apportionment of it under section 131.

(3) Notices deposited under this section shall be local land charges, and for the purposes of the Local Land Charges Act 1975 the council with whom any such notice is deposited shall be treated as the originating authority as respects the charge constituted by it. 1975 c. 76.

(4) In relation to compensation specified in a notice registered under this section, references in this Part to so much of the compensation as is attributable to a part of the land to which the notice relates shall be construed as follows—

(a) if the notice does not include an apportionment under section 131, the amount of the compensation shall be treated as distributed rateably according to area over the land to which the notice relates;

(b) if the notice includes such an apportionment—

(i) the compensation shall be treated as distributed in accordance with that apportionment as between the different parts of the land by reference to which the apportionment is made; and

(ii) so much of the compensation as, in accordance with the apportionment, is attributed to a part of the land shall be treated as distributed rateably according to area over that part.

Recovery of compensation on subsequent development.

133.—(1) No person shall carry out any new development to which this section applies, on land in respect of which a notice ("a compensation notice") is registered under section 132, until any amount which is recoverable under this section in accordance with section 134 in respect of the compensation specified in the notice has been paid or secured to the satisfaction of the Secretary of State.

(2) Subject to subsections (3) and (4), this section applies to any new development—

(a) which is development of a residential, commercial or industrial character and consists wholly or mainly of the construction of houses, flats, shop or office premises, or industrial buildings (including warehouses), or any combination of them; or

(b) which consists in the winning and working of minerals; or

(c) to which, having regard to the probable value of the development, it is in the opinion of the Secretary of State reasonable that this section should apply.

(3) This section shall not apply to any development by virtue of subsection (2)(c) if, on an application made to him for the purpose, the Secretary of State has certified that, having regard to the probable value of the development, it is not in his opinion reasonable that this section should apply to it.

PART V

(4) Where the compensation specified in the compensation notice became payable in respect of the imposition of conditions on the granting of permission to develop land, this section shall not apply to the development for which that permission was granted.

Amount recoverable and provisions for payment or remission of it.

134.—(1) Subject to the following provisions of this section, the amount recoverable under section 133 in respect of the compensation specified in a compensation notice—

(a) if the land on which the development is to be carried out ("the development area") is identical with, or includes (with other land) the whole of, the land comprised in the compensation notice, shall be the amount of compensation specified in that notice;

(b) if the development area forms part of the land comprised in the compensation notice, or includes part of that land together with other land not comprised in that notice, shall be so much of the amount of the compensation specified in that notice as is attributable to land comprised in that notice and falling within the development area.

(2) Where, in the case of any land in respect of which a compensation notice has been registered, the Secretary of State is satisfied, having regard to the probable value of any proper development of that land, that no such development is likely to be carried out unless he exercises his powers under this subsection, he may, in the case of any particular development, remit the whole or part of any amount otherwise recoverable under section 133.

(3) Where part only of any such amount has been remitted in respect of any land, the Secretary of State shall cause the compensation notice to be amended by substituting in it, for the statement of the amount of the compensation, in so far as it is attributable to that land, a statement of the amount which has been remitted under subsection (2).

(4) Where, in connection with the development of any land, an amount becomes recoverable under section 133 in respect of the compensation specified in a compensation notice, then, except where, and to the extent that, payment of that amount has been remitted under subsection (2), no amount shall be recoverable under section 133 in respect of that compensation, in so far as it is attributable to that land, in connection with any subsequent development of it.

(5) No amount shall be recoverable under section 133 in respect of any compensation by reference to which a sum has become recoverable by the Secretary of State under section 308.

(6) An amount recoverable under section 133 in respect of any compensation shall be payable to the Secretary of State either—

(a) as a single capital payment, or

(b) as a series of instalments of capital and interest combined, or

(c) as a series of other annual or periodical payments, of such amounts, and payable at such times, as the Secretary of State may direct.

(7) Before giving a direction under subsection (6)(c) the Secretary of State shall take into account any representations made by the person by whom the development is to be carried out.

(8) Except where the amount payable under subsection (6) is payable as a single capital payment, it shall be secured by the person by whom the development is to be carried out in such manner (whether by mortgage, covenant or otherwise) as the Secretary of State may direct.

(9) If any person initiates any new development to which section 133 applies in contravention of subsection (1) of that section, the Secretary of State may serve a notice on him—

(a) specifying the amount appearing to the Secretary of State to be the amount recoverable under that section in respect of the compensation in question, and

(b) requiring him to pay that amount to the Secretary of State within such period as may be specified in the notice.

(10) The period specified under subsection (9)(b) must not be less than three months after the service of the notice.

Supplementary provisions

135.—(1) Regulations made under this section may make provision— Mortgages, rent-charges and settlements.

(a) as to the exercise of the right to claim compensation under this Part,

(b) as to the person to whom such compensation or any part of it is to be paid, and

(c) as to the application of any such compensation or any part of it,

in cases where, apart from this section, the right to claim the compensation is exercisable by reference to an interest in land which is subject to a mortgage, or to a rentcharge, or to the trusts of a settlement, or which was so subject at a time specified in the regulations.

(2) In relation to any case where by virtue of any such regulations compensation or a part of it is to be paid to the owner of a rentcharge, the regulations may—

(a) make similar provision to that made by section 25 of the War Damage Act 1943 (rights of owners of rentcharges as to payments for war damage) but with such adaptations and modifications as may be prescribed, and 1943 c.21.

(b) provide for disputes arising under the regulations, so far as they relate to rentcharges, to be referred to the Lands Tribunal for determination by it.

136.—(1) In calculating value for any of the purposes of this Part— Calculation of value.

(a) subject to subsection (2), rules (2) to (4) of the rules set out in section 5 of the Land Compensation Act 1961 shall apply with the necessary modifications; and 1961 c. 33.

(b) any mortgage to which the interest to be valued is subject shall be disregarded.

(2) Rule (3) of those rules shall not apply for the purposes of paragraph 15 of Schedule 12.

(3) Where for the purposes of any of the provisions of this Part—

(a) value falls to be calculated by reference to the duration of a tenancy, and

PART V

(b) by reason of any option or other contractual right with respect to the determination, renewal or continuance of the tenancy, the date of expiry of the tenancy is not ascertainable with certainty,

that date shall be taken to be such as appears reasonable and probable having regard to the interests of the party by whom the option is exercisable, or in whose favour the right operates, and to any other material considerations subsisting at the time when the calculation of value falls to be made.

PART VI

RIGHTS OF OWNERS ETC. TO REQUIRE PURCHASE OF INTERESTS

CHAPTER I

INTERESTS AFFECTED BY PLANNING DECISIONS OR ORDERS

Service of purchase notices

Circumstances in which purchase notices may be served.

137.—(1) This section applies where—

(a) on an application for planning permission to develop any land, permission is refused or is granted subject to conditions; or

(b) by an order under section 97 planning permission in respect of any land is revoked, or is modified by the imposition of conditions; or

(c) an order is made under section 102 or paragraph 1 of Schedule 9 in respect of any land.

(2) If—

(a) in the case mentioned in subsection (1)(a) or (b), any owner of the land claims that the conditions mentioned in subsection (3) are satisfied with respect to it, or

(b) in the case mentioned in subsection (1)(c), any person entitled to an interest in land in respect of which the order is made claims that the conditions mentioned in subsection (4) are satisfied with respect to it,

he may, within the prescribed time and in the prescribed manner, serve on the council of the district or London borough in which the land is situated a notice (in this Act referred to as "a purchase notice") requiring that council to purchase his interest in the land in accordance with this Chapter.

(3) The conditions mentioned in subsection (2)(a) are—

(a) that the land has become incapable of reasonably beneficial use in its existing state; and

(b) in a case where planning permission was granted subject to conditions or was modified by the imposition of conditions, that the land cannot be rendered capable of reasonably beneficial use by the carrying out of the permitted development in accordance with those conditions; and

(c) in any case, that the land cannot be rendered capable of reasonably beneficial use by the carrying out of any other development for which planning permission has been granted or for which the local planning authority or the Secretary of State has undertaken to grant planning permission.

(4) The conditions mentioned in subsection (2)(b) are—

(a) that by reason of the order the land is incapable of reasonably beneficial use in its existing state; and

(b) that it cannot be rendered capable of reasonably beneficial use by the carrying out of any development for which planning permission has been granted, whether by that order or otherwise.

(5) For the purposes of subsection (1)(a) and any claim arising in the circumstances mentioned in that subsection, the conditions referred to in sections 91 and 92 shall be disregarded.

(6) A person on whom a repairs notice has been served under section 48 of the Planning (Listed Buildings and Conservation Areas) Act 1990 shall not be entitled to serve a notice under this section in the circumstances mentioned in subsection (1)(a) in respect of the building in question—

1990 c. 9

(a) until the expiration of three months beginning with the date of the service of the repairs notice; and

(b) if during that period the compulsory acquisition of the building is begun in the exercise of powers under section 47 of that Act, unless and until the compulsory acquisition is discontinued.

(7) For the purposes of subsection (6) a compulsory acquisition—

(a) is started when the the notice required by section 12 of the Acquisition of Land Act 1981 or, as the case may be, paragraph 3 of Schedule 1 to that Act is served; and

1981 c. 67.

(b) is discontinued—

(i) in the case of acquisition by the Secretary of State, when he decides not to make the compulsory purchase order; and

(ii) in any other case, when the order is withdrawn or the Secretary of State decides not to confirm it.

(8) No purchase notice shall be served in respect of an interest in land while the land is incapable of reasonably beneficial use by reason only of such an order as is mentioned in subsection (1)(c), except by virtue of a claim under subsection (2)(b).

Circumstances in which land incapable of reasonably beneficial use.

138.—(1) Where, for the purpose of determining whether the conditions specified in section 137(3) or (4) are satisfied in relation to any land, any question arises as to what is or would in any particular circumstances be a reasonably beneficial use of that land, then, in determining that question for that purpose, no account shall be taken of any unauthorised prospective use of that land.

(2) A prospective use of land shall be regarded as unauthorised for the purposes of subsection (1)—

(a) if it would involve the carrying out of new development, or

(b) in the case of a purchase notice served in consequence of a refusal or conditional grant of planning permission, if it would contravene the condition set out in Schedule 10.

PART VI

Duties of authorities on service of purchase notice

Action by council on whom purchase notice is served.

139.—(1) The council on whom a purchase notice is served shall serve on the owner by whom the purchase notice was served a notice (a "response notice") stating either—

(a) that the council are willing to comply with the purchase notice; or

(b) that another local authority or statutory undertakers specified in the response notice have agreed to comply with it in their place; or

(c) that for reasons so specified the council are not willing to comply with the purchase notice and have not found any other local authority or statutory undertakers who will agree to comply with it in their place, and that they have sent the Secretary of State a copy of the purchase notice and of the response notice.

(2) A response notice must be served before the end of the period of three months beginning with the date of service of the purchase notice.

(3) Where the council on whom a purchase notice is served by an owner have served a response notice on him in accordance with subsection (1)(a) or (b), the council or, as the case may be, the other local authority or statutory undertakers specified in the response notice shall be deemed—

(a) to be authorised to acquire the interest of the owner compulsorily in accordance with the relevant provisions, and

(b) to have served a notice to treat in respect of it on the date of service of the response notice.

(4) Where the council propose to serve such a response notice as is mentioned in subsection (1)(c), they must first send the Secretary of State a copy—

(a) of the proposed response notice, and

(b) of the purchase notice.

1961 c. 33.

(5) A notice to treat which is deemed to have been served by virtue of subsection (3)(b) may not be withdrawn under section 31 of the Land Compensation Act 1961.

Procedure on reference of purchase notice to Secretary of State.

140.—(1) Where a copy of a purchase notice is sent to the Secretary of State under section 139(4), he shall consider whether to confirm the notice or to take other action under section 141 in respect of it.

(2) Before confirming a purchase notice or taking such other action, the Secretary of State must give notice of his proposed action—

(a) to the person who served the purchase notice;

(b) to the council on whom it was served;

(c) outside Greater London—

(i) to the county planning authority and also, where that authority is a joint planning board, to the county council; and

(ii) if the district council on whom the purchase notice in question was served is a constituent member of a joint planning board, to that board; and

(d) if the Secretary of State proposes to substitute any other local authority or statutory undertakers for the council on whom the notice was served, to them.

(3) A notice under subsection (2) shall specify the period (which must not be less than 28 days from its service) within which any of the persons on whom it is served may require the Secretary of State to give those persons an opportunity of appearing before, and being heard by, a person appointed by the Secretary of State for the purpose.

(4) If within that period any of those persons so require, before the Secretary of State confirms the purchase notice or takes any other action under section 141 in respect of it he must give those persons such an opportunity.

(5) If, after any of those persons have appeared before and been heard by the appointed person, it appears to the Secretary of State to be expedient to take action under section 141 otherwise than in accordance with the notice given by him, the Secretary of State may take that action accordingly.

Action by Secretary of State in relation to purchase notice.

141.—(1) Subject to the following provisions of this section and to section 142(3), if the Secretary of State is satisfied that the conditions specified in subsection (3) or, as the case may be, subsection (4) of section 137 are satisfied in relation to a purchase notice, he shall confirm the notice.

(2) If it appears to the Secretary of State to be expedient to do so, he may, instead of confirming the purchase notice—

(a) in the case of a notice served on account of the refusal of planning permission, grant planning permission for the development in question;

(b) in the case of a notice served on account of planning permission for development being granted subject to conditions, revoke or amend those conditions so far as appears to him to be required in order to enable the land to be rendered capable of reasonably beneficial use by the carrying out of that development;

(c) in the case of a notice served on account of the revocation of planning permission by an order under section 97, cancel the order;

(d) in the case of a notice served on account of the modification of planning permission by such an order by the imposition of conditions, revoke or amend those conditions so far as appears to him to be required in order to enable the land to be rendered capable of reasonably beneficial use by the carrying out of the development in respect of which the permission was granted; or

(e) in the case of a notice served on account of the making of an order under section 102 or paragraph 1 of Schedule 9, revoke the order or, as the case may be, amend the order so far as appears to him to be required in order to prevent the land from being rendered incapable of reasonably beneficial use by the order.

(3) If it appears to the Secretary of State that the land, or any part of the land, could be rendered capable of reasonably beneficial use within a reasonable time by the carrying out of any other development for which planning permission ought to be granted, he may, instead of confirming

PART VI

the purchase notice, or, as the case may be, of confirming it so far as it relates to that part of the land, direct that, if an application for planning permission for that development is made, it must be granted.

(4) If it appears to the Secretary of State, having regard to the probable ultimate use of the land, that it is expedient to do so, he may, if he confirms the notice, modify it, either in relation to the whole or any part of the land, by substituting another local authority or statutory undertakers for the council on whom the notice was served.

(5) Any reference in section 140 to the taking of action by the Secretary of State under this section includes a reference to the taking by him of a decision not to confirm the purchase notice either on the grounds that any of the conditions referred to in subsection (1) are not satisfied or by virtue of section 142.

Power to refuse to confirm purchase notice where land has restricted use by virtue of previous planning permission.

142.—(1) This section applies where a purchase notice is served in respect of land which consists in whole or in part of land which has a restricted use by virtue of an existing planning permission.

(2) For the purposes of this section, land is to be treated as having a restricted use by virtue of an existing planning permission if it is part of a larger area in respect of which planning permission has previously been granted (and has not been revoked) and either—

(a) it remains a condition of the planning permission (however expressed) that that part shall remain undeveloped or be preserved or laid out in a particular way as amenity land in relation to the remainder; or

(b) the planning permission was granted on an application which contemplated (expressly or by necessary implication) that the part should not be comprised in the development for which planning permission was sought, or should be preserved or laid out as mentioned in paragraph (a).

(3) Where a copy of the purchase notice is sent to the Secretary of State under section 139(4), he need not confirm the notice under section 141(1) if it appears to him that the land having a restricted use by virtue of an existing planning permission ought, in accordance with that permission, to remain undeveloped or, as the case may be, remain or be preserved or laid out as amenity land in relation to the remainder of the large area for which that planning permission was granted.

Effect of Secretary of State's action in relation to purchase notice.

143.—(1) Where the Secretary of State confirms a purchase notice—

(a) the council on whom the purchase notice was served, or

(b) if under section 141(4) the Secretary of State modified the purchase notice by substituting another local authority or statutory undertakers for that council, that other authority or those undertakers,

shall be deemed to be authorised to acquire the interest of the owner compulsorily in accordance with the relevant provisions, and to have served a notice to treat in respect of it on such date as the Secretary of State may direct.

(2) If, before the end of the relevant period, the Secretary of State has neither—

(a) confirmed the purchase notice, nor

(b) taken any such action in respect of it as is mentioned in section 141(2) or (3), nor

(c) notified the owner by whom the notice was served that he does not propose to confirm the notice,

the notice shall be deemed to be confirmed at the end of that period, and the council on whom the notice was served shall be deemed to be authorised as mentioned in subsection (1) and to have served a notice to treat in respect of the owner's interest at the end of that period.

(3) Subject to subsection (4), for the purposes of subsection (2) the relevant period is—

(a) the period of nine months beginning with the date of service of the purchase notice; or

(b) if it ends earlier, the period of six months beginning with the date on which a copy of the purchase notice was sent to the Secretary of State.

(4) The relevant period does not run if the Secretary of State has before him at the same time both—

(a) a copy of the purchase notice sent to him under section 139(4); and

(b) a notice of appeal under section 78, 174 or 195 of this Act or under section 20 or 39 of the Planning (Listed Buildings and Conservation Areas) Act 1990 (appeals against refusal of listed building consent, etc. and appeals against listed building enforcement notices) or under section 21 of the Planning (Hazardous Substances) Act 1990 (appeals against decisions and failure to take decisions relating to hazardous substances) relating to any of the land to which the purchase notice relates.

1990 c. 9.

1990 c. 10.

(5) Where—

(a) the Secretary of State has notified the owner by whom a purchase notice has been served of a decision on his part to confirm, or not to confirm, the notice; and

(b) that decision is quashed under Part XII,

the purchase notice shall be treated as cancelled, but the owner may serve a further purchase notice in its place.

(6) The reference in subsection (5) to a decision to confirm, or not to confirm, the purchase notice includes—

(a) any decision not to confirm the notice in respect of any part of the land to which it relates, and

(b) any decision to grant any permission, or give any direction, instead of confirming the notice, either wholly or in part.

(7) For the purposes of determining whether a further purchase notice under subsection (5) was served within the period prescribed for the service of purchase notices, the planning decision in consequence of which the notice was served shall be treated as having been made on the date on which the decision of the Secretary of State was quashed.

(8) A notice to treat which is deemed to have been served by virtue of subsection (1) or (2) may not be withdrawn under section 31 of the Land Compensation Act 1961.

1961 c. 33.

PART VI

Compensation

Special provisions as to compensation where purchase notice served.

144.—(1) Where compensation is payable by virtue of section 107 in respect of expenditure incurred in carrying out any works on land, any compensation payable in respect of the acquisition of an interest in the land in pursuance of a purchase notice shall be reduced by an amount equal to the value of those works.

(2) Where—

(a) the Secretary of State directs under section 141(3) that, if an application for it is made, planning permission must be granted for the development of any land, and

(b) on a claim made to the local planning authority within the prescribed time and in the prescribed manner, it is shown that the permitted development value of the interest in that land in respect of which the purchase notice was served is less than its existing use value,

that authority shall pay the person entitled to that interest compensation of an amount equal to the difference.

(3) If the planning permission mentioned in subsection (2)(a) would be granted subject to conditions for regulating the design or external appearance, or the size or height of buildings, or for regulating the number of buildings to be erected on the land, the Secretary of State may direct that in assessing any compensation payable under subsection (2) those conditions must be disregarded, either altogether or to such extent as may be specified in the direction.

(4) The Secretary of State may only give a direction under subsection (3) if it appears to him to be reasonable to do so having regard to the local circumstances.

(5) Sections 117 and 118 shall have effect in relation to compensation under subsection (2) as they have effect in relation to compensation to which those sections apply.

(6) In this section—

"permitted development value", in relation to an interest in land in respect of which a direction is given under section 141(3), means the value of that interest calculated with regard to that direction, but on the assumption that no planning permission would be granted otherwise than in accordance with that direction, and

"existing use value", in relation to such an interest, means the value of that interest as (for the purpose of ascertaining the compensation payable on an acquisition of the interest in pursuance of the purchase notice) that value would have been assessed in accordance with the provisions of the Acquisition of Land (Assessment of Compensation) Act 1919, as modified by the provisions of sections 51 to 54 of the 1947 Act, if no enactment repealing, modifying or superseding any of those provisions had been passed after the passing of the 1947 Act.

1919 c. 57.

(7) Where a purchase notice in respect of an interest in land is served in consequence of an order under section 102 or paragraph 1 of Schedule 9, then if—

(a) that interest is acquired in accordance with this Chapter; or

(b) compensation is payable in respect of that interest under subsection (2),

no compensation shall be payable in respect of that order under section 115.

Special provisions for requiring purchase of whole of partially affected agricultural unit

Counter-notice requiring purchase of remainder of agricultural unit.

145.—(1) This section applies where—

(a) an acquiring authority is deemed under this Chapter to have served notice to treat in respect of any agricultural land on a person ("the claimant") who has a greater interest in the land than as tenant for a year or from year to year (whether or not he is in occupation of the land), and

(b) the claimant has such an interest in other agricultural land ("the unaffected area") comprised in the same agricultural unit as that to which the notice relates.

(2) Where this section applies the claimant may serve on the acquiring authority a counter-notice—

(a) claiming that the unaffected area is not reasonably capable of being farmed, either by itself or in conjunction with other relevant land, as a separate agricultural unit; and

(b) requiring the acquiring authority to purchase his interest in the whole of the unaffected area.

(3) Subject to subsection (4), "other relevant land" in subsection (2) means—

(a) land which is comprised in the same agricultural unit as the land to which the notice to treat relates and in which the claimant does not have such an interest as is mentioned in subsection (1); and

(b) land which is comprised in any other agricultural unit occupied by the claimant on the date on which the notice to treat is deemed to have been served and in respect of which he is then entitled to a greater interest than as tenant for a year or from year to year.

(4) Where a notice to treat has been served or is deemed under this Chapter or under Part III of the Compulsory Purchase (Vesting Declarations) Act 1981 to have been served in respect of any of the unaffected area or in respect of other relevant land as defined in subsection (3), then, unless and until the notice to treat is withdrawn, this section and section 146 shall have effect as if that land did not form part of the unaffected land or, as the case may be, did not constitute other relevant land. 1981 c. 66.

(5) Where a counter-notice is served under subsection (2) the claimant shall also serve a copy of it on any other person who has an interest in the unaffected area (but failure to comply with this subsection shall not invalidate the counter-notice).

(6) A counter-notice under subsection (2) and any copy of that notice required to be served under subsection (5) must be served within the period of two months beginning with the date on which the notice to treat is deemed to have been served.

PART VI

1845 c. 18.
1965 c. 56.

(7) This section is without prejudice to the rights conferred by sections 93 and 94 of the Lands Clauses (Consolidation) Act 1845 or section 8(2) and (3) of the Compulsory Purchase Act 1965 (provisions as to divided land).

Effect of counter-notice under s. 145.

146.—(1) If the acquiring authority do not within the period of two months beginning with the date of service of a counter-notice under section 145 agree in writing to accept the counter-notice as valid, the claimant or the authority may, within two months after the end of that period, refer it to the Lands Tribunal.

(2) On such a reference the Tribunal shall determine whether the claim in the counter-notice is justified and declare the counter-notice valid or invalid accordingly.

(3) Where a counter-notice is accepted as valid under subsection (1) or declared to be valid under subsection (2), the acquiring authority shall be deemed—

(a) to be authorised to acquire compulsorily the interest of the claimant in the land to which the requirement in the counter-notice relates under the same provision of this Chapter as they are authorised to acquire the other land in the agricultural unit in question; and

(b) to have served a notice to treat in respect of it on the date on which notice to treat is deemed to have been served under that provision.

(4) A claimant may withdraw a counter-notice at any time before the compensation payable in respect of a compulsory acquisition in pursuance of the counter-notice has been determined by the Lands Tribunal or at any time before the end of six weeks beginning with the date on which it is determined.

(5) Where a counter-notice is withdrawn by virtue of subsection (4) any notice to treat deemed to have been served in consequence of it shall be deemed to have been withdrawn.

1961 c. 33.

(6) Without prejudice to subsection (5), a notice to treat deemed to have been served by virtue of this section may not be withdrawn under section 31 of the Land Compensation Act 1961.

1973 c. 26.

(7) The compensation payable in respect of the acquisition of an interest in land in pursuance of a notice to treat deemed to have been served by virtue of this section shall be assessed on the assumptions mentioned in section 5(2), (3) and (4) of the Land Compensation Act 1973.

(8) Where by virtue of this section the acquiring authority become or will become entitled to a lease of any land but not to the interest of the lessor—

(a) the authority shall offer to surrender the lease to the lessor on such terms as the authority consider reasonable;

(b) the question of what is reasonable may be referred to the Lands Tribunal by the authority or the lessor and, if at the expiration of the period of three months after the date of the offer mentioned in paragraph (a) the authority and the lessor have not agreed on that question and that question has not been referred to the Tribunal by the lessor, it shall be so referred by the authority;

(c) if that question is referred to the Tribunal, the lessor shall be deemed—

(i) to have accepted the surrender of the lease at the expiry of one month after the date of the determination of the Tribunal or on such other date as the Tribunal may direct, and

(ii) to have agreed with the authority on the terms of surrender which the Tribunal has held to be reasonable.

(9) For the purposes of subsection (8) any terms as to surrender contained in the lease shall be disregarded.

(10) Where the lessor—

(a) refuses to accept any sum payable to him by virtue of subsection (8), or

(b) refuses or fails to make out his title to the satisfaction of the acquiring authority,

they may pay into court any such sum payable to the lessor and section 9(2) and (5) of the Compulsory Purchase Act 1965 (deposit of compensation in cases of refusal to convey etc.) shall apply to that sum with the necessary modifications. 1965 c. 56

(11) Where an acquiring authority who become entitled to the lease of any land as mentioned in subsection (8) are a body incorporated by or under any enactment, the corporate powers of the authority shall, if they would not otherwise do so, include the power to farm that land.

Provisions supplemental to ss. 145 and 146.

147.—(1) Sections 145 and 146 apply in relation to the acquisition of interests in land by government departments which possess compulsory purchase powers as they apply in relation to the acquisition of interests in land by authorities who are not government departments.

(2) In sections 145, 146 and this section—

"agricultural" and "agricultural land" have the meaning given in section 109 of the Agriculture Act 1947 and references to the farming of land include references to the carrying on in relation to the land of any agricultural activities; 1947 c. 48.

"agricultural unit" has the meaning given in section 171(1);

"acquiring authority" has the same meaning as in the Land Compensation Act 1961 ; and 1961 c. 33.

"government departments which possess compulsory purchase powers" means government departments being authorities possessing compulsory purchase powers within the meaning of that Act.

Supplemental

Interpretation of Chapter I.

148.—(1) In this Chapter—

"the relevant provisions" means—

(a) the provisions of Part IX, or

PART VI

(b) in the case of statutory undertakers, any statutory provision (however expressed) under which they have power, or may be authorised, to purchase land compulsorily for the purposes of their undertaking; and

"statutory undertakers" includes public telecommunications operators.

(2) In the case of a purchase notice served by such a person as is mentioned in subsection (2)(b) of section 137, references in this Chapter to the owner of the land include references to that person unless the context otherwise requires.

CHAPTER II

INTERESTS AFFECTED BY PLANNING PROPOSALS: BLIGHT

Preliminary

Scope of Chapter II.

149.—(1) This Chapter shall have effect in relation to land falling within any paragraph of Schedule 13 (land affected by planning proposals of public authorities etc.); and in this Chapter such land is referred to as "blighted land".

(2) Subject to the provisions of sections 161 and 162, an interest qualifies for protection under this Chapter if—

(a) it is an interest in a hereditament or part of a hereditament and on the relevant date it satisfies one of the conditions mentioned in subsection (3); or

(b) it is an interest in an agricultural unit or part of an agricultural unit and on the relevant date it is the interest of an owner-occupier of the unit;

and in this Chapter such an interest is referred to as "a qualifying interest".

(3) The conditions mentioned in subsection (2)(a) are—

(a) that the annual value of the hereditament does not exceed such amount as may be prescribed for the purposes of this paragraph by an order made by the Secretary of State, and the interest is the interest of an owner-occupier of the hereditament; or

(b) that the interest is the interest of a resident owner-occupier of the hereditament.

(4) In this section "the relevant date", in relation to an interest, means the date of service of a notice under section 150 in respect of it.

(5) In this Chapter "blight notice" means a notice served under section 150, 161 or 162.

Blight notices

Notices requiring purchase of blighted land.

150.—(1) Where the whole or part of a hereditament or agricultural unit is comprised in blighted land and a person claims that—

(a) he is entitled to a qualifying interest in that hereditament or unit;

(b) he has made reasonable endeavours to sell that interest; and

(c) in consequence of the fact that the hereditament or unit or a part of it was, or was likely to be, comprised in blighted land, he has been unable to sell that interest except at a price substantially lower than that for which it might reasonably have been expected to sell if no part of the hereditament or unit were, or were likely to be, comprised in such land,

he may serve on the appropriate authority a notice in the prescribed form requiring that authority to purchase that interest to the extent specified in, and otherwise in accordance with, this Chapter.

(2) Subject to subsection (3), subsection (1) shall apply in relation to an interest in part of a hereditament or unit as it applies in relation to an interest in the whole of a hereditament or unit.

(3) Subsection (2) shall not enable any person—

(a) if he is entitled to an interest in the whole of a hereditament or agricultural unit, to make any claim or serve any notice under this section in respect of his interest in part of a hereditament or unit; or

(b) if he is entitled to an interest only in part of a hereditament or agricultural unit, to make or serve any such claim or notice in respect of his interest in less than the whole of that part.

(4) In this Chapter—

(a) subject to section 161(1), "the claimant", in relation to a blight notice, means the person who served that notice, and

(b) any reference to the interest of the claimant, in relation to a blight notice, is a reference to the interest which the notice requires the appropriate authority to purchase as mentioned in subsection (1).

Counter-notices objecting to blight notices.

151.—(1) Where a blight notice has been served in respect of a hereditament or an agricultural unit, the appropriate authority may serve on the claimant a counter-notice in the prescribed form objecting to the notice.

(2) A counter-notice under subsection (1) may be served at any time before the end of the period of two months beginning with the date of service of the blight notice.

(3) Such a counter-notice shall specify the grounds on which the appropriate authority object to the blight notice (being one or more of the grounds specified in subsection (4) or, as relevant, in section 159(1), 161(5) or 162(5)).

(4) Subject to the following provisions of this Act, the grounds on which objection may be made in a counter-notice to a notice served under section 150 are—

(a) that no part of the hereditament or agricultural unit to which the notice relates is comprised in blighted land;

(b) that the appropriate authority (unless compelled to do so by virtue of this Chapter) do not propose to acquire any part of the hereditament, or in the case of an agricultural unit any part of the affected area, in the exercise of any relevant powers;

(c) that the appropriate authority propose in the exercise of relevant powers to acquire a part of the hereditament or, in the case of an agricultural unit, a part of the affected area specified in the

PART VI

counter-notice, but (unless compelled to do so by virtue of this Chapter) do not propose to acquire any other part of that hereditament or area in the exercise of any such powers;

(d) in the case of land falling within paragraph 1, 3 or 13 but not 14, 15 or 16 of Schedule 13, that the appropriate authority (unless compelled to do so by virtue of this Chapter) do not propose to acquire in the exercise of any relevant powers any part of the hereditament or, in the case of an agricultural unit, any part of the affected area during the period of 15 years from the date of the counter-notice or such longer period from that date as may be specified in the counter-notice;

(e) that, on the date of service of the notice under section 150, the claimant was not entitled to an interest in any part of the hereditament or agricultural unit to which the notice relates;

(f) that (for reasons specified in the counter-notice) the interest of the claimant is not a qualifying interest;

(g) that the conditions specified in paragraphs (b) and (c) of section 150(1) are not fulfilled.

(5) Where the appropriate enactment confers power to acquire rights over land, subsection (4) shall have effect as if—

(a) in paragraph (b) after the word "acquire" there were inserted the words "or to acquire any rights over";

(b) in paragraph (c) for the words "do not propose to acquire" there were substituted the words "propose neither to acquire, nor to acquire any right over";

(c) in paragraph (d) after the words "affected area" there were inserted "or to acquire any right over any part of it".

(6) An objection may not be made on the grounds mentioned in paragraph (d) of subsection (4) if it may be made on the grounds mentioned in paragraph (b) of that subsection.

(7) The grounds on which objection may be made in a counter-notice to a blight notice served by virtue of paragraph 19 of Schedule 13 shall not include those mentioned in subsection (4)(b) or (c).

(8) In this section "relevant powers", in relation to blighted land falling within any paragraph of Schedule 13, means any powers under which the appropriate authority are or could be authorised—

(a) to acquire that land or to acquire any rights over it compulsorily as being land falling within that paragraph; or

(b) to acquire that land or any rights over it compulsorily for any of the relevant purposes;

and "the relevant purposes", in relation to any such land, means the purposes for which, in accordance with the circumstances by virtue of which that land falls within the paragraph in question, it is liable to be acquired or is indicated as being proposed to be acquired.

Further counter-notices where certain proposals have come into force.

152.—(1) Where—

(a) an appropriate authority have served a counter-notice objecting to a blight notice in respect of any land falling within paragraph 1, 2, 3, 4 or 14 of Schedule 13 by virtue of Note (1) to that paragraph, and

(b) the relevant plan or alterations or, as the case may be, the relevant order or scheme comes into force (whether in its original form or with modifications),

the appropriate authority may serve on the claimant, in substitution for the counter-notice already served, a further counter-notice specifying different grounds of objection.

(2) Such a further counter-notice shall not be served—

(a) at any time after the end of the period of two months beginning with the date on which the relevant plan or alterations come into force; or

(b) if the objection in the counter-notice already served has been withdrawn or the Lands Tribunal has already determined whether or not to uphold that objection.

Reference of objection to Lands Tribunal: general.

153.—(1) Where a counter-notice has been served under section 151 objecting to a blight notice, the claimant may require the objection to be referred to the Lands Tribunal.

(2) Such a reference may be required under subsection (1) at any time before the end of the period of two months beginning with the date of service of the counter-notice.

(3) On any such reference, if the objection is not withdrawn, the Lands Tribunal shall consider—

(a) the matters set out in the notice served by the claimant, and

(b) the grounds of the objection specified in the counter-notice;

and, subject to subsection (4), unless it is shown to the satisfaction of the Tribunal that the objection is not well-founded, the Tribunal shall uphold the objection.

(4) An objection on the grounds mentioned in section 151(4)(b), (c) or (d) shall not be upheld by the Tribunal unless it is shown to the satisfaction of the Tribunal that the objection is well-founded.

(5) If the Tribunal determines not to uphold the objection, the Tribunal shall declare that the notice to which the counter-notice relates is a valid notice.

(6) If the Tribunal upholds the objection, but only on the grounds mentioned in section 151(4)(c), the Tribunal shall declare that the notice is a valid notice in relation to the part of the hereditament, or in the case of an agricultural unit the part of the affected area, specified in the counter-notice as being the part which the appropriate authority propose to acquire as mentioned in that notice, but not in relation to any other part of the hereditament or affected area.

(7) In a case falling within subsection (5) or (6), the Tribunal shall give directions specifying the date on which notice to treat (as mentioned in section 154) is to be deemed to have been served.

(8) This section shall have effect in relation to a further counter-notice served by virtue of section 152(1) as it has effect in relation to the counter-notice for which it is substituted.

PART VI

Effect of valid blight notice.

154.—(1) Subsection (2) applies where a blight notice has been served and either—

(a) no counter-notice objecting to that notice is served in accordance with this Chapter; or

(b) where such a counter-notice has been served, the objection is withdrawn or, on a reference to the Lands Tribunal, is not upheld by the Tribunal.

(2) Where this subsection applies, the appropriate authority shall be deemed—

(a) to be authorised to acquire compulsorily under the appropriate enactment the interest of the claimant in the hereditament, or in the case of an agricultural unit the interest of the claimant in so far as it subsists in the affected area, and

(b) to have served a notice to treat in respect of it on the date mentioned in subsection (3).

(3) The date referred to in subsection (2)—

(a) in a case where, on a reference to the Lands Tribunal, the Tribunal determines not to uphold the objection, is the date specified in directions given by the Tribunal in accordance with section 153(7);

(b) in any other case, is the date on which the period of two months beginning with the date of service of the blight notice comes to an end.

(4) Subsection (5) applies where the appropriate authority have served a counter-notice objecting to a blight notice on the grounds mentioned in section 151(4)(c) and either—

(a) the claimant, without referring that objection to the Lands Tribunal, and before the time for so referring it has expired—

(i) gives notice to the appropriate authority that he accepts the proposal of the authority to acquire the part of the hereditament or affected area specified in the counter-notice, and

(ii) withdraws his claim as to the remainder of that hereditament or area; or

(b) on a reference to the Lands Tribunal, the Tribunal makes a declaration in accordance with section 153(6) in respect of that part of the hereditament or affected area.

(5) Where this subsection applies, the appropriate authority shall be deemed—

(a) to be authorised to acquire compulsorily under the appropriate enactment the interest of the claimant in so far as it subsists in the part of the hereditament or affected area specified in the counter-notice (but not in so far as it subsists in any other part of that hereditament or area), and

(b) to have served a notice to treat in respect of it on the date mentioned in subsection (6).

(6) The date referred to in subsection (5)—

(a) in a case falling within paragraph (a) of subsection (4), is the date on which notice is given in accordance with that paragraph; and

(b) in a case falling within paragraph (b) of that subsection, is the date specified in directions given by the Lands Tribunal in accordance with section 153(7).

Effect on powers of compulsory acquisition of counter-notice disclaiming intention to acquire.

155.—(1) Subsection (2) shall have effect where the grounds of objection specified in a counter-notice served under section 151 consist of or include the grounds mentioned in paragraph (b) or (d) of subsection (4) of that section and either—

(a) the objection on the grounds mentioned in that paragraph is referred to and upheld by the Lands Tribunal; or

(b) the time for referring that objection to the Lands Tribunal expires without its having been so referred.

(2) If—

(a) a compulsory purchase order has been made under the appropriate enactment in respect of land which consists of or includes the whole or part of the hereditament or agricultural unit to which the counter-notice relates, or

(b) the land in question falls within paragraph 21 of Schedule 13,

any power conferred by that order or, as the case may be, by special enactment for the compulsory acquisition of the interest of the claimant in the hereditament or agricultural unit or any part of it shall cease to have effect.

(3) Subsection (4) shall have effect where the grounds of objection specified in a counter-notice under section 151 consist of or include the grounds mentioned in paragraph (c) of subsection (4) of that section and either—

(a) the objection on the grounds mentioned in that paragraph is referred to and upheld by the Lands Tribunal; or

(b) the time for referring that objection to the Lands Tribunal expires without its having been so referred;

and in subsection (4) any reference to "the part of the hereditament or affected area not required" is a reference to the whole of that hereditament or area except the part specified in the counter-notice as being the part which the appropriate authority propose to acquire as mentioned in the counter-notice.

(4) If—

(a) a compulsory purchase order has been made under the appropriate enactment in respect of land which consists of or includes any of the part of the hereditament or affected area not required, or

(b) the land in question falls within paragraph 21 of Schedule 13,

any power conferred by that order or, as the case may be, by the special enactment for the compulsory acquisition of the interest of the claimant in any land comprised in the part of the hereditament or affected area not required shall cease to have effect.

PART VI

Withdrawal of blight notice.

156.—(1) Subject to subsection (3), the person by whom a blight notice has been served may withdraw the notice at any time before the compensation payable in respect of a compulsory acquisition in pursuance of the notice has been determined by the Lands Tribunal or, if there has been such a determination, at any time before the end of the period of six weeks beginning with the date of the determination.

(2) Where a blight notice is withdrawn by virtue of subsection (1) any notice to treat deemed to have been served in consequence of it shall be deemed to have been withdrawn.

(3) A person shall not be entitled by virtue of subsection (1) to withdraw a notice after the appropriate authority have exercised a right of entering and taking possession of land in pursuance of a notice to treat deemed to have been served in consequence of that notice.

(4) No compensation shall be payable in respect of the withdrawal of a notice to treat which is deemed to have been withdrawn by virtue of subsection (2).

Compensation

Special provisions as to compensation for acquisitions in pursuance of blight notices.
1981 c.67.
1990 c. 9.

157.—(1) Where—

(a) an interest in land is acquired in pursuance of a blight notice, and

(b) the interest is one in respect of which a compulsory purchase order is in force under section 1 of the Acquisition of Land Act 1981, as applied by section 47 of the Planning (Listed Buildings and Conservation Areas) Act 1990, containing a direction for minimum compensation under section 50 of that Act of 1990,

the compensation payable for the acquisition shall be assessed in accordance with that direction and as if the notice to treat deemed to have been served in respect of the interest under section 154 had been served in pursuance of the compulsory purchase order.

(2) Where—

(a) an interest in land is acquired in pursuance of a blight notice, and

1985 c.68.

(b) the interest is one in respect of which a compulsory purchase order is in force under section 290 of the Housing Act 1985 (acquisition of land for clearance);

the compensation payable for the acquisition shall be assessed in accordance with that Act and as if the notice to treat deemed to have been served in respect of the interest under section 154 had been served in pursuance of the compulsory purchase order.

(3) The compensation payable in respect of the acquisition by virtue of section 160 of an interest in land comprised in—

(a) the unaffected area of an agricultural unit; or

(b) if the appropriate authority have served a counter-notice objecting to the blight notice on the grounds mentioned in section 151(4)(c), so much of the affected area of the unit as is not specified in the counter-notice,

1973 c.26.

shall be assessed on the assumptions mentioned in section 5(2), (3) and (4) of the Land Compensation Act 1973.

(4) In subsection (3) the reference to "the appropriate authority" shall be construed as if the unaffected area of an agricultural unit were part of the affected area.

Special provisions for requiring purchase of whole of partially affected agricultural unit

Inclusion in blight notices of requirement to purchase parts of agricultural units unaffected by blight.

158.—(1) This section applies where—

(a) a blight notice is served in respect of an interest in the whole or part of an agricultural unit, and

(b) on the date of service that unit or part contains land ("the unaffected area") which is not blighted land as well as land ("the affected area") which is such land.

(2) Where this section applies the claimant may include in the blight notice—

(a) a claim that the unaffected area is not reasonably capable of being farmed, either by itself or in conjunction with other relevant land, as a separate agricultural unit; and

(b) a requirement that the appropriate authority shall purchase his interest in the whole of the unit or, as the case may be, in the whole of the part of it to which the notice relates.

(3) Subject to section 159(4), "other relevant land" in subsection (2) means—

(a) if the blight notice is served only in respect of part of land comprised in the agricultural unit, the remainder of it; and

(b) land which is comprised in any other agricultural unit occupied by the claimant on the date of service and in respect of which he is then entitled to an owner's interest as defined in section 168(4).

Objections to s. 158 notices.

159.—(1) The grounds on which objection may be made in a counter-notice to a blight notice served by virtue of section 158 shall include the ground that the claim made in the notice is not justified.

(2) Objection shall not be made to a blight notice served by virtue of section 158 on the grounds mentioned in section 151(4)(c) unless it is also made on the grounds mentioned in subsection (1).

(3) The Lands Tribunal shall not uphold an objection to a notice served by virtue of section 158 on the grounds mentioned in section 151(4)(c) unless it also upholds the objection on the grounds mentioned in subsection (1).

(4) Where objection is made to a blight notice served by virtue of section 158 on the ground mentioned in subsection (1) and also on those mentioned in section 151(4)(c), the Lands Tribunal, in determining whether or not to uphold the objection, shall treat that part of the affected area which is not specified in the counter-notice as included in "other relevant land" as defined in section 158(3).

(5) If the Lands Tribunal upholds an objection but only on the ground mentioned in subsection (1), the Tribunal shall declare that the blight notice is a valid notice in relation to the affected area but not in relation to the unaffected area.

PART VI

(6) If the Tribunal upholds an objection both on the ground mentioned in subsection (1) and on the grounds mentioned in section 151(4)(c) (but not on any other grounds) the Tribunal shall declare that the blight notice is a valid notice in relation to the part of the affected area specified in the counter-notice as being the part which the appropriate authority propose to acquire as mentioned in that notice but not in relation to any other part of the affected area or in relation to the unaffected area.

(7) In a case falling within subsection (5) or (6), the Tribunal shall give directions specifying a date on which notice to treat (as mentioned in sections 154 and section 160) is to be deemed to have been served.

(8) Section 153(6) shall not apply to any blight notice served by virtue of section 158.

Effect of notices served by virtue of s. 158.

160.—(1) In relation to a blight notice served by virtue of section 158—

(a) subsection (2) of section 154 shall have effect as if for the words "or in the case of an agricultural unit the interest of the claimant in so far as it subsists in the affected area" there were substituted the words "or agricultural unit"; and

(b) subsections (4) and (5) of that section shall not apply to any such blight notice.

(2) Where the appropriate authority have served a counter-notice objecting to a blight notice on the grounds mentioned in section 159(1), then if either—

(a) the claimant, without referring that objection to the Lands Tribunal and before the time for so referring it has expired, gives notice to the appropriate authority that he withdraws his claim as to the unaffected area; or

(b) on a reference to the Tribunal, the Tribunal makes a declaration in accordance with section 159(5),

the appropriate authority shall be deemed—

(i) to be authorised to acquire compulsorily under the appropriate enactment the interest of the claimant in so far as it subsists in the affected area (but not in so far as it subsists in the unaffected area), and

(ii) to have served a notice to treat in respect of it on the date mentioned in subsection (3).

(3) The date referred to in subsection (2)—

(a) in a case falling within paragraph (a) of subsection (2), is the date on which notice is given in accordance with that paragraph; and

(b) in a case falling within paragraph (b) of that subsection, is the date specified in directions given by the Tribunal in accordance with section 159(7).

(4) Where the appropriate authority have served a counter-notice objecting to a blight notice on the grounds mentioned in section 159(1) and also on the grounds mentioned in section 151(4)(c), then if either—

(a) the claimant, without referring that objection to the Lands Tribunal and before the time for so referring it has expired—

(i) gives notice to the appropriate authority that he accepts the proposal of the authority to acquire the part of the affected area specified in the counter-notice, and

(ii) withdraws his claim as to the remainder of that area and as to the unaffected area; or

(b) on a reference to the Tribunal, the Tribunal makes a declaration in accordance with section 159(6) in respect of that part of the affected area,

the appropriate authority shall be deemed to be authorised to acquire compulsorily under the appropriate enactment the interest of the claimant in so far as it subsists in the part of the affected area specified in the counter-notice (but not in so far as it subsists in any other part of that area or in the unaffected area) and to have served a notice to treat in respect of it on the date mentioned in subsection (5).

(5) The date referred to in subsection (4)—

(a) in a case falling within paragraph (a) of that subsection, is the date on which notice is given in accordance with that paragraph; and

(b) in a case falling within paragraph (b) of that subsection, is the date specified in directions given by the Tribunal in accordance with section 159(7).

(6) In relation to a blight notice served by virtue of section 158 references to "the appropriate authority" and "the appropriate enactment" shall be construed as if the unaffected area of an agricultural unit were part of the affected area.

Personal representatives, mortgagees and partnerships

Powers of personal representatives in respect of blight notice.

161.—(1) In relation to any time after the death of a person who has served a blight notice, sections 151(1), 152(1), 153(1), 154(4) and (5), 156(1) and 160(2) and (4) shall apply as if any reference in them to the claimant were a reference to the claimant's personal representatives.

(2) Where the whole or part of a hereditament or agricultural unit is comprised in blighted land and a person claims that—

(a) he is the personal representative of a person ("the deceased") who at the date of his death was entitled to an interest in that hereditament or unit;

(b) the interest was one which would have been a qualifying interest if a notice under section 150 had been served in respect of it on that date;

(c) he has made reasonable endeavours to sell that interest;

(d) in consequence of the fact that the hereditament or unit or a part of it was, or was likely to be, comprised in blighted land, he has been unable to sell that interest except at a price substantially lower than that for which it might reasonably have been expected to sell if no part of the hereditament or unit were, or were likely to be, comprised in such land; and

PART VI

(e) one or more individuals are (to the exclusion of any body corporate) beneficially entitled to that interest,

he may serve on the appropriate authority a notice in the prescribed form requiring that authority to purchase that interest to the extent specified in, and otherwise in accordance with, this Chapter.

(3) Subject to subsection (4), subsection (2) shall apply in relation to an interest in part of a hereditament or agricultural unit as it applies in relation to an interest in the whole of a hereditament or agricultural unit.

(4) Subsection (3) shall not enable any person—

(a) if the deceased was entitled to an interest in the whole of a hereditament or agricultural unit, to make any claim or serve any notice under this section in respect of the deceased's interest in part of the hereditament or unit; or

(b) if the deceased was entitled to an interest only in part of the hereditament or agricultural unit, to make or serve any such claim or notice in respect of the deceased's interest in less than the whole of that part.

(5) Subject to sections 151(7) and 159(2) and (3), the grounds on which objection may be made in a counter-notice under section 151 to a notice under this section are those specified in paragraphs (a) to (c) of subsection (4) of that section and, in a case to which it applies, the grounds specified in paragraph (d) of that subsection and also the following grounds—

(a) that the claimant is not the personal representative of the deceased or that, on the date of the deceased's death, the deceased was not entitled to an interest in any part of the hereditament or agricultural unit to which the notice relates;

(b) that (for reasons specified in the counter-notice) the interest of the deceased is not such as is specified in subsection (2)(b);

(c) that the conditions specified in subsection (2)(c), (d) or (e) are not satisfied.

Power of mortgagees to serve blight notice.

162.—(1) Where the whole or part of a hereditament or agricultural unit is comprised in blighted land and a person claims that—

(a) he is entitled as mortgagee (by virtue of a power which has become exercisable) to sell an interest in the hereditament or unit, giving immediate vacant possession of the land;

(b) he has made reasonable endeavours to sell that interest; and

(c) in consequence of the fact that the hereditament or unit or a part of it was, or was likely to be, comprised in blighted land, he has been unable to sell that interest except at a price substantially lower than that for which it might reasonably have been expected to sell if no part of the hereditament or unit were, or were likely to be, comprised in such land,

then, subject to the provisions of this section, he may serve on the appropriate authority a notice in the prescribed form requiring that authority to purchase that interest to the extent specified in, and otherwise in accordance with, this Chapter.

(2) Subject to subsection (3), subsection (1) shall apply in relation to an interest in part of a hereditament or unit as it applies in relation to an interest in the whole of a hereditament or unit.

(3) Subsection (2) shall not enable a person—

(a) if his interest as mortgagee is in the whole of a hereditament or agricultural unit, to make any claim or serve any notice under this section in respect of any interest in part of the hereditament or unit; or

(b) if his interest as mortgagee is only in part of a hereditament or agricultural unit, to make or serve any such notice or claim in respect of any interest in less than the whole of that part.

(4) Notice under this section shall not be served unless the interest which the mortgagee claims he has the power to sell—

(a) could be the subject of a notice under section 150 served by the person entitled to it on the date of service of the notice under this section; or

(b) could have been the subject of such a notice served by that person on a date not more than six months before the date of service of the notice under this section.

(5) Subject to sections 151(7) and 159(2) and (3), the grounds on which objection may be made in a counter-notice under section 151 to a notice under this section are those specified in paragraphs (a) to (c) of subsection (4) of that section and, in a case to which it applies, the grounds specified in paragraph (d) of that subsection and also the following grounds—

(a) that, on the date of service of the notice under this section, the claimant had no interest as mortgagee in any part of the hereditament or agricultural unit to which the notice relates;

(b) that (for reasons specified in the counter-notice) the claimant had not on that date the power referred to in subsection (1)(a);

(c) that the conditions specified in subsection (1)(b) and (c) are not fulfilled;

(d) that (for reasons specified in the counter-notice) neither of the conditions specified in subsection (4) was, on the date of service of the notice under this section, satisfied with regard to the interest referred to in that subsection.

Prohibition on service of simultaneous notices under ss. 150, 161 and 162.

163.—(1) No notice shall be served under section 150 or 161 in respect of a hereditament or agricultural unit, or any part of it, at a time when a notice already served under section 162 is outstanding with respect to it, and no notice shall be served under section 162 at a time when a notice already served under section 150 or 161 is outstanding with respect to the relevant hereditament, unit or part.

(2) For the purposes of subsection (1), a notice shall be treated as outstanding with respect to a hereditament, unit or part—

(a) until it is withdrawn in relation to the hereditament, unit or part; or

(b) in a case where an objection to the notice has been made by a counter-notice under section 151, until either—

(i) the period of two months specified in section 153 elapses without the claimant having required the objection to be referred to the Lands Tribunal under that section; or

(ii) the objection, having been so referred, is upheld by the Tribunal with respect to the hereditament, unit or part.

PART VI

Special provisions as to partnerships.

164.—(1) This section shall have effect for the purposes of the application of this Chapter to a hereditament or agricultural unit occupied for the purposes of a partnership firm.

(2) Occupation for the purposes of the firm shall be treated as occupation by the firm, and not as occupation by any one or more of the partners individually, and the definitions of "owner-occupier" in section 168(1) and (2) shall apply in relation to the firm accordingly.

(3) If, after the service by the firm of a blight notice, any change occurs (whether by death or otherwise) in the constitution of the firm, any proceedings, rights or obligations consequential upon that notice may be carried on or exercised by or against, or, as the case may be, shall be incumbent upon, the partners for the time being constituting the firm.

1978 c. 30.

(4) Nothing in this Chapter shall be construed as indicating an intention to exclude the operation of the definition of "person" in Schedule 1 to the Interpretation Act 1978 (by which, unless the contrary intention appears, "person" includes any body of persons corporate or unincorporate) in relation to any provision of this Chapter.

(5) Subsection (2) shall not affect the definition of "resident owner-occupier" in section 168(3).

Miscellaneous and supplementary provisions

Power of Secretary of State to acquire land affected by orders relating to new towns etc. where blight notice served.

165.—(1) Where a blight notice has been served in respect of land falling within paragraph 7, 8 or 9 of Schedule 13, then until such time as a development corporation is established for the new town or, as the case may be, an urban development corporation is established for the urban development area the Secretary of State shall have power to acquire compulsorily any interest in the land in pursuance of the blight notice served by virtue of that paragraph.

(2) Where the Secretary of State acquires an interest under subsection (1), then—

- (a) if the land is or becomes land within paragraph 8 or, as the case may be, paragraph 9(b) of Schedule 13, the interest shall be transferred by him to the development corporation established for the new town or, as the case may be, the urban development corporation established for the urban development area; and
- (b) in any other case, the interest may be disposed of by him in such manner as he thinks fit.

1961 c. 33.

(3) The Land Compensation Act 1961 shall have effect in relation to the compensation payable in respect of the acquisition of an interest by the Secretary of State under subsection (1) as if—

1981 c. 64.
1980 c. 65.

- (a) the acquisition were by a development corporation under the New Towns Act 1981 or, as the case may be, by an urban development corporation under Part XVI of the Local Government, Planning and Land Act 1980;
- (b) in the case of land within paragraph 7 of Schedule 13, the land formed part of an area designated as the site of a new town by an order which has come into operation under section 1 of the New Towns Act 1981; and

PART VI

(c) in the case of land within paragraph 9(a) of Schedule 13, the land formed part of an area designated as an urban development area by an order under section 134 of the Local Government, Planning and Land Act 1980 which has come into operation. 1980 c. 65.

Saving for claimant's right to sell whole hereditament, etc.

166.—(1) The provisions of sections 151(4)(c), 153(6), 154(4) and (5) and 155(3) and (4) relating to hereditaments shall not affect—

(a) the right of a claimant under section 92 of the Lands Clauses Consolidation Act 1845 to sell the whole of the hereditament or, in the case of an agricultural unit, the whole of the affected area, which he has required the authority to purchase; or 1845 c. 18.

(b) the right of a claimant under section 8 of the Compulsory Purchase Act 1965 to sell (unless the Lands Tribunal otherwise determines) the whole of the hereditament or, as the case may be, affected area which he has required that authority to purchase. 1965 c. 56.

(2) In accordance with subsection (1)(b), in determining whether or not to uphold an objection relating to a hereditament on the grounds mentioned in section 151(4)(c), the Lands Tribunal shall consider (in addition to the other matters which they are required to consider) whether—

(a) in the case of a house, building or factory, the part proposed to be acquired can be taken without material detriment to the house, building or factory; or

(b) in the case of a park or garden belonging to a house, the part proposed to be acquired can be taken without seriously affecting the amenity or convenience of the house.

No withdrawal of constructive notice to treat.

167. Without prejudice to the provisions of section 156(1) and (2), a notice to treat which is deemed to have been served by virtue of this Chapter may not be withdrawn under section 31 of the Land Compensation Act 1961. 1961 c. 33.

Meaning of "owner-occupier" and "resident owner-occupier".

168.—(1) Subject to the following provisions of this section, in this Chapter "owner-occupier", in relation to a hereditament, means—

(a) a person who occupies the whole or a substantial part of the hereditament in right of an owner's interest in it, and has so occupied the hereditament or that part of it during the whole of the period of six months ending with the date of service; or

(b) if the whole or a substantial part of the hereditament was unoccupied for a period of not more than 12 months ending with that date, a person who so occupied the hereditament or, as the case may be, that part of it during the whole of a period of six months ending immediately before the period when it was not occupied.

(2) Subject to the following provisions of this section, in this Chapter "owner-occupier", in relation to an agricultural unit, means a person who—

(a) occupies the whole of that unit and has occupied it during the whole of the period of six months ending with the date of service; or

PART VI

(b) occupied the whole of that unit during the whole of a period of six months ending not more than 12 months before the date of service,

and, at all times material for the purposes of paragraph (a) or, as the case may be, paragraph (b) has been entitled to an owner's interest in the whole or part of that unit.

(3) In this Chapter "resident owner-occupier", in relation to a hereditament, means—

(a) an individual who occupies the whole or a substantial part of the hereditament as a private dwelling in right of an owner's interest in it, and has so occupied the hereditament or, as the case may be, that part during the whole of the period of six months ending with the date of service; or

(b) if the whole or a substantial part of the hereditament was unoccupied for a period of not more than 12 months ending with that date, an individual who so occupied the hereditament or, as the case may be, that part during the whole of a period of six months ending immediately before the period when it was not occupied.

(4) In this section—

"owner's interest", in relation to a hereditament or agricultural unit, means a freehold interest in it or a tenancy of it granted or extended for a term of years certain not less than three years of which remain unexpired on the date of service; and

"date of service", in relation to a hereditament or agricultural unit, means the date of service of a notice in respect of it under section 150.

"Appropriate authority" for purposes of Chapter II.

169.—(1) Subject to the following provisions of this section, in this Chapter "the appropriate authority", in relation to any land, means the government department, local authority or other body or person by whom, in accordance with the circumstances by virtue of which the land falls within any paragraph of Schedule 13, the land is liable to be acquired or is indicated as being proposed to be acquired or, as the case may be, any right over the land is proposed to be acquired.

(2) If any question arises—

(a) whether the appropriate authority in relation to any land for the purposes of this Chapter is the Secretary of State or a local highway authority; or

(b) which of two or more local highway authorities is the appropriate authority in relation to any land for those purposes; or

(c) which of two or more local authorities is the appropriate authority in relation to any land for those purposes,

that question shall be referred to the Secretary of State, whose decision shall be final.

PART VI

(3) If any question arises which authority is the appropriate authority for the purposes of this Chapter—

(a) section 151(2) shall have effect as if the reference to the date of service of the blight notice were a reference to that date or, if it is later, the date on which that question is determined;

(b) section 162(4)(b) shall apply with the substitution for the period of six months of a reference to that period extended by so long as it takes to obtain a determination of the question; and

(c) section 168(1)(b), (2)(b) and (3)(b) shall apply with the substitution for the reference to 12 months before the date of service of a reference to that period extended by so long as it takes to obtain a determination of the question.

(4) In relation to land falling within paragraph 7, 8 or 9 of Schedule 13, until such time as a development corporation is established for the new town or, as the case may be, an urban development corporation is established for the urban development area, this Chapter shall have effect as if "the appropriate authority" were the Secretary of State.

(5) In relation to land falling within paragraph 19 of Schedule 13, "the appropriate authority" shall be the highway authority for the highway in relation to which the order mentioned in that paragraph was made.

"Appropriate enactment" for purposes of Chapter II.

170.—(1) Subject to the following provisions of this section, in this Chapter "the appropriate enactment", in relation to land falling within any paragraph of Schedule 13, means the enactment which provides for the compulsory acquisition of land as being land falling within that paragraph or, as respects paragraph 22(b), the enactment under which the compulsory purchase order referred to in that paragraph was made.

(2) In relation to land falling within paragraph 2, 3 or 4 of that Schedule, an enactment shall for the purposes of subsection (1) be taken to be an enactment which provides for the compulsory acquisition of land as being land falling within that paragraph if—

(a) the enactment provides for the compulsory acquisition of land for the purposes of the functions which are indicated in the development plan as being the functions for the purposes of which the land is allocated or is proposed to be developed; or

(b) where no particular functions are so indicated in the development plan, the enactment provides for the compulsory acquisition of land for the purposes of any of the functions of the government department, local authority or other body for the purposes of whose functions the land is allocated or is defined as the site of proposed development.

(3) In relation to land falling within paragraph 2, 3 or 4 of that Schedule by virtue of Note (1) to that paragraph, "the appropriate enactment" shall be determined in accordance with subsection (2) as if references in that subsection to the development plan were references to any such plan, proposal or modifications as are mentioned in paragraph (a), (b) or (c) of that Note.

(4) In relation to land falling within paragraph 5 or 6 of that Schedule, "the appropriate enactment" shall be determined in accordance with subsection (2) as if references in that subsection to the development plan were references to the resolution or direction in question.

PART VI

(5) In relation to land falling within paragraph 7, 8 or 9 of that Schedule, until such time as a development corporation is established for the new town or, as the case may be, an urban development corporation is established for the urban development area, this Chapter shall have effect as if "the appropriate enactment" were section 165(1).

(6) In relation to land falling within paragraph 10 or 11 of that Schedule, "the appropriate enactment" shall be section 290 of the Housing Act 1985.

1985 c. 68.

(7) In relation to land falling within paragraph 19 of that Schedule, "the appropriate enactment" shall be section 239(6) of the Highways Act 1980.

1980 c. 66.

(8) In relation to land falling within paragraph 22 of that Schedule by virtue of Note (1) to that paragraph, "the appropriate enactment" shall be the enactment which would provide for the compulsory acquisition of the land or of the rights over the land if the relevant compulsory purchase order were confirmed or made.

(9) Where, in accordance with the circumstances by virtue of which any land falls within any paragraph of that Schedule, it is indicated that the land is proposed to be acquired for highway purposes, any enactment under which a highway authority are or (subject to the fulfilment of the relevant conditions) could be authorised to acquire that land compulsorily for highway purposes shall, for the purposes of subsection (1), be taken to be an enactment providing for the compulsory acquisition of that land as being land falling within that paragraph.

(10) In subsection (9) the reference to the fulfilment of the relevant conditions is a reference to such one or more of the following as are applicable to the circumstances in question—

(a) the coming into operation of any requisite order or scheme made, or having effect as if made, under the provisions of Part II of the Highways Act 1980;

(b) the coming into operation of any requisite scheme made, or having effect as if made, under section 106(3) of that Act;

(c) the making or approval of any requisite plans.

(11) If, apart from this subsection, two or more enactments would be the appropriate enactment in relation to any land for the purposes of this Chapter, the appropriate enactment for those purposes shall be taken to be that one of those enactments under which, in the circumstances in question, it is most likely that (apart from this Chapter) the land would have been acquired by the appropriate authority.

(12) If any question arises as to which enactment is the appropriate enactment in relation to any land for the purposes of this Chapter, that question shall be referred—

(a) where the appropriate authority are a government department, to the Minister in charge of that department;

(b) where the appropriate authority are statutory undertakers, to the appropriate Minister; and

(c) in any other case, to the Secretary of State,

and the decision of the Minister or, as the case may be, the Secretary of State shall be final.

PART VI

General interpretation of Chapter II.

171.—(1) Subject to the following provisions of this section, in this Chapter—

"the affected area", in relation to an agricultural unit, means so much of that unit as, on the date of service, consists of land falling within any paragraph of Schedule 13;

"agricultural" has the same meaning as in section 109 of the Agriculture Act 1947 and references to the farming of land include references to the carrying on in relation to the land of agricultural activities; 1947 c.48.

"agricultural unit" means land which is occupied as a unit for agricultural purposes, including any dwellinghouse or other building occupied by the same person for the purpose of farming the land;

"annual value" means—

(a) in the case of a hereditament which is shown in a local non-domestic rating list and none of which consists of domestic property or property exempt from local non-domestic rating, the value shown in that list as the rateable value of that hereditament on the date of service;

(b) in the case of a hereditament which is shown in a local non-domestic rating list and which includes domestic property or property exempt from local non-domestic rating, the sum of—

(i) the value shown in that list as the rateable value of that hereditament on the date of service; and

(ii) the value attributable to the non-rateable part of that hereditament in accordance with subsections (2) and (3);

(c) in the case of any other hereditament, the value attributable to that hereditament in accordance with subsections (2) and (3);

"blight notice" has the meaning given in section 149(5);

"the claimant" has the meaning given in section 150(4);

"hereditament" means a relevant hereditament within the meaning of section 64(4)(a) to (c) of the Local Government Finance Act 1988; 1988 c. 41.

"special enactment" means a local enactment, or a provision contained in an Act other than a local or private Act, which is a local enactment or provision authorising the compulsory acquisition of land specifically identified in it; and in this definition "local enactment" means a local or private Act, or an order confirmed by Parliament or brought into operation in accordance with special parliamentary procedure.

(2) The value attributable to a hereditament, or the non-rateable part of it, in respect of domestic property shall be the value certified by the relevant valuation officer as being 5 per cent. of the compensation which would be payable in respect of the value of that property if it were purchased compulsorily under statute with vacant possession and the compensation payable were calculated in accordance with Part II of the Land Compensation Act 1961 by reference to the relevant date. 1961 c. 33.

(3) The value attributable to a hereditament, or the non-rateable part of it, in respect of property exempt from local non-domestic rating shall be the value certified by the relevant valuation officer as being the value which would have been shown as the rateable value of that property on

PART VI

the date of service if it were a relevant non-domestic hereditament consisting entirely of non-domestic property, none of which was exempt from local non-domestic rating.

(4) Land which (apart from this subsection) would comprise separate hereditaments solely by reason of being divided by a boundary between rating areas shall be treated for the purposes of the definition of "hereditament" in subsection (1) as if it were not so divided.

(5) In this section—

"date of service" has the same meaning as in section 168;

"relevant valuation officer" means the valuation officer who would have determined the rateable value in respect of the hereditament for the purposes of Part III of the Local Government Finance Act 1988 if the hereditament had fulfilled the conditions set out in section 42(1)(b) to (d) of that Act;

1988 c.41.

"relevant date" is the date by reference to which that determination would have been made;

and expressions used in the definition of "annual value" in subsection (1) or in subsection (2) or (3) which are also used in Part III of that Act have the same meaning as in that Part.

PART VII

ENFORCEMENT

Enforcement notices

Power to issue enforcement notice.

172.—(1) Where—

(a) it appears to the local planning authority that there has been a breach of planning control after the end of 1963; and

(b) the authority consider it expedient to do so having regard to the provisions of the development plan and to any other material considerations,

they may issue a notice requiring the breach to be remedied.

(2) A notice under this section is referred to in this Act as an "enforcement notice".

(3) There is a breach of planning control—

(a) if development has been carried out, whether before or after the commencement of this Act, without the grant of the planning permission required for that development in accordance with Part III (or, as the case may be, Part III of the 1962 Act or Part III of the 1971 Act); or

(b) if any conditions or limitations subject to which planning permission was granted have not been complied with.

(4) An enforcement notice which relates to a breach of planning control consisting in—

(a) the carrying out without planning permission of building, engineering, mining or other operations in, on, over or under land; or

(b) the failure to comply with any condition or limitation which relates to the carrying out of such operations and subject to which planning permission was granted for the development of that land; or

(c) the making without planning permission of a change of use of any building to use as a single dwellinghouse; or

(d) the failure to comply with a condition which prohibits or has the effect of preventing a change of use of a building to use as a single dwellinghouse,

may be issued only within the period of four years from the date of the breach.

(5) Subject to section 175(4), an enforcement notice shall take effect on a date specified in it (in this Part referred to as the "specified date").

(6) A copy of an enforcement notice shall be served not later than 28 days after the date of its issue and not later than 28 days before the specified date—

(a) on the owner and on the occupier of the land to which it relates; and

(b) on any other person having an interest in that land, which in the opinion of the authority is an interest materially affected by the notice.

(7) The local planning authority may withdraw an enforcement notice (without prejudice to their powers to issue another) at any time before it takes effect.

(8) If they do so, they shall immediately give notice of the withdrawal to every person who was served with a copy of the notice.

Contents of enforcement notice.

173.—(1) An enforcement notice shall specify the matters alleged to constitute a breach of planning control.

(2) An enforcement notice shall also specify—

(a) any steps the local planning authority require to be taken in order to remedy the breach; and

(b) any such steps as are mentioned in subsection (4) which the authority require to be taken.

(3) In this section "steps to be taken in order to remedy the breach" means (according to the particular circumstances of the breach) steps for the purpose—

(a) of restoring the land to its condition before the development took place; or

(b) of securing compliance with the conditions or limitations subject to which planning permission was granted,

including—

(i) the demolition or alteration of any building or works;

(ii) the discontinuance of any use of land; and

(iii) the carrying out on land of any building or other operations.

PART VII

(4) The steps referred to in subsection (2)(b) are steps for the purpose—

(a) of making the development comply with the terms of any planning permission which has been granted in respect of the land; or

(b) of removing or alleviating any injury to amenity which has been caused by the development.

(5) An enforcement notice shall specify the period within which any such step as is mentioned in subsection (2) is to be taken and may specify different periods for the taking of different steps.

(6) Where the matters which an enforcement notice alleges to constitute a breach of planning control include development which has involved the making of a deposit of refuse or waste materials on land, the notice may require that the contour of the deposit shall be modified by altering the gradient or gradients of its sides in such manner as may be specified in the notice.

(7) The Secretary of State may by regulations direct—

(a) that enforcement notices shall specify matters additional to those which they are required to specify by this section; and

(b) that every copy of an enforcement notice served under section 172 shall be accompanied by an explanatory note giving such information as may be specified in the regulations with regard to the right of appeal conferred by section 174.

(8) Where—

(a) an enforcement notice has been issued in respect of development consisting of the erection of a building or the carrying out of works without the grant of planning permission; and

(b) the notice has required the taking of steps for a purpose mentioned in subsection (4)(b); and

(c) the steps have been taken,

for the purposes of the planning Acts planning permission for the retention of the building or works as they are as a result of compliance with the notice shall be deemed to have been granted on an application for such permission made to the local planning authority.

Appeal against enforcement notice.

174.—(1) A person having an interest in the land to which an enforcement notice relates or a relevant occupier may appeal to the Secretary of State against the notice, whether or not a copy of it has been served on him.

(2) An appeal may be brought on any of the following grounds—

(a) that planning permission ought to be granted for the development to which the notice relates or, as the case may be, that a condition or limitation alleged in the enforcement notice not to have been complied with ought to be discharged;

(b) that the matters alleged in the notice do not constitute a breach of planning control;

(c) that the breach of planning control alleged in the notice has not taken place;

PART VII

(d) in the case of a notice to which section 172(4) applies, that the period of four years from the date of the breach of planning control to which the notice relates had elapsed at the date when the notice was issued;

(e) in the case of a notice not falling within paragraph (d), that the breach of planning control alleged by the notice occurred before the beginning of 1964;

(f) that copies of the enforcement notice were not served as required by section 172(6);

(g) that the steps required by the notice to be taken exceed what is necessary to remedy any breach of planning control or to achieve a purpose specified in section 173(4);

(h) that the period specified in the notice as the period within which any step is to be taken falls short of what should reasonably be allowed.

(3) An appeal under this section shall be made by notice in writing to the Secretary of State before the specified date.

(4) A person who gives notice under subsection (3) shall submit to the Secretary of State, either when giving the notice or within the prescribed time, a statement in writing—

(a) specifying the grounds on which he is appealing against the enforcement notice; and

(b) giving such further information as may be prescribed.

(5) If, where more than one ground is specified in that statement, the appellant does not give information required under subsection (4)(b) in relation to each of those grounds within the prescribed time, the Secretary of State may determine the appeal without considering any ground as to which the appellant has failed to give such information within that time.

(6) In this section "relevant occupier" means a person who—

(a) on the date on which the enforcement notice is issued occupies the land to which the notice relates by virtue of a licence in writing; and

(b) continues so to occupy the land when the appeal is brought.

Appeals: supplementary provisions.

175.—(1) The Secretary of State may by regulations prescribe the procedure which is to be followed on appeals under section 174 and, in particular, but without prejudice to the generality of this subsection, may—

(a) require the local planning authority to submit, within such time as may be prescribed, a statement indicating the submissions which they propose to put forward on the appeal;

(b) specify the matters to be included in such a statement;

(c) require the authority or the appellant to give such notice of such an appeal as may be prescribed;

(d) require the authority to send to the Secretary of State, within such period from the date of the bringing of the appeal as may be prescribed, a copy of the enforcement notice and a list of the persons served with copies of it.

PART VII

(2) The notice to be prescribed under subsection (1)(c) shall be such notice as in the opinion of the Secretary of State is likely to bring the appeal to the attention of persons in the locality in which the land to which the enforcement notice relates is situated.

(3) Subject to section 176(4), the Secretary of State shall, if either the appellant or the local planning authority so desire, give each of them an opportunity of appearing before and being heard by a person appointed by the Secretary of State for the purpose.

(4) Where an appeal is brought under section 174 the enforcement notice shall be of no effect pending the final determination or the withdrawal of the appeal.

(5) Where any person has appealed to the Secretary of State against an enforcement notice, no person shall be entitled, in any other proceedings instituted after the making of the appeal, to claim that the notice was not duly served on the person who appealed.

(6) Schedule 6 applies to appeals under section 174, including appeals under that section as applied by regulations under any other provisions of this Act.

General provisions relating to determination of appeals.

176.—(1) On the determination of an appeal under section 174, the Secretary of State shall give directions for giving effect to the determination, including, where appropriate, directions for quashing the enforcement notice or for varying its terms.

(2) On such an appeal if the Secretary of State is satisfied that to do so will not cause the appellant or the local planning authority injustice, he may—

(a) correct any informality, defect or error in the enforcement notice; or

(b) give directions for varying its terms.

(3) The Secretary of State—

(a) may dismiss an appeal if the appellant fails to comply with section 174(4) within the prescribed time; and

(b) may allow an appeal and quash the enforcement notice if the local planning authority fail to comply with any requirement of regulations made by virtue of paragraph (a), (b), or (d) of section 175(1) within the prescribed period.

(4) If the Secretary of State proposes to dismiss an appeal under paragraph (a) of subsection (3) or to allow an appeal and quash the enforcement notice under paragraph (b) of that subsection, he need not comply with section 175(3).

(5) Where it would otherwise be a ground for determining an appeal under section 174 in favour of the appellant that a person required to be served with a copy of the enforcement notice was not served, the Secretary of State may disregard that fact if neither the appellant nor that person has been substantially prejudiced by the failure to serve him.

PART VII

Grant or modification of planning permission on appeals against enforcement notices.

177.—(1) On the determination of an appeal under section 174, the Secretary of State may—

(a) grant planning permission for the development to which the enforcement notice relates or for part of that development or for the development of part of the land to which the enforcement notice relates;

(b) discharge any condition or limitation subject to which planning permission was granted;

(c) determine any purpose for which the land may, in the circumstances obtaining at the time of the determination, be lawfully used having regard to any past use of it and to any planning permission relating to it.

(2) In considering whether to grant planning permission under subsection (1), the Secretary of State shall have regard to the provisions of the development plan, so far as material to the subject matter of the enforcement notice, and to any other material considerations.

(3) Any planning permission granted by the Secretary of State under subsection (1) may—

(a) include permission to retain or complete any buildings or works on the land, or to do so without complying with some condition attached to a previous planning permission;

(b) be granted subject to such conditions as the Secretary of State thinks fit;

and section 72(1) and (5) shall apply with any necessary modifications in relation to the grant of permission under subsection (1) as it applies to a grant of permission under section 70(1).

(4) Where under subsection (1) the Secretary of State discharges a condition or limitation, he may substitute another condition or limitation for it, whether more or less onerous.

(5) Where an appeal against an enforcement notice is brought under section 174, the appellant shall be deemed to have made an application for planning permission for the development to which the notice relates.

(6) Any planning permission granted under subsection (1) on an appeal shall be treated as granted on the application deemed to have been made by the appellant.

(7) In relation to a grant of planning permission or a determination under subsection (1) the Secretary of State's decision shall be final.

(8) For the purposes of section 69 the Secretary of State's decision shall be treated as having been given by him in dealing with an application for planning permission made to the local planning authority.

Execution and cost of works required by enforcement notice.

178.—(1) If any steps which by virtue of section 173(2)(a) are required by an enforcement notice to be taken (other than the discontinuance of a use of land) have not been taken within the compliance period, the local planning authority may—

(a) enter the land and take those steps, and

(b) recover from the person who is then the owner of the land any expenses reasonably incurred by them in doing so.

PART VII

(2) Where a copy of an enforcement notice has been served in respect of any breach of planning control (as defined in section 172(3))—

(a) any expenses incurred by the owner or occupier of any land for the purpose of complying with the notice, and

(b) any sums paid by the owner of any land under subsection (1) in respect of expenses incurred by the local planning authority in taking steps required by such a notice to be taken,

shall be deemed to be incurred or paid for the use and at the request of the person by whom the breach of planning control was committed.

(3) Regulations made under this Act may provide that—

1936 c. 49.

(a) section 276 of the Public Health Act 1936, (power of local authorities to sell materials removed in executing works under that Act subject to accounting for the proceeds of sale);

(b) section 289 of that Act (power to require the occupier of any premises to permit works to be executed by the owner of the premises); and

(c) section 294 of that Act (limit on liability of persons holding premises as agents or trustees in respect of the expenses recoverable under that Act),

shall apply, subject to such adaptations and modifications as may be specified in the regulations, in relation to any steps required to be taken by an enforcement notice.

(4) Regulations under subsection (3) applying section 289 of the Public Health Act 1936 may include adaptations and modifications for the purpose of giving the owner of land to which an enforcement notice relates the right, as against all other persons interested in the land, to comply with the requirements of the enforcement notice.

(5) Regulations under subsection (3) may also provide for the charging on the land of any expenses recoverable by a local planning authority under subsection (1).

(6) Where by virtue of this section any expenses are recoverable by a local planning authority, those expenses shall be recoverable as a simple contract debt in any court of competent jurisdiction.

(7) In this section and in sections 179, 183 and 184 any reference to the compliance period, in relation to an enforcement notice, is a reference to the period specified in the notice for compliance with it or such extended period as the local planning authority may allow for compliance with it.

Penalties for non-compliance with enforcement notice.

179.—(1) Where—

(a) a copy of an enforcement notice has been served on the person who at the time when the copy was served was the owner of the land to which the notice relates, and

(b) any steps required by the notice to be taken (other than the discontinuance of a use of land) have not been taken within the compliance period,

then, subject to the provisions of this section, that person shall be guilty of an offence.

PART VII

(2) A person who is guilty of an offence under subsection (1) shall be liable—

(a) on summary conviction, to a fine not exceeding the statutory maximum, or

(b) on conviction on indictment, to a fine.

(3) Where proceedings have been brought under subsection (1) against a person ("the original owner") who has, at some time before the end of the compliance period, ceased to be the owner of the land, if he—

(a) duly lays information to that effect, and

(b) gives the prosecution not less than three clear days' notice of his intention,

he shall be entitled to have the person who then became the owner of the land ("the subsequent owner") brought before the court in the proceedings.

(4) Where in such proceedings—

(a) it has been proved that any steps required by the enforcement notice have not been taken within the compliance period, and

(b) the original owner proves that the failure to take those steps was attributable, in whole or in part, to the default of the subsequent owner

then—

(i) the subsequent owner may be convicted of the offence; and

(ii) if the original owner also proves that he took all reasonable steps to secure compliance with the enforcement notice, he shall be acquitted of the offence.

(5) If, after a person has been convicted under the previous provisions of this section, he does not as soon as practicable do everything in his power to secure compliance with the enforcement notice, he shall be guilty of a further offence and liable—

(a) on summary conviction to a fine not exceeding £200 for each day following his first conviction on which any of the requirements of the notice (other than the discontinuance of the use of land) remain unfulfilled; or

(b) on conviction on indictment, to a fine.

(6) Where, by virtue of an enforcement notice—

(a) a use of land is required to be discontinued, or

(b) any conditions or limitations are required to be complied with in respect of a use of land or in respect of the carrying out of operations on it,

then, if any person uses the land or causes or permits it to be used, or carries out those operations or causes or permits them to be carried out, in contravention of the notice, he shall be guilty of an offence.

(7) A person who is guilty of an offence under subsection (6) shall be liable—

(a) on summary conviction, to a fine not exceeding the statutory maximum, or

(b) on conviction on indictment, to a fine.

(8) Where a person is convicted under subsection (6) in respect of any use of land and the use is continued after the conviction he shall be guilty of a further offence and liable—

(a) on summary conviction, to a fine not exceeding £200 for each day on which the use is so continued, or

(b) on conviction on indictment, to a fine.

Effect of planning permission on enforcement notice.

180.—(1) If, after the service of a copy of an enforcement notice, planning permission is granted—

(a) for the retention on land of buildings or works, or

(b) for the continuance of a use of land, to which the enforcement notice relates,

the enforcement notice shall cease to have effect in so far as it requires steps to be taken for the demolition or alteration of those buildings or works or, as the case may be, the discontinuance of that use.

(2) If the planning permission granted as mentioned in subsection (1) is granted so as to permit the retention of buildings or works, or the continuance of a use of land, without complying with some condition subject to which a previous planning permission was granted, the enforcement notice shall cease to have effect in so far as it requires steps to be taken for complying with that condition.

(3) The fact that an enforcement notice has wholly or partly ceased to have effect under subsection (1) or (2) shall not affect the liability of any person for an offence in respect of a previous failure to comply with the notice.

Enforcement notice to have effect against subsequent development.

181.—(1) Compliance with an enforcement notice, whether in respect of—

(a) the completion, demolition or alteration of any buildings or works;

(b) the discontinuance of any use of land; or

(c) any other requirements contained in the notice,

shall not discharge the notice.

(2) Without prejudice to subsection (1), any provision of an enforcement notice requiring a use of land to be discontinued shall operate as a requirement that it shall be discontinued permanently, to the extent that it is in contravention of Part III; and accordingly the resumption of that use at any time after it has been discontinued in compliance with the enforcement notice shall to that extent be in contravention of the enforcement notice.

(3) Without prejudice to subsection (1), if any development is carried out on land by way of reinstating or restoring buildings or works which have been demolished or altered in compliance with an enforcement notice, the notice shall, notwithstanding that its terms are not apt for the purpose, be deemed to apply in relation to the buildings or works as reinstated or restored as it applied in relation to the buildings or works before they were demolished or altered; and, subject to subsection (4), the provisions of section 178(1) and (2) shall apply accordingly.

(4) Where, at any time after an enforcement notice takes effect—

(a) any development is carried out on land by way of reinstating or restoring buildings or works which have been demolished or altered in compliance with the notice; and

(b) the local planning authority propose, under section 178(1), to take any steps required by the enforcement notice for the demolition or alteration of the buildings or works in consequence of the reinstatement or restoration,

the local planning authority shall, not less than 28 days before taking any such steps, serve on the owner and occupier of the land a notice of their intention to do so.

(5) Where without planning permission a person carries out any development on land by way of reinstating or restoring buildings or works which have been demolished or altered in compliance with an enforcement notice—

(a) he shall be guilty of an offence and shall be liable on summary conviction to a fine not exceeding level 5 on the standard scale, and

(b) no person shall be liable under any of the provisions of section 179(1) to (5) for failure to take any steps required to be taken by an enforcement notice by way of demolition or alteration of what has been so reinstated or restored.

Enforcement by the Secretary of State.

182.—(1) If it appears to the Secretary of State to be expedient that an enforcement notice should be issued in respect of any land, he may issue such a notice.

(2) The Secretary of State shall not issue such a notice without consulting the local planning authority.

(3) An enforcement notice issued by the Secretary of State shall have the same effect as a notice issued by the local planning authority.

(4) In relation to an enforcement notice issued by the Secretary of State, sections 178 and 181 shall apply as if for any reference in those sections to the local planning authority there were substituted a reference to the Secretary of State.

Stop notices

Stop notices.

183.—(1) Where in respect of any land the local planning authority—

(a) have served a copy of an enforcement notice requiring a breach of planning control to be remedied; but

(b) consider it expedient to prevent, before the expiry of the compliance period, the carrying out of any activity which is, or is included in, a matter alleged by the notice to constitute the breach,

they may at any time before the notice takes effect serve a notice prohibiting the carrying out of that activity on the land, or any part of it specified in the notice.

(2) A notice under subsection (1) is in this Act referred to as a "stop notice".

PART VII

(3) A stop notice shall not prohibit—

(a) the use of any building as a dwellinghouse, or

(b) the use of land as the site for a caravan occupied by any person as his only or main residence, or

(c) the taking of any steps specified in the enforcement notice as required to be taken in order to remedy the breach of planning control.

1960 c. 62.

(4) For the purposes of subsection (3) "caravan" has the same meaning as it has for the purposes of Part I of the Caravan Sites and Control of Development Act 1960.

(5) Where the period during which an activity has been carried out on land (whether continuously or otherwise) began more than 12 months earlier, a stop notice shall not prohibit the carrying out of that activity on that land unless it is, or is incidental to, building, engineering, mining or other operations or the deposit of refuse or waste materials.

(6) A stop notice may be served by the local planning authority on any person who appears to them to have an interest in the land or to be engaged in any activity prohibited by the notice.

(7) The local planning authority may at any time withdraw a stop notice (without prejudice to their power to serve another) by serving notice to that effect on persons served with the stop notice.

Stop notices: supplementary provisions.

184.—(1) A stop notice must refer to the enforcement notice to which it relates and have a copy of that notice annexed to it.

(2) A stop notice must specify the date on which it will take effect (and it cannot be contravened until that date).

(3) That date must not be earlier than three nor later than 28 days from the day on which the notice is first served on any person.

(4) A stop notice shall cease to have effect when—

(a) the enforcement notice to which it relates is withdrawn or quashed; or

(b) the compliance period expires; or

(c) notice of the withdrawal of the stop notice is first served under section 183(7).

(5) A stop notice shall also cease to have effect if or to the extent that the activities prohibited by it cease, on a variation of the enforcement notice, to be included in the matters alleged by the enforcement notice to constitute a breach of planning control.

(6) Where a stop notice has been served in respect of any land, the local planning authority may display there a notice (in this section and section 187 referred to as a "site notice")—

(a) stating that a stop notice has been served and that any person contravening it may be prosecuted for an offence under section 187,

(b) giving the date when the stop notice takes effect, and

(c) indicating its requirements.

PART VII

(7) If under section 183(7) the local planning authority withdraw a stop notice in respect of which a site notice was displayed, they must display a notice of the withdrawal in place of the site notice.

(8) A stop notice shall not be invalid by reason that a copy of the enforcement notice to which it relates was not served as required by section 172(6) if it is shown that the local planning authority took all such steps as were reasonably practicable to effect proper service.

Service of stop notices by Secretary of State.

185.—(1) If it appears to the Secretary of State to be expedient that a stop notice should be served in respect of any land, he may himself serve such a notice.

(2) A notice served by the Secretary of State under subsection (1) shall have the same effect as if it had been served by the local planning authority.

(3) The Secretary of State shall not serve such a notice without consulting the local planning authority.

Compensation for loss due to stop notice.

186.—(1) Where a stop notice is served under section 183 compensation may be payable under this section in respect of a prohibition contained in the notice only if—

(a) the enforcement notice is quashed on grounds other than those mentioned in paragraph (a) of section 174(2);

(b) the enforcement notice is varied (otherwise than on the grounds mentioned in that paragraph) so that matters alleged to constitute a breach of planning control cease to include one or more of the activities prohibited by the stop notice;

(c) the enforcement notice is withdrawn by the local planning authority otherwise than in consequence of the grant by them of planning permission for the development to which the notice relates or for its retention or continuance without compliance with a condition or limitation subject to which a previous planning permission was granted; or

(d) the stop notice is withdrawn.

(2) A person who, when the stop notice is first served, has an interest in or occupies the land to which the notice relates shall be entitled to be compensated by the local planning authority in respect of any loss or damage directly attributable to the prohibition contained in the notice or, in a case within subsection (1)(b), so much of that prohibition as ceases to have effect.

(3) A claim for compensation under this section shall be made to the local planning authority within the prescribed time and in the prescribed manner.

(4) The loss or damage in respect of which compensation is payable under this section in respect of a prohibition shall include any sum payable in respect of a breach of contract caused by the taking of action necessary to comply with the prohibition.

(5) In the assessment of compensation under this section, account shall be taken of the extent (if any) to which the claimant's entitlement is attributable—

PART VII

(a) to his failure to comply with a notice under section 330, or

(b) to any mis-statement made by him in response to such a notice.

(6) Except in so far as may be otherwise provided by any regulations made under this Act, any question of disputed compensation under this Part shall be referred to and determined by the Lands Tribunal.

1961 c.33.

(7) In relation to the determination of any such question, the provisions of sections 2 and 4 of the Land Compensation Act 1961 shall apply subject to any necessary modifications and to the provisions of any regulations made under this Act.

Penalties for contravention of stop notice.

187.—(1) If any person contravenes or causes or permits the contravention of a stop notice—

(a) after a site notice has been displayed, or

(b) if a site notice has not been displayed, more than two days after the stop notice has been served on him,

then, subject to subsection (3), he shall be guilty of an offence.

(2) A person who is guilty of an offence under subsection (1) shall be liable—

(a) on summary conviction to a fine not exceeding the statutory maximum, or

(b) on conviction on indictment to a fine;

and if the offence is continued after conviction he shall be guilty of a further offence and liable—

(i) on summary conviction to a fine not exceeding £200 for each day on which the offence is continued, or

(ii) on conviction on indictment to a fine.

(3) In proceedings for an offence under this section it shall be a defence for the accused to prove—

(a) that the stop notice was not served on him, and

(b) that he did not know, and could not reasonably have been expected to know, of its existence.

Registers

Register of enforcement and stop notices.

188.—(1) Every district planning authority and the council of every metropolitan district or London borough shall keep, in such manner as may be prescribed by a development order, a register containing such information as may be so prescribed with respect—

(a) to enforcement notices; and

(b) to stop notices,

which relate to land in their area.

(2) A development order may make provision—

(a) for the entry relating to any enforcement notice or stop notice, and everything relating to any such notice, to be removed from the register in such circumstances as may be specified in the order; and

(b) for requiring a county planning authority to supply to a district planning authority such information as may be so specified with regard to enforcement notices issued and stop notices served by the county planning authority.

(3) Every register kept under this section shall be available for inspection by the public at all reasonable hours.

Enforcement of orders for discontinuance of use, etc.

Penalties for contravention of orders under s. 102 and Schedule 9.

189.—(1) Any person who without planning permission—

(a) uses land, or causes or permits land to be used—

(i) for any purpose for which an order under section 102 or paragraph 1 of Schedule 9 has required that its use shall be discontinued; or

(ii) in contravention of any condition imposed by such an order by virtue of subsection (1) of that section or, as the case may be, sub-paragraph (1) of that paragraph; or

(b) resumes, or causes or permits to be resumed, development consisting of the winning and working of minerals the resumption of which an order under paragraph 3 of that Schedule has prohibited; or

(c) contravenes, or causes or permits to be contravened, any such requirement as is specified in sub-paragraph (3) or (4) of that paragraph,

shall be guilty of an offence.

(2) Any person who contravenes any requirement of an order under paragraph 5 or 6 of that Schedule or who causes or permits any requirement of such an order to be contravened shall be guilty of an offence.

(3) Any person guilty of an offence under this section shall be liable—

(a) on summary conviction, to a fine not exceeding the statutory maximum; and

(b) on conviction on indictment, to a fine.

(4) It shall be a defence for a person charged with an offence under this section to prove that he took all reasonable measures and exercised all due diligence to avoid commission of the offence by himself or by any person under his control.

(5) If in any case the defence provided by subsection (4) involves an allegation that the commission of the offence was due to the act or default of another person or due to reliance on information supplied by another person, the person charged shall not, without the leave of the court, be entitled to rely on the defence unless, within a period ending seven clear days before the hearing, he has served on the prosecutor a notice in writing giving such information identifying or assisting in the identification of the other person as was then in his possession.

Enforcement of orders under s. 102 and Schedule 9.

190.—(1) This section applies where—

(a) any step required by an order under section 102 or paragraph 1 of Schedule 9 to be taken for the alteration or removal of any buildings or works or any plant or machinery;

PART VII

(b) any step required by an order under paragraph 3 of that Schedule to be taken—

(i) for the alteration or removal of plant or machinery; or

(ii) for the removal or alleviation of any injury to amenity; or

(c) any step for the protection of the environment required to be taken by an order under paragraph 5 or 6 of that Schedule,

has not been taken within the period specified in the order or within such extended period as the local planning authority or, as the case may be, the mineral planning authority may allow.

(2) Where this section applies the local planning authority or, as the case may be, the mineral planning authority may enter the land and take the required step.

(3) Where the local planning authority or, as the case may be, the mineral planning authority have exercised their power under subsection (2) they may recover from the person who is then the owner of the land any expenses reasonably incurred by them in doing so.

(4) Any expenses recoverable by a local planning authority or a mineral planning authority under subsection (3) shall be recoverable as a simple contract debt in any court of competent jurisdiction.

1936 c.49.

(5) Section 276 of the Public Health Act 1936 shall apply in relation to any works executed by an authority under subsection (2) as it applies in relation to works executed by a local authority under that Act.

Established use certificates

Meaning of "established use".

191. For the purposes of this Part a use of land is established if—

(a) it was begun before the beginning of 1964 without planning permission and has continued since the end of 1963;

(b) it was begun before the beginning of 1964 under a planning permission granted subject to conditions or limitations, which either have never been complied with or have not been complied with since the end of 1963; or

(c) it was begun after the end of 1963 as the result of a change of use not requiring planning permission and there has been, since the end of 1963, no change of use requiring planning permission.

Applications for established use certificates.

192.—(1) Subject to subsection (3), where a person having an interest in land claims that a particular use of it has become established, he may apply to the local planning authority for a certificate to that effect.

(2) Such a certificate is in this Act referred to as an "established use certificate".

(3) No application may be made under subsection (1)—

(a) in respect of the use of land as a single dwellinghouse, or

(b) in respect of any use not subsisting at the time of the application.

PART VII

(4) An established use certificate shall, as respects any matters stated in it, be conclusive for the purposes of an appeal to the Secretary of State against an enforcement notice a copy of which has been served in respect of any land to which the certificate relates, if the copy of the notice is served after the date of the application on which the certificate was granted.

(5) The Secretary of State may give directions requiring applications for established use certificates to be referred to him instead of being dealt with by local planning authorities.

(6) In section 69 references to applications for planning permission shall include references to applications for established use certificates.

Supplementary provisions as to applications.

193.—(1) An application for an established use certificate shall be made in such manner as may be prescribed by a development order and shall include such particulars, and be verified by such evidence, as may be required by such an order or by any directions given under such an order, or by the local planning authority or, in the case of an application referred to the Secretary of State, by him.

(2) A development order may provide that an application for an established use certificate shall not be entertained unless it is accompanied by a certificate in such form as may be prescribed by the order and corresponding to one of those described in section 66(1) or section 67(3).

(3) Any such order may also—

(a) include requirements corresponding to section 66(2) to (6) (or, as the case may be, section 67(5), (6) and (11)) and section 71(2); and

(b) make provision as to who, in the case of any land, is to be treated as the owner for the purposes of any provision of the order made by virtue of subsection (2) or this subsection.

(4) If any person—

(a) issues a certificate which purports to comply with any provision of a development order made by virtue of subsection (2) or (3) and contains a statement which he knows to be false or misleading in a material particular, or

(b) recklessly issues a certificate which purports to comply with any such provision and contains a statement which is false or misleading in a material particular,

he shall be guilty of an offence.

(5) A person guilty of such an offence shall be liable on summary conviction to a fine not exceeding level 3 on the standard scale.

(6) If any person, for the purpose of procuring a particular decision on an application (whether by himself or another) for an established use certificate—

(a) knowingly or recklessly makes a statement which is false in a material particular; or

(b) with intent to deceive, produces, furnishes, sends or otherwise makes use of any document which is false in a material particular; or

PART VII

(c) with intent to deceive, withholds any material information,

he shall be guilty of an offence.

(7) A person guilty of such an offence shall be liable—

(a) on summary conviction, to a fine not exceeding the statutory maximum, or

(b) on conviction on indictment, to imprisonment for a term not exceeding two years or a fine, or both.

Determination of applications.

194.—(1) On an application to the local planning authority under section 192, or on a reference to the Secretary of State under subsection (5) of that section, the authority or, as the case may be, the Secretary of State shall—

(a) if and so far as they are or he is satisfied that the applicant's claim is made out, grant him an established use certificate accordingly; and

(b) if and so far as they are or he is not so satisfied, refuse the application.

(2) An established use certificate may be granted—

(a) either for the whole of the land specified in the application, or for a part of it;

(b) in the case of an application specifying two or more uses, either for all those uses or for some one or more of them.

(3) An established use certificate shall be in such form as may be prescribed by a development order and shall specify—

(a) the land to which the certificate relates and any use of it which is certified by the certificate as established;

(b) by reference to the paragraphs of section 191, the grounds on which that use is so certified; and

(c) the date on which the application for the certificate was made.

(4) The date mentioned in subsection (3)(c) shall be the date at which the use is certified as established.

(5) Provision may be made by a development order for regulating the manner in which applications for established use certificates are to be dealt with by local planning authorities.

(6) Such an order may in particular provide for requiring the authority—

(a) to give to any applicant within such time as may be prescribed by the order such notice as may be so prescribed as to the manner in which his application has been dealt with;

(b) to give to the Secretary of State and to such other persons as may be prescribed by or under the order, such information as may be so prescribed with respect to such applications made to the authority, including information as to the manner in which any application has been dealt with.

Appeals against refusal or failure to give decision on application.

195.—(1) Where an application is made to a local planning authority for an established use certificate and—

(a) the application is refused or is refused in part, or

(b) the authority do not give notice to the applicant of their decision on the application within such period as may be prescribed by a development order or within such extended period as may at any time be agreed upon in writing between the applicant and the authority,

the applicant may by notice appeal to the Secretary of State.

(2) On any such appeal, if and so far as the Secretary of State is satisfied—

(a) in the case of an appeal under subsection (1)(a), that the authority's refusal is not well-founded, or

(b) in the case of an appeal under subsection (1)(b), that if the authority had refused the application their refusal would not have been well-founded,

he shall grant the appellant an established use certificate accordingly or, in the case of a refusal in part, modify the certificate granted by the authority on the application.

(3) If and so far as the Secretary of State is satisfied that the authority's refusal is or, as the case may be, would have been well-founded, he shall dismiss the appeal.

(4) In section 193(2) and (6) references to applications for established use certificates include references to appeals arising out of such applications.

(5) For the purposes of the application of section 288(10)(b) in relation to an appeal in a case within subsection (1)(b) it shall be assumed that the authority decided to refuse the application in question.

(6) Schedule 6 applies to appeals under this section.

Further provisions as to references and appeals to the Secretary of State.

196.—(1) Before determining an application referred to him under section 192(5) or an appeal to him under section 195(1), the Secretary of State shall, if either the applicant or appellant (as the case may be) or the local planning authority so wish, give each of them an opportunity of appearing before, and being heard by, a person appointed by the Secretary of State for the purpose.

(2) Where the Secretary of State grants an established use certificate on such a reference or such an appeal, he shall give notice to the local planning authority of that fact.

(3) The decision of the Secretary of State on such an application or appeal shall be final.

(4) The information which may be prescribed as being required to be contained in a register kept under section 69 shall include information with respect to established use certificates granted by the Secretary of State.

(5) On such an application or appeal the Secretary of State may, in respect of any use of land for which an established use certificate is not granted (either by him or by the local planning authority), grant planning permission for that use or, as the case may be, for the continuance of that use without complying with some condition subject to which a previous planning permission was granted.

PART VII

(6) In the case of any use of land for which the Secretary of State has power to grant planning permission under this section, the applicant or appellant shall be deemed to have made an application for such planning permission.

(7) Any planning permission so granted shall be treated as granted on that application.

PART VIII

SPECIAL CONTROLS

CHAPTER I

TREES

General duty of planning authorities as respects trees

Planning permission to include appropriate provision for preservation and planting of trees.

197. It shall be the duty of the local planning authority—

(a) to ensure, whenever it is appropriate, that in granting planning permission for any development adequate provision is made, by the imposition of conditions, for the preservation or planting of trees; and

(b) to make such orders under section 198 as appear to the authority to be necessary in connection with the grant of such permission, whether for giving effect to such conditions or otherwise.

Tree preservation orders

Power to make tree preservation orders.

198.—(1) If it appears to a local planning authority that it is expedient in the interests of amenity to make provision for the preservation of trees or woodlands in their area, they may for that purpose make an order with respect to such trees, groups of trees or woodlands as may be specified in the order.

(2) An order under subsection (1) is in this Act referred to as a "tree preservation order".

(3) A tree preservation order may, in particular, make provision—

(a) for prohibiting (subject to any exemptions for which provision may be made by the order) the cutting down, topping, lopping, uprooting, wilful damage or wilful destruction of trees except with the consent of the local planning authority, and for enabling that authority to give their consent subject to conditions;

(b) for securing the replanting, in such manner as may be prescribed by or under the order, of any part of a woodland area which is felled in the course of forestry operations permitted by or under the order;

(c) for applying, in relation to any consent under the order, and to applications for such consent, any of the provisions of this Act mentioned in subsection (4), subject to such adaptations and modifications as may be specified in the order.

(4) The provisions referred to in subsection (3)(c) are—

(a) the provisions of Part III relating to planning permission and to applications for planning permission, except sections 56, 62, 65 to 68, 69(3) and (4), 71, 80, 81, 91 to 96, 100 and 101 and Schedule 8; and

(b) sections 137 to 141, 143 and 144 (except so far as they relate to purchase notices served in consequence of such orders as are mentioned in section 137(1)(b) or (c));

(c) section 316.

(5) A tree preservation order may be made so as to apply, in relation to trees to be planted pursuant to any such conditions as are mentioned in section 197(a), as from the time when those trees are planted.

(6) Without prejudice to any other exemptions for which provision may be made by a tree preservation order, no such order shall apply—

(a) to the cutting down, uprooting, topping or lopping of trees which are dying or dead or have become dangerous, or

(b) to the cutting down, uprooting, topping or lopping of any trees in compliance with any obligations imposed by or under an Act of Parliament or so far as may be necessary for the prevention or abatement of a nuisance.

(7) This section shall have effect subject to—

(a) section 39(2) of the Housing and Planning Act 1986 (saving for effect of section 2(4) of the Opencast Coal Act 1958 on land affected by a tree preservation order despite its repeal); and 1986 c. 63. 1958 c.69.

(b) section 15 of the Forestry Act 1967 (licences under that Act to fell trees comprised in a tree preservation order). 1967 c.10.

Form of and procedure applicable to orders.

199.—(1) A tree preservation order shall not take effect until it is confirmed by the local planning authority and the local planning authority may confirm any such order either without modification or subject to such modifications as they consider expedient.

(2) Provision may be made by regulations under this Act with respect—

(a) to the form of tree preservation orders, and

(b) to the procedure to be followed in connection with the making and confirmation of such orders.

(3) Without prejudice to the generality of subsection (2), the regulations may make provision—

(a) that, before a tree preservation order is confirmed by the local planning authority, notice of the making of the order shall be given to the owners and occupiers of land affected by the order and to such other persons, if any, as may be specified in the regulations;

(b) that objections and representations with respect to the order, if duly made in accordance with the regulations, shall be considered before the order is confirmed by the local planning authority; and

(c) that copies of the order, when confirmed by the authority, shall be served on such persons as may be specified in the regulations.

PART VIII

Orders affecting land where Forestry Commissioners interested.

200.—(1) In relation to land in which the Forestry Commissioners have an interest, a tree preservation order may be made only if—

(a) there is not in force in respect of the land a plan of operations or other working plan approved by the Commissioners under a forestry dedication covenant; and

(b) the Commissioners consent to the making of the order.

(2) For the purposes of subsection (1), the Forestry Commissioners are only to be regarded as having an interest in land if—

1979 c. 21.

(a) they have made a grant or loan under section 1 of the Forestry Act 1979 in respect of it, or

(b) there is a forestry dedication covenant in force in respect of it.

(3) A tree preservation order in respect of such land shall not have effect so as to prohibit, or to require any consent for, the cutting down of a tree in accordance with a plan of operations or other working plan approved by the Forestry Commissioners, and for the time being in force, under a forestry dedication covenant or under the conditions of a grant or loan made under section 1 of the Forestry Act 1979.

(4) In this section—

1967 c. 10.

(a) "a forestry dedication covenant" means a covenant entered into with the Commissioners under section 5 of the Forestry Act 1967; and

(b) references to provisions of the Forestry Act 1967 and the Forestry Act 1979 include references to any corresponding provisions replaced by those provisions or by earlier corresponding provisions.

Provisional tree preservation orders.

201.—(1) If it appears to a local planning authority that a tree preservation order proposed to be made by that authority should take effect immediately without previous confirmation, they may include in the order as made by them a direction that this section shall apply to the order.

(2) Notwithstanding section 199(1), an order which contains such a direction—

(a) shall take effect provisionally on such date as may be specified in it, and

(b) shall continue in force by virtue of this section until—

(i) the expiration of a period of six months beginning with the date on which the order was made; or

(ii) the date on which the order is confirmed,

whichever first occurs.

Power for Secretary of State to make tree preservation orders.

202.—(1) If it appears to the Secretary of State, after consultation with the local planning authority, to be expedient that a tree preservation order or an order amending or revoking such an order should be made, he may himself make such an order.

(2) Any order so made by the Secretary of State shall have the same effect as if it had been made by the local planning authority and confirmed by them under this Chapter.

PART VIII

(3) The provisions of this Chapter and of any regulations made under it with respect to the procedure to be followed in connection with the making and confirmation of any order to which subsection (1) applies and the service of copies of it as confirmed shall have effect, subject to any necessary modifications—

(a) in relation to any proposal by the Secretary of State to make such an order,

(b) in relation to the making of it by the Secretary of State, and

(c) in relation to the service of copies of it as so made.

Compensation for loss or damage caused by orders, etc.

Compensation in respect of tree preservation orders.

203. A tree preservation order may make provision for the payment by the local planning authority, subject to such exceptions and conditions as may be specified in the order, of compensation in respect of loss or damage caused or incurred in consequence—

(a) of the refusal of any consent required under the order, or

(b) of the grant of any such consent subject to conditions.

Compensation in respect of requirement as to replanting of trees.

204.—(1) This section applies where—

(a) in pursuance of provision made by a tree preservation order, a direction is given by the local planning authority or the Secretary of State for securing the replanting of all or any part of a woodland area which is felled in the course of forestry operations permitted by or under the order; and

(b) the Forestry Commissioners decide not to make any grant or loan under section 1 of the Forestry Act 1979 in respect of the replanting by reason that the direction frustrates the use of the woodland area for the growing of timber or other forest products for commercial purposes and in accordance with the rules or practice of good forestry. 1979 c. 21.

(2) Where this section applies, the local planning authority exercising functions under the tree preservation order shall be liable, on the making of a claim in accordance with this section, to pay compensation in respect of such loss or damage, if any, as is caused or incurred in consequence of compliance with the direction.

(3) The Forestry Commissioners shall, at the request of the person under a duty to comply with such a direction as is mentioned in subsection (1)(a), give a certificate stating—

(a) whether they have decided not to make such a grant or loan as is mentioned in subsection (1)(b), and

(b) if so, the grounds for their decision.

(4) A claim for compensation under this section must be served on the local planning authority—

(a) within 12 months from the date on which the direction was given, or

PART VIII

(b) where an appeal has been made to the Secretary of State against the decision of the local planning authority, within 12 months from the date of the decision of the Secretary of State on the appeal,

but subject in either case to such extension of that period as the local planning authority may allow.

Determination of compensation claims.

205.—(1) Except in so far as may be otherwise provided by any tree preservation order or any regulations made under this Act, any question of disputed compensation under section 203 or 204 shall be referred to and determined by the Lands Tribunal.

1961 c.33.

(2) In relation to the determination of any such question, the provisions of sections 2 and 4 of the Land Compensation Act 1961 shall apply subject to any necessary modifications and to the provisions of any regulations made under this Act.

Consequences of tree removal, etc.

Replacement of trees.

206.—(1) If any tree in respect of which a tree preservation order is for the time being in force—

(a) is removed, uprooted or destroyed in contravention of the order, or

(b) except in the case of a tree to which the order applies as part of a woodland, is removed, uprooted or destroyed or dies at a time when its cutting down or uprooting is authorised only by virtue of section 198(6)(a),

it shall be the duty of the owner of the land to plant another tree of an appropriate size and species at the same place as soon as he reasonably can.

(2) The duty imposed by subsection (1) does not apply to an owner if on application by him the local planning authority dispense with it.

(3) In respect of trees in a woodland it shall be sufficient for the purposes of this section to replace the trees removed, uprooted or destroyed by planting the same number of trees—

(a) on or near the land on which the trees removed, uprooted or destroyed stood, or

(b) on such other land as may be agreed between the local planning authority and the owner of the land,

and in such places as may be designated by the local planning authority.

(4) In relation to any tree planted pursuant to this section, the relevant tree preservation order shall apply as it applied to the original tree.

(5) The duty imposed by subsection (1) on the owner of any land shall attach to the person who is from time to time the owner of the land.

Enforcement of duties as to replacement of trees.

207.—(1) If it appears to the local planning authority that—

(a) the provisions of section 206, or

(b) any conditions of a consent given under a tree preservation order which require the replacement of trees,

are not complied with in the case of any tree or trees, that authority may serve on the owner of the land a notice requiring him, within such period as may be specified in the notice, to plant a tree or trees of such size and species as may be so specified.

(2) A notice under subsection (1) may only be served within four years from the date of the alleged failure to comply with those provisions or conditions.

(3) Subject to section 208, a notice under this section shall take effect at the end of such period as may be specified in it.

(4) The period so specified must not be less than 28 days after the service of the notice.

(5) The duty imposed by section 206(1) may only be enforced as provided by this section and not otherwise.

Appeals against s. 207 notices.

208.—(1) A person on whom a notice under section 207(1) is served may appeal to the Secretary of State against the notice on any of the following grounds—

(a) that the provisions of section 206 or, as the case may be, the conditions mentioned in section 207(1)(b) are not applicable or have been complied with;

(b) that the requirements of the notice are unreasonable in respect of the period or the size or species of trees specified in it;

(c) that the planting of a tree or trees in accordance with the notice is not required in the interests of amenity or would be contrary to the practice of good forestry;

(d) that the place on which the tree is or trees are required to be planted is unsuitable for that purpose.

(2) An appeal under subsection (1) may be made at any time within the period specified in the notice as the period at the end of which it is to take effect.

(3) Such an appeal shall be made by notice in writing to the Secretary of State.

(4) The notice shall indicate the grounds of the appeal and state the facts on which it is based.

(5) On any such appeal the Secretary of State shall, if either the appellant or the local planning authority so desire, give each of them an opportunity of appearing before and being heard by a person appointed by the Secretary of State for the purpose.

(6) Where such an appeal is brought, the notice under section 207(1) shall be of no effect pending the final determination or the withdrawal of the appeal.

(7) On the determination of such an appeal the Secretary of State shall give directions for giving effect to the determination, including, where appropriate, directions for quashing the notice under section 207(1) or for varying its terms.

PART VIII

(8) On such an appeal the Secretary of State may—

(a) correct any informality, defect or error in the notice under section 207(1), or

(b) give directions varying the terms,

if he is satisfied that the correction or, as the case may be, the variation can be made without injustice to the appellant or the local planning authority.

(9) Schedule 6 applies to appeals under this section.

(10) Where any person has appealed to the Secretary of State under this section against a notice, neither that person nor any other shall be entitled, in any other proceedings instituted after the making of the appeal, to claim that the notice was not duly served on the person who appealed.

Execution and cost of works required by s. 207 notice.

209.—(1) If, within the period specified in a notice under section 207(1) for compliance with it, or within such extended period as the local planning authority may allow, any trees which are required to be planted by a notice under that section have not been planted, the local planning authority may—

(a) enter the land and plant those trees, and

(b) recover from the person who is then the owner of the land any expenses reasonably incurred by them in doing so.

(2) Where such a notice has been served—

(a) any expenses incurred by the owner of any land for the purpose of complying with the notice, and

(b) any sums paid by the owner of any land under subsection (1) in respect of expenses incurred by the local planning authority in planting trees required by such a notice to be planted,

shall be deemed to be incurred or paid for the use and at the request of any person, other than the owner, responsible for the cutting down, destruction or removal of the original tree or trees.

(3) Regulations made under this Act may provide that—

1936 c.49.

(a) section 276 of the Public Health Act 1936 (power of local authorities to sell materials removed in executing works under that Act subject to accounting for the proceeds of sale);

(b) section 289 of that Act (power to require the occupier of any premises to permit works to be executed by the owner of the premises); or

(c) section 294 of that Act (limit on liability of persons holding premises as agents or trustees in respect of the expenses recoverable under that Act),

shall apply, subject to such adaptations and modifications as may be specified in the regulations, in relation to any steps required to be taken by a notice under section 207(1).

(4) Regulations under subsection (3) applying section 289 of the Public Health Act 1936 may include adaptations and modifications for the purpose of giving the owner of land to which such a notice relates the right, as against all other persons interested in the land, to comply with the requirements of the notice.

PART VIII

(5) Regulations under subsection (3) may also provide for the charging on the land of any expenses recoverable by a local authority under subsection (1).

(6) Where by virtue of this section any expenses are recoverable by a local planning authority, those expenses shall be recoverable as a simple contract debt in any court of competent jurisdiction.

Penalties for non-compliance with tree preservation order.

210.—(1) If any person, in contravention of a tree preservation order—

(a) cuts down, uproots or wilfully destroys a tree, or

(b) wilfully damages, tops or lops a tree in such a manner as to be likely to destroy it,

he shall be guilty of an offence.

(2) A person guilty of an offence under subsection (1) shall be liable—

(a) on summary conviction to a fine not exceeding the statutory maximum or twice the sum which appears to the court to be the value of the tree, whichever is the greater; or

(b) on conviction on indictment, to a fine.

(3) In determining the amount of any fine to be imposed on a person convicted on indictment of an offence under subsection (1), the court shall in particular have regard to any financial benefit which has accrued or appears likely to accrue to him in consequence of the offence.

(4) If any person contravenes the provisions of a tree preservation order otherwise than as mentioned in subsection (1), he shall be guilty of an offence and liable on summary conviction to a fine not exceeding level 4 on the standard scale.

(5) If, in the case of a continuing offence under this section, the contravention is continued after the conviction, the offender shall be guilty of a further offence and liable on summary conviction to an additional fine not exceeding £5 for each day on which the contravention is so continued.

Trees in conservation areas

Preservation of trees in conservation areas.

211.—(1) Subject to the provisions of this section and section 212, any person who, in relation to a tree to which this section applies, does any act which might by virtue of section 198(3)(a) be prohibited by a tree preservation order shall be guilty of an offence.

(2) Subject to section 212, this section applies to any tree in a conservation area in respect of which no tree preservation order is for the time being in force.

(3) It shall be a defence for a person charged with an offence under subsection (1) to prove—

(a) that he served notice of his intention to do the act in question (with sufficient particulars to identify the tree) on the local planning authority in whose area the tree is or was situated; and

(b) that he did the act in question—

(i) with the consent of the local planning authority in whose area the tree is or was situated, or

PART VIII

(ii) after the expiry of the period of six weeks from the date of the notice but before the expiry of the period of two years from that date.

(4) Section 210 shall apply to an offence under this section as it applies to a contravention of a tree preservation order.

Power to disapply s. 211.

212.—(1) The Secretary of State may by regulations direct that section 211 shall not apply in such cases as may be specified in the regulations.

(2) Without prejudice to the generality of subsection (1), the regulations may be framed so as to exempt from the application of that section cases defined by reference to all or any of the following matters—

(a) acts of such descriptions or done in such circumstances or subject to such conditions as may be specified in the regulations;

(b) trees in such conservation areas as may be so specified;

(c) trees of a size or species so specified; or

(d) trees belonging to persons or bodies of a description so specified.

(3) The regulations may, in relation to any matter by reference to which an exemption is conferred by them, make different provision for different circumstances.

(4) Regulations under subsection (1) may in particular, but without prejudice to the generality of that subsection, exempt from the application of section 211 cases exempted from section 198 by subsection (6) of that section.

Enforcement of controls as respects trees in conservation areas.

213.—(1) If any tree to which section 211 applies—

(a) is removed, uprooted or destroyed in contravention of that section; or

(b) is removed, uprooted or destroyed or dies at a time when its cutting down or uprooting is authorised only by virtue of the provisions of such regulations under subsection (1) of section 212 as are mentioned in subsection (4) of that section,

it shall be the duty of the owner of the land to plant another tree of an appropriate size and species at the same place as soon as he reasonably can.

(2) The duty imposed by subsection (1) does not apply to an owner if on application by him the local planning authority dispense with it.

(3) The duty imposed by subsection (1) on the owner of any land attaches to the person who is from time to time the owner of the land and may be enforced as provided by section 207 and not otherwise.

Registers of s. 211 notices.

214. It shall be the duty of a local planning authority to compile and keep available for public inspection free of charge at all reasonable hours and at a convenient place a register containing such particulars as the Secretary of State may determine of notices under section 211 affecting trees in their area.

CHAPTER II

PART VIII

LAND ADVERSELY AFFECTING AMENITY OF NEIGHBOURHOOD

Power to require proper maintenance of land.

215.—(1) If it appears to the local planning authority that the amenity of a part of their area, or of an adjoining area, is adversely affected by the condition of land in their area, they may serve on the owner and occupier of the land a notice under this section.

(2) The notice shall require such steps for remedying the condition of the land as may be specified in the notice to be taken within such period as may be so specified.

(3) Subject to the following provisions of this Chapter, the notice shall take effect at the end of such period as may be specified in the notice.

(4) That period shall not be less than 28 days after the service of the notice.

Penalty for non-compliance with s. 215 notice.

216.—(1) The provisions of this section shall have effect where a notice has been served under section 215.

(2) If any owner or occupier of the land on whom the notice was served fails to take steps required by the notice within the period specified in it for compliance with it, he shall be guilty of an offence and liable on summary conviction to a fine not exceeding level 3 on the standard scale.

(3) Where proceedings have been brought under subsection (2) against a person as the owner of the land and he has, at some time before the end of the compliance period, ceased to be the owner of the land, if he—

(a) duly lays information to that effect, and

(b) gives the prosecution not less than three clear days' notice of his intention,

he shall be entitled to have the person who then became the owner of the land brought before the court in the proceedings.

(4) Where proceedings have been brought under subsection (2) against a person as the occupier of the land and he has, at some time before the end of the compliance period, ceased to be the occupier of the land, if he—

(a) duly lays information to that effect, and

(b) gives the prosecution not less than three clear days' notice of his intention,

he shall be entitled to have brought before the court in the proceedings the person who then became the occupier of the land or, if nobody then became the occupier, the person who is the owner at the date of the notice.

(5) Where in such proceedings—

(a) it has been proved that any steps required by the notice under section 215 have not been taken within the compliance period, and

(b) the original defendant proves that the failure to take those steps was attributable, in whole or in part, to the default of a person specified in a notice under subsection (3) or (4),

then—

(i) that person may be convicted of the offence; and

PART VIII

(ii) if the original defendant also proves that he took all reasonable steps to ensure compliance with the notice, he shall be acquitted of the offence.

(6) If, after a person has been convicted under the previous provisions of this section, he does not as soon as practicable do everything in his power to secure compliance with the notice, he shall be guilty of a further offence and liable on summary conviction to a fine not exceeding £40 for each day following his first conviction on which any of the requirements of the notice remain unfulfilled.

(7) Any reference in this section to the compliance period, in relation to a notice, is a reference to the period specified in the notice for compliance with it or such extended period as the local planning authority who served the notice may allow for compliance.

Appeal to magistrates' court against s. 215 notice.

217.—(1) A person on whom a notice under section 215 is served, or any other person having an interest in the land to which the notice relates, may, at any time within the period specified in the notice as the period at the end of which it is to take effect, appeal against the notice on any of the following grounds—

(a) that the condition of the land to which the notice relates does not adversely affect the amenity of any part of the area of the local planning authority who served the notice, or of any adjoining area;

(b) that the condition of the land to which the notice relates is attributable to, and such as results in the ordinary course of events from, the carrying on of operations or a use of land which is not in contravention of Part III;

(c) that the requirements of the notice exceed what is necessary for preventing the condition of the land from adversely affecting the amenity of any part of the area of the local planning authority who served the notice, or of any adjoining area;

(d) that the period specified in the notice as the period within which any steps required by the notice are to be taken falls short of what should reasonably be allowed.

(2) Any appeal under this section shall be made to a magistrates' court acting for the petty sessions area in which the land in question is situated.

(3) Where such an appeal is brought, the notice to which it relates shall be of no effect pending the final determination or withdrawal of the appeal.

(4) On such an appeal the magistrates' court may correct any informality, defect or error in the notice if satisfied that the informality, defect or error is not material.

(5) On the determination of such an appeal the magistrates' court shall give directions for giving effect to their determination, including, where appropriate, directions for quashing the notice or for varying the terms of the notice in favour of the appellant.

(6) Where any person has appealed to a magistrates' court under this section against a notice, neither that person nor any other shall be entitled, in any other proceedings instituted after the making of the appeal, to claim that the notice was not duly served on the person who appealed.

Part VIII

Further appeal to the Crown Court.

218. Where an appeal has been brought under section 217, an appeal against the decision of the magistrates' court on that appeal may be brought to the Crown Court by the appellant or by the local planning authority who served the notice in question under section 215.

Execution and cost of works required by s. 215 notice.

219.—(1) If, within the period specified in a notice under section 215 in accordance with subsection (2) of that section, or within such extended period as the local planning authority who served the notice may allow, any steps required by the notice to be taken have not been taken, the local planning authority who served the notice may—

(a) enter the land and take those steps, and

(b) recover from the person who is then the owner of the land any expenses reasonably incurred by them in doing so.

(2) Where a notice has been served under section 215—

(a) any expenses incurred by the owner or occupier of any land for the purpose of complying with the notice, and

(b) any sums paid by the owner of any land under subsection (1) in respect of expenses incurred by the local planning authority in taking steps required by such a notice,

shall be deemed to be incurred or paid for the use and at the request of the person who caused or permitted the land to come to be in the condition in which it was when the notice was served.

(3) Regulations made under this Act may provide that—

(a) section 276 of the Public Health Act 1936 (power of local authorities to sell materials removed in executing works under that Act subject to accounting for the proceeds of sale); 1936 c.49.

(b) section 289 of that Act (power to require the occupier of any premises to permit works to be executed by the owner of the premises); or

(c) section 294 of that Act (limit on liability of persons holding premises as agents or trustees in respect of the expenses recoverable under that Act),

shall apply, subject to such adaptations and modifications as may be specified in the regulations, in relation to any steps required to be taken by a notice under section 215.

(4) Regulations under subsection (3) applying section 289 of the Public Health Act 1936 may include adaptations and modifications for the purpose of giving the owner of land to which a notice under section 215 relates the right, as against all other persons interested in the land, to comply with the requirements of the enforcement notice.

(5) Regulations under subsection (3) may also provide for the charging on the land of any expenses recoverable by a local authority under subsection (1).

(6) Where by virtue of this section any expenses are recoverable by a local planning authority, those expenses shall be recoverable as a simple contract debt in any court of competent jurisdiction.

PART VIII

CHAPTER III

ADVERTISEMENTS

Advertisement regulations

Regulations controlling display of advertisements.

220.—(1) Regulations under this Act shall make provision for restricting or regulating the display of advertisements so far as appears to the Secretary of State to be expedient in the interests of amenity or public safety.

(2) Without prejudice to the generality of subsection (1), any such regulations may provide—

(a) for regulating the dimensions, appearance and position of advertisements which may be displayed, the sites on which advertisements may be displayed and the manner in which they are to be affixed to the land;

(b) for requiring the consent of the local planning authority to be obtained for the display of advertisements, or of advertisements of any class specified in the regulations;

(c) for applying, in relation to any such consent and to applications for such consent, any of the provisions mentioned in subsection (3), subject to such adaptations and modifications as may be specified in the regulations;

(d) for the constitution, for the purposes of the regulations, of such advisory committees as may be prescribed by the regulations, and for determining the manner in which the expenses of any such committee are to be defrayed.

(3) The provisions referred to in subsection (2)(c) are—

(a) the provisions of Part III relating to planning permission and to applications for planning permission, except sections 56, 62, 65 to 68, 69(3) and (4), 71, 80, 81, 91 to 96, 100 and 101 and Schedule 8;

(b) sections 137 to 141, 143 and 144 (except so far as they relate to purchase notices served in consequence of such orders as are mentioned in section 137(1)(b) or (c));

(c) section 316.

(4) Without prejudice to the generality of the powers conferred by this section, regulations made for the purposes of this section may provide that any appeal from the decision of the local planning authority, on an application for their consent under the regulations, shall be to an independent tribunal constituted in accordance with the regulations, instead of being an appeal to the Secretary of State.

(5) If any tribunal is so constituted, the Secretary of State may pay to the chairman and members of the tribunal such remuneration, whether by way of salaries or by way of fees, and such reasonable allowances in respect of expenses properly incurred in the performance of their duties, as he may with the consent of the Treasury determine.

Power to make different advertisement regulations for different areas.

221.—(1) Regulations made for the purposes of section 220 may make different provision with respect to different areas, and in particular may make special provision—

(a) with respect to conservation areas;

(b) with respect to areas defined for the purposes of the regulations as experimental areas, and

(c) with respect to areas defined for the purposes of the regulations as areas of special control.

(2) An area may be defined as an experimental area for a prescribed period for the purpose of assessing the effect on amenity or public safety of advertisements of a prescribed description.

(3) An area may be defined as an area of special control if it is—

(a) a rural area, or

(b) an area which appears to the Secretary of State to require special protection on grounds of amenity.

(4) Without prejudice to the generality of subsection (1), the regulations may prohibit the display in an area of special control of all advertisements except advertisements of such classes (if any) as may be prescribed.

(5) Areas of special control for the purposes of regulations under this section may be defined by means of orders made or approved by the Secretary of State in accordance with the provisions of the regulations.

(6) Where the Secretary of State is authorised by the regulations to make or approve any such order as is mentioned in subsection (5), the regulations shall provide—

(a) for the publication of notice of the proposed order in such manner as may be prescribed,

(b) for the consideration of objections duly made to it, and

(c) for the holding of such inquiries or other hearings as may be prescribed,

before the order is made or approved.

(7) Subject to subsection (8), regulations made under section 220 may be made so as to apply—

(a) to advertisements which are being displayed on the date on which the regulations come into force, or

(b) to the use for the display of the advertisements of any site which was being used for that purpose on that date.

(8) Any regulations made in accordance with subsection (7) shall provide for exempting from them—

(a) the continued display of any such advertisements as there mentioned; and

(b) the continued use for the display of advertisements of any such site as there mentioned,

during such period as may be prescribed.

(9) Different periods may be prescribed under subsection (8) for the purposes of different provisions of the regulations.

PART VIII

Planning permission not needed for advertisements complying with regulations.

222. Where the display of advertisements in accordance with regulations made under section 220 involves development of land—

(a) planning permission for that development shall be deemed to be granted by virtue of this section, and

(b) no application shall be necessary for that development under Part III.

Repayment of expense of removing prohibited advertisements

Repayment of expense of removing prohibited advertisements.

223.—(1) Where, for the purpose of complying with any regulations made under section 220, works are carried out by any person—

(a) for removing an advertisement which was being displayed on 1st August 1948; or

(b) for discontinuing the use for the display of advertisements of a site used for that purpose on that date,

that person shall, on a claim made to the local planning authority within such time and in such manner as may be prescribed, be entitled to recover from that authority compensation in respect of any expenses reasonably incurred by him in carrying out those works.

(2) Except in so far as may be otherwise provided by any regulations made under this Act, any question of disputed compensation under this section shall be referred to and determined by the Lands Tribunal.

1961 c.33.

(3) In relation to the determination of any such question, the provisions of sections 2 and 4 of the Land Compensation Act 1961 shall apply subject to any necessary modifications and to the provisions of any regulations made under this Act.

Enforcement of control over advertisements

Enforcement of control as to advertisements.

224.—(1) Regulations under section 220 may make provision for enabling the local planning authority to require—

(a) the removal of any advertisement which is displayed in contravention of the regulations, or

(b) the discontinuance of the use for the display of advertisements of any site which is being so used in contravention of the regulations.

(2) For that purpose the regulations may apply any of the provisions of Part VII with respect to enforcement notices or the provisions of section 186, subject to such adaptations and modifications as may be specified in the regulations.

(3) Without prejudice to any provisions included in such regulations by virtue of subsection (1) or (2), if any person displays an advertisement in contravention of the regulations he shall be guilty of an offence and liable on summary conviction to a fine of such amount as may be prescribed, not exceeding level 3 on the standard scale and, in the case of a continuing offence, £40 for each day during which the offence continues after conviction.

(4) Without prejudice to the generality of subsection (3), a person shall be deemed to display an advertisement for the purposes of that subsection if—

(a) he is the owner or occupier of the land on which the advertisement is displayed; or

(b) the advertisement gives publicity to his goods, trade, business or other concerns.

(5) A person shall not be guilty of an offence under subsection (3) by reason only—

(a) of his being the owner or occupier of the land on which an advertisement is displayed, or

(b) of his goods, trade, business or other concerns being given publicity by the advertisement,

if he proves that it was displayed without his knowledge or consent.

Power to remove or obliterate placards and posters.

225.—(1) Subject to subsections (2) and (3), the local planning authority may remove or obliterate any placard or poster—

(a) which is displayed in their area; and

(b) which in their opinion is so displayed in contravention of regulations made under section 220.

(2) Subsection (1) does not authorise the removal or obliteration of a placard or poster displayed within a building to which there is no public right of access.

(3) Subject to subsection (4), where a placard or poster identifies the person who displayed it or caused it to be displayed, the local planning authority shall not exercise any power conferred by subsection (1) unless they have first given him notice in writing—

(a) that in their opinion it is displayed in contravention of regulations made under section 220; and

(b) that they intend to remove or obliterate it on the expiry of a period specified in the notice.

(4) Subsection (3) does not apply if—

(a) the placard or poster does not give his address, and

(b) the authority do not know it and are unable to ascertain it after reasonable inquiry.

(5) The period specified in a notice under subsection (3) must be not less than two days from the date of service of the notice.

PART IX

ACQUISITION AND APPROPRIATION OF LAND FOR PLANNING PURPOSES, ETC.

Acquisition for planning and public purposes

Compulsory acquisition of land for development and other planning purposes.

226.—(1) A local authority to whom this section applies shall, on being authorised to do so by the Secretary of State, have power to acquire compulsorily any land in their area which—

(a) is suitable for and required in order to secure the carrying out of development, redevelopment or improvement; or

(b) is required for a purpose which it is necessary to achieve in the interests of the proper planning of an area in which the land is situated.

PART IX

(2) A local authority and the Secretary of State in considering for the purposes of subsection (1)(a) whether land is suitable for development, re-development or improvement shall have regard—

(a) to the provisions of the development plan, so far as material;

(b) to whether planning permission for any development on the land is in force; and

(c) to any other considerations which would be material for the purpose of determining an application for planning permission for development on the land.

(3) Where a local authority exercise their power under subsection (1) in relation to any land, they shall, on being authorised to do so by the Secretary of State, have power to acquire compulsorily—

(a) any land adjoining that land which is required for the purpose of executing works for facilitating its development or use; or

(b) where that land forms part of a common or open space or fuel or field garden allotment, any land which is required for the purpose of being given in exchange for the land which is being acquired.

(4) It is immaterial by whom the local authority propose that any activity or purpose mentioned in subsection (1) or (3)(a) should be undertaken or achieved (and in particular the local authority need not propose to undertake an activity or to achieve that purpose themselves).

(5) Where under subsection (1) the Secretary of State has power to authorise a local authority to whom this section applies to acquire any land compulsorily he may, after the requisite consultation, authorise the land to be so acquired by another authority, being a local authority within the meaning of this Act.

(6) Before giving an authorisation under subsection (5), the Secretary of State shall—

(a) if the land is in a non-metropolitan county, consult with the councils of the county and the district;

(b) if the land is in a metropolitan district, consult with the council of the district; and

(c) if the land is in a London borough, consult with the council of the borough.

1981 c.67.

(7) The Acquisition of Land Act 1981 shall apply to the compulsory acquisition of land under this section.

(8) The local authorities to whom this section applies are the councils of counties, districts and London boroughs.

Acquisition of land by agreement.

227.—(1) The council of any county, district or London borough may acquire by agreement any land which they require for any purpose for which a local authority may be authorised to acquire land under section 226.

1965 c.56.

(2) The provisions of Part 1 of the Compulsory Purchase Act 1965 (so far as applicable), other than sections 4 to 8, section 10 and section 31, shall apply in relation to the acquisition of land under this section.

Compulsory acquisition of land by the Secretary of State for the Environment.

228.—(1) The Secretary of State for the Environment may acquire compulsorily—

(a) any land necessary for the public service; and

(b) any land which it is proposed to use not only for the public service but also—

(i) to meet the interests of proper planning of the area, or

(ii) to secure the best or most economic development or use of the land,

otherwise than for the public service.

(2) Where the Secretary of State has acquired or proposes to acquire any land under subsection (1) ("the primary land") and in his opinion other land ought to be acquired together with the primary land—

(a) in the interests of the proper planning of the area concerned; or

(b) for the purpose of ensuring that the primary land can be used, or developed and used, (together with that other land) in what appears to him to be the best or most economic way; or

(c) where the primary land or any land acquired, or which he proposes to acquire, by virtue of paragraph (a) or (b) of this subsection or of section 122(1)(a) or (b) of the Local Government, Planning and Land Act 1980, forms part of a common, open space or fuel or field garden allotment, for the purpose of being given in exchange for that land, 1980 c. 65.

he may compulsorily acquire that other land.

(3) Subject to subsection (4), the power of acquiring land compulsorily under this section shall include power to acquire an easement or other right over land by the grant of a new right.

(4) Subsection (3) shall not apply to an easement or other right over any land which would for the purposes of the Acquisition of Land Act 1981 form part of a common, open space or fuel or field garden allotment. 1981 c. 67.

(5) References in this section to the public service include the service in the United Kingdom—

(a) of any international organisation or institution whether or not the United Kingdom or Her Majesty's Government in the United Kingdom is or is to become a member;

(b) of any office or agency established by such an organisation or institution or for its purposes, or established in pursuance of a treaty (whether or not the United Kingdom is or is to become a party to the treaty);

(c) of a foreign sovereign Power or the Government of such a Power.

(6) For the purposes of subsection (5)(b) "treaty" includes any international agreement and any protocol or annex to a treaty or international agreement.

(7) The Acquisition of Land Act 1981 shall apply to any compulsory acquisition by the Secretary of State for the Environment under this section.

PART IX

Appropriation of land forming part of common, etc.

229.—(1) Any local authority may be authorised, by an order made by that authority and confirmed by the Secretary of State, to appropriate for any purpose for which that authority can be authorised to acquire land under any enactment any land to which this subsection applies which is for the time being held by them for other purposes.

(2) Subsection (1) applies to land which is or forms part of a common or fuel or field garden allotment (including any such land which is specially regulated by any enactment, whether public general or local or private), other than land which is Green Belt land within the meaning of the Green Belt (London and Home Counties) Act 1938.

1938 c. xciii.

1981 c. 67.

(3) Section 19 of the Acquisition of Land Act 1981 (special provision with respect to compulsory purchase orders under that Act relating to land forming part of a common, open space or fuel or field garden allotment) shall apply to an order under this section authorising the appropriation of land as it applies to a compulsory purchase order under that Act.

(4) Where land appropriated under this section was acquired under an enactment incorporating the Lands Clauses Acts, any works executed on the land after the appropriation has been effected shall, for the purposes of section 68 of the Lands Clauses Consolidation Act 1845 and section 10 of the Compulsory Purchase Act 1965, be deemed to have been authorised by the enactment under which the land was acquired.

1845 c.18.

1965 c.56.

(5) On an appropriation of land by a local authority under this section, where—

(a) the authority is not an authority to whom Part II of the 1959 Act applies;

(b) the land was immediately before the appropriation held by the authority for the purposes of a grant-aided function (within the meaning of that Act); or

(c) the land is appropriated by the authority for the purposes of such a function,

such adjustments shall be made in the accounts of the local authority as the Secretary of State may direct.

(6) On an appropriation under this section which does not fall within subsection (5), such adjustment of accounts shall be made as is required by section 24(1) of the 1959 Act.

Acquisition of land for purposes of exchange.

230.—(1) Without prejudice to the generality of the powers conferred by sections 226 and 227, any power of a local authority to acquire land under those sections, whether compulsorily or by agreement, shall include power to acquire land required for giving in exchange—

(a) for land appropriated under section 229; or

(b) for Green Belt land appropriated in accordance with the Green Belt (London and Home Counties) Act 1938 for any purpose specified in a development plan.

(2) In subsection (1) "Green Belt land" has the same meaning as in that Act.

PART IX

Power of Secretary of State to require acquisition or development of land.

231.—(1) If the Secretary of State is satisfied after holding a local inquiry that the council of a county, district or London borough have failed to take steps for the acquisition of any land which in his opinion ought to be acquired by them under section 226 for a purpose which it is necessary to achieve in the interests of the proper planning of an area in which the land is situated, he may by order require the council to take such steps as may be specified in the order for acquiring the land.

(2) If the Secretary of State is satisfied after holding a local inquiry that a local authority have failed to carry out, on land acquired by them under section 226 (or section 68 of the 1962 Act or section 112 of the 1971 Act) or appropriated by them under section 229 (or section 121 of the 1971 Act), any development which in his opinion ought to be carried out, he may by order require the authority to take such steps as may be specified in the order for carrying out the development.

(3) An order under this section shall be enforceable on the application of the Secretary of State by mandamus.

Appropriation, disposal and development of land held for planning purposes, etc.

Appropriation of land held for planning purposes.

232.—(1) Where any land has been acquired or appropriated by a local authority for planning purposes and is for the time being held by them for the purposes for which it was so acquired or appropriated, the authority may appropriate the land for any purpose for which they are or may be authorised in any capacity to acquire land by virtue of or under any enactment not contained in this Part or in Chapter V of Part I of the Planning (Listed Buildings and Conservation Areas) Act 1990. 1990 c. 9.

(2) Land which consists or forms part of a common, or formerly consisted or formed part of a common, and is held or managed by a local authority in accordance with a local Act shall not be appropriated under this section without the consent of the Secretary of State.

(3) Such consent may be given—

(a) either in respect of a particular appropriation or in respect of appropriations of any class, and

(b) either subject to or free from any conditions or limitations.

(4) Before appropriating under this section any land which consists of or forms part of an open space, a local authority—

(a) shall publish a notice of their intention to do so for at least two consecutive weeks in a newspaper circulating in their area; and

(b) shall consider any objections to the proposed appropriation which may be made to them.

(5) In relation to any appropriation under this section—

(a) subsection (4) of section 122 of the Local Government Act 1972 (which relates to the operation of section 68 of the Lands Clauses Consolidation Act 1845 and section 10 of the Compulsory Purchase Act 1965) shall have effect as it has effect in relation to appropriations under section 122 of that Act of 1972; and 1972 c.70. 1845 c.18. 1965 c.56.

(b) subsections (5) and (6) of section 229 of this Act shall have effect as they have effect in relation to appropriations under that section.

PART IX

(6) In relation to any such land as is mentioned in subsection (1), this section shall have effect to the exclusion of the provisions of section 122(1) of the Local Government Act 1972.

1972 c.70.

Disposal by local authorities of land held for planning purposes.

233.—(1) Where any land has been acquired or appropriated by a local authority for planning purposes and is for the time being held by them for the purposes for which it was so acquired or appropriated, the authority may dispose of the land to such person, in such manner and subject to such conditions as appear to them to be expedient in order—

(a) to secure the best use of that or other land and any buildings or works which have been, or are to be, erected, constructed or carried out on it (whether by themselves or by any other person), or

(b) to secure the erection, construction or carrying out on it of any buildings or works appearing to them to be needed for the proper planning of the area of the authority.

(2) Land which consists of or forms part of a common, or formerly consisted or formed part of a common, and is held or managed by a local authority in accordance with a local Act shall not be disposed of under this section without the consent of the Secretary of State.

(3) The consent of the Secretary of State is also required where the disposal is to be for a consideration less than the best that can reasonably be obtained and is not—

(a) the grant of a term of seven years or less; or

(b) the assignment of a term of years of which seven years or less are unexpired at the date of the assignment.

(4) Before disposing under this section of any land which consists of or forms part of an open space, a local authority—

(a) shall publish a notice of their intention to do so for at least two consecutive weeks in a newspaper circulating in their area; and

(b) shall consider any objections to the proposed disposal which may be made to them.

(5) In relation to land acquired or appropriated for planning purposes for a reason mentioned in section 226(1)(a) or (3) the powers conferred by this section on a local authority, and on the Secretary of State in respect of the giving of consent to disposals under this section, shall be so exercised as to secure to relevant occupiers, so far as may be practicable, a suitable opportunity for accommodation.

(6) A person is a relevant occupier for the purposes of subsection (5) if—

(a) he was living or carrying on business or other activities on any such land as is mentioned in that subsection which the authority have acquired as mentioned in subsection (1),

(b) he desires to obtain accommodation on such land, and

(c) he is willing to comply with any requirements of the authority as to the development and use of such land;

and in this subsection "development" includes redevelopment.

PART IX

(7) In subsection (5) a suitable opportunity for accommodation means, in relation to any person, an opportunity to obtain accommodation on the land in question which is suitable to his reasonable requirements on terms settled with due regard to the price at which any such land has been acquired from him.

(8) In relation to any such land as is mentioned in subsection (1), this section shall have effect to the exclusion of section 123 of the Local Government Act 1972 (disposal of land by principal councils). 1972 c. 70.

Disposal by Secretary of State of land acquired under s. 228.

234.—(1) The Secretary of State may dispose of land held by him and acquired by him or any other Minister under section 228 to such person, in such manner and subject to such conditions as appear to him expedient.

(2) In particular, the Secretary of State may under subsection (1) dispose of land held by him for any purpose in order to secure its use for that purpose.

Development of land held for planning purposes.

235.—(1) A local authority may—

(a) erect, construct or carry out on any land to which this section applies any building or work other than a building or work for the erection, construction or carrying out of which, whether by that local authority or by any other person, statutory power exists by virtue of, or could be conferred under, an alternative enactment; and

(b) repair, maintain and insure any buildings or works on such land and generally deal with such land in a proper course of management.

(2) This section applies to any land which—

(a) has been acquired or appropriated by a local authority for planning purposes, and

(b) is for the time being held by the authority for the purposes for which it was so acquired or appropriated.

(3) A local authority may exercise the powers conferred by subsection (1) notwithstanding any limitation imposed by law on their capacity by virtue of their constitution.

(4) A local authority may enter into arrangements with an authorised association for the carrying out by the association of any operation which, apart from the arrangements, the local authority would have power under this section to carry out, on such terms (including terms as to the making of payments or loans by the authority to the association) as may be specified in the arrangements.

(5) Nothing in this section shall be construed—

(a) as authorising any act or omission on the part of a local authority which is actionable at the suit of any person on any grounds other than such a limitation as is mentioned in subsection (3); or

(b) as authorising an authorised association to carry out any operation which they would not have power to carry out apart from subsection (4).

PART IX

(6) In this section—

1963 c.29.
1982 c.52.
1990 c. 9.

"alternative enactment" means any enactment which is not contained in this Part, in section 2, 5 or 6 of the Local Authorities (Land) Act 1963, in section 14(1) or (4) or 17(3) of the Industrial Development Act 1982 or in Chapter V of Part I of the Planning (Listed Buildings and Conservation Areas) Act 1990; and

"authorised association" means any society, company or body of persons—

(a) whose objects include the promotion, formation or management of garden cities, garden suburbs or garden villages and the erection, improvement or management of buildings for the working classes and others, and

(b) which does not trade for profit or whose constitution forbids the issue of any share or loan capital with interest or dividend exceeding the rate for the time being fixed by the Treasury.

Extinguishment of certain rights affecting acquired or appropriated land

Extinguishment of rights over land compulsorily acquired.

236.—(1) Subject to the provisions of this section, upon the completion of a compulsory acquisition of land under section 226, 228 or 230—

(a) all private rights of way and rights of laying down, erecting, continuing or maintaining any apparatus on, under or over the land shall be extinguished, and

(b) any such apparatus shall vest in the acquiring authority.

(2) Subsection (1) shall not apply—

(a) to any right vested in, or apparatus belonging to, statutory undertakers for the purpose of the carrying on of their undertaking, or

(b) to any right conferred by or in accordance with the telecommunications code on the operator of a telecommunications code system, or

(c) to any telecommunications apparatus kept installed for the purposes of any such system.

(3) In respect of any right or apparatus not falling within subsection (2), subsection (1) shall have effect subject—

(a) to any direction given by the acquiring authority before the completion of the acquisition that subsection (1) shall not apply to any right or apparatus specified in the direction; and

(b) to any agreement which may be made (whether before or after the completion of the acquisition) between the acquiring authority and the person in or to whom the right or apparatus in question is vested or belongs.

(4) Any person who suffers loss by the extinguishment of a right or the vesting of any apparatus under this section shall be entitled to compensation from the acquiring authority.

1961 c.33.

(5) Any compensation payable under this section shall be determined in accordance with the Land Compensation Act 1961.

PART IX

Power to override easements and other rights.

237.—(1) Subject to subsection (3), the erection, construction or carrying out or maintenance of any building or work on land which has been acquired or appropriated by a local authority for planning purposes (whether done by the local authority or by a person deriving title under them) is authorised by virtue of this section if it is done in accordance with planning permission, notwithstanding that it involves—

(a) interference with an interest or right to which this section applies, or

(b) a breach of a restriction as to the user of land arising by virtue of a contract.

(2) Subject to subsection (3), the interests and rights to which this section applies are any easement, liberty, privilege, right or advantage annexed to land and adversely affecting other land, including any natural right to support.

(3) Nothing in this section shall authorise interference with any right of way or right of laying down, erecting, continuing or maintaining apparatus on, under or over land which is—

(a) a right vested in or belonging to statutory undertakers for the purpose of the carrying on of their undertaking, or

(b) a right conferred by or in accordance with the telecommunications code on the operator of a telecommunications code system.

(4) In respect of any interference or breach in pursuance of subsection (1), compensation—

(a) shall be payable under section 63 or 68 of the Lands Clauses Consolidation Act 1845 or under section 7 or 10 of the Compulsory Purchase Act 1965, and

1845 c.18.

1965 c.56.

(b) shall be assessed in the same manner and subject to the same rules as in the case of other compensation under those sections in respect of injurious affection where—

(i) the compensation is to be estimated in connection with a purchase under those Acts, or

(ii) the injury arises from the execution of works on land acquired under those Acts.

(5) Where a person deriving title under the local authority by whom the land in question was acquired or appropriated—

(a) is liable to pay compensation by virtue of subsection (4), and

(b) fails to discharge that liability,

the liability shall be enforceable against the local authority.

(6) Nothing in subsection (5) shall be construed as affecting any agreement between the local authority and any other person for indemnifying the local authority against any liability under that subsection.

(7) Nothing in this section shall be construed as authorising any act or omission on the part of any person which is actionable at the suit of any person on any grounds other than such an interference or breach as is mentioned in subsection (1).

PART IX

Use and development of consecrated land.

238.—(1) Notwithstanding any obligation or restriction imposed under ecclesiastical law or otherwise in respect of consecrated land, any such land, which has been the subject of a relevant acquisition or appropriation, may subject to the following provisions of this section—

(a) if it has been acquired by a Minister, be used in any manner by him or on his behalf for any purpose for which he acquired the land; and

(b) in any other case, be used by any person in any manner in accordance with planning permission.

(2) Subsection (1) applies whether or not the land includes a building but it does not apply to land which consists of or forms part of a burial ground.

(3) Any use of consecrated land authorised by subsection (1) shall be subject—

(a) to compliance with the prescribed requirements with respect—

(i) to the removal and reinterment of any human remains, and

(ii) to the disposal of monuments and fixtures and furnishings; and

(b) to such provisions as may be prescribed for prohibiting or restricting the use of the land, either absolutely or until the prescribed consent has been obtained, so long as any church or other building used or formerly used for religious worship, or any part of it, remains on the land.

(4) Any use of land other than consecrated land which—

(a) has been the subject of a relevant acquisition or appropriation, and

(b) at the time of acquisition or appropriation included a church or other building used or formerly used for religious worship or the site of such a church or building,

shall be subject to compliance with such requirements as are mentioned in subsection (3)(a).

(5) Any regulations made for the purposes of subsection (3) or (4)—

(a) shall contain such provisions as appear to the Secretary of State to be requisite for securing that any use of land which is subject to compliance with the regulations shall, as nearly as may be, be subject to the same control as is imposed by law in the case of a similar use authorised by an enactment not contained in this Act or by a Measure, or as it would be proper to impose on a disposal of the land in question otherwise than in pursuance of an enactment or Measure;

(b) shall contain such requirements relating to the disposal of any such land as is mentioned in subsection (3) or (4) as appear to the Secretary of State requisite for securing that the provisions of those subsections are complied with in relation to the use of the land; and

(c) may contain such incidental and consequential provisions (including provision as to the closing of registers) as appear to the Secretary of State to be expedient for the purposes of the regulations.

PART IX

(6) Nothing in this section shall be construed as authorising any act or omission on the part of any person which is actionable at the suit of any person on any grounds other than contravention of any such obligation, restriction or enactment as is mentioned in subsection (1).

Use and development of burial grounds.

239.—(1) Notwithstanding anything in any enactment relating to burial grounds or any obligation or restriction imposed under ecclesiastical law or otherwise in respect of them, any land consisting of a burial ground or part of a burial ground, which has been the subject of a relevant acquisition or appropriation, may—

(a) if it has been acquired by a Minister, be used in any manner by him or on his behalf for any purpose for which he acquired the land; and

(b) in any other case, be used by any person in any manner in accordance with planning permission.

(2) This section does not apply to land which has been used for the burial of the dead until the prescribed requirements with respect to the removal and reinterment of human remains, and the disposal of monuments, in or upon the land have been complied with.

(3) Nothing in this section shall be construed as authorising any act or omission on the part of any person which is actionable at the suit of any person on any grounds other than contravention of any such enactment, obligation or restriction as is mentioned in subsection (1).

Provisions supplemental to ss. 238 and 239.

240.—(1) Provision shall be made by any regulations made for the purposes of sections 238(3) and (4) and 239(2)—

(a) for requiring the persons in whom the land is vested to publish notice of their intention to carry out the removal and reinterment of any human remains or the disposal of any monuments;

(b) for enabling the personal representatives or relatives of any deceased person themselves to undertake—

(i) the removal and reinterment of the remains of the deceased, and

(ii) the disposal of any monument commemorating the deceased,

and for requiring the persons in whom the land is vested to defray the expenses of such removal, reinterment and disposal (not exceeding such amount as may be prescribed);

(c) for requiring compliance—

(i) with such reasonable conditions (if any) as may be imposed in the case of consecrated land, by the bishop of the diocese, with respect to the manner of removal and the place and manner of reinterment of any human remains and the disposal of any monuments, and

(ii) with any directions given in any case by the Secretary of State with respect to the removal and reinterment of any human remains.

PART IX

(2) Subject to the provisions of any such regulations, no faculty is required—

(a) for the removal and reinterment in accordance with the regulations of any human remains, or

(b) for the removal or disposal of any monuments,

1857 c. 81.

and section 25 of the Burial Act 1857 (prohibition of removal of human remains without the licence of the Secretary of State except in certain cases) does not apply to a removal carried out in accordance with the regulations.

(3) In sections 238 and 239 and this section—

"burial ground" includes any churchyard, cemetery or other ground, whether consecrated or not, which has at any time been set apart for the purposes of interment,

"monument" includes a tombstone or other memorial, and

1990 c. 9.

"relevant acquisition or appropriation" means an acquisition made by a Minister, a local authority or statutory undertakers under this Part or Chapter V of Part I of the Planning (Listed Buildings and Conservation Areas) Act 1990 or compulsorily under any other enactment, or an appropriation by a local authority for planning purposes.

Use and development of open spaces.

241.—(1) Notwithstanding anything in any enactment relating to land which is or forms part of a common, open space or fuel or field garden allotment or in any enactment by which the land is specially regulated, such land which has been acquired by a Minister, a local authority or statutory undertakers under this Part or under Chapter V of Part I of the Planning (Listed Buildings and Conservation Areas) Act 1990 or compulsorily under any other enactment, or which has been appropriated by a local authority for planning purposes—

(a) if it has been acquired by a Minister, may be used in any manner by him or on his behalf for any purpose for which he acquired the land; and

(b) in any other case, may be used by any person in any manner in accordance with planning permission.

(2) Nothing in this section shall be construed as authorising any act or omission on the part of any person which is actionable at the suit of any person on any grounds other than contravention of any such enactment as is mentioned in subsection (1).

Overriding of rights of possession.

242. If the Secretary of State certifies that possession of a house which—

(a) has been acquired or appropriated by a local authority for planning purposes, and

(b) is for the time being held by the authority for the purposes for which it was acquired or appropriated,

1977 c.42.
1988 c. 50.

is immediately required for those purposes, nothing in the Rent Act 1977 or Part I of the Housing Act 1988 shall prevent the acquiring or appropriating authority from obtaining possession of the house.

Constitution of joint body to hold land for planning purposes

PART IX

243.—(1) If it appears to the Secretary of State, after consultation with the local authorities concerned, to be expedient that any land acquired by a local authority for planning purposes should be held by a joint body, consisting of representatives of that authority and of any other local authority, he may by order provide for the establishment of such a joint body and for the transfer to that body of the land so acquired.

Constitution of joint body to hold land for planning purposes.

(2) Any order under this section providing for the establishment of a joint body may make such provision as the Secretary of State considers expedient with respect to the constitution and functions of that body.

(3) The provisions which may be included under subsection (2) include provisions—

(a) for incorporating the joint body;

(b) for conferring on them, in relation to land transferred to them as mentioned in subsection (1), any of the powers conferred on local authorities by this Part or Chapter V of Part I of the Planning (Listed Buildings and Conservation Areas) Act 1990 in relation to land acquired and held by such authorities for the purposes of this Part or that Chapter;

1990 c. 9.

(c) for determining the manner in which their expenses are to be defrayed.

(4) Regulations under this Act may make such provision consequential upon or supplementary to the provisions of this section as appears to the Secretary of State to be necessary or expedient.

General and supplementary provisions

244.—(1) A joint planning board or a board reconstituted under Schedule 17 to the Local Government Act 1972 shall, on being authorised to do so by the Secretary of State, have the same power to acquire land compulsorily as the local authorities to whom section 226 applies have under that section.

Powers of joint planning boards under Part IX.
1972 c.70.

(2) Such a board shall have the same power to acquire land by agreement as the local authorities mentioned in subsection (1) of section 227 have under that subsection.

(3) Sections 226(1) and (7), 227, 229, 230, 232, 233 and 235 to 242 apply with the necessary modifications as if any such board were a local authority to which those sections applied.

(4) On being authorised to do so by the Secretary of State such a board shall have, for any purpose for which by virtue of this section they may acquire land compulsorily, the power which section 13 of the Local Government (Miscellaneous Provisions) Act 1976 confers on the local authorities to whom subsection (1) of that section applies to purchase compulsorily rights over land not in existence when their compulsory purchase is authorised, and subsections (2) to (5) of that section shall accordingly apply to the purchase of rights under this subsection as they apply to the purchase of rights under subsection (1) of that section.

1976 c.57.

245.—(1) Where—

Modification of incorporated enactments for purposes of this Part.

(a) it is proposed that land should be acquired compulsorily under section 226 or 228, and

PART IX

1981 c.67.

(b) a compulsory purchase order relating to that land is submitted to the confirming authority in accordance with Part II of the Acquisition of Land Act 1981 or, as the case may be, is made in draft by the Secretary of State for the Environment in accordance with Schedule 1 to that Act,

the confirming authority or, as the case may be, that Secretary of State may disregard for the purposes of that Part or, as the case may be, that Schedule any objection to the order or draft which, in the opinion of that authority or Secretary of State, amounts in substance to an objection to the provisions of the development plan defining the proposed use of that or any other land.

(2) Where a compulsory purchase order authorising the acquisition of any land under section 226 is submitted to the Secretary of State in accordance with Part II of the Acquisition of Land Act 1981, then if the Secretary of State—

(a) is satisfied that the order ought to be confirmed so far as it relates to part of the land comprised in it; but

(b) has not for the time being determined whether it ought to be confirmed so far as it relates to any other such land,

he may confirm the order so far as it relates to the land mentioned in paragraph (a) and give directions postponing consideration of the order, so far as it relates to any other land specified in the directions, until such time as may be so specified.

(3) Where the Secretary of State gives directions under subsection (2), the notices required by section 15 of the Acquisition of Land Act 1981 to be published and served shall include a statement of the effect of the directions.

1965 c.56.

(4) In construing the Compulsory Purchase Act 1965 in relation to any of the provisions of this Part—

(a) references to the execution of the works shall be construed as including references to any erection, construction or carrying out of buildings or works authorised by section 237;

(b) in relation to the erection, construction or carrying out of any buildings or works so authorised, references in section 10 of that Act to the acquiring authority shall be construed as references to the person by whom the buildings or works in question are erected, constructed or carried out; and

(c) references to the execution of the works shall be construed as including also references to any erection, construction or carrying out of buildings or works on behalf of a Minister or statutory undertakers on land acquired by that Minister or those undertakers, where the buildings or works are erected, constructed or carried out for the purposes for which the land was acquired.

Interpretation of Part IX.

246.—(1) In this Part—

1990 c. 9.

(a) any reference to the acquisition of land for planning purposes is a reference to the acquisition of it under section 226 or 227 of this Act or section 52 of the Planning (Listed Buildings and Conservation Areas) Act 1990 (or, as the case may be, under section 112 or 119 of the 1971 Act or section 68 or 71 of the 1962 Act); and

(b) any reference to the appropriation of land for planning purposes is a reference to the appropriation of it for purposes for which land can be (or, as the case may be, could have been) acquired under those sections.

(2) Nothing in sections 237 to 241 shall be construed as authorising any act or omission on the part of a local authority or body corporate in contravention of any limitation imposed by law on their capacity by virtue of their constitution.

(3) Any power conferred by section 238, 239 or 241 to use land in a manner mentioned in those sections shall be construed as a power so to use the land, whether or not it involves the erection, construction or carrying out of any building or work or the maintenance of any building or work.

PART X

HIGHWAYS

Orders made by Secretary of State

Highways affected by development: orders by Secretary of State.

247.—(1) The Secretary of State may by order authorise the stopping up or diversion of any highway if he is satisfied that it is necessary to do so in order to enable development to be carried out—

(a) in accordance with planning permission granted under Part III, or

(b) by a government department.

(2) Such an order may make such provision as appears to the Secretary of State to be necessary or expedient for the provision or improvement of any other highway.

(3) Such an order may direct—

(a) that any highway provided or improved by virtue of it shall for the purposes of the Highways Act 1980 be a highway maintainable at the public expense; 1980 c. 66.

(b) that the Secretary of State, or any county council, metropolitan district council or London borough council specified in the order or, if it is so specified, the Common Council of the City of London, shall be the highway authority for that highway;

(c) in the case of a highway for which the Secretary of State is to be the highway authority, that the highway shall, on such date as may be specified in the order, become a trunk road within the meaning of the Highways Act 1980.

(4) An order made under this section may contain such incidental and consequential provisions as appear to the Secretary of State to be necessary or expedient, including in particular—

(a) provision for authorising the Secretary of State, or requiring any other authority or person specified in the order—

(i) to pay, or to make contributions in respect of, the cost of doing any work provided for by the order or any increased expenditure to be incurred which is attributable to the doing of any such work; or

PART X

1935 c. 67.

(ii) to repay, or to make contributions in respect of, any compensation paid by the highway authority in respect of restrictions imposed under section 1 or 2 of the Restriction of Ribbon Development Act 1935 in relation to any highway stopped up or diverted under the order;

(b) provision for the preservation of any rights of statutory undertakers in respect of any apparatus of theirs which immediately before the date of the order is under, in, on, over, along or across the highway to which the order relates.

(5) An order may be made under this section authorising the stopping up or diversion of any highway which is temporarily stopped up or diverted under any other enactment.

(6) The provisions of this section shall have effect without prejudice to—

(a) any power conferred on the Secretary of State by any other enactment to authorise the stopping up or diversion of a highway;

1981 c. 67.

(b) the provisions of Part VI of the Acquisition of Land Act 1981; or

(c) the provisions of section 251(1).

Highways crossing or entering route of proposed new highway, etc.

248.—(1) This section applies where—

(a) planning permission is granted under Part III for constructing or improving, or the Secretary of State proposes to construct or improve, a highway ("the main highway"); and

(b) another highway crosses or enters the route of the main highway or is, or will be, otherwise affected by the construction or improvement of the main highway.

(2) Where this section applies, if it appears to the Secretary of State expedient to do so—

(a) in the interests of the safety of users of the main highway; or

(b) to facilitate the movement of traffic on the main highway,

he may by order authorise the stopping up or diversion of the other highway.

(3) Subsections (2) to (6) of section 247 shall apply to an order under this section as they apply to an order under that section, taking the reference in subsection (2) of that section to any other highway as a reference to any highway other than that which is stopped up or diverted under this section and the references in subsection (3) to a highway provided or improved by virtue of an order under that section as including a reference to the main highway.

Order extinguishing right to use vehicles on highway.

249.—(1) This section applies where—

(a) a local planning authority by resolution adopt a proposal for improving the amenity of part of their area, and

(b) the proposal involves the public ceasing to have any right of way with vehicles over a highway in that area, being a highway which is neither a trunk road nor a road classified as a principal road.

(2) The Secretary of State may, on an application by a local planning authority who have so resolved, by order provide for the extinguishment of any right which persons may have to use vehicles on that highway.

(3) An order under subsection (2) may include such provision as the Secretary of State (after consultation with every authority who are a local planning authority for the area in question and the highway authority) thinks fit for permitting the use on the highway of vehicles (whether mechanically propelled or not) in such cases as may be specified in the order, notwithstanding the extinguishment of any such right as is mentioned in that subsection.

(4) Such provision as is mentioned in subsection (3) may be framed by reference to—

(a) particular descriptions of vehicles, or

(b) particular persons by whom, or on whose authority, vehicles may be used, or

(c) the circumstances in which, or the times at which, vehicles may be used for particular purposes.

(5) No provision contained in, or having effect under, any enactment, being a provision prohibiting or restricting the use of footpaths, footways or bridleways shall affect any use of a vehicle on a highway in relation to which an order under subsection (2) has effect, where the use is permitted in accordance with provisions of the order included by virtue of subsection (3).

(6) If any authority who are a local planning authority for the area in which a highway to which an order under subsection (2) relates is situated apply to the Secretary of State in that behalf, he may by order revoke that order, and, if he does so, any right to use vehicles on the highway in relation to which the order was made which was extinguished by virtue of the order under that subsection shall be reinstated.

(7) Such an order as is mentioned in subsection (6) may make provision requiring the removal of any obstruction of a highway resulting from the exercise of powers under Part VIIA of the Highways Act 1980. 1980 c. 66.

(8) Before making an application under subsection (2) or (6) the local planning authority shall consult with the highway authority (if different) and any other authority who are a local planning authority for the area in question.

(9) Subsections (2), (3), (4) and (6) of section 247 shall apply to an order under this section as they apply to an order under that section.

Compensation for orders under s. 249.

250.—(1) Any person who, at the time of an order under section 249(2) coming into force, has an interest in land having lawful access to a highway to which the order relates shall be entitled to be compensated by the local planning authority on whose application the order was made in respect of—

(a) any depreciation in the value of his interest which is directly attributable to the order; and

(b) any other loss or damage which is so attributable.

(2) In subsection (1) "lawful access" means access authorised by planning permission or access in respect of which no such permission is necessary.

PART X

(3) A claim for compensation under this section shall be made to the local planning authority on whose application the order was made within the prescribed time and in the prescribed manner.

1961 c. 33.

(4) For the purpose of assessing any such compensation the rules set out in section 5 of the Land Compensation Act 1961 shall, so far as applicable and subject to any necessary modifications, have effect as they have effect for the purpose of assessing compensation for the compulsory acquisition of an interest in land.

(5) Where an interest in land is subject to a mortgage—

(a) any compensation to which this section applies which is payable in respect of depreciation of the value of that interest shall be assessed as if the interest were not subject to the mortgage;

(b) a claim for any such compensation may be made by any mortgagee of the interest, but without prejudice to the making of a claim by the person entitled to the interest;

(c) no compensation to which this section applies shall be payable in respect of the interest of the mortgagee (as distinct from the interest which is subject to the mortgage); and

(d) any compensation to which this section applies which is payable in respect of the interest which is subject to the mortgage shall be paid to the mortgagee (or, if there is more than one mortgagee, to the first mortgagee) and shall in either case be applied by him as if it were proceeds of sale.

(6) Except in so far as may be otherwise provided by any regulations made under this Act, any question of disputed compensation under this section shall be referred to and determined by the Lands Tribunal.

(7) In relation to the determination of any such question, the provisions of sections 2 and 4 of the Land Compensation Act 1961 shall apply subject to any necessary modifications and to the provisions of any regulations made under this Act.

Extinguishment of public rights of way over land held for planning purposes.

251.—(1) Where any land has been acquired or appropriated for planning purposes and is for the time being held by a local authority for the purposes for which it was acquired or appropriated, the Secretary of State may by order extinguish any public right of way over the land if he is satisfied—

(a) that an alternative right of way has been or will be provided; or

(b) that the provision of an alternative right of way is not required.

(2) In this section any reference to the acquisition or appropriation of land for planning purposes shall be construed in accordance with section 246(1) as if this section were in Part IX.

(3) Subsection (1) shall also apply (with the substitution of a reference to the Broads Authority for the reference to the local authority) in relation to any land within the Broads which is held by the Broads Authority and which was acquired by, or vested in, the Authority for any purpose connected with the discharge of any of its functions.

Procedure for making of orders.

252.—(1) Before making an order under section 247, 248, 249 or 251 the Secretary of State shall publish in at least one local newspaper circulating in the relevant area, and in the London Gazette, a notice—

(a) stating the general effect of the order;

(b) specifying a place in the relevant area where a copy of the draft order and of any relevant map or plan may be inspected by any person free of charge at all reasonable hours during a period of 28 days from the date of the publication of the notice ("the publication date"); and

(c) stating that any person may within that period by notice to the Secretary of State object to the making of the order.

(2) Not later than the publication date, the Secretary of State shall serve a copy of the notice, together with a copy of the draft order and of any relevant map or plan—

(a) on every local authority in whose area any highway or, as the case may be, any land to which the order relates is situated, and

(b) on any water, sewerage, hydraulic power or electricity undertakers or public gas supplier having any cables, mains, sewers, pipes or wires laid along, across, under or over any highway to be stopped up or diverted, or, as the case may be, any land over which a right of way is proposed to be extinguished, under the order.

(3) Not later than the publication date, the Secretary of State shall also cause a copy of the notice to be displayed in a prominent position at the ends of so much of any highway as is proposed to be stopped up or diverted or, as the case may be, of the right of way proposed to be extinguished under the order.

(4) If before the end of the period of 28 days mentioned in subsection (1)(b) an objection is received by the Secretary of State from any local authority or undertakers or public gas supplier on whom a notice is required to be served under subsection (2), or from any other person appearing to him to be affected by the order, and the objection is not withdrawn, then unless subsection (5) applies the Secretary of State shall cause a local inquiry to be held.

(5) If, in a case where the objection is made by a person other than such a local authority or undertakers or supplier, the Secretary of State is satisfied that in the special circumstances of the case the holding of such an inquiry is unnecessary he may dispense with the inquiry.

(6) Subsections (2) to (5) of section 250 of the Local Government Act 1972 (local inquiries: evidence and costs) shall apply in relation to an inquiry caused to be held by the Secretary of State under subsection (4). 1972 c. 70.

(7) Where publication of the notice mentioned in subsection (1) takes place on more than one day, the references in this section to the publication date are references to the latest date on which it is published.

(8) After considering any objections to the order which are not withdrawn and, where a local inquiry is held, the report of the person who held the inquiry, the Secretary of State may, subject to subsection (9), make the order either without modification or subject to such modifications as he thinks fit.

(9) Where—

(a) the order contains a provision requiring any such payment, repayment or contribution as is mentioned in section 247(4)(a); and

PART X

(b) objection to that provision is duly made by an authority or person who would be required by it to make such a payment, repayment or contribution; and

(c) the objection is not withdrawn,

the order shall be subject to special parliamentary procedure.

(10) Immediately after the order has been made, the Secretary of State shall publish, in the manner specified in subsection (1), a notice stating that the order has been made and naming a place where a copy of the order may be seen at all reasonable hours.

(11) Subsections (2), (3) and (7) shall have effect in relation to a notice under subsection (10) as they have effect in relation to a notice under subsection (1).

(12) In this section—

"the relevant area", in relation to an order, means the area in which any highway or land to which the order relates is situated;

"local authority" means the council of a county, district, parish or London borough, a joint authority established by Part IV of the Local Government Act 1985, a housing action trust established under Part III of the Housing Act 1988 and the parish meeting of a rural parish not having a separate parish council;

1985 c. 51.
1988 c. 50.

and in subsection (2)—

(i) the reference to water undertakers shall be construed as including a reference to the National Rivers Authority, and

(ii) the reference to electricity undertakers shall be construed as a reference to holders of licences under section 6 of the Electricity Act 1989 who are entitled to exercise any power conferred by paragraph 1 of Schedule 4 to that Act.

1989 c. 29.

Procedure in anticipation of planning permission.

253.—(1) Where—

(a) the Secretary of State would, if planning permission for any development had been granted under Part III, have power to make an order under section 247 or 248 authorising the stopping up or diversion of a highway in order to enable that development to be carried out, and

(b) subsection (2), (3) or (4) applies,

then, notwithstanding that such permission has not been granted, the Secretary of State may publish notice of the draft of such an order in accordance with section 252.

(2) This subsection applies where the relevant development is the subject of an application for planning permission and either—

(a) that application is made by a local authority or statutory undertakers or the British Coal Corporation; or

(b) that application stands referred to the Secretary of State in pursuance of a direction under section 77; or

(c) the applicant has appealed to the Secretary of State under section 78 against a refusal of planning permission or of approval required under a development order or against a condition of any such permission or approval.

PART X

(3) This subsection applies where—

(a) the relevant development is to be carried out by a local authority or statutory undertakers and requires, by virtue of an enactment, the authorisation of a government department; and

(b) the developers have made an application to the department for that authorisation and also requested a direction under section 90(1) that planning permission be deemed to be granted for that development.

(4) This subsection applies where the council of a county, metropolitan district or London borough or a joint planning board certify that they have begun to take such steps, in accordance with regulations made by virtue of section 316, as are required to enable them to obtain planning permission for the relevant development.

(5) Section 252(8) shall not be construed as authorising the Secretary of State to make an order under section 247 or 248 of which notice has been published by virtue of subsection (1) until planning permission is granted for the development which occasions the making of the order.

Compulsory acquisition of land in connection with highways.

254.—(1) The Secretary of State, or a local highway authority on being authorised by the Secretary of State to do so, may acquire land compulsorily—

(a) for the purpose of providing or improving any highway which is to be provided or improved in pursuance of an order under section 247, 248 or 249 or for any other purpose for which land is required in connection with the order; or

(b) for the purpose of providing any public right of way which is to be provided as an alternative to a right of way extinguished under an order under section 251.

(2) The Acquisition of Land Act 1981 shall apply to the acquisition of land under this section. 1981 c. 67.

Concurrent proceedings in connection with highways.

255.—(1) In relation to orders under sections 247, 248 and 249, regulations made under this Act may make provision for securing that any proceedings required to be taken for the purposes of the acquisition of land under section 254 (as mentioned in subsection (1)(a) of that section) may be taken concurrently with any proceedings required to be taken for the purposes of the order.

(2) In relation to orders under section 251, regulations made under this Act may make provision for securing—

(a) that any proceedings required to be taken for the purposes of such an order may be taken concurrently with any proceedings required to be taken for the purposes of the acquisition of the land over which the right of way is to be extinguished; or

(b) that any proceedings required to be taken for the purposes of the acquisition of any other land under section 254 (as mentioned in subsection (1)(b) of that section) may be taken concurrently with either or both of the proceedings referred to in paragraph (a).

PART X

Telecommunication apparatus: orders by Secretary of State.

256.—(1) Where—

(a) in pursuance of an order under section 247, 248 or 249 a highway is stopped up or diverted or, as the case may be, any right to use vehicles on that highway is extinguished; and

(b) immediately before the date on which the order came into force there was under, in, on, over, along or across the highway any telecommunication apparatus kept installed for the purposes of a telecommunications code system,

the operator of that system shall have the same powers in respect of the apparatus as if the order had not come into force.

(2) Notwithstanding subsection (1), any person entitled to land over which the highway subsisted shall be entitled to require the alteration of the apparatus.

(3) Where—

(a) any such order provides for the improvement of a highway, other than a trunk road, and

(b) immediately before the date on which the order came into force there was under, in, on, over, along or across the highway any telecommunication apparatus kept installed for the purposes of a telecommunications code system,

the local highway authority shall be entitled to require the alteration of the apparatus.

(4) Subsection (3) does not have effect so far as it relates to the alteration of any apparatus for the purpose of authority's works as defined in Part II of the Public Utilities Street Works Act 1950.

1950 c. 39.

(5) Paragraph 1(2) of the telecommunications code (alteration of apparatus to include moving, removal or replacement of apparatus) shall apply for the purposes of this section as it applies for the purposes of that code.

(6) Paragraph 21 of the telecommunications code (restriction on removal of telecommunication apparatus) shall apply in relation to any entitlement conferred by this section to require the alteration, moving or replacement of any telecommunication apparatus as it applies in relation to an entitlement to require the removal of any such apparatus.

Orders by other authorities

Footpaths and bridleways affected by development: orders by other authorities.

257.—(1) Subject to section 259, a competent authority may by order authorise the stopping up or diversion of any footpath or bridleway if they are satisfied that it is necessary to do so in order to enable development to be carried out—

(a) in accordance with planning permission granted under Part III, or

(b) by a government department.

(2) An order under this section may, if the competent authority are satisfied that it should do so, provide—

(a) for the creation of an alternative highway for use as a replacement for the one authorised by the order to be stopped up or diverted, or for the improvement of an existing highway for such use;

(b) for authorising or requiring works to be carried out in relation to any footpath or bridleway for whose stopping up or diversion, creation or improvement provision is made by the order;

(c) for the preservation of any rights of statutory undertakers in respect of any apparatus of theirs which immediately before the date of the order is under, in, on, over, along or across any such footpath or bridleway;

(d) for requiring any person named in the order to pay, or make contributions in respect of, the cost of carrying out any such works.

(3) An order may be made under this section authorising the stopping up or diversion of a footpath or bridleway which is temporarily stopped up or diverted under any other enactment.

(4) In this section "competent authority" means—

(a) in the case of development authorised by a planning permission, the local planning authority who granted the permission or, in the case of a permission granted by the Secretary of State, who would have had power to grant it; and

(b) in the case of development carried out by a government department, the local planning authority who would have had power to grant planning permission on an application in respect of the development in question if such an application had fallen to be made.

Extinguishment of public rights of way over land held for planning purposes.

258.—(1) Where any land has been acquired or appropriated for planning purposes and is for the time being held by a local authority for the purposes for which it was acquired or appropriated, then, subject to section 259, the local authority may by order extinguish any public right of way over the land, being a footpath or bridleway, if they are satisfied—

(a) that an alternative right of way has been or will be provided; or

(b) that the provision of an alternative right of way is not required.

(2) In this section any reference to the acquisition or appropriation of land for planning purposes shall be construed in accordance with section 246(1) as if this section were in Part IX.

(3) Subsection (1) shall also apply (with the substitution of a reference to the Broads Authority for the reference to the local authority) in relation to any land within the Broads which is held by the Broads Authority and which was acquired by, or vested in, the Authority for any purpose connected with the discharge of any of its functions.

Confirmation of orders made by other authorities.

259.—(1) An order made under section 257 or 258 shall not take effect unless confirmed by the Secretary of State or unless confirmed, as an unopposed order, by the authority who made it.

(2) The Secretary of State shall not confirm any such order unless satisfied as to every matter as to which the authority making the order are required under section 257 or, as the case may be, section 258 to be satisfied.

(3) The time specified—

(a) in an order under section 257 as the time from which a footpath or bridleway is to be stopped up or diverted; or

PART X

(b) in an order under section 258 as the time from which a right of way is to be extinguished,

shall not be earlier than confirmation of the order.

(4) Schedule 14 shall have effect with respect to the confirmation of orders under section 257 or 258 and the publicity for such orders after they are confirmed.

Telecommunication apparatus: orders by or on application of other authorities.

260.—(1) This section applies where—

(a) any order is made by a local authority under section 258(1), or on the application of a local authority under section 251(1), which extinguishes a public right of way; or

(b) any order is made by a competent authority under section 257 which authorises the stopping up or diversion of a footpath or bridleway,

and at the time of the publication of the notice required by section 252(1) or, as the case may be, paragraph 1 of Schedule 14 any telecommunication apparatus was kept installed for the purposes of a telecommunications code system under, in, on, over, along or across the land over which the right of way subsisted.

(2) In subsection (1) "competent authority" has the same meaning as in section 257 and in the following provisions of this section references to the authority are to the authority who made the order or, as the case may be, to the authority on whose application it was made.

(3) The power of the operator of the telecommunications code system to remove the apparatus—

(a) shall, notwithstanding the making of the order, be exercisable at any time not later than the end of the period of three months from the date on which the right of way is extinguished or authorised to be stopped up or diverted; and

(b) if before the end of that period the operator of the system has given notice to the authority of his intention to remove the apparatus or a part of it, shall be exercisable in respect of the whole or, as the case may be, that part of the apparatus after the end of that period.

(4) The operator of the system may by notice given in that behalf to the authority not later than the end of that period abandon the telecommunication apparatus or any part of it.

(5) Subject to subsection (4), the operator of the system shall be deemed at the end of that period to have abandoned any part of the apparatus which the operator has then neither removed nor given notice of his intention to remove.

(6) The operator of the system shall be entitled to recover from the authority the expense of providing, in substitution for the apparatus and any other telecommunication apparatus connected with it which is rendered useless in consequence of the removal or abandonment of the first-mentioned apparatus, any telecommunication apparatus in such other place as the operator may require.

PART X

(7) Where under the previous provisions of this section the operator of the system has abandoned the whole or any part of any telecommunication apparatus, that apparatus or that part of it shall vest in the authority and shall be deemed, with its abandonment, to cease to be kept installed for the purposes of a telecommunications code system.

(8) As soon as reasonably practicable after the making of any such order as is mentioned in paragraph (a) or (b) of subsection (1) in circumstances in which that subsection applies in relation to the operator of any telecommunications code system, the person by whom the order was made shall give notice to the operator of the making of the order.

(9) Subsections (5) and (6) of section 256 apply for the purposes of this section as they apply for the purposes of that section.

Temporary highway orders: mineral workings

Temporary stopping up of highways for mineral workings.

261.—(1) Where the Secretary of State is satisfied—

(a) that an order made by him under section 247 for the stopping up or diversion of a highway is required for the purpose of enabling minerals to be worked by surface working; and

(b) that the highway can be restored, after the minerals have been worked, to a condition not substantially less convenient to the public,

the order may provide for the stopping up or diversion of the highway during such period as may be prescribed by or under the order and for its restoration at the expiration of that period.

(2) Where a competent authority within the meaning of section 257 are satisfied—

(a) that an order made by them under that section for the stopping up or diversion of a footpath or bridleway is required for the purpose of enabling minerals to be worked by surface working; and

(b) that the footpath or bridleway can be restored, after the minerals have been worked, to a condition not substantially less convenient to the public,

the order may provide for the stopping up or diversion of the footpath or bridleway during such period as may be prescribed by or under the order and for its restoration at the expiration of that period.

(3) Without prejudice to the provisions of section 247 or 257, any such order as is authorised by subsection (1) or (2) may contain such provisions as appear to the Secretary of State or, as the case may be, the competent authority to be expedient—

(a) for imposing upon persons who, apart from the order, would be subject to any liability with respect to the repair of the original highway during the period prescribed by or under the order a corresponding liability in respect of any highway provided in pursuance of the order;

PART X

(b) for the stopping up at the expiry of that period of any highway so provided and for the reconstruction and maintenance of the original highway;

and any provision included in the order in accordance with subsection (4) of section 247 or subsection (2) of section 257 requiring payment to be made in respect of any cost or expenditure under the order may provide for the payment of a capital sum in respect of the estimated amount of that cost or expenditure.

(4) In relation to any highway which is stopped up or diverted by virtue of an order under section 247 or 248, sections 271 and 272 shall have effect—

(a) as if for references to land which has been acquired as there mentioned and to the acquiring or appropriating authority there were substituted respectively references to land over which the highway subsisted and to the person entitled to possession of that land; and

(b) as if references in subsection (5) of each of those sections to a local authority or statutory undertakers included references to any person (other than a Minister) who is entitled to possession of that land,

and sections 275 to 278 shall have effect accordingly.

(5) Subsection (4) shall not apply to land constituting the site of a highway in respect of which opencast planning permission (within the meaning of section 51 of the Opencast Coal Act 1958) has been granted.

1958 c. 69.

PART XI

STATUTORY UNDERTAKERS

Preliminary

Meaning of "statutory undertakers".

262.—(1) Subject to the following provisions of this section, in this Act "statutory undertakers" means persons authorised by any enactment to carry on any railway, light railway, tramway, road transport, water transport, canal, inland navigation, dock, harbour, pier or lighthouse undertaking or any undertaking for the supply of hydraulic power and a relevant airport operator (within the meaning of Part V of the Airports Act 1986).

1986 c. 31.

(2) Subject to the following provisions of this section, in this Act "statutory undertaking" shall be construed in accordance with subsection (1) and, in relation to a relevant airport operator (within the meaning of that Part), means an airport to which that Part of that Act applies.

(3) Subject to subsection (5), for the purposes of the provisions mentioned in subsection (4) any public gas supplier, water or sewerage undertaker, the National Rivers Authority, the Post Office and the Civil Aviation Authority shall be deemed to be statutory undertakers and their undertakings statutory undertakings.

(4) The provisions referred to in subsection (3) are sections 55, 90, 101, 108(3), 123, 139 to 141, 143, 148, 170(12)(b), 236(2)(a), 237 to 241, 245, 247(4)(b), 253, 257(2), 263(1) and (2), 264, 266 to 283, 288(10)(a), 306, 325(9), 336(2) and (3), paragraph 18 of Schedule 1 and Schedules 8, 13 and 14.

(5) Subsection (4) shall apply— PART XI

(a) as respects the Post Office, as if the reference to sections 55, 247(4)(b), 253 and 257(2) were omitted; and

(b) as respects the Post Office and the Civil Aviation Authority as if—

(i) the references to sections 245, 263(1) and (2) and 336(2) and (3) were omitted; and

(ii) after the words " 266 to 283" there were inserted the words "(except section 271 as applied by section 13 of the Opencast Coal Act 1958)".

(6) Any holder of a licence under section 6 of the Electricity Act 1989 shall be deemed to be a statutory undertaker and his undertaking a statutory undertaking— 1989 c. 29.

(a) for the purposes of the provisions mentioned in subsection (7)(a), if he holds a licence under subsection (1) of that section;

(b) for the purposes of the provisions mentioned in subsection (7)(b), if he is entitled to exercise any power conferred by Schedule 3 to that Act; and

(c) for the purposes of the provisions mentioned in subsection (7)(c), if he is entitled to exercise any power conferred by paragraph 1 of Schedule 4 to that Act.

(7) The provisions referred to in subsection (6) are—

(a) sections 55, 108(3), 123, 139 to 141, 143, 148, 236(2)(a), 237, 245, 253, 263(1) and (2), 264, 266 to 283, 288(10)(a), 306, 325(9) and 336(2) and (3), paragraph 18 of Schedule 1 and Schedule 13;

(b) sections 170(12)(b) and 238 to 241; and

(c) sections 247(4) and 257(2) and Schedule 14.

Meaning of "operational land".

263.—(1) Subject to the following provisions of this section and to section 264, in this Act "operational land" means, in relation to statutory undertakers—

(a) land which is used for the purpose of carrying on their undertaking; and

(b) land in which an interest is held for that purpose.

(2) Paragraphs (a) and (b) of subsection (1) do not include land which, in respect of its nature and situation, is comparable rather with land in general than with land which is used, or in which interests are held, for the purpose of the carrying on of statutory undertakings.

(3) In sections 108(3), 123(3) and (4), 266 to 283 and Part II of Schedule 8 "operational land", in relation to the Post Office and the Civil Aviation Authority, means land of the Post Office's or, as the case may be, of the Authority's of any such class as may be prescribed by regulations.

(4) Such regulations—

(a) shall be made—

(i) in the case of the Post Office, by the appropriate Minister and the Secretary of State acting jointly; and

(ii) in the case of the Civil Aviation Authority, by the appropriate Minister;

PART XI

(b) may define a class of land by reference to any circumstances whatsoever, and

(c) in the case of the Civil Aviation Authority, may make provision for different circumstances, including prescribing different classes of land for the purposes of different provisions.

Cases in which land is to be treated as not being operational land.

264.—(1) This section applies where an interest in land is held by statutory undertakers for the purpose of carrying on their undertaking and—

(a) the interest was acquired by them on or after 6th December 1968; or

(b) it was held by them immediately before that date but the circumstances were then such that the land did not fall to be treated as operational land for the purposes of the 1962 Act.

(2) Where this section applies in respect of any land then, notwithstanding the provisions of section 263, the land shall not be treated as operational land for the purposes of this Act unless it falls within subsection (3) or (4).

(3) Land falls within this subsection if—

(a) there is, or at some time has been, in force with respect to it a specific planning permission for its development; and

(b) that development, if carried out, would involve or have involved its use for the purpose of the carrying on of the statutory undertakers' undertaking.

(4) Land falls within this subsection if—

1968 c. 73.
1969 c. 35.
1986 c. 44.
1986 c. 31.
1989 c. 15.

(a) the undertakers' interest in the land was acquired by them as the result of a transfer under the provisions of the Transport Act 1968, the Transport (London) Act 1969, the Gas Act 1986, the Airports Act 1986 or the Water Act 1989 from other statutory undertakers; and

(b) immediately before transfer the land was operational land of those other undertakers.

(5) A specific planning permission for the purpose of subsection (3)(a) is a planning permission—

(a) granted on an application in that behalf made under Part III; or

(b) granted by provisions of a development order granting planning permission generally for development which has received specific parliamentary approval; or

(c) granted by a special development order in respect of development specifically described in the order; or

(d) deemed to be granted by virtue of a direction of a government department under section 90(1).

(6) In subsection (5)—

(a) the reference in paragraph (a) to Part III includes a reference to Part III of the 1971 Act and the enactments in force before the commencement of that Act and replaced by Part III of it; and

(b) the reference in paragraph (b) to development which has received specific parliamentary approval is a reference to development authorised—

(i) by a local or private Act of Parliament, PART XI

(ii) by an order approved by both Houses of Parliament; or

(iii) by an order which has been brought into operation in accordance with the provisions of the Statutory Orders (Special Procedure) Act 1945, 1945 c. 18.

being an Act or order which designates specifically both the nature of the development authorised by it and the land upon which it may be carried out;

(c) the reference in paragraph (d) to section 90(1) includes a reference to section 40 of the 1971 Act, section 41 of the 1962 Act and section 35 of the 1947 Act.

(7) This section shall not apply to land in the case of which an interest of the Postmaster General's vested in the Post Office by virtue of section 16 of the Post Office Act 1969. 1969 c. 49.

(8) Where an interest in land is held by the Civil Aviation Authority this section shall not apply for the purpose of determining whether the land is operational land in relation to the Authority for the purposes of this Act.

Meaning of "the appropriate Minister".

265.—(1) Subject to the following provisions of this section, in this Act "the appropriate Minister" means—

(a) in relation to statutory undertakers carrying on any railway, light railway, tramway, road transport, dock, harbour, pier or lighthouse undertaking, the Civil Aviation Authority or a relevant airport operator (within the meaning of Part V of the Airports Act 1986), the Secretary of State for Transport; 1986 c. 31.

(b) in relation to statutory undertakers carrying on an undertaking for the supply of hydraulic power, the Secretary of State for Energy;

(c) in relation to the Post Office, the Secretary of State for Trade and Industry; and

(d) in relation to any other statutory undertakers, the Secretary of State for the Environment.

(2) For the purposes of sections 170(12), 266 to 280, 325(9) and 336(2) and (3) and Part II of Schedule 8, "the appropriate Minister", in relation to a public gas supplier or a holder of a licence under section 6 of the Electricity Act 1989, means the Secretary of State for Energy. 1989 c. 29.

(3) For the purposes of sections 170(12), 266 to 280, 325(9) and 336(2) and (3) and Part II of Schedule 8 and Schedule 14 "the appropriate Minister"—

(a) in relation to the National Rivers Authority, means the Secretary of State or the Minister of Agriculture, Fisheries and Food; and

(b) in relation to a water or sewerage undertaker, means the Secretary of State.

PART XI

(4) References in this Act to the Secretary of State and the appropriate Minister—

(a) if the appropriate Minister is not the one concerned as the Secretary of State, shall be construed as references to the Secretary of State and the appropriate Minister; and

(b) if the one concerned as the Secretary of State is also the appropriate Minister, shall be construed as references to him alone,

and similarly with references to a Minister and the appropriate Minister and with any provision requiring the Secretary of State to act jointly with the appropriate Minister.

Application of Part III to statutory undertakers

Applications for planning permission by statutory undertakers.

266.—(1) Where—

(a) an application for planning permission to develop land to which this subsection applies is made by statutory undertakers and is referred to the Secretary of State under Part III; or

(b) an appeal is made to the Secretary of State under that Part from the decision on such an application; or

(c) such an application is deemed to be made under subsection (5) of section 177 on an appeal under section 174 by statutory undertakers,

the application or appeal shall be dealt with by the Secretary of State and the appropriate Minister.

(2) Subsection (1) applies—

(a) to operational land; and

(b) to land in which the statutory undertakers hold or propose to acquire an interest with a view to its being used for the purpose of carrying on their undertaking, where the planning permission, if granted on the application or appeal, would be for development involving the use of the land for that purpose.

(3) An application for planning permission which is deemed to have been made by virtue of section 196(6) shall be determined by the Secretary of State and the appropriate Minister.

(4) Subject to the provisions of this Part as to compensation, the provisions of this Act shall apply to an application which is dealt with under this section by the Secretary of State and the appropriate Minister as if it had been dealt with by the Secretary of State.

(5) Subsection (2)(b) shall have effect in relation to the Civil Aviation Authority as if for the reference to development involving the use of land for the purpose of carrying on the Civil Aviation Authority's undertaking there were substituted a reference to development involving the use of land for such of the purposes of carrying on that undertaking as may be prescribed by the appropriate Minister.

Conditional grants of planning permission.

267. Notwithstanding anything in Part III, planning permission to develop operational land of statutory undertakers shall not, except with their consent, be granted subject to conditions requiring—

(a) that any buildings or works authorised by the permission shall be removed, or

(b) that any use of the land so authorised shall be discontinued,

at the end of a specified period.

Development requiring authorisation of government department.

268.—(1) The Secretary of State and the appropriate Minister shall not be required under section 266(1) to deal with an application for planning permission for the development of operational land if the authorisation of a government department is required in respect of that development.

(2) Subsection (1) does not apply where the relevant authorisation has been granted without any direction as to the grant of planning permission.

(3) For the purposes of this section development shall be taken to be authorised by a government department if—

(a) any consent, authority or approval to or for the development is granted by the department in pursuance of an enactment;

(b) a compulsory purchase order is confirmed by the department authorising the purchase of land for the purpose of the development;

(c) consent is granted by the department to the appropriation of land for the purpose of the development or the acquisition of land by agreement for that purpose;

(d) authority is given by the department for the borrowing of money for the purpose of the development, or for the application for that purpose of any money not otherwise so applicable; or

(e) any undertaking is given by the department to pay a grant in respect of the development in accordance with an enactment authorising the payment of such grants,

and references in this section to the authorisation of a government department shall be construed accordingly.

Revocation or modification of permission to develop operational land.

269. In relation to any planning permission granted on the application of statutory undertakers for the development of operational land, the provisions of Part III with respect to the revocation and modification of planning permission shall have effect as if for any reference in them to the Secretary of State there were substituted a reference to the Secretary of State and the appropriate Minister.

Order requiring discontinuance of use etc. of operational land.

270. The provisions of Part III with respect to the making of orders—

(a) requiring the discontinuance of any use of land;

(b) imposing conditions on the continuance of it; or

(c) requiring buildings or works on land to be altered or removed,

and the provisions of Schedule 9 with respect to the making of orders under that Schedule shall have effect in relation to operational land of statutory undertakers as if for any reference in them to the Secretary of State there were substituted a reference to the Secretary of State and the appropriate Minister.

PART XI

Extinguishment of rights of statutory undertakers, etc.

Extinguishment of rights of statutory undertakers: preliminary notices. 1990 c. 9.

271.—(1) This section applies where any land has been acquired by a Minister, a local authority or statutory undertakers under Part IX of this Act or Chapter V of Part I of the Planning (Listed Buildings and Conservation Areas) Act 1990 or compulsorily under any other enactment or has been appropriated by a local authority for planning purposes, and—

(a) there subsists over that land a right vested in or belonging to statutory undertakers for the purpose of the carrying on of their undertaking, being a right of way or a right of laying down, erecting, continuing or maintaining apparatus on, under or over the land; or

(b) there is on, under or over the land apparatus vested in or belonging to statutory undertakers for the purpose of the carrying on of their undertaking.

(2) If the acquiring or appropriating authority is satisfied that the extinguishment of the right or, as the case may be, the removal of the apparatus, is necessary for the purpose of carrying out any development with a view to which the land was acquired or appropriated, they may serve on the statutory undertakers a notice—

(a) stating that at the end of the relevant period the right will be extinguished; or

(b) requiring that before the end of that period the apparatus shall be removed.

(3) The statutory undertakers on whom a notice is served under subsection (2) may, before the end of the period of 28 days from the date of service of the notice, serve a counter-notice on the acquiring or appropriating authority—

(a) stating that they object to all or any of the provisions of the notice; and

(b) specifying the grounds of their objection.

(4) If no counter-notice is served under subsection (3)—

(a) any right to which the notice relates shall be extinguished at the end of the relevant period; and

(b) if at the end of that period any requirement of the notice as to the removal of any apparatus has not been complied with, the acquiring or appropriating authority may remove the apparatus and dispose of it in any way the authority may think fit.

(5) If a counter-notice is served under subsection (3) on a local authority or on statutory undertakers, the authority or undertakers may either—

(a) withdraw the notice (without prejudice to the service of a further notice); or

(b) apply to the Secretary of State and the appropriate Minister for an order under this section embodying the provisions of the notice, with or without modification.

(6) If a counter-notice is served under subsection (3) on a Minister—

(a) he may withdraw the notice (without prejudice to the service of a further notice); or

(b) he and the appropriate Minister may make an order under this section embodying the provisions of the notice, with or without modification.

(7) In this section any reference to the appropriation of land for planning purposes shall be construed in accordance with section 246(1) as if this section were in Part IX.

(8) For the purposes of this section the relevant period, in relation to a notice served in respect of any right or apparatus, is the period of 28 days from the date of service of the notice or such longer period as may be specified in it in relation to that right or apparatus.

Extinguishment of rights of telecommunications code system operators: preliminary notices.

1990 c. 9.

272.—(1) This section applies where any land has been acquired by a Minister, a local authority or statutory undertakers under Part IX of this Act or under Chapter V of Part I of the Planning (Listed Buildings and Conservation Areas) Act 1990 or compulsorily under any other enactment or has been appropriated by a local authority for planning purposes, and—

(a) there subsists over that land a right conferred by or in accordance with the telecommunications code on the operator of a telecommunications code system, being a right of way or a right of laying down, erecting, continuing or maintaining apparatus on, under or over the land; or

(b) there is on, under or over the land telecommunication apparatus kept installed for the purposes of any such system.

(2) If the acquiring or appropriating authority is satisfied that the extinguishment of the right or, as the case may be, the removal of the apparatus is necessary for the purpose of carrying out any development with a view to which the land was acquired or appropriated, they may serve on the operator of the telecommunications code system a notice—

(a) stating that at the end of the relevant period the right will be extinguished; or

(b) requiring that before the end of that period the apparatus shall be removed.

(3) The operator of the telecommunications code system on whom a notice is served under subsection (2) may, before the end of the period of 28 days from the date of service of the notice, serve a counter-notice on the acquiring or appropriating authority—

(a) stating that he objects to all or any of the provisions of the notice; and

(b) specifying the grounds of his objection.

(4) If no counter-notice is served under subsection (3)—

(a) any right to which the notice relates shall be extinguished at the end of the relevant period; and

(b) if at the end of that period any requirement of the notice as to the removal of any apparatus has not been complied with, the acquiring or appropriating authority may remove the apparatus and dispose of it in any way the authority may think fit.

(5) If a counter-notice is served under subsection (3) on a local authority or on statutory undertakers, the authority or undertakers may either—

PART XI

(a) withdraw the notice (without prejudice to the service of a further notice); or

(b) apply to the Secretary of State and the Secretary of State for Trade and Industry for an order under this section embodying the provisions of the notice, with or without modification.

(6) If a counter-notice is served under subsection (3) on a Minister—

(a) he may withdraw the notice (without prejudice to the service of a further notice); or

(b) he and the Secretary of State for Trade and Industry may make an order under this section embodying the provisions of the notice, with or without modification.

(7) In this section any reference to the appropriation of land for planning purposes shall be construed in accordance with section 246(1) as if this section were in Part IX.

(8) For the purposes of this section the relevant period, in relation to a notice served in respect of any right or apparatus, is the period of 28 days from the date of service of the notice or such longer period as may be specified in it in relation to that right or apparatus.

Notice for same purposes as ss. 271 and 272 but given by undertakers to developing authority.

273.—(1) Subject to the provisions of this section, where land has been acquired or appropriated as mentioned in section 271(1), and—

(a) there is on, under or over the land any apparatus vested in or belonging to statutory undertakers; and

(b) the undertakers claim that development to be carried out on the land is such as to require, on technical or other grounds connected with the carrying on of their undertaking, the removal or re-siting of the apparatus affected by the development,

the undertakers may serve on the acquiring or appropriating authority a notice claiming the right to enter on the land and carry out such works for the removal or re-siting of the apparatus or any part of it as may be specified in the notice.

(2) No notice under this section shall be served later than 21 days after the beginning of the development of land which has been acquired or appropriated as mentioned in section 271(1).

(3) Where a notice is served under this section, the authority on whom it is served may, before the end of the period of 28 days from the date of service, serve on the statutory undertakers a counter-notice—

(a) stating that they object to all or any of the provisions of the notice; and

(b) specifying the grounds of their objection.

(4) If no counter-notice is served under subsection (3), the statutory undertakers shall, after the end of that period, have the rights claimed in their notice.

(5) If a counter-notice is served under subsection (3), the statutory undertakers who served the notice under this section may either withdraw it or may apply to the Secretary of State and the appropriate Minister for an order under this section conferring on the undertakers the rights claimed in the notice or such modified rights as the Secretary of State and the appropriate Minister think it expedient to confer on them.

PART XI

(6) Where, by virtue of this section or of an order of Ministers under it, statutory undertakers have the right to execute works for the removal or re-siting of apparatus, they may arrange with the acquiring or appropriating authority for the works to be carried out by that authority, under the superintendence of the undertakers, instead of by the undertakers themselves.

(7) In subsection (1)(a), the reference to apparatus vested in or belonging to statutory undertakers shall include a reference to telecommunication apparatus kept installed for the purposes of a telecommunications code system.

(8) For the purposes of subsection (7), in this section—

(a) references (except in subsection (1)(a)) to statutory undertakers shall have effect as references to the operator of any such system; and

(b) references to the appropriate Minister shall have effect as references to the Secretary of State for Trade and Industry.

Orders under ss. 271 and 272.

274.—(1) Where a Minister and the appropriate Minister propose to make an order under section 271(6) or 272(6), they shall prepare a draft of the order.

(2) Before making an order under subsection (5) or (6) of section 271, or under subsection (5) or (6) of section 272, the Ministers proposing to make the order shall give the statutory undertakers or, as the case may be, the operator of the telecommunications code system on whom notice was served under subsection (2) of section 271 or, as the case may be, under subsection (2) of section 272 an opportunity of objecting to the application for, or proposal to make, the order.

(3) If any such objection is made, before making the order the Ministers shall consider the objection and give those statutory undertakers or, as the case may be, that operator (and, in a case falling within subsection (5) of either of those sections, the local authority or statutory undertakers on whom the counter-notice was served) an opportunity of appearing before, and being heard by, a person appointed for the purpose by the Secretary of State and the appropriate Minister.

(4) After complying with subsections (2) and (3) the Ministers may, if they think fit, make the order in accordance with the application or, as the case may be, in accordance with the draft order, either with or without modification.

(5) Where an order is made under section 271 or 272—

(a) any right to which the order relates shall be extinguished at the end of the period specified in that behalf in the order; and

(b) if, at the end of the period so specified in relation to any apparatus, any requirement of the order as to the removal of the apparatus has not been complied with, the acquiring or appropriating authority may remove the apparatus and dispose of it in any way the authority may think fit.

(6) In this section references to the appropriate Minister shall in the case of an order under section 272 be taken as references to the Secretary of State for Trade and Industry.

PART XI

Extension or modification of statutory undertakers' functions

Extension or modification of functions of statutory' undertakers.

275.—(1) The powers conferred by this section shall be exercisable where, on a representation made by statutory undertakers, it appears to the Secretary of State and the appropriate Minister to be expedient that the powers and duties of those undertakers should be extended or modified, in order—

(a) to secure the provision of services which would not otherwise be provided, or satisfactorily provided, for any purpose in connection with which a local authority or Minister may be authorised under Part IX of this Act or under Chapter V of Part I of the Planning (Listed Buildings and Conservation Areas) Act 1990 to acquire land or in connection with which any such person may compulsorily acquire land under any other enactment; or

1990 c. 9.

(b) to facilitate an adjustment of the carrying on of the undertaking necessitated by any of the acts and events mentioned in subsection (2).

(2) The said acts and events are—

(a) the acquisition under Part IX of this Act or that Chapter or compulsorily under any other enactment of any land in which an interest was held, or which was used, for the purpose of the carrying on of the undertaking of the statutory undertakers in question;

(b) the extinguishment of a right or the imposition of any requirement by virtue of section 271 or 272;

(c) a decision on an application made by the statutory undertakers for planning permission to develop any such land as is mentioned in paragraph (a);

(d) the revocation or modification of planning permission granted on any such application;

(e) the making of an order under section 102 or paragraph 1 of Schedule 9 in relation to any such land.

(3) The powers conferred by this section shall also be exercisable where, on a representation made by a local authority or Minister, it appears to the Secretary of State and the appropriate Minister to be expedient that the powers and duties of statutory undertakers should be extended or modified in order to secure the provision of new services, or the extension of existing services, for any purpose in connection with which the local authority or Minister making the representation may be authorised under Part IX of this Act or under Chapter V of Part I of the Planning (Listed Buildings and Conservation Areas) Act 1990 to acquire land or in connection with which the local authority or Minister may compulsorily acquire land under any other enactment.

(4) Where the powers conferred by this section are exercisable, the Secretary of State and the appropriate Minister may, if they think fit, by order provide for such extension or modification of the powers and duties of the statutory undertakers as appears to them to be requisite in order—

(a) to secure the services in question, as mentioned in subsection (1)(a) or (3), or

(b) to secure the adjustment in question, as mentioned in subsection (1)(b),

as the case may be.

(5) Without prejudice to the generality of subsection (4), an order under this section may make provision—

(a) for empowering the statutory undertakers—

(i) to acquire (whether compulsorily or by agreement) any land specified in the order, and

(ii) to erect or construct any buildings or works so specified;

(b) for applying in relation to the acquisition of any such land or the construction of any such works enactments relating to the acquisition of land and the construction of works;

(c) where it has been represented that the making of the order is expedient for the purposes mentioned in subsection (1)(a) or (3), for giving effect to such financial arrangements between the local authority or Minister and the statutory undertakers as they may agree, or as, in default of agreement, may be determined to be equitable in such manner and by such tribunal as may be specified in the order;

(d) for such incidental and supplemental matters as appear to the Secretary of State and the appropriate Minister to be expedient for the purposes of the order.

Procedure in relation to orders under s. 275.

276.—(1) As soon as possible after making such a representation as is mentioned in subsection (1) or subsection (3) of section 275 the statutory undertakers, the local authority or Minister making the representation shall—

(a) publish notice of the representation; and

(b) if the Secretary of State and the appropriate Minister so direct, serve a similar notice on such persons, or persons of such classes, as they may direct.

(2) A notice under subsection (1)—

(a) shall be published in such form and manner as the Secretary of State and the appropriate Minister may direct;

(b) shall give such particulars as they may direct of the matters to which the representation relates; and

(c) shall specify the time within which, and the manner in which, objections to the making of an order on the representation may be made.

(3) Orders under section 275 shall be subject to special parliamentary procedure.

Relief of statutory undertakers from obligations rendered impracticable.

277.—(1) Where, on a representation made by statutory undertakers, the appropriate Minister is satisfied that the fulfilment of any obligation incurred by those undertakers in connection with the carrying on of their undertaking has been rendered impracticable by an act or event to which this subsection applies, the appropriate Minister may, if he thinks fit, by

PART XI

order direct that the statutory undertakers shall be relieved of the fulfilment of that obligation, either absolutely or to such extent as may be specified in the order.

(2) Subsection (1) applies to the following acts and events—

(a) the compulsory acquisition under Part IX of this Act or under Chapter V of Part I of the Planning (Listed Buildings and Conservation Areas) Act 1990 or under any other enactment of any land in which an interest was held, or which was used, for the purpose of the carrying on of the undertaking of the statutory undertakers; and

1990 c. 9.

(b) the acts and events specified in section 275(2)(b) to (e).

(3) The appropriate Minister may direct statutory undertakers who have made a representation to him under subsection (1) to publicise it in either or both of the following ways—

(a) by publishing in such form and manner as he may direct a notice, giving such particulars as he may direct of the matters to which the representation relates and specifying the time within which, and the manner in which, objections to the making of an order on the representation may be made;

(b) by serving such a notice on such persons, or persons of such classes, as he may direct.

(4) The statutory undertakers shall comply with any direction given to them under subsection (3) as soon as possible after the making of the representation under subsection (1).

(5) If any objection to the making of an order under this section is duly made and is not withdrawn before the order is made, the order shall be subject to special parliamentary procedure.

(6) Immediately after an order is made under this section by the appropriate Minister, he shall—

(a) publish a notice stating that the order has been made and naming a place where a copy of it may be seen at all reasonable hours; and

(b) serve a similar notice—

(i) on any person who duly made an objection to the order and has sent to the appropriate Minister a request in writing to serve him with the notice required by this subsection, specifying an address for service; and

(ii) on such other persons (if any) as the appropriate Minister thinks fit.

(7) Subject to subsection (8), and to the provisions of Part XII, an order under this section shall become operative on the date on which the notice required by subsection (6) is first published.

(8) Where in accordance with subsection (5) the order is subject to special parliamentary procedure, subsection (7) shall not apply.

PART XI

Objections to orders under ss. 275 and 277.

278.—(1) For the purposes of sections 275 to 277, an objection to the making of an order shall not be treated as duly made unless—

(a) the objection is made within the time and in the manner specified in the notice required by section 276 or, as the case may be, section 277; and

(b) a statement in writing of the grounds of the objection is comprised in or submitted with the objection.

(2) Where an objection to the making of such an order is duly made in accordance with subsection (1) and is not withdrawn, the following provisions of this section shall have effect in relation to it.

(3) Unless the appropriate Minister decides without regard to the objection not to make the order, or decides to make a modification which is agreed to by the objector as meeting the objection, before he makes a final decision he—

(a) shall consider the grounds of the objection as set out in the statement; and

(b) may, if he thinks fit, require the objector to submit within a specified period a further statement in writing as to any of the matters to which the objection relates.

(4) In so far as the appropriate Minister, after considering the grounds of the objection as set out in the original statement and in any such further statement, is satisfied that the objection relates to a matter which can be dealt with in the assessment of compensation, the appropriate Minister may treat the objection as irrelevant for the purpose of making a final decision.

(5) If—

(a) after considering the grounds of the objection as so set out, the appropriate Minister is satisfied that, for the purpose of making a final decision, he is sufficiently informed as to the matters to which the objection relates; or

(b) in a case where a further statement has been required, it is not submitted within the specified period,

the appropriate Minister may make a final decision without further investigation as to those matters.

(6) Subject to subsections (4) and (5), before making a final decision the appropriate Minister shall give the objector an opportunity of appearing before, and being heard by, a person appointed for the purpose by the appropriate Minister.

(7) If the objector takes that opportunity, the appropriate Minister shall give an opportunity of appearing and being heard on the same occasion to the statutory undertakers, local authority or Minister on whose representation the order is proposed to be made, and to any other persons to whom it appears to him to be expedient to give such an opportunity.

(8) Notwithstanding anything in the previous provisions of this section, if it appears to the appropriate Minister that the matters to which the objection relates are such as to require investigation by public local inquiry before he makes a final decision, he shall cause such an inquiry to be held.

PART XI

(9) Where the appropriate Minister determines to cause such an inquiry to be held, any of the requirements of subsections (3) to (7) to which effect has not been given at the time of that determination shall be dispensed with.

(10) In this section any reference to making a final decision in relation to an order is a reference to deciding whether to make the order or what modification (if any) ought to be made.

(11) In the application of this section to an order under section 275, any reference to the appropriate Minister shall be construed as a reference to the Secretary of State and the appropriate Minister.

Compensation

Right to compensation in respect of certain decisions and orders.

279.—(l) Statutory undertakers shall, subject to the following provisions of this Part, be entitled to compensation from the local planning authority—

(a) in respect of any decision made in accordance with section 266 by which planning permission to develop operational land of those undertakers is refused or is granted subject to conditions where—

(i) planning permission for that development would have been granted by a development order but for a direction given under such an order that planning permission so granted should not apply to the development; and

(ii) it is not development which has received specific parliamentary approval (within the meaning of section 264(6));

(b) in respect of any order under section 97, as modified by section 269, by which planning permission which was granted on the application of those undertakers for the development of any such land is revoked or modified.

(2) Where by virtue of section 271—

(a) any right vested in or belonging to statutory undertakers is extinguished; or

(b) any requirement is imposed on statutory undertakers,

those undertakers shall be entitled to compensation from the acquiring or appropriating authority at whose instance the right was extinguished or the requirement imposed.

(3) Where by virtue of section 272—

(a) any right vested in or belonging to an operator of a telecommunications code system is extinguished; or

(b) any requirement is imposed on such an operator,

the operator shall be entitled to compensation from the acquiring or appropriating authority at whose instance the right was extinguished or the requirement imposed.

(4) Where—

(a) works are carried out for the removal or re-siting of statutory undertakers' apparatus; and

(b) the undertakers have the right to carry out those works by virtue of section 273 or an order of Ministers under that section,

the undertakers shall be entitled to compensation from the acquiring or appropriating authority.

(5) Subsection (1) shall not apply in respect of a decision or order if—

(a) it relates to land acquired by the statutory undertakers after 7th January 1947; and

(b) the Secretary of State and the appropriate Minister include in the decision or order a direction that subsection (1) shall not apply to it.

(6) The Secretary of State and the appropriate Minister may only give a direction under subsection (5) if they are satisfied, having regard to the nature, situation and existing development of the land and of any neighbouring land, and to any other material considerations, that it is unreasonable that compensation should be recovered in respect of the decision or order in question.

(7) For the purposes of this section the conditions referred to in sections 91 and 92 shall be disregarded.

Measure of compensation to statutory undertakers, etc.

280.—(1) Where statutory undertakers are entitled to compensation—

(a) as mentioned in subsection (1), (2) or (4) of section 279;

(b) under the provisions of section 115 in respect of an order made under section 102 or paragraph 1, 3, 5 or 6 of Schedule 9, as modified by section 270; or

(c) in respect of a compulsory acquisition of land which has been acquired by those undertakers for the purposes of their undertaking, where the first-mentioned acquisition is effected under a compulsory purchase order confirmed or made without the appropriate Minister's certificate,

or the operator of a telecommunications code system is entitled to compensation as mentioned in section 279(3), the amount of the compensation shall (subject to section 281) be an amount calculated in accordance with this section.

(2) Subject to subsections (4) to (6), that amount shall be the aggregate of—

(a) the amount of any expenditure reasonably incurred in acquiring land, providing apparatus, erecting buildings or doing work for the purpose of any adjustment of the carrying on of the undertaking or, as the case may be, the running of the telecommunications code system rendered necessary by the proceeding giving rise to compensation (a "business adjustment");

(b) the appropriate amount for loss of profits; and

(c) where the compensation is under section 279(2) or (3), and is in respect of the imposition of a requirement to remove apparatus, the amount of any expenditure reasonably incurred by the statutory undertakers or, as the case may be, the operator in complying with the requirement, reduced by the value after removal of the apparatus removed.

PART XI

(3) In subsection (2) "the appropriate amount for loss of profits" means—

(a) where a business adjustment is made, the aggregate of—

(i) the estimated amount of any decrease in net receipts from the carrying on of the undertaking or, as the case may be, the running of the telecommunications code system pending the adjustment, in so far as the decrease is directly attributable to the proceeding giving rise to compensation; and

(ii) such amount as appears reasonable compensation for any estimated decrease in net receipts from the carrying on of the undertaking or, as the case may be, the running of the telecommunications code system in the period after the adjustment has been completed, in so far as the decrease is directly attributable to the adjustment;

(b) where no business adjustment is made, such amount as appears reasonable compensation for any estimated decrease in net receipts from the carrying on of the undertaking or, as the case may be, the running of the telecommunications code system which is directly attributable to the proceeding giving rise to compensation.

(4) Where a business adjustment is made, the aggregate amount mentioned in subsection (2) shall be reduced by such amount (if any) as appears to the Lands Tribunal to be appropriate to offset—

(a) the estimated value of any property (whether moveable or immoveable) belonging to the statutory undertakers or the operator and used for the carrying on of their undertaking or, as the case may be, the running of the telecommunications code system which in consequence of the adjustment ceases to be so used, in so far as the value of the property has not been taken into account under paragraph (c) of that subsection; and

(b) the estimated amount of any increase in net receipts from the carrying on of the undertaking or the running of the telecommunications code system in the period after the adjustment has been completed, in so far as that amount has not been taken into account in determining the amount mentioned in paragraph (b) of that subsection and is directly attributable to the adjustment.

(5) Where a business adjustment is made the aggregate amount mentioned in subsection (2) shall be further reduced by any amount which appears to the Lands Tribunal to be appropriate, having regard to any increase in the capital value of immoveable property belonging to the statutory undertakers or the operator which is directly attributable to the adjustment, allowance being made for any reduction made under subsection (4)(b).

(6) Where—

(a) the compensation is under section 279(4); and

(b) the acquiring or appropriating authority carry out the works,

then, in addition to any reduction falling to be made under subsection (4) or (5), the aggregate amount mentioned in subsection (2) shall be reduced by the actual cost to the authority of carrying out the works.

(7) References in this section to a decrease in net receipts shall be construed as references—

(a) to the amount by which a balance of receipts over expenditure is decreased;

(b) to the amount by which a balance of expenditure over receipts is increased; or

(c) where a balance of receipts over expenditure is converted into a balance of expenditure over receipts, to the aggregate of the two balances;

and references to an increase in net receipts shall be construed accordingly.

(8) In this section—

"proceeding giving rise to compensation" means—

(a) except in relation to compensation under section 279(4), the particular action (that is to say, the decision, order, extinguishment of a right, imposition of a requirement or acquisition) in respect of which compensation falls to be assessed, as distinct from any development or project in connection with which that action may have been taken;

(b) in relation to compensation under section 279(4), the circumstances making it necessary for the apparatus in question to be removed or re-sited;

"the appropriate Minister's certificate" means such a certificate as is mentioned in section 16 of or paragraph 3 of Schedule 3 to the Acquisition of Land Act 1981. 1981 c. 67.

Exclusion of s. 280 at option of statutory undertakers.

281.—(1) Where statutory undertakers are entitled to compensation in respect of such a compulsory acquisition as is mentioned in section 280(1)(c), the statutory undertakers may by notice in writing under this section elect that the compensation shall be ascertained in accordance with the enactments (other than rule (5) of the rules set out in section 5 of the Land Compensation Act 1961) which would be applicable apart from section 280. 1961 c. 33.

(2) If the statutory undertakers so elect the compensation shall be ascertained accordingly.

(3) An election under this section may be made either in respect of the whole of the land comprised in the compulsory acquisition in question or in respect of part of that land.

(4) Any notice under this section shall be given to the acquiring authority before the end of the period of two months from the date of service of notice to treat in respect of the interest of the statutory undertakers.

Procedure for assessing compensation.

282.—(1) Where the amount of any such compensation as is mentioned in subsection (1) of section 280 falls to be ascertained in accordance with the provisions of that section, the compensation shall, in default of agreement, be assessed by the Lands Tribunal, if apart from this section it would not fall to be so assessed.

PART XI

1961 c.33.

(2) For the purposes of any proceedings arising before the Lands Tribunal in respect of compensation falling to be ascertained as mentioned in subsection (1), the provisions of sections 2 and 4 of the Land Compensation Act 1961 shall apply as they apply to proceedings on a question referred to the Tribunal under section 1 of that Act, but with the substitution in section 4 of that Act, for references to the acquiring authority, of references to the person from whom the compensation is claimed.

Advertisements

Display of advertisements on operational land.

283. Sections 266 to 270 and 279(1), (5) and (6) do not apply in relation to the display of advertisements on operational land of statutory undertakers.

PART XII

VALIDITY

Validity of development plans and certain orders, decisions and directions.

284.—(1) Except in so far as may be provided by this Part, the validity of—

(a) a structure plan, local plan or unitary development plan or any alteration, repeal or replacement of any such plan, whether before or after the plan, alteration, repeal or replacement has been approved or adopted; or

(b) a simplified planning zone scheme or an alteration of such a scheme, whether before or after the adoption or approval of the scheme or alteration; or

(c) an order under any provision of Part X except section 251(1), whether before or after the order has been made; or

(d) an order under section 277, whether before or after the order has been made; or

(e) any such order as is mentioned in subsection (2), whether before or after it has been confirmed; or

(f) any such action on the part of the Secretary of State as is mentioned in subsection (3),

shall not be questioned in any legal proceedings whatsoever.

(2) The orders referred to in subsection (1)(e) are—

(a) any order under section 97 or under the provisions of that section as applied by or under any other provision of this Act;

(b) any order under section 102;

(c) any tree preservation order;

(d) any order made in pursuance of section 221(5);

(e) any order under paragraph 1, 3, 5 or 6 of Schedule 9.

(3) The action referred to in subsection (1)(f) is action on the part of the Secretary of State of any of the following descriptions—

(a) any decision on an application for planning permission referred to him under section 77;

(b) any decision on an appeal under section 78;

(c) the giving of any direction under section 80;

PART XII

(d) any decision to confirm a completion notice under section 95;

(e) any decision to grant planning permission under paragraph (a) of section 177(1) or to discharge a condition or limitation under paragraph (b) of that section;

(f) any decision to confirm or not to confirm a purchase notice including—

(i) any decision not to confirm such a notice in respect of part of the land to which it relates, or

(ii) any decision to grant any permission, or give any direction, instead of confirming such a notice, either wholly or in part;

(g) any decision on an application for an established use certificate referred to the Secretary of State under subsection (5) of section 192 or on an appeal under section 195(1);

(h) any decision relating—

(i) to an application for consent under a tree preservation order,

(ii) to an application for consent under any regulations made in accordance with section 220 or 221, or

(iii) to any certificate or direction under any such order or regulations,

whether it is a decision on appeal or a decision on an application referred to the Secretary of State for determination in the first instance.

(4) Nothing in this section shall affect the exercise of any jurisdiction of any court in respect of any refusal or failure on the part of the Secretary of State to take any such action as is mentioned in subsection (3).

Validity of enforcement notices and similar notices.

285.—(1) Subject to the provisions of this section, the validity of an enforcement notice shall not, except by way of an appeal under Part VII, be questioned in any proceedings whatsoever on any of the grounds on which such an appeal may be brought.

(2) Subsection (1) shall not apply to proceedings brought under section 179(6) to (8) against a person who—

(a) has held an interest in the land since before the enforcement notice was issued under that Part;

(b) did not have a copy of the enforcement notice served on him under that Part; and

(c) satisfies the court—

(i) that he did not know and could not reasonably have been expected to know that the enforcement notice had been issued; and

(ii) that his interests have been substantially prejudiced by the failure to serve him with a copy of it.

(3) Subject to subsection (4), the validity of a notice which has been served under section 215 on the owner and occupier of the land shall not, except by way of an appeal under Chapter II of Part VIII, be questioned in any proceedings whatsoever on either of the grounds specified in section 217(1)(a) or (b).

PART XII

(4) Subsection (3) shall not prevent the validity of such a notice being questioned on either of those grounds in proceedings brought under section 216 against a person on whom the notice was not served, but who has held an interest in the land since before the notice was served on the owner and occupier of the land, if he did not appeal against the notice under that Chapter.

(5) The validity of a notice purporting to be an enforcement notice shall not depend on whether any non-compliance to which the notice relates was a non-compliance with conditions, or with limitations, or with both.

(6) Any reference in such a notice to non-compliance with conditions or limitations (whether both expressions are used in the notice or only one of them) shall be construed as a reference to non-compliance with conditions, or with limitations, or with both conditions and limitations, as the case may require.

Challenges to validity on ground of authority's powers.

286.—(1) The validity of any permission, determination or certificate granted, made or issued or purporting to have been granted, made or issued by a local planning authority in respect of—

(a) an application for planning permission;

(b) an application for determining under section 64 whether an application for such permission is required;

(c) an application for an established use certificate under section 192;

(d) an application for consent to the display of advertisements under section 220; or

(e) a determination under section 302 or Schedule 15,

shall not be called in question in any legal proceedings, or in any proceedings under this Act which are not legal proceedings, on the ground that the permission, determination or certificate should have been granted, made or given by some other local planning authority.

(2) The validity of any order under section 97 revoking or modifying planning permission, any order under section 102 or paragraph 1 of Schedule 9 requiring discontinuance of use, or imposing conditions on continuance of use, or requiring the alteration or removal of buildings or works, or any enforcement notice under section 172 or stop notice under section 183, being an order or notice purporting to have been made, issued or served by a local planning authority, shall not be called in question in any such proceedings on the ground—

(a) in the case of an order or notice purporting to have been made, issued or served by a district planning authority, that they failed to comply with paragraph 11(2) of Schedule 1;

(b) in the case of an order or notice purporting to have been made, issued or served by a county planning authority, that they had no power to make, issue or serve it because it did not relate to a county matter within the meaning of that Schedule.

Proceedings for questioning validity of development plans and certain schemes and orders.

287.—(1) If any person aggrieved by a unitary development plan or a local plan or by any alteration, repeal or replacement of any such plan or structure plan, desires to question the validity of the plan or, as the case may be, the alteration, repeal or replacement on the ground—

PART XII

(a) that it is not within the powers conferred by Part II, or

(b) that any requirement of that Part or of any regulations made under it has not been complied with in relation to the approval or adoption of the plan or, as the case may be, its alteration, repeal or replacement,

he may make an application to the High Court under this section.

(2) On any application under this section the High Court—

(a) may by interim order wholly or in part suspend the operation of the plan, or, as the case may be, the alteration, repeal or replacement, either generally or in so far as it affects any property of the applicant, until the final determination of the proceedings;

(b) if satisfied that the plan or, as the case may be, the alteration, repeal or replacement is wholly or to any extent outside the powers conferred by Part II, or that the interests of the applicant have been substantially prejudiced by the failure to comply with any requirement of that Part or of any regulations made under it, may wholly or in part quash the plan or, as the case may be, the alteration, repeal or replacement either generally or in so far as it affects any property of the applicant.

(3) Subsections (1) and (2) shall apply, subject to any necessary modifications, to a simplified planning zone scheme or an alteration of such a scheme or to an order under section 247, 248, 249, 251, 257, 258 or 277 as they apply to any plan or any alteration, repeal or replacement there mentioned.

(4) An application under this section must be made within six weeks from the relevant date.

(5) For the purposes of subsection (4) the relevant date is—

(a) in the case of an application in respect of such a plan as is mentioned in subsection (1), the date of the publication of the first notice of the approval or adoption of the plan, alteration, repeal or replacement required by regulations under section 26 or, as the case may be, section 53,

(b) in the case of an application by virtue of subsection (3) in respect of a simplified planning zone scheme or an alteration of such a scheme, the date of the publication of the first notice of the approval or adoption of the scheme or alteration required by regulations under paragraph 13 of Schedule 7,

(c) in the case of an application by virtue of subsection (3) in respect of an order under section 247, 248, 249, or 251, the date on which the notice required by section 252(10) is first published,

(d) in the case of an application by virtue of subsection (3) in respect of an order under section 257 or 258, the date on which the notice required by paragraph 7 of Schedule 14 is first published in accordance with that paragraph,

(e) in the case of an application by virtue of subsection (3) in respect of an order under section 277, the date on which the notice required by subsection (6) of that section is first published;

but subject, in the case of those orders mentioned in paragraphs (c) and (e) to which section 292 applies, to that section.

PART XII

(6) In their application to simplified planning zone schemes and their alteration, subsections (1) and (2) shall have effect as if they referred to Part III instead of Part II.

Proceedings for questioning the validity of other orders, decisions and directions.

288.—(1) If any person—

(a) is aggrieved by any order to which this section applies and wishes to question the validity of that order on the grounds—

(i) that the order is not within the powers of this Act, or

(ii) that any of the relevant requirements have not been complied with in relation to that order; or

(b) is aggrieved by any action on the part of the Secretary of State to which this section applies and wishes to question the validity of that action on the grounds—

(i) that the action is not within the powers of this Act, or

(ii) that any of the relevant requirements have not been complied with in relation to that action,

he may make an application to the High Court under this section.

(2) Without prejudice to subsection (1), if the authority directly concerned with any order to which this section applies, or with any action on the part of the Secretary of State to which this section applies, wish to question the validity of that order or action on any of the grounds mentioned in subsection (1), the authority may make an application to the High Court under this section.

(3) An application under this section must be made within six weeks from the date on which the order is confirmed (or, in the case of an order under section 97 which takes effect under section 99 without confirmation, the date on which it takes effect) or, as the case may be, the date on which the action is taken.

(4) This section applies to any such order as is mentioned in subsection (2) of section 284 and to any such action on the part of the Secretary of State as is mentioned in subsection (3) of that section.

(5) On any application under this section the High Court—

(a) may, subject to subsection (6), by interim order suspend the operation of the order or action, the validity of which is questioned by the application, until the final determination of the proceedings;

(b) if satisfied that the order or action in question is not within the powers of this Act, or that the interests of the applicant have been substantially prejudiced by a failure to comply with any of the relevant requirements in relation to it, may quash that order or action.

(6) Paragraph (a) of subsection (5) shall not apply to applications questioning the validity of tree preservation orders.

(7) In relation to a tree preservation order, or to an order made in pursuance of section 221(5), the powers conferred on the High Court by subsection (5) shall be exercisable by way of quashing or (where applicable) suspending the operation of the order either in whole or in part, as the court may determine.

(8) References in this section to the confirmation of an order include the confirmation of an order subject to modifications as well as the confirmation of an order in the form in which it was made.

(9) In this section "the relevant requirements", in relation to any order or action to which this section applies, means any requirements of this Act or of the Tribunals and Inquiries Act 1971, or of any order, regulations or rules made under this Act or under that Act which are applicable to that order or action. 1971 c. 62.

(10) Any reference in this section to the authority directly concerned with any order or action to which this section applies—

(a) in relation to any such decision as is mentioned in section 284(3)(f), is a reference to the council on whom the notice in question was served and, in a case where the Secretary of State has modified such a notice, wholly or in part, by substituting another local authority or statutory undertakers for that council, includes a reference to that local authority or those statutory undertakers;

(b) in any other case, is a reference to the authority who made the order in question or made the decision or served the notice to which the proceedings in question relate, or who referred the matter to the Secretary of State, or, where the order or notice in question was made or served by him, the authority named in the order or notice.

Appeals to High Court relating to enforcement notices and notices under s. 207.

289.—(1) Where the Secretary of State gives a decision in proceedings on an appeal under Part VII against an enforcement notice the appellant or the local planning authority or any other person having an interest in the land to which the notice relates may, according as rules of court may provide, either appeal to the High Court against the decision on a point of law or require the Secretary of State to state and sign a case for the opinion of the High Court.

(2) Where the Secretary of State gives a decision in proceedings on an appeal under Part VIII against a notice under section 207, the appellant or the local planning authority or any person (other than the appellant) on whom the notice was served may, according as rules of court may provide, either appeal to the High Court against the decision on a point of law or require the Secretary of State to state and sign a case for the opinion of the High Court.

(3) At any stage of the proceedings on any such appeal as is mentioned in subsection (1), the Secretary of State may state any question of law arising in the course of the proceedings in the form of a special case for the decision of the High Court.

(4) A decision of the High Court on a case stated by virtue of subsection (3) shall be deemed to be a judgment of the court within the meaning of section 16 of the Supreme Court Act 1981 (jurisdiction of the Court of Appeal to hear and determine appeals from any judgment of the High Court). 1981 c. 54.

(5) In relation to any proceedings in the High Court or the Court of Appeal brought by virtue of this section the power to make rules of court shall include power to make rules—

PART XII

(a) prescribing the powers of the High Court or the Court of Appeal with respect to the remitting of the matter with the opinion or direction of the court for re-hearing and determination by the Secretary of State; and

(b) providing for the Secretary of State, either generally or in such circumstances as may be prescribed by the rules, to be treated as a party to any such proceedings and to be entitled to appear and to be heard accordingly.

(6) No appeal to the Court of Appeal shall be brought by virtue of this section except with the leave of the High Court or the Court of Appeal.

(7) In this section "decision" includes a direction or order, and references to the giving of a decision shall be construed accordingly.

Appeals to High Court against decisions under s. 64.

290.—(1) If, in the case of any decision to which this section applies, the person who made the application to which the decision relates or the local planning authority is dissatisfied with the decision in point of law, that person or, as the case may be, the local planning authority may, according as rules of court may provide, either appeal against the decision to the High Court or require the Secretary of State to state and sign a case for the opinion of the High Court.

(2) This section applies to any decision of the Secretary of State—

(a) on an application under section 64 which is referred to the Secretary of State under the provisions of section 77 as applied by that section; or

(b) on an appeal brought under the provisions of section 78 as applied by section 64.

(3) Where an application under section 64 is made as part of an application for planning permission, subsections (1) and (2) shall have effect in relation to that application in so far as it is an application under the said section 64, but not in so far as it is an application for planning permission.

(4) In relation to proceedings in the High Court or the Court of Appeal brought by virtue of this section, the power to make rules of court shall include power to make rules prescribing the powers of the High Court or the Court of Appeal with respect to—

(a) the giving of any decision which might have been given by the Secretary of State;

(b) the remitting of the matter, with the opinion or direction of the court, for re-hearing and determination by the Secretary of State;

(c) the giving of directions to the Secretary of State.

(5) No appeal to the Court of Appeal shall be brought by virtue of this section except with the leave of the High Court or of the Court of Appeal.

(6) Without prejudice to the previous provisions of this section, rules of court in relation to proceedings in the High Court or the Court of Appeal brought by virtue of this section may provide for the Secretary of State, either generally or in such circumstances as may be prescribed by the rules, to be treated as a party to any such proceedings and to be entitled to appear and to be heard accordingly.

PART XII

Special provisions as to decisions relating to statutory undertakers.

291. In relation to any action which—

(a) apart from the provisions of Part XI would fall to be taken by the Secretary of State and, if so taken, would be action falling within section 284(3); but

(b) by virtue of that Part, is required to be taken by the Secretary of State and the appropriate Minister,

the provisions of sections 284 and 288 shall have effect (subject to section 292) as if any reference in those provisions to the Secretary of State were a reference to the Secretary of State and the appropriate Minister.

Special provisions as to orders subject to special parliamentary procedure. 1945 c. 18.

292.—(1) Where an order under section 247, 248, 249 or 277 is subject to special parliamentary procedure, then—

(a) if the order is confirmed by Act of Parliament under section 6 of the Statutory Orders (Special Procedure) Act 1945, sections 284 and 287 shall not apply to the order;

(b) in any other case, section 287 shall have effect in relation to the order as if, in subsection (4) of that section, for the reference to the date there mentioned there were substituted a reference to the date on which the order becomes operative under section 6 of that Act ("the operative date").

(2) Where by virtue of Part XI any such action as is mentioned in section 291 is required to be embodied in an order, and that order is subject to special parliamentary procedure, then—

(a) if the order in which the action is embodied is confirmed by Act of Parliament under section 6 of that Act, sections 284 and 288 shall not apply;

(b) in any other case, section 288 shall apply with the substitution for any reference to the date on which the action is taken of a reference to the operative date.

PART XIII

APPLICATION OF ACT TO CROWN LAND

Preliminary

Preliminary definitions.

293.—(1) In this Part—

"Crown land" means land in which there is a Crown interest or a Duchy interest;

"Crown interest" means an interest belonging to Her Majesty in right of the Crown or belonging to a government department or held in trust for Her Majesty for the purposes of a government department;

"Duchy interest" means an interest belonging to Her Majesty in right of the Duchy of Lancaster or belonging to the Duchy of Cornwall;

"private interest" means an interest which is neither a Crown interest nor a Duchy interest.

PART XIII

(2) For the purposes of this Part "the appropriate authority", in relation to any land—

(a) in the case of land belonging to Her Majesty in right of the Crown and forming part of the Crown Estate, means the Crown Estate Commissioners;

(b) in relation to any other land belonging to Her Majesty in right of the Crown, means the government department having the management of that land;

(c) in relation to land belonging to Her Majesty in right of the Duchy of Lancaster, means the Chancellor of the Duchy;

(d) in relation to land belonging to the Duchy of Cornwall, means such person as the Duke of Cornwall, or the possessor for the time being of the Duchy of Cornwall, appoints;

(e) in the case of land belonging to a government department or held in trust for Her Majesty for the purposes of a government department, means that department.

(3) If any question arises as to what authority is the appropriate authority in relation to any land, that question shall be referred to the Treasury, whose decision shall be final.

(4) A person who is entitled to occupy Crown land by virtue of a licence in writing shall be treated for the purposes of section 296(1)(c), so far as applicable to Parts III, VII and VIII, and sections 294(2) to (7), 295, 299 and 300 as having an interest in land and references in section 299 to the disposal of an interest in Crown land, and in that section and sections 294(2) and 300 to a private interest in such land, shall be construed accordingly.

Application of Act as respects Crown land

Control of development on Crown land: special enforcement notices.

294.—(1) No enforcement notice shall be issued under section 172 in respect of development carried out by or on behalf of the Crown after 1st July 1948 on land which was Crown land at the time when the development was carried out.

(2) The following provisions of this section apply to development of Crown land carried out otherwise than by or on behalf of the Crown at a time when no person is entitled to occupy it by virtue of a private interest.

(3) Where—

(a) it appears to a local planning authority that development to which this subsection applies has taken place in their area, and

(b) they consider it expedient to do so having regard to the provisions of the development plan and to any other material considerations,

they may issue a notice under this section (a "special enforcement notice").

(4) No special enforcement notice shall be issued except with the consent of the appropriate authority.

(5) A special enforcement notice shall specify—

(a) the matters alleged to constitute development to which this section applies; and

(b) the steps which the authority issuing the notice require to be taken for restoring the land to its condition before the development took place or for discontinuing any use of the land which has been instituted by the development.

(6) A special enforcement notice shall also specify—

(a) the date on which it is to take effect ("the specified date"), and

(b) the period within which any such steps as are mentioned in subsection (5)(b) are to be taken.

(7) A special enforcement notice may specify different periods for the taking of different steps.

Supplementary provisions as to special enforcement notices.

295.—(1) Not later than 28 days after the date of the issue of a special enforcement notice and not later than 28 days before the specified date, the local planning authority who issued it shall serve a copy of it—

(a) on the person who carried out the development alleged in the notice;

(b) on any person who is occupying the land when the notice is issued; and

(c) on the appropriate authority.

(2) The local planning authority need not serve a copy of the notice on the person mentioned in subsection (1)(a) if they are unable after reasonable enquiry to identify or trace him.

(3) Any such person as mentioned in subsection (1)(a) or (b) may appeal against the notice to the Secretary of State on the ground that the matters alleged in the notice—

(a) have not taken place, or

(b) do not constitute development to which section 294 applies.

(4) A person may appeal against a special enforcement notice under subsection (3) whether or not he was served with a copy of it.

(5) The provisions contained in or having effect under sections 174(3) to (5), 175(1) to (4) and 176(1) to (4) shall apply to special enforcement notices issued by local planning authorities and to appeals against them under subsection (3) as they apply to enforcement notices and to appeals under section 174.

(6) The Secretary of State may by regulations apply to special enforcement notices and to appeals under subsection (3) such other provisions of this Act (with such modifications as he thinks fit) as he thinks necessary or expedient.

Exercise of powers in relation to Crown land.

296.—(1) Notwithstanding any interest of the Crown in Crown land, but subject to the following provisions of this section—

(a) a plan approved, adopted or made under Part II of this Act or Part II of the 1971 Act may include proposals relating to the use of Crown land;

(b) any power to acquire land compulsorily under Part IX may be exercised in relation to any interest in Crown land which is for the time being held otherwise than by or on behalf of the Crown;

PART XIII

(c) any restrictions or powers imposed or conferred by Part III, VII or VIII, by the provisions of Part VI relating to purchase notices, or by any of the provisions of sections 266 to 270, shall apply and be exercisable in relation to Crown land, to the extent of any interest in it for the time being held otherwise than by or on behalf of the Crown.

(2) Except with the consent of the appropriate authority—

(a) no order or notice shall be made, issued or served under any of the provisions of section 102, 103, 172, 198, 199 or 215 or Schedule 9 or under any of those provisions as applied by any order or regulations made under Part VIII, in relation to land which for the time being is Crown land;

(b) no interest in land which for the time being is Crown land shall be acquired compulsorily under Part IX.

(3) No purchase notice shall be served in relation to any interest in Crown land unless—

(a) an offer has been previously made by the owner of that interest to dispose of it to the appropriate authority on equivalent terms, and

(b) that offer has been refused by the appropriate authority.

(4) In subsection (3) "equivalent terms" means that the price payable for the interest shall be equal to (and shall, in default of agreement, be determined in the same manner as) the compensation which would be payable in respect of it if it were acquired in pursuance of a purchase notice.

(5) The rights conferred by the provisions of Chapter II of Part VI shall be exercisable by a person who (within the meaning of those provisions) is an owner-occupier of a hereditament or agricultural unit which is Crown land, or is a resident owner-occupier of a hereditament which is Crown land, in the same way as they are exercisable in respect of a hereditament or agricultural unit which is not Crown land, and those provisions shall apply accordingly.

Agreements relating to Crown land.

297.—(1) The appropriate authority and the local planning authority for the area in which any Crown land is situated may make agreements for securing the use of the land, so far as may be prescribed by any such agreement, in conformity with the provisions of the development plan applicable to it.

(2) Any such agreement may contain such consequential provisions, including provisions of a financial character, as may appear to be necessary or expedient having regard to the purposes of the agreement.

(3) An agreement made under this section by a government department shall not have effect unless it is approved by the Treasury.

(4) In considering whether to make or approve an agreement under this section relating—

(a) to land belonging to a government department, or

(b) to land held in trust for Her Majesty for the purposes of a government department,

the department and the Treasury shall have regard to the purposes for which the land is held by or for the department.

PART XIII

Supplementary provisions as to Crown and Duchy interests.

298.—(1) Subject to the following provisions of this section—

(a) where there is a Crown interest in any land, the provisions of sections 109 to 113 and Part V and the provisions of Schedule 3 to the Planning (Consequential Provisions) Act 1990 in so far as they relate to those sections or that Part, or to Part VII or sections 166 to 168 of the 1971 Act, shall have effect in relation to any private interest or Duchy interest as if the Crown interest were a private interest; and

1990 c. 11

(b) where there is a Duchy interest in any land, those provisions shall have effect in relation to that interest, and to any private interest, as if the Duchy interest were a private interest.

(2) References in this Act to claims established under Part VI of the 1947 Act include references to claims so established in accordance with arrangements made under section 88(2) of that Act (which provided for the application of Part VI of that Act to Duchy interests and for the payment of sums in lieu of development charges in respect of such interests); references to development charges include references to sums determined in accordance with such arrangements to be appropriate in substitution for development charges; and references to the amount of an established claim or of a development charge shall be construed accordingly.

(3) Where, in accordance with an agreement under section 297, the approval of a local planning authority is required in respect of any development of land in which there is a Duchy interest, the provisions of this Act referred to in subsection (1)(a) shall have effect in relation to the withholding of that approval, or the giving of it subject to conditions, as if it were a refusal of planning permission or, as the case may be, a grant of planning permission subject to conditions.

Provisions relating to anticipated disposal of Crown land

Application for planning permission etc. in anticipation of disposal of Crown land.

299.—(1) This section has effect for the purpose of enabling Crown land, or an interest in Crown land, to be disposed of with the benefit of planning permission or a determination under section 64.

(2) Notwithstanding the interest of the Crown in the land in question, an application for any such permission or determination may be made by—

(a) the appropriate authority; or

(b) any person authorised by that authority in writing;

and, subject to subsections (3) to (5), all the statutory provisions relating to the making and determination of any such application shall accordingly apply as if the land were not Crown land.

(3) Any planning permission granted by virtue of this section shall apply only—

(a) to development carried out after the land in question has ceased to be Crown land; and

(b) so long as that land continues to be Crown land, to development carried out by virtue of a private interest in the land.

PART XIII

(4) In relation to any application made by virtue of this section for any determination under section 64, subsection (1) of that section shall have effect as if for the reference to an application for planning permission being required there were substituted a reference to such an application being required in the event of the proposed operations or change of use being carried out or made otherwise than by or on behalf of the Crown.

(5) The Secretary of State may by regulations—

(a) modify or exclude any of the statutory provisions referred to in subsection (2) in their application by virtue of that subsection and any other statutory provisions in their application to permissions or determinations granted or made by virtue of this section;

(b) make provision for requiring a local planning authority to be notified of any disposal of, or of an interest in, any Crown land in respect of which an application has been made by virtue of this section; and

(c) make such other provision in relation to the making and determination of applications by virtue of this section as he thinks necessary or expedient.

(6) This section shall not be construed as affecting any right to apply for any such permission or determination as is mentioned in subsection (1) in respect of Crown land in a case in which such an application can be made by virtue of a private interest in the land.

(7) In this section "statutory provisions" means provisions contained in or having effect under any enactment.

Tree preservation orders in anticipation of disposal of Crown land.

300.—(1) A local planning authority may make a tree preservation order in respect of Crown land in which no interest is for the time being held otherwise than by or on behalf of the Crown, if they consider it expedient to do so for the purpose of preserving trees or woodlands on the land in the event of its ceasing to be Crown land or becoming subject to a private interest.

(2) No tree preservation order shall be made by virtue of this section except with the consent of the appropriate authority.

(3) A tree preservation order made by virtue of this section shall not take effect until the first occurrence of a relevant event.

(4) For the purposes of subsection (3), a relevant event occurs in relation to any land if it ceases to be Crown land or becomes subject to a private interest.

(5) A tree preservation order made by virtue of this section—

(a) shall not require confirmation under section 199 until after the occurrence of the event by virtue of which it takes effect; and

(b) shall by virtue of this subsection continue in force until—

(i) the expiration of the period of six months beginning with the occurrence of that event; or

(ii) the date on which the order is confirmed,

whichever first occurs.

(6) Where a tree preservation order takes effect in accordance with subsection (3), the appropriate authority shall as soon as practicable give to the authority who made the order a notice in writing of the name and address of the person who has become entitled to the land in question or to a private interest in it.

(7) The procedure prescribed under section 199 in connection with the confirmation of a tree preservation order shall apply in relation to an order made by virtue of this section as if the order were made on the date on which the notice under subsection (6) is received by the authority who made it.

Requirement of planning permission for continuance of use instituted by the Crown.

301.—(1) A local planning authority in whose area any Crown land is situated may agree with the appropriate authority that subsection (2) shall apply to such use of land by the Crown as is specified in the agreement, being a use resulting from a material change made or proposed to be made by the Crown in the use of the land.

(2) Where an agreement is made under subsection (1) in respect of any Crown land, then, if at any time the land ceases to be used by the Crown for the purposes specified in the agreement, this Act shall have effect in relation to any subsequent private use of the land as if—

(a) the specified use by the Crown had required planning permission, and

(b) that use had been authorised by planning permission granted subject to a condition requiring its discontinuance at that time.

(3) The condition referred to in subsection (2) shall not be enforceable against any person who had a private interest in the land at the time when the agreement was made unless the local planning authority by whom the agreement was made have notified him of the making of the agreement and of the effect of that subsection.

(4) An agreement made under subsection (1) by a local planning authority shall be a local land charge, and for the purposes of the Local Land Charges Act 1975 the local planning authority by whom such an agreement is made shall be treated as the originating authority as respects the charge constituted by the agreement. 1975 c. 76.

(5) In this section "private use" means use otherwise than by or on behalf of the Crown, and references to the use of land by the Crown include references to its use on behalf of the Crown.

Enforcement in respect of war-time breaches of planning control by the Crown

Enforcement in respect of war-time breaches of planning control by the Crown.

302.—(1) This section applies where during the war period—

(a) works not complying with planning control were carried out on land, or

(b) a use of land not complying with planning control was begun by or on behalf of the Crown.

(2) Subject to subsection (4), if at any time after the end of the war period there subsists in the land a permanent or long-term interest which is neither held by or on behalf of the Crown nor subject to any interest or right to possession so held, the planning control shall, so long as such an interest subsists in the land, be enforceable in respect of those works or that use notwithstanding—

PART XIII

(a) that the works were carried out or the land used by or on behalf of the Crown, or

(b) the subsistence in the land of any interest held by or on behalf of the Crown in reversion (whether immediate or not) expectant on the termination of that permanent or long-term interest.

(3) A person entitled to make an application under this subsection with respect to any land may apply at any time before the relevant date to an authority responsible for enforcing any planning control for a determination—

(a) whether works on the land carried out, or a use of the land begun, during the war period fail to comply with any planning control which the authority are responsible for enforcing, and

(b) if so, whether the works or use should be deemed to comply with that control.

(4) Where any works on land carried out, or use of land begun, during the war period remain or continues after the relevant date and no such determination has been given, the works or use shall by virtue of this subsection be treated for all purposes as complying with that control unless steps for enforcing the control have been begun before that date.

(5) Schedule 15 shall have effect for the purpose of making supplementary provision concerning the enforcement of breaches of planning control to which this section applies and the making and determination of applications under subsection (3).

(6) In this section and that Schedule—

"authority responsible for enforcing planning control" means, in relation to any works on land or use of land, the authority empowered by virtue of section 75 of the 1947 Act or of paragraph 34 of Schedule 24 to the 1971 Act (including that paragraph as it continues in effect by virtue of Schedule 3 to the Planning (Consequential Provisions) Act 1990) to serve an enforcement notice in respect of it or the authority who would be so empowered if the works had been carried out, or the use begun, otherwise than in compliance with planning control;

1990 c. 11

"the relevant date", in relation to any land, means the date with which the period of five years from the end of the war period ends, but for the purposes of this definition any time during which, notwithstanding subsection (2), planning control is unenforceable by reason of the subsistence in or over the land of any interest or right to possession held by or on behalf of the Crown shall be disregarded;

1985 c. 68.

"owner" has the same meaning as in the Housing Act 1985 and "owned" shall be construed accordingly;

"permanent or long-term interest", in relation to any land, means the fee simple in the land, a tenancy of the land granted for a term of more than ten years and not subject to a subsisting right of the landlord to determine the tenancy at or before the expiration of ten years from the beginning of the term, or a tenancy granted for a term of ten years or less with a right of renewal which would enable the tenant to prolong the term of the tenancy beyond ten years;

"tenancy" includes a tenancy under an underlease and a tenancy under an agreement for a lease or underlease, but does not include an option to take a tenancy and does not include a mortgage;

"war period" means the period extending from 3rd September 1939 to 26th March 1946;

"works" includes any building, structure, excavation or other work on land.

(7) References in this section and that Schedule to non-compliance with planning control mean—

(a) in relation to works on land carried out, or a use of land begun, at a time when the land was subject to a resolution to prepare a scheme under the Town and Country Planning Act 1932, that the works were carried out or the use begun otherwise than in accordance with the terms of an interim development order or of permission granted under such an order; 1932 c. 48.

(b) in relation to works on land carried out, or a use of land begun, at a time when the land was subject to such a scheme, that the works were carried out or the use begun otherwise than in conformity with the provisions of the scheme;

and references in this Act to compliance with planning control shall be construed accordingly.

(8) References in this section and that Schedule to the enforcement of planning control shall be construed as references to the exercise of the powers conferred by section 75 of the 1947 Act or by paragraph 34 of Schedule 24 to the 1971 Act (including that paragraph as it continues in effect by virtue of Schedule 3 to the Planning (Consequential Provisions) Act 1990). 1990 c. 11

PART XIV

FINANCIAL PROVISIONS

Fees for planning applications, etc.

303.—(1) The Secretary of State may by regulations make such provision as he thinks fit for the payment of a fee of the prescribed amount to a local planning authority in respect of an application made to them under the planning Acts or any order or regulations made under them for any permission, consent, approval, determination or certificate.

(2) Regulations under subsection (1) may provide for the transfer of prescribed fees received in respect of any description of application by an authority to whom applications fall to be made to any other authority by whom applications of that description fall to be dealt with.

(3) The Secretary of State may by regulations make such provision as he thinks fit for the payment to him of a fee of the prescribed amount in respect of an application for planning permission which is deemed to be made to him under this Act or any order or regulations made under it.

(4) Regulations under subsection (1) or (3) may provide for the remission or refunding of a prescribed fee (in whole or in part) in prescribed circumstances.

(5) No such regulations shall be made unless a draft of the regulations has been laid before and approved by a resolution of each House of Parliament.

PART XIV

(6) The reference to the planning Acts in subsection (1) does not include a reference to section 302 of this Act.

Grants for research and education.

304. The Secretary of State may, with the consent of the Treasury, make grants for assisting establishments engaged in promoting or assisting research relating to, and education with respect to, the planning and design of the physical environment.

Contributions by Ministers towards compensation paid by local authorities.

305.—(1) Where—

(a) compensation is payable by a local authority under this Act in consequence of any decision or order to which this section applies, and

(b) that decision or order was given or made wholly or partly in the interest of a service which is provided by a government department and the cost of which is defrayed out of money provided by Parliament,

the Minister responsible for the administration of that service may pay to that authority a contribution of such amount as he may with the consent of the Treasury determine.

(2) This section applies to any decision or order given or made under Part III, the provisions of Part VI relating to purchase notices, Part VII, Part VIII or Schedule 5, 6 or 9.

Contributions by local authorities and statutory undertakers.

1980 c. 66.

1990 c. 9.

306.—(1) Without prejudice to section 274 of the Highways Act 1980 (contributions by local authorities to expenses of highway authorities), any local authority may contribute towards any expenses incurred by a local highway authority—

(a) in the acquisition of land under Part IX of this Act or Chapter V of Part I of the Planning (Listed Buildings and Conservation Areas) Act 1990,

(b) in the construction or improvement of roads on land so acquired, or

(c) in connection with any development required in the interests of the proper planning of the area of the local authority.

(2) Any local authority and any statutory undertakers may contribute towards—

(a) any expenses incurred by a local planning authority in or in connection with the carrying out of a survey or the preparation of a unitary development plan or a local plan or the alteration, repeal or replacement of such a plan or a structure plan under Part II;

(b) any expenses incurred by a local planning authority or a mineral planning authority in or in connection with the performance of any of their functions under Part III, the provisions of Part VI relating to purchase notices, Part VII, Part VIII (except section 207), Part IX or Schedule 5 or 9.

(3) Where any expenses are incurred by a local authority in the payment of compensation payable in consequence of anything done under Part III, the provisions of Part VI relating to purchase notices, Part VII, Part VIII, or Schedule 5 or 9, the Secretary of State may, if it appears to him to be expedient to do so, require any other local authority to

contribute towards those expenses such sum as appears to him to be reasonable, having regard to any benefit accruing to that authority by reason of the proceeding giving rise to the compensation.

(4) Subsection (3) shall apply in relation to payments made by a local authority to any statutory undertakers in accordance with financial arrangements to which effect is given under section 275(5)(c), as it applies in relation to compensation payable by such an authority in consequence of anything done under Part III, Part VIII or Schedule 5 or 9, and the reference in that subsection to the proceeding giving rise to the compensation shall be construed accordingly.

(5) For the purposes of this section, contributions made by a local planning authority towards the expenditure of a joint advisory committee shall be deemed to be expenses incurred by that authority for the purposes for which that expenditure is incurred by the committee.

Assistance for acquisition of property where objection made to blight notice in certain cases.

307.—(1) The council of a county, district or London borough may advance money to any person for the purposes of enabling him to acquire a hereditament or agricultural unit in respect of which a counter-notice has been served under section 151 specifying the grounds mentioned in subsection (4)(d) of that section as, or as one of, the grounds of objection.

(2) No advance may be made under subsection (1) in the case of a hereditament if its annual value exceeds such amount as may be prescribed for the purposes of section 149(3)(a).

(3) An advance under subsection (1) may be made subject to such conditions as the council may think fit.

Recovery from acquiring authorities of sums paid by way of compensation.

308.—(1) This section applies where—

(a) an interest in land is compulsorily acquired or is sold to an authority possessing compulsory purchase powers, and

(b) a notice is registered under section 110(2) or 132(1) in respect of any of the land acquired or sold (whether before or after the completion of the acquisition or sale) in consequence of a planning decision or order made before the service of the notice to treat, or the making of the contract, in pursuance of which the acquisition or sale is effected.

(2) Where this section applies the Secretary of State shall, subject to the following provisions of this section, be entitled to recover from the acquiring authority a sum equal to so much of the amount of the compensation specified in the notice as (in accordance with section 110(5) or, as the case may be, section 132(4)) is to be treated as attributable to that land.

(3) If, immediately after the completion of the acquisition or sale, there is outstanding some interest in the land acquired or sold to which a person other than the acquiring authority is entitled, the sum referred to in subsection (2) shall not accrue due until that interest either ceases to exist or becomes vested in the acquiring authority.

(4) No sum shall be recoverable under this section in the case of a compulsory acquisition or sale where the Secretary of State is satisfied that the interest in question is being acquired for the purposes of the use of the land as a public open space.

PART XIV

(5) Where the Secretary of State recovers a sum under this section in respect of any land by reason that it is land in respect of which a notice is registered under the provisions of section 110, section 112(11) to (13) shall have effect in relation to that sum as if it were a sum recovered as mentioned in section 112(11).

(6) In this section and in section 309 "interest" (where the reference is to an interest in land) means the fee simple or a tenancy of the land and does not include any other interest in it.

Recovery from acquiring authorities of sums paid in respect of war-damaged land.

309.—(1) Where an interest in land is compulsorily acquired by, or sold to, an authority possessing compulsory purchase powers, and a payment exceeding £20 has become or becomes payable under section 59 of the 1947 Act in respect of that interest, the Secretary of State shall, subject to the following provisions of this section, be entitled to recover the amount of the payment from the acquiring authority.

(2) If, before 18th November 1952, operations were begun in, on, over or under the land, or a use of the land was instituted, and—

(a) a development charge has at any time been determined to be payable in respect of the operations or use, or it has at any time been determined that no development charge was payable; or

(b) the operations or use were comprised in a scheme of development exempt from development charge,

subsection (1) shall not apply to so much of any payment referred to in that subsection as was attributable to any land in relation to which the determination was made or, as the case may be, which is included in that scheme of development.

(3) No amount shall be recoverable under this section in respect of any land in relation to which an amount has become recoverable by the Secretary of State under the provisions of section 133 as applied by section 327.

(4) If the acquisition or sale in question does not extend to the whole of the land to which the payment under section 59 of the 1947 Act related, the amount recoverable under this section shall be so much of that payment as in accordance with subsection (5) is to be treated as apportioned to the land in which the interest acquired or sold subsists.

(5) For the purposes of this section a payment under section 59 of the 1947 Act shall be treated as apportioned, as between different parts of the land to which it related, in the way in which it might reasonably be expected to have been so apportioned if, under the scheme made under that section, the authority determining the amount of the payment had been required (in accordance with the same principles as applied to the determination of that amount) to apportion it between different parts of that land.

(6) In this section references to a scheme of development exempt from development charge are references to a scheme of development such that, if the operations and uses of land comprised in the scheme had all been begun or instituted before 18th November 1952, all those operations and uses would have been exempt from the provisions of Part VII of the 1947 Act by virtue of regulations made under it.

(7) References in this section to the amount of a payment shall be construed as including any interest payable on the principal amount of the payment. PART XIV

Sums recoverable from acquiring authorities reckonable for purposes of grant.

310. Where—

(a) a sum is recoverable from any authority under section 308 or 309 by reference to an acquisition or purchase of an interest in land, and

(b) a grant became or becomes payable to that or some other authority under an enactment in respect of that acquisition or purchase or of a subsequent appropriation of the land,

the power conferred by that enactment to pay the grant shall include, and shall be deemed always to have included, power to pay a grant in respect of that sum as if it had been expenditure incurred by the acquiring authority in connection with the acquisition or purchase.

Expenses of government departments.

311.—(1) The following expenses of the Secretary of State shall be paid out of money provided by Parliament—

(a) any expenses incurred by the Secretary of State under subsection (5) of section 220 or in the payment of expenses of any committee established under that section;

(b) any sums necessary to enable the Secretary of State to make any payments becoming payable by him under Part IV or V;

(c) any expenses incurred by the Secretary of State under Part X;

(d) any expenses incurred by the Secretary of State in the making of grants under section 304;

(e) any administrative expenses incurred by the Secretary of State for the purposes of this Act.

(2) There shall be paid out of money provided by Parliament any expenses incurred by any government department (including the Secretary of State)—

(a) in the acquisition of land under Part IX;

(b) in the payment of compensation under section 236(4), 279(2) or 325;

(c) under section 240(1)(b); or

(d) under section 305.

Payments under s. 59 of 1947 Act and Parts I and V of 1954 Act.

312.—(1) The Secretary of State shall pay out of money provided by Parliament any payments falling to be made by him on or after 1st April 1968 under—

(a) section 59 of the 1947 Act (war-damaged land); or

(b) any provision of Part I or Part V of the 1954 Act.

(2) Any sums received by the Secretary of State by virtue of—

(a) the provisions of section 133, as applied by virtue of Schedule 24 to the 1971 Act and Schedule 3 to the Planning (Consequential Provisions) Act 1990 to compensation paid under Part V of the 1954 Act; or 1990 c. 11.

PART XIV

(b) the provisions of section 308 as so applied,

shall be paid into the Consolidated Fund.

General provision as to receipts of Secretary of State.

313. Without prejudice to section 312, and subject to the provisions of section 112, any sums received by the Secretary of State under any provision of this Act shall be paid into the Consolidated Fund.

Expenses of county councils.

314. The council of a county may direct that any expenses incurred by them under the provisions specified in Parts I and II of Schedule 16 shall be treated as special expenses of a county council chargeable upon such part of the county as may be specified in the directions.

PART XV

MISCELLANEOUS AND GENERAL PROVISIONS

Application of Act in special cases

Power to modify Act in relation to minerals.

315.—(1) In relation to development consisting of the winning and working of minerals, the provisions specified in Parts I and II of Schedule 16 shall have effect subject to such adaptations and modifications as may be prescribed.

(2) In relation to interests in land consisting of or comprising minerals (being either the fee simple or tenancies of such land) and in relation to claims established (as mentioned in paragraph 1(2) of Schedule 12) wholly or partly in respect of such land, the provisions specified in Part III of Schedule 16 shall have effect subject to such adaptations and modifications as may be prescribed.

(3) Regulations made for the purposes of this section may only be made with the consent of the Treasury and shall be of no effect unless they are approved by resolution of each House of Parliament.

(4) Any regulations made by virtue of subsection (1) shall not apply—

(a) to the winning and working, on land held or occupied with land used for the purposes of agriculture, of any minerals reasonably required for the purposes of that use, including the fertilisation of the land so used and the maintenance, improvement or alteration of buildings or works on it which are occupied or used for those purposes; or

(b) to development consisting of the winning and working of any minerals vested in the British Coal Corporation, being development to which any of the provisions of the planning Acts relating to operational land of statutory undertakers apply by virtue of regulations made under section 317.

(5) Nothing in subsection (1) or (4) shall be construed as affecting the prerogative right of Her Majesty (whether in right of the Crown or of the Duchy of Lancaster) or of the Duke of Cornwall to any gold or silver mine.

Application of certain provisions to local planning authorities.

316.—(1) In relation to land of local planning authorities and to the development by local authorities of land in respect of which they are the local planning authorities, the provisions specified in Part V of Schedule 16 shall have effect subject to such exceptions and modifications as may be prescribed by regulations.

(2) Subject to section 90, any such regulations may in particular provide for securing—

(a) that any application by such an authority for planning permission to develop such land, or for any other consent required in relation to such land under those provisions, shall be made to the Secretary of State and not to the local planning authority;

(b) that any order or notice authorised to be made, issued or served under those provisions in relation to such land shall be made or served by the Secretary of State and not by the local planning authority.

(3) Sections 65 to 68 and 71(1) and (2) shall apply, with the necessary modifications, in relation to applications made to the Secretary of State in pursuance of regulations made for the purposes of subsection (1), as they apply in relation to applications for planning permission which fall to be determined by the local planning authority.

(4) In relation to statutory undertakers who are local planning authorities, section 283 and the provisions specified in that section shall have effect subject to such exceptions and modifications as may be prescribed.

(5) In relation to an urban development corporation which is the local planning authority by virtue of an order under section 149(1) of the Local Government, Planning and Land Act 1980 and a housing action trust established under Part III of the Housing Act 1988 which is a local planning authority by virtue of an order under section 67(1) of that Act, subsections (1) to (3) shall have effect for the purposes of Part III of this Act specified in the order, and in relation to the kinds of development so specified as if—

1980 c. 65.

1988 c. 50.

(a) in subsection (1) the reference to development by local authorities of land in respect of which they are the local planning authorities included a reference to development by the corporation or, as the case may be, the trust of land in respect of which it is the local planning authority; and

(b) in subsection (2)—

(i) in paragraph (a) the words "the corporation" or, as the case may be, "the trust" were substituted for the words "such an authority", and the word "corporation" or, as the case may be, "trust" were substituted for the words "local planning authority"; and

(ii) in paragraph (b) the word "corporation" or, as the case may be, "trust" were substituted for the words "local planning authority".

PART XV

The British Coal Corporation.

317.—(1) The Secretary of State for the Environment and the Secretary of State for Energy may by regulations made with the consent of the Treasury direct that any of the provisions specified in Part I of Schedule 16 or of section 264 relating to statutory undertakers and to land of such undertakers—

(a) shall apply to the British Coal Corporation as if it were a statutory undertaker; and

(b) shall apply to land (including mines) of that Corporation of any such class as may be specified in the regulations as if it were operational land.

(2) Such regulations may apply those provisions subject to such adaptations, modifications and exceptions as may be specified in the regulations.

(3) Without prejudice to the generality of subsection (2), where such regulations apply any provisions by virtue of which any compensation is payable to the British Coal Corporation which if it were payable to statutory undertakers would be assessable in accordance with the provisions of section 280, they may provide for an alternative basis of assessment.

Ecclesiastical property.
1981 c. 67.

318.—(1) Without prejudice to the provisions of the Acquisition of Land Act 1981 with respect to notices served under that Act, where under any of the provisions of this Act a notice or copy of a notice is required to be served on an owner of land, and the land is ecclesiastical property, a similar notice or copy of a notice shall be served on the Church Commissioners.

(2) Where the fee simple of any ecclesiastical property is in abeyance—

(a) if the property is situated elsewhere than in Wales, then for the purposes of the provisions specified in Part VI of Schedule 16 the fee simple shall be treated as being vested in the Church Commissioners;

(b) in any case, the fee simple shall, for the purposes of a compulsory acquisition of the property under Part IX, be treated as being vested in the Church Commissioners, and any notice to treat shall be served, or be deemed to have been served, accordingly.

(3) Any compensation payable under Part IV, section 186, Part VIII (except section 204) or section 250 in respect of land which is ecclesiastical property—

(a) shall be paid to the Church Commissioners, and

(b) shall be applied by them for the purposes for which the proceeds of a sale by agreement of the land would be applicable under any enactment or Measure authorising or disposing of the proceeds of such a sale.

(4) Any sum which under any of the provisions specified in Part III of Schedule 16 is payable in relation to land which is, or on 1st July 1948 was, ecclesiastical property, and apart from this subsection would be payable to an incumbent—

(a) shall be paid to the Church Commissioners, and

(b) shall be applied by them for the purposes mentioned in subsection (3)(b).

(5) Where any sum is recoverable under section 111, 112, 133 or 327 in respect of any such land, the Church Commissioners may apply any money or securities held by them in the payment of that sum.

(6) In this section "ecclesiastical property" means land belonging to an ecclesiastical benefice, or being or forming part of a church subject to the jurisdiction of a bishop of any diocese or the site of such a church, or being or forming part of a burial ground subject to such jurisdiction.

Application of Act to Isles of Scilly.

319.—(1) The Secretary of State shall by order provide for the application to the Isles of Scilly of the provisions specified in Parts I and II of Schedule 16, sections 1(4), 67, 72(5), 97(5), 102(8), 105, 116, 190 (in so far as it applies to orders under Schedule 9), 294(2) to (7), 295, 299 to 301 and 303, the definitions of "development consisting of the winning and working of minerals" and "mineral working deposit" in section 336(1), paragraph 11(4) of Schedule 1 and Schedules 5, 9 and 11, as if those Isles were a separate county.

(2) In relation to land in the Isles of Scilly, the provisions specified in Part III of Schedule 16 and section 225 shall have effect as if those Isles were a district and the Council of the Isles were the council of that district.

(3) The Secretary of State may by order provide for the application to the Isles of Scilly of the provisions specified in Part IV of that Schedule as if those Isles were a separate county or district.

(4) Before making an order under subsection (1) or (3) the Secretary of State shall consult with the Council of the Isles of Scilly.

(5) Any order under subsection (1) or (3) may provide for the application of provisions to the Isles subject to such modifications as may be specified in the order.

Local inquiries and other hearings

Local inquiries.

320.—(1) The Secretary of State may cause a local inquiry to be held for the purposes of the exercise of any of his functions under any of the provisions of this Act.

(2) Subsections (2) to (5) of section 250 of the Local Government Act 1972 (local inquiries: evidence and costs) apply to an inquiry held by virtue of this section. 1972 c. 70.

Planning inquiries to be held in public subject to certain exceptions.

321.—(1) This section applies to any inquiry held under section 320(1), paragraph 6 of Schedule 6 or paragraph 5 of Schedule 8.

(2) Subject to subsection (3), at any such inquiry oral evidence shall be heard in public and documentary evidence shall be open to public inspection.

(3) If the Secretary of State is satisfied in the case of any such inquiry—

(a) that giving evidence of a particular description or, as the case may be, making it available for inspection would be likely to result in the disclosure of information as to any of the matters mentioned in subsection (4); and

PART XV

(b) that the public disclosure of that information would be contrary to the national interest,

he may direct that evidence of the description indicated in the direction shall only be heard or, as the case may be, open to inspection at that inquiry by such persons or persons of such descriptions as he may specify in the direction.

(4) The matters referred to in subsection (3)(a) are—

(a) national security; and

(b) the measures taken or to be taken to ensure the security of any premises or property.

Orders as to costs of parties where no local inquiry held.

322.—(1) This section applies to proceedings under this Act where the Secretary of State is required, before reaching a decision, to give any person an opportunity of appearing before and being heard by a person appointed by him.

1972 c. 70.

(2) The Secretary of State has the same power to make orders under section 250(5) of the Local Government Act 1972 (orders with respect to the costs of the parties) in relation to proceedings to which this section applies which do not give rise to a local inquiry as he has in relation to a local inquiry.

Procedure on certain appeals and applications.

323.—(1) The Secretary of State may by regulations prescribe the procedure to be followed in connection with proceedings under this Act where he is required, before reaching a decision, to give any person an opportunity of appearing before and being heard by a person appointed by him and which are to be disposed of without an inquiry or hearing to which rules under section 11 of the Tribunals and Inquiries Act 1971 apply.

1971 c. 62.

(2) The regulations may in particular make provision as to the procedure to be followed—

(a) where steps have been taken with a view to the holding of such an inquiry or hearing which does not take place, or

(b) where steps have been taken with a view to the determination of any matter by a person appointed by the Secretary of State and the proceedings are the subject of a direction that the matter shall instead be determined by the Secretary of State, or

(c) where steps have been taken in pursuance of such a direction and a further direction is made revoking that direction,

and may provide that such steps shall be treated as compliance, in whole or in part, with the requirements of the regulations.

(3) The regulations may also—

(a) provide for a time limit within which any party to the proceedings must submit representations in writing and any supporting documents;

(b) prescribe the time limit (which may be different for different classes of proceedings) or enable the Secretary of State to give directions setting the time limit in a particular case or class of case;

(c) empower the Secretary of State to proceed to a decision taking into account only such written representations and supporting documents as were submitted within the time limit; and

(d) empower the Secretary of State, after giving the parties written notice of his intention to do so, to proceed to a decision notwithstanding that no written representations were made within the time limit, if it appears to him that he has sufficient material before him to enable him to reach a decision on the merits of the case.

Rights of entry

Rights of entry.

324.—(1) Any person duly authorised in writing by the Secretary of State or by a local planning authority may at any reasonable time enter any land for the purpose of surveying it in connection with—

(a) the preparation, approval, adoption or making of a unitary development plan or a local plan relating to the land under Part II or the alteration of such a plan or a structure plan relating to the land under that Part, including the carrying out of any survey under that Part;

(b) any application under Part III or sections 198 to 200, 220 or 221 or under any order or regulations made under any of those provisions, for any permission, consent or determination to be given or made in connection with that land or any other land under that Part or any of those sections or under any such order or regulations;

(c) any proposal by the local planning authority or by the Secretary of State to make, issue or serve any order or notice under Part III (other than sections 94 and 96), Part VII or Part VIII or under any order or regulations made under any of those provisions.

(2) Any person duly authorised in writing by the Secretary of State or a local authority may at any reasonable time enter any land for the purpose of ascertaining whether any of the functions conferred by sections 207 to 209 should or may be exercised in connection with the land or for the purpose of exercising any of those functions in connection with the land.

(3) Any person duly authorised in writing by the local planning authority may at any reasonable time enter any land for the purpose of exercising a power conferred on the authority by section 225 if—

(a) the land is unoccupied; and

(b) it would be impossible to exercise the power without entering the land.

(4) Any person who is an officer of the Valuation Office or is duly authorised in writing by the Secretary of State may at any reasonable time enter any land for the purpose of surveying it, or estimating its value, in connection with a claim for compensation under Part V in respect of that land or any other land.

(5) Any person who is an officer of the Valuation Office or is duly authorised in writing by a local planning authority may at any reasonable time enter any land for the purpose of surveying it, or estimating its value, in connection with a claim for compensation in respect of that land or any

PART XV

other land which is payable by the local planning authority under Part IV, section 186, Part VIII (other than section 204), section 250(1) or Part XI (other than section 279(2) or (3) or 280(1)(c)).

(6) Any person who is an officer of the Valuation Office or is duly authorised in writing by a local authority or Minister authorised to acquire land under section 226 or 228 or by a local authority who have power to acquire land under Part IX may at any reasonable time enter any land for the purpose of surveying it, or estimating its value, in connection with any proposal to acquire that land or any other land or in connection with any claim for compensation in respect of any such acquisition.

(7) Any person duly authorised in writing by the Secretary of State or by a local planning authority may at any reasonable time enter any land in respect of which an order or notice has been made or served as mentioned in subsection (1)(c) for the purpose of ascertaining whether the order or notice has been complied with.

(8) Subject to section 325, any power conferred by this section to survey land shall be construed as including power to search and bore for the purpose of ascertaining the nature of the subsoil or the presence of minerals in it.

(9) In subsections (1)(c) and (7) references to a local planning authority include, in relation to a building situated in Greater London, a reference to the Historic Buildings and Monuments Commission for England.

Supplementary provisions as to rights of entry.

325.—(1) A person authorised under section 324 to enter any land—

(a) shall, if so required, produce evidence of his authority before so entering, and

(b) shall not demand admission as of right to any land which is occupied unless 24 hours' notice of the intended entry has been given to the occupier.

(2) Any person who wilfully obstructs a person acting in the exercise of his powers under section 324 shall be guilty of an offence and liable on summary conviction to a fine not exceeding level 2 on the standard scale.

(3) If any person who, in compliance with the provisions of section 324, is admitted into a factory, workshop or workplace discloses to any person any information obtained by him in it as to any manufacturing process or trade secret, he shall be guilty of an offence.

(4) Subsection (3) does not apply if the disclosure is made by a person in the course of performing his duty in connection with the purpose for which he was authorised to enter the premises.

(5) A person who is guilty of an offence under subsection (3) shall be liable on summary conviction to a fine not exceeding the statutory maximum or on conviction on indictment to imprisonment for a term not exceeding two years or a fine or both.

(6) Where any land is damaged—

(a) in the exercise of a right of entry conferred under section 324, or

(b) in the making of any survey for the purpose of which any such right of entry has been so conferred,

compensation in respect of that damage may be recovered by any person interested in the land from the Secretary of State or authority on whose behalf the entry was effected.

(7) The provisions of section 118 shall apply in relation to compensation under subsection (6) as they apply in relation to compensation under Part IV.

(8) No person shall carry out under section 324 any works authorised by virtue of subsection (8) of that section unless notice of his intention to do so was included in the notice required by subsection (1).

(9) The authority of the appropriate Minister shall be required for the carrying out under that section of works so authorised if the land in question is held by statutory undertakers, and they object to the proposed works on the ground that the execution of the works would be seriously detrimental to the carrying on of their undertaking.

Miscellaneous and general provisions

Assumptions as to planning permission in determining value of interests in land.

326.—(1) In any case where the value or depreciation in value of an interest in land falls to be determined on the assumption that planning permission would be granted for development of any class specified in Schedule 3, it shall be further assumed, as regards development of any class specified in paragraph 1 or 3 of that Schedule, that such permission would be granted subject to the condition set out in Schedule 10.

(2) For the purposes of subsection (1), so far as applicable to any determination of existing use value as defined in section 144(6)—

(a) references to Schedule 3 and to paragraphs 1 and 3 of that Schedule shall be construed as references to Schedule 3 to the 1947 Act and to the corresponding paragraphs of that Schedule; and

(b) that Schedule shall have effect as if it contained a paragraph corresponding to paragraph 13 of Schedule 3.

(3) Except as provided in section 111(5), nothing in subsections (1) and (2) or in paragraph 13 or 14(2) of Schedule 3 affects the meaning of "new development" in this Act or any determination to be made for the purpose of Part V.

(4) For the avoidance of doubt it is hereby declared that where, under any provision of this Act, the value of an interest in land is required to be assessed on the assumption that planning permission would be granted for development of any class specified in Schedule 3, that assumption is to be made on the footing that any such development must comply with the provisions of any enactment, other than the planning Acts, which would be applicable to it.

Recovery on subsequent development of payments in respect of war-damaged land.

327.—(1) In relation to notices registered under section 57 of the 1954 Act (which provided for the registration of notices of payments made under section 59 of the 1947 Act) sections 133 and 134 shall have effect as they have effect in relation to notices registered under section 132 but subject to the following provisions.

(2) Any reference in section 133 or 134 to the compensation specified in a notice shall be construed as a reference to the payment so specified.

PART XV

(3) Section 133 shall be assumed to apply to every description of new development.

(4) No amount shall be recoverable by the Secretary of State by virtue of this section in respect of any land in relation to which an amount has become recoverable under section 309.

(5) For the purposes of this section a payment under section 59 of the 1947 Act shall be treated as apportioned, as between different parts of the land to which it related, in the way in which it might reasonably be expected to have been so apportioned if, under the scheme made under that section, the authority determining the amount of the payment had been required (in accordance with the same principles as applied to the determination of that amount) to apportion it between different parts of that land.

Settled land and land of universities and colleges.
1925 c. 18.
1925 c. 20.
1925 c. 24.

328.—(1) The purposes authorised for the application of capital money—

(a) by section 73 of the Settled Land Act 1925 and by that section as applied by section 28 of the Law of Property Act 1925 in relation to trusts for sale; and

(b) by section 26 of the Universities and College Estates Act 1925,

shall include the payment of any sum recoverable under section 111, 112, 133 or 327.

(2) The purposes authorised as purposes for which money may be raised by mortgage—

(a) by section 71 of the Settled Land Act 1925 and by that section as so applied; and

(b) by section 30 of the Universities and College Estates Act 1925,

shall include the payment of any sum so recoverable.

Service of notices.

329.—(1) Any notice or other document required or authorised to be served or given under this Act may be served or given either—

(a) by delivering it to the person on whom it is to be served or to whom it is to be given; or

(b) by leaving it at the usual or last known place of abode of that person or, in a case where an address for service has been given by that person, at that address; or

(c) by sending it in a prepaid registered letter, or by the recorded delivery service, addressed to that person at his usual or last known place of abode or, in a case where an address for service has been given by that person, at that address; or

(d) in the case of an incorporated company or body, by delivering it to the secretary or clerk of the company or body at their registered or principal office or sending it in a prepaid registered letter, or by the recorded delivery service, addressed to the secretary or clerk of the company or body at that office.

(2) Where the notice or document is required or authorised to be served on any person as having an interest in premises, and the name of that person cannot be ascertained after reasonable inquiry, or where the notice or document is required or authorised to be served on any person as an occupier of premises, the notice or document shall be taken to be duly served if—

(a) it is addressed to him either by name or by the description of "the owner" or, as the case may be, "the occupier" of the premises (describing them) and is delivered or sent in the manner specified in subsection (1)(a), (b) or (c); or

(b) it is so addressed and is marked in such a manner as may be prescribed for securing that it is plainly identifiable as a communication of importance and—

(i) it is sent to the premises in a prepaid registered letter or by the recorded delivery service and is not returned to the authority sending it, or

(ii) it is delivered to some person on those premises, or is affixed conspicuously to some object on those premises.

(3) Where—

(a) the notice or other document is required to be served on or given to all persons who have interests in or are occupiers of premises comprised in any land, and

(b) it appears to the authority required or authorised to serve or give the notice or other document that any part of that land is unoccupied,

the notice or document shall be taken to be duly served on all persons having interests in, and on any occupiers of, premises comprised in that part of the land (other than a person who has given to that authority an address for the service of the notice or document on him) if it is addressed to "the owners and any occupiers" of that part of the land (describing it) and is affixed conspicuously to some object on the land.

Power to require information as to interests in land.

330.—(1) For the purpose of enabling the Secretary of State or a local authority to make an order or issue or serve any notice or other document which, by any of the provisions of this Act, he or they are authorised or required to make, issue or serve, the Secretary of State or the local authority may by notice in writing require the occupier of any premises and any person who, either directly or indirectly, receives rent in respect of any premises to give in writing such information as to the matters mentioned in subsection (2) as may be so specified.

(2) Those matters are—

(a) the nature of the interest in the premises of the person on whom the notice is served;

(b) the name and address of any other person known to him as having an interest in the premises;

(c) the purpose for which the premises are being used;

(d) the time when that use began;

(e) the name and address of any person known to the person on whom the notice is served as having used the premises for that purpose;

PART XV

(f) the time when any activities being carried out on the premises began.

(3) A notice under subsection (1) may require information to be given within 21 days after the date on which it is served, or such longer time as may be specified in it, or as the Secretary of State or, as the case may be, the local authority may allow.

(4) Any person who, without reasonable excuse, fails to comply with a notice served on him under subsection (1) shall be guilty of an offence and liable on summary conviction to a fine not exceeding level 3 on the standard scale.

(5) Any person who, having been required by a notice under subsection (1) to give any information, knowingly makes any misstatement in respect of it shall be guilty of an offence and liable on summary conviction to a fine not exceeding the statutory maximum or on conviction on indictment to imprisonment for a term not exceeding two years or to a fine, or both.

Offences by corporations.

331.—(1) Where an offence under this Act which has been committed by a body corporate is proved to have been committed with the consent or connivance of, or to be attributable to any neglect on the part of—

(a) a director, manager, secretary or other similar officer of the body corporate, or

(b) any person who was purporting to act in any such capacity,

he as well as the body corporate shall be guilty of that offence and be liable to be proceeded against accordingly.

(2) In subsection (1) "director", in relation to any body corporate—

(a) which was established by or under an enactment for the purpose of carrying on under national ownership an industry or part of an industry or undertaking, and

(b) whose affairs are managed by its members,

means a member of that body corporate.

Combined applications.

332.—(1) Regulations made under this Act may provide for the combination in a single document, made in such form and transmitted to such authority as may be prescribed, of—

(a) an application for planning permission in respect of any development; and

(b) an application required, under any enactment specified in the regulations, to be made to a local authority in respect of that development.

(2) Before making any regulations under this section, the Secretary of State shall consult with such local authorities or associations of local authorities as appear to him to be concerned.

(3) Different provision may be made by any such regulations in relation to areas in which different enactments are in force.

(4) If an application required to be made to a local authority under an enactment specified in any such regulations is made in accordance with the provisions of the regulations, it shall be valid notwithstanding anything in that enactment prescribing, or enabling any authority to prescribe, the form in which, or the manner in which, such an application is to be made.

(5) Subsection (4) shall have effect without prejudice to—

(a) the validity of any application made in accordance with the enactment in question; or

(b) any provision of that enactment enabling a local authority to require further particulars of the matters to which the application relates.

(6) In this section "application" includes a submission.

Regulations and orders.

333.—(1) The Secretary of State may make regulations under this Act—

(a) for prescribing the form of any notice, order or other document authorised or required by this Act to be served, made or issued by any local authority;

(b) for any purpose for which regulations are authorised or required to be made under this Act (other than a purpose for which regulations are authorised or required to be made by another Minister).

(2) Any power conferred by this Act to make regulations shall be exercisable by statutory instrument.

(3) Any statutory instrument containing regulations made under this Act (except regulations under section 88 and regulations which by virtue of this Act are of no effect unless approved by a resolution of each House of Parliament) shall be subject to annulment in pursuance of a resolution of either House of Parliament.

(4) The power to make development orders and orders under sections 2, 28, 55(2)(f), 87, 149(3)(a) and 319 shall be exercisable by statutory instrument.

(5) Any statutory instrument—

(a) which contains an order under section 2 which has been made after a local inquiry has been held in accordance with subsection (2) of that section; or

(b) which contains a development order or an order under section 28, 87 or 149(3)(a),

shall be subject to annulment in pursuance of a resolution of either House of Parliament.

(6) Without prejudice to subsection (5), where a development order makes provision for excluding or modifying any enactment contained in a public general Act (other than any of the enactments specified in Schedule 17) the order shall not have effect until that provision is approved by a resolution of each House of Parliament.

PART XV

1978 c. 30.

(7) Without prejudice to section 14 of the Interpretation Act 1978, any power conferred by any of the provisions of this Act to make an order, shall include power to vary or revoke any such order by a subsequent order.

Licensing planning areas.

1964 c. 26.

334.—(1) Where the united district for which, by an order under section 2, a joint planning board is constituted comprises a licensing planning area, or the whole or part of such a united district is included in a licensing planning area, the Secretary of State may by order revoke or vary any order in force under Part VII of the Licensing Act 1964 so far as may be necessary or expedient in consequence of the order under section 2.

(2) Subject to subsection (1), nothing in any order made under section 2 shall affect the validity of any order in force under Part VII of the Licensing Act 1964 if made before the date of the order under section 2.

Act not excluded by special enactments.

335. For the avoidance of doubt it is hereby declared that the provisions of this Act, and any restrictions or powers imposed or conferred by it in relation to land, apply and may be exercised in relation to any land notwithstanding that provision is made by any enactment in force at the passing of the 1947 Act, or by any local Act passed at any time during the Session of Parliament held during the regnal years 10 & 11 Geo. 6, for authorising or regulating any development of the land.

Interpretation.

1990 c. 11.

336.—(1) In this Act, except in so far as the context otherwise requires and subject to the following provisions of this section and to any transitional provision made by the Planning (Consequential Provisions) Act 1990—

1944 c. 47. "the 1944 Act" means the Town and Country Planning Act 1944;

1947 c. 51. "the 1947 Act" means the Town and Country Planning Act 1947;

1954 c. 72. "the 1954 Act" means the Town and Country Planning Act 1954;

1959 c. 53. "the 1959 Act" means the Town and Country Planning Act 1959;

1962 c. 38. "the 1962 Act" means the Town and Country Planning Act 1962;

1968 c. 72. "the 1968 Act" means the Town and Country Planning Act 1968;

1971 c. 78. "the 1971 Act" means the Town and Country Planning Act 1971;

"acquiring authority", in relation to the acquisition of an interest in land (whether compulsorily or by agreement) or to a proposal so to acquire such an interest, means the government department, local authority or other body by whom the interest is, or is proposed to be, acquired;

"advertisement" means any word, letter, model, sign, placard, board, notice, device or representation, whether illuminated or not, in the nature of, and employed wholly or partly for the purposes of, advertisement, announcement or direction, and (without prejudice to the previous provisions of this definition) includes any hoarding or similar structure used, or adapted for use, for the display of advertisements, and references to the display of advertisements shall be construed accordingly;

"aftercare condition" has the meaning given in paragraph 2(2) of Schedule 5;

"aftercare scheme" has the meaning given in paragraph 2(3) of Schedule 5;

Part XV

"agriculture" includes horticulture, fruit growing, seed growing, dairy farming, the breeding and keeping of livestock (including any creature kept for the production of food, wool, skins or fur, or for the purpose of its use in the farming of land), the use of land as grazing land, meadow land, osier land, market gardens and nursery grounds, and the use of land for woodlands where that use is ancillary to the farming of land for other agricultural purposes, and "agricultural" shall be construed accordingly;

"the appropriate Minister" has the meaning given in section 265;

"authority possessing compulsory purchase powers", in relation to the compulsory acquisition of an interest in land, means the person or body of persons effecting the acquisition and, in relation to any other transaction relating to an interest in land, means any person or body of persons who could be or have been authorised to acquire that interest compulsorily for the purposes for which the transaction is or was effected or a body (being a parish council, community council or parish meeting) on whose behalf a district council or county council could be or have been so authorised;

"authority to whom Part II of the 1959 Act applies" means a body of any of the descriptions specified in Part I of Schedule 4 to the 1959 Act;

"bridleway" has the same meaning as in the Highways Act 1980; 1980 c. 66.

"the Broads" has the same meaning as in the Norfolk and Suffolk Broads Act 1988; 1988 c. 4.

"building" includes any structure or erection, and any part of a building, as so defined, but does not include plant or machinery comprised in a building;

"buildings or works" includes waste materials, refuse and other matters deposited on land, and references to the erection or construction of buildings or works shall be construed accordingly;

"building operations" includes rebuilding operations, structural alterations of or additions to buildings, and other operations normally undertaken by a person carrying on business as a builder;

"caravan site" has the meaning given in section 1(4) of the Caravan Sites and Control of Development Act 1960; 1960 c. 62.

"clearing", in relation to land, means the removal of buildings or materials from the land, the levelling of the surface of the land, and the carrying out of such other operations in relation to it as may be prescribed;

"common" includes any land subject to be enclosed under the Inclosure Acts 1845 to 1882, and any town or village green;

"compulsory acquisition" does not include the vesting in a person by an Act of Parliament of property previously vested in some other person;

"conservation area" means an area designated under section 69 of the Planning (Listed Buildings and Conservation Areas) Act 1990; 1990 c. 9.

"development" has the meaning given in section 55, and "develop" shall be construed accordingly;

"development consisting of the winning and working of minerals" includes the extraction of minerals from a mineral-working deposit;

PART XV

"development order" has the meaning given in section 59;

"development plan" shall be construed in accordance with sections 27 and 54 (but subject to the transitional provisions in Schedule 2);

"disposal" means disposal by way of sale, exchange or lease, or by way of the creation of any easement, right or privilege, or in any other manner, except by way of appropriation, gift or mortgage, and "dispose of" shall be construed accordingly;

"enactment" includes an enactment in any local or private Act of Parliament and an order, rule, regulation, byelaw or scheme made under an Act of Parliament;

"enforcement notice" means a notice under section 172;

"engineering operations" includes the formation or laying out of means of access to highways;

"enterprise zone scheme" means a scheme or modified scheme having effect to grant planning permission in accordance with section 88;

"erection", in relation to buildings as defined in this subsection, includes extension, alteration and re-erection;

"established use certificate" has the meaning given in section 192;

1980 c. 66. "footpath" has the same meaning as in the Highways Act 1980;

"fuel or field garden allotment" means any allotment set out as a fuel allotment, or a field garden allotment, under an Inclosure Act;

"functions" includes powers and duties;

"government department" includes any Minister of the Crown;

"the Greater London Development Plan" means the development plan submitted to the Minister of Housing and Local Government under section 25 of the London Government Act 1963 and approved by the Secretary of State under section 5 of the 1962 Act or the corresponding provision of the 1971 Act; (1963 c. 33.)

1980 c. 66. "highway" has the same meaning as in the Highways Act 1980 ;

"improvement", in relation to a highway, has the same meaning as in the Highways Act 1980;

"joint planning board" has the meaning given in section 2;

"land" means any corporeal hereditament, including a building, and, in relation to the acquisition of land under Part IX, includes any interest in or right over land;

"lease" includes an underlease and an agreement for a lease or underlease, but does not include an option to take a lease or a mortgage, and "leasehold interest" means the interest of the tenant under a lease as so defined;

"local authority" (except in section 252 and subject to subsection (10)) means—

(a) a charging authority, a precepting authority (except the Receiver for the Metropolitan Police District), a combined police authority or a combined fire authority, as those expressions are defined in section 144 of the Local Government Finance Act 1988; (1988 c. 41.)

(b) a levying body within the meaning of section 74 of that Act; and

PART XV

(c) a body as regards which section 75 of that Act applies;

and includes any joint board or joint committee if all the constituent authorities are local authorities within paragraph (a), (b) or (c);

"local highway authority" means a highway authority other than the Secretary of State;

"local planning authority" shall be construed in accordance with Part I;

"London borough" includes the City of London, references to the council of a London borough or the clerk to such a council being construed, in relation to the City, as references to the Common Council of the City and the town clerk of the City respectively;

"means of access" includes any means of access, whether private or public, for vehicles or for foot passengers, and includes a street;

"mineral compensation modifications" has the meaning given in paragraph 1 of Schedule 11;

"mineral planning authority" has the meaning given in section 1(4);

"mineral-working deposit" means any deposit of material remaining after minerals have been extracted from land or otherwise deriving from the carrying out of operations for the winning and working of minerals in, on or under land;

"minerals" includes all minerals and substances in or under land of a kind ordinarily worked for removal by underground or surface working, except that it does not include peat cut for purposes other than sale;

"Minister" means any Minister of the Crown or other government department;

"mortgage" includes any charge or lien on any property for securing money or money's worth;

"new development" has the meaning given in section 55(6);

"open space" means any land laid out as a public garden, or used for the purposes of public recreation, or land which is a disused burial ground;

"operational land" has the meaning given in section 263;

"owner", in relation to any land, means (except in sections 66, 67 and 71) a person, other than a mortgagee not in possession, who, whether in his own right or as trustee for any other person, is entitled to receive the rack rent of the land or, where the land is not let at a rack rent, would be so entitled if it were so let;

"the planning Acts" means this Act, the Planning (Listed Buildings and Conservation Areas) Act 1990, the Planning (Hazardous Substances) Act 1990 and the Planning (Consequential Provisions) Act 1990; 1990 c. 9. 1990 c. 10. 1990 c. 11.

"planning decision" means a decision made on an application under Part III;

"planning permission" means permission under Part III, and in construing references to planning permission to develop land or to carry out any development of land, or to applications for such permission, regard shall be had to section 63(3) and (5);

"planning permission granted for a limited period" has the meaning given in section 72(2);

PART XV

"prescribed" (except in relation to matters expressly required or authorised by this Act to be prescribed in some other way) means prescribed by regulations under this Act;

"previous apportionment", in relation to an apportionment for any of the purposes of the relevant provisions, means an apportionment made before the apportionment in question, being—

(a) an apportionment for any of the purposes of the relevant provisions as made, confirmed or varied by the Lands Tribunal on a reference to that Tribunal; or

(b) an apportionment for any of those purposes which might have been referred to the Lands Tribunal by virtue of any of the relevant provisions, where the time for such a reference has expired without its being required to be so referred or where, after it had been so referred, the reference was withdrawn before the Tribunal gave their decision on it; or

1953 c. 16.

(c) an apportionment made by or with the approval of the Central Land Board in connection with the approval by the Board under section 2(2) of the Town and Country Planning Act 1953 of an assignment of part of the benefit of an established claim (as defined by paragraph 1(4) of Schedule 12 to this Act),

and in this definition "the relevant provisions" means any of the provisions of Part V of this Act, or of Part VII of the 1971 Act, or of Part VI of the 1962 Act, any of those provisions as applied by any other provision of this Act or of those Acts, and any of the provisions of the 1954 Act;

1986 c. 44.

"public gas supplier" has the same meaning as in Part I of the Gas Act 1986;

"purchase notice" has the meaning given in section 137;

"relevant order" has the meaning given in paragraph 11 of Schedule 11;

"replacement of open space", in relation to any area, means the rendering of land available for use as an open space, or otherwise in an undeveloped state, in substitution for land in that area which is so used;

"restoration condition" has the meaning given in paragraph 2(2) of Schedule 5;

"restriction on the winning and working of minerals" has the meaning given in paragraph 10 of Schedule 11;

"simplified planning zone" and "simplified planning zone scheme" shall be construed in accordance with sections 82 and 83;

"special consultations" has the meaning given in paragraph 12 of Schedule 11;

"statutory undertakers" and "statutory undertaking" have the meanings given in section 262;

"steps for the protection of the environment" has the meaning given in paragraph 5(4) of Schedule 9;

"stop notice" has the meaning given in section 183;

"suspension order" has the meaning given in paragraph 5 of Schedule 9; and

"supplementary suspension order" has the meaning given in paragraph 6 of Schedule 9;

PART XV

"tenancy" has the same meaning as in the Landlord and Tenant Act 1954 ; 1954 c. 56.

"tree preservation order" has the meaning given in section 198;

"urban development area" and "urban development corporation" have the same meanings as in Part XVI of the Local Government, Planning and Land Act 1980; 1980 c. 65.

"use", in relation to land, does not include the use of land for the carrying out of any building or other operations on it;

"Valuation Office" means the Valuation Office of the Inland Revenue Department;

"war damage" has the meaning given in the War Damage Act 1943. 1943 c. 21.

(2) If, in relation to anything required or authorised to be done under this Act, any question arises as to which Minister is or was the appropriate Minister in relation to any statutory undertakers, that question shall be determined by the Treasury.

(3) If any question so arises whether land of statutory undertakers is operational land, that question shall be determined by the Minister who is the appropriate Minister in relation to those undertakers.

(4) Words in this Act importing a reference to service of a notice to treat shall be construed as including a reference to the constructive service of such a notice which, by virtue of any enactment, is to be deemed to be served.

(5) With respect to references in this Act to planning decisions—

(a) in relation to a decision altered on appeal by the reversal or variation of the whole or part of it, such references shall be construed as references to the decision as so altered;

(b) in relation to a decision upheld on appeal, such references shall be construed as references to the decision of the local planning authority and not to the decision of the Secretary of State on the appeal;

(c) in relation to a decision given on an appeal in the circumstances mentioned in section 78(2), such references shall be construed as references to the decision so given;

(d) the time of a planning decision, in a case where there is or was an appeal, shall be taken to be or have been the time of the decision as made by the local planning authority (whether or not that decision is or was altered on that appeal) or, in the case of a decision given on an appeal in the circumstances mentioned in section 78(2), the end of the period there mentioned.

(6) Section 56 shall apply for determining for the purposes of this Act when development of land shall be taken to be initiated.

(7) In relation to the sale or acquisition of an interest in land—

(a) in a case where the interest is or was conveyed or assigned without a preliminary contract, references in this Act to a contract are references to the conveyance or assignment; and

(b) references to the making of a contract are references to the execution of it.

(8) In this Act—

(a) references to a person from whom title is derived by another person include references to any predecessor in title of that other person;

PART XV

(b) references to a person deriving title from another person include references to any successor in title of that other person;

(c) references to deriving title are references to deriving title either directly or indirectly.

(9) References in the planning Acts to any of the provisions in Part V of Schedule 16 include, except where the context otherwise requires, references to those provisions as modified under section 316(1) to (3).

(10) In section 90, Chapter I of Part VI, and sections 324(2) and 330 "local authority", in relation to land in the Broads, includes the Broads Authority.

Short title, commencement and extent.

337.—(1) This Act may be cited as the Town and Country Planning Act 1990.

1990 c. 11.

(2) Except as provided in Part II and in Schedule 4 to the Planning (Consequential Provisions) Act 1990, this Act shall come into force at the end of the period of three months beginning with the day on which it is passed.

(3) This Act extends to England and Wales only.

SCHEDULES

SCHEDULE 1

Section 1.

LOCAL PLANNING AUTHORITIES: DISTRIBUTION OF FUNCTIONS

Preliminary

1.—(1) In this Schedule "county matter" means in relation to any application, order or notice—

(a) the winning and working of minerals in, on or under land (whether by surface or underground working) or the erection of any building, plant or machinery—

(i) which it is proposed to use in connection with the winning and working of minerals or with their treatment or disposal in or on land adjoining the site of the working; or

(ii) which a person engaged in mining operations proposes to use in connection with the grading, washing, grinding or crushing of minerals;

(b) the use of land, or the erection of any building, plant or machinery on land, for the carrying out of any process for the preparation or adaptation for sale of any mineral or the manufacture of any article from a mineral where—

(i) the land forms part of or adjoins a site used or proposed to be used for the winning and working of minerals; or

(ii) the mineral is, or is proposed to be, brought to the land from a site used, or proposed to be used, for the winning and working of minerals by means of a pipeline, conveyor belt, aerial ropeway, or similar plant or machinery, or by private road, private waterway or private railway;

(c) the carrying out of searches and tests of mineral deposits or the erection of any building, plant or machinery which it is proposed to use in connection with them;

(d) the disposal of mineral waste;

(e) the use of land for any purpose required in connection with the transport by rail or water of aggregates (that is to say, any of the following, namely—

(i) sand and gravel;

(ii) crushed rock;

(iii) artificial materials of appearance similar to sand, gravel or crushed rock and manufactured or otherwise derived from iron or steel slags, pulverised fuel ash, clay or mineral waste),

or the erection of any building, plant or machinery which it is proposed to use in connection with them;

(f) the erection of any building, plant or machinery which it is proposed to use for the coating of roadstone or the production of concrete or of concrete products or artificial aggregates, where the building, plant or machinery is to be erected in or on land which forms part of or adjoins a site used or proposed to be used—

(i) for the winning and working of minerals; or

(ii) for any of the purposes mentioned in paragraph (e) above;

(g) the erection of any building, plant or machinery which it is proposed to use for the manufacture of cement;

SCH. 1

(h) the carrying out of operations in, on, over or under land, or a use of land, where the land is or forms part of a site used or formerly used for the winning and working of minerals and where the operations or use would conflict with or prejudice compliance with a restoration condition or an aftercare condition;

(i) the carrying out of operations in, on, over or under land, or any use of land, which is situated partly in and partly outside a National Park;

(j) the carrying out of any operation which is, as respects the area in question, a prescribed operation or an operation of a prescribed class or any use which is, as respects that area, a prescribed use or use of a prescribed class.

(2) In sub-paragraph (1) "the winning and working of minerals" includes the extraction of minerals from a mineral-working deposit.

Development plans

2. The functions of a local planning authority under sections 30 to 33 and 50(1) to (5) shall be exercisable by the county planning authority and references in those sections to a local planning authority shall be construed accordingly.

Planning and special control

3.—(1) The functions of a local planning authority of determining—

(a) applications for planning permission;

(b) applications for determining under section 64 whether an application for such permission is required;

(c) applications for an established use certificate under section 192;

shall, subject to sub-paragraph (2), be exercised by the district planning authority.

(2) The functions of a local planning authority of determining any such application as is mentioned in sub-paragraph (1) which appears to the district planning authority to relate to a county matter shall be exercised by the county planning authority.

(3) Every application mentioned in sub-paragraph (1) shall be made to the district planning authority.

(4) The district planning authority shall send to the county planning authority, as soon as possible and in any case not later than seven days after they have received it, a copy of any application for planning permission which appears to them to relate to a county matter.

(5) Subject to sub-paragraph (6), the district planning authority shall send to the local highway authority, as soon as may be after they have received it, a copy of any application for planning permission which does not appear to them to relate to a county matter.

(6) If the local highway authority specify any case or class of case in which a copy of such an application as is mentioned in sub-paragraph (5) need not be sent to them, the duty imposed on the district planning authority by that sub-paragraph shall not extend to any application to which the direction relates.

(7) The previous provisions of this paragraph shall not apply to applications relating to land in a National Park, but paragraph 4 shall apply to such applications instead.

4.—(1) Each of the following applications, namely—

(a) applications for planning permission;

(b) applications for determining under section 64 whether an application for such permission is required; Sch. 1

(c) applications for an established use certificate under section 192; and

(d) applications for consent to the display of advertisements under section 220,

shall, if relating to land in a National Park, be made to the district planning authority who shall, unless it falls to be determined by them, send it on to the county planning authority and, in the case of an application for planning permission, shall send a copy to the local highway authority, except where the local highway authority are a local planning authority and except in any case or class of case with respect to which the local highway authority otherwise direct.

(2) Where any such application relating to land in a National Park or an application so relating for approval of a matter reserved under an outline planning permission within the meaning of section 92 falls to be determined by a county planning authority, that authority shall before determining it consult with the district planning authority for the area in which the land to which the application relates is situated.

5.—(1) The Secretary of State may include in a development order such provisions as he thinks fit enabling a local highway authority to impose restrictions on the grant by the local planning authority of planning permission for the following descriptions of development relating to land in the area of the local highway authority—

(a) the formation, laying out or alteration of any means of access to a road classified under section 12(3) of the Highways Act 1980 or section 27 of the Local Government Act 1966 or to a proposed road the route of which has been adopted by resolution of the local highway authority and notified as such to the local planning authority; 1980 c. 66. 1966 c. 42.

(b) any other operations or use of land which appear to the local highway authority to be likely to result in a material increase in the volume of traffic entering or leaving such a classified or proposed road, to prejudice the improvement or construction of such a road or to result in a material change in the character of traffic entering, leaving or using such a road.

(2) The reference to a local planning authority in sub-paragraph (1) shall not be construed as including a reference to an urban development corporation who are the local planning authority by virtue of an order under section 149 of the Local Government, Planning and Land Act 1980, and no provision of a development order which is included in it by virtue of that paragraph is to be construed as applying to such a corporation. 1980 c. 65.

(3) The Secretary of State may include in a development order provision enabling a local highway authority to impose restrictions on the grant by an urban development corporation who are the local planning authority of planning permission for such descriptions of development as may be specified in the order.

6.—(1) A development order may also include provision requiring a county planning authority who are determining any application mentioned in paragraph 3 and relating to a county matter, or an application for approval of a matter reserved under an outline planning permission within the meaning of section 92 and so relating, to give the district planning authority for the area in which the land to which the application relates is situated an opportunity to make recommendations to the county planning authority as to the manner in which the application is determined, and to take into account any such recommendations.

SCH. 1

(2) It may also include provision requiring a county or district planning authority who have received any application so mentioned or any application for such approval (including any such application relating to land in a National Park) to notify the district or, as the case may be, county planning authority of the terms of their decision, or, where the application is referred to the Secretary of State, the date when it was so referred and, when notified to them, the terms of his decision.

7.—(1) It shall be the duty of a local planning authority in a non-metropolitan county when exercising their functions under sections 70 and 71 to seek the achievement of the general objectives of the structure plan for the time being in force in their area.

(2) Subject to sub-paragraph (4), the district planning authority shall consult the county planning authority for their area before determining any application to which this sub-paragraph applies.

(3) Sub-paragraph (2) applies to any application for planning permission for the carrying out—

(a) of any development of land which would materially conflict with or prejudice the implementation—

(i) of any policy or general proposal contained in a structure plan which has been approved by the Secretary of State;

(ii) of any policy or general proposal contained in proposals for the alteration or repeal and replacement of a structure plan which have been submitted to the Secretary of State for approval;

(iii) of any proposal for the alteration or repeal and replacement of a structure plan so as to include in the plan any matter to which the county planning authority have given publicity under section 33;

(iv) of a fundamental provision of a development plan to which paragraph 2 of Part III of Schedule 2 applies, so far as the development plan is in force in the district planning authority's area;

(v) of any proposal contained in a local plan which has been prepared by the county planning authority (whether or not the plan has been adopted by the authority or approved by the Secretary of State);

(vi) of any proposal to include in a local plan which the county planning authority are preparing any matter to which they have given publicity under section 39 or 40;

(vii) of any proposal to include in alterations which the county planning authority are proposing for a local plan any matter to which they have given publicity under section 39 or 40;

(b) of any development of land which would, by reason of its scale or nature or the location of the land, be of major importance for the implementation of a structure plan;

(c) of any development of land in an area which the county planning authority have notified to the district planning authority, in writing, as an area in which development is likely to affect or be affected by the winning and working of minerals, other than coal;

(d) of any development of land which the county planning authority have notified the district planning authority, in writing, that they themselves propose to develop;

(e) of any development of land which would prejudice the carrying out of development proposed by the county planning authority and notified to the district planning authority under paragraph (d);

(f) of any development of land in England in respect of which the county planning authority have notified the district planning authority, in writing, that it is proposed that it shall be used for waste disposal;

(g) of any development of land which would prejudice a proposed use of land for waste disposal notified to the district planning authority under paragraph (f).

(4) The district planning authority may determine any application to which sub-paragraph (2) applies without the consultation required by that sub-paragraph if the county planning authority have given them directions authorising them to do so.

(5) A direction under sub-paragraph (4) may relate to a class of applications or to a particular application.

(6) Subject to sub-paragraph (7), where the district planning authority are required to consult the county planning authority before determining an application for planning permission—

(a) they shall give the county planning authority notice that they propose to consider the application and send them a copy of it; and

(b) they shall not determine it until the expiration of such period from the date of the notice as a development order may provide.

(7) A district planning authority may determine an application for planning permission before the expiration of such a period as is mentioned in sub-paragraph (6)(b)—

(a) if they have received representations concerning the application from the county planning authority before the expiration of that period; or

(b) if the county planning authority have notified them that they do not wish to make representations.

(8) Where a district planning authority are required to consult the county planning authority before determining an application for planning permission, they shall in determining it take into account any representations relating to it which they have received from the county planning authority before the expiration of the period mentioned in sub-paragraph (6)(b).

8.—(1) Where a district planning authority or, in a metropolitan county, a local planning authority have been notified in writing by the council of a parish or community wholly or partly situated in the area of that authority that the council wish to be informed—

(a) of every application for planning permission relating to land in the parish or community,

(b) of every application so relating for approval of a matter reserved under an outline planning permission within the meaning of section 92, or

(c) of any description of such applications,

if the authority receive any such application or, as the case may be, an application of any such description they shall inform the council in writing of the application, indicating the nature of the development to which the application relates and identifying the land to which it relates.

(2) The provisions which may be contained in a development order shall include provision requiring—

(a) a local planning authority, who are determining any application of which the council of a parish or community are entitled to be informed, to give that council an opportunity to make representations to the local planning authority as to the manner in which the application should be determined and to take into account any such representations;

(b) the district planning authority or, in a metropolitan county, a local planning authority to notify that council of the terms of their or, in a non-metropolitan county, the county planning authority's decision on

SCH. 1

any such application or, where the application is referred to the Secretary of State, the date when it was so referred and, when notified to them, the terms of his decision.

9.—(1) The functions of local planning authorities under the provisions of this Act relating to simplified planning zone schemes shall be exercised in non-metropolitan counties by the district planning authorities.

(2) Where a district planning authority in a non-metropolitan county are proceeding in accordance with paragraph 5 of Schedule 7, before they prepare the proposed scheme or alterations they shall consult the county council as planning authority and as to the effect of their proposals on existing or future highways; and when they have prepared the proposed scheme or alterations they shall send the county council a copy.

(3) Where a district planning authority in a non-metropolitan county are proceeding in accordance with paragraph 6 of Schedule 7, they shall send a copy of the proposed alterations to the county council.

10. Elsewhere than in a National Park, the functions of a local planning authority under section 94 shall be exercisable by the district planning authority, except that where the relevant planning permission was granted by the county planning authority, those functions, so far as relating to that permission, shall be exercisable by the county planning authority and also by the district planning authority after consulting the county planning authority.

11.—(1) The functions of a local planning authority of—

(a) making orders under section 97 revoking or modifying planning permission, or under section 102 requiring discontinuance of use, imposing conditions on continuance of use or requiring the alteration or removal of buildings or works, or

(b) issuing enforcement notices under section 172 or serving stop notices under section 183,

shall, subject to sub-paragraphs (2) to (4), be exercisable by the district planning authority.

(2) In a case where it appears to the district planning authority of a district in a non-metropolitan county that the functions mentioned in sub-paragraph (1) relate to county matters, they shall not exercise those functions without first consulting the county planning authority.

(3) Subject to sub-paragraph (4), in a non-metropolitan county those functions shall also be exercisable by a county planning authority in a case where it appears to that authority that they relate to a matter which should properly be considered a county matter.

(4) In relation to a matter which is a county matter by virtue of any of the provisions of paragraph 1(1)(a) to (h) the functions of a local planning authority specified in sub-paragraph (1)(b) shall only be exercisable by the county planning authority in their capacity as mineral planning authority.

12. In sections 178(1), 181(4)(b) and 190(2) to (5) any reference to the local planning authority shall be construed as a reference to the authority who issued the notice or made the order in question or, in the case of an notice issued or an order made by the Secretary of State, the authority named in the notice or order.

13.—(1) A county planning authority may only make a tree preservation order—

(a) if they make it in pursuance of section 197(b);

(b) if it relates to land which does not lie wholly within the area of a single district planning authority; SCH. 1

(c) if it relates to land in which the county planning authority hold an interest; or

(d) if it relates to land in a National Park.

(2) Where a local planning authority have made a tree preservation order under section 198 or the Secretary of State has made such an order by virtue of section 202, the powers of varying or revoking the order and the powers of dispensing with section 206 or serving, or appearing on an appeal relating to, a notice under section 207 shall be exercisable only by the authority who made the order or, in the case of an order made by the Secretary of State, the authority named in the order.

14. The functions of local planning authorities under sections 69, 211, 214, 220, 221, 224 and 225, and in non-metropolitan counties the functions under section 215, are exercisable by district planning authorities.

15.—(1) The copy of the notice required to be served by paragraph 4(5) of Schedule 8 on a local planning authority shall, in the case of a proposal that a government department should give a direction under section 90(1) or that development should be carried out by or on behalf of a government department, be served on the local planning authority who, in the opinion of the Secretary of State, would have been responsible for dealing with an application for planning permission for the development in question if such an application had fallen to be made.

(2) References in paragraphs 3(2) and 5(1) of that Schedule to the local planning authority shall be construed as references to the local planning authority on whom that copy is required to be served.

Compensation

16.—(1) Claims for payment of compensation under section 107 (including that section as applied by section 108) and sections 114, 115(1) to (4), 186 and 223 shall, subject to sub-paragraph (3), be made to and paid by the local planning authority who took the action by virtue of which the claim arose or, where that action was taken by the Secretary of State, the local planning authority from whom the appeal was made to him or who referred the matter to him or, in the case of an order made or notice served by him by virtue of section 100, 104 or 185, the appropriate authority, and references in those sections to a local planning authority shall be construed accordingly.

(2) In this paragraph "appropriate authority" means—

(a) in the case of a claim for compensation under section 107 or 108, the local planning authority who granted, or are to be treated for the purposes of section 107 as having granted, the planning permission the revocation or modification of which gave rise to the claim;

(b) in the case of a claim for compensation under section 115(1) to (4) or 186, the local planning authority named in the relevant order or stop notice of the Secretary of State;

(c) in the case of a claim for compensation under section 223, the district planning authority.

(3) The Secretary of State may after consultation with all the authorities concerned direct that where a local planning authority is liable to pay compensation under any of the provisions mentioned in sub-paragraph (1) in any particular case or class of case they shall be entitled to be reimbursed the whole of the compensation or such proportion of it as he may direct from one or more authorities specified in the direction.

SCH. 1

(4) The local planning authority by whom compensation is to be paid and to whom claims for compensation are to be made under section 144(2) shall be the district planning authority.

17. Claims for payment of compensation under a tree preservation order by virtue of section 203, and claims for payment of compensation under section 204 by virtue of directions given in pursuance of such an order, shall be made to and paid by the local planning authority who made the order or, in the case of an order made by the Secretary of State, the authority named in the order; and the reference in section 204(2) to the authority exercising functions under the tree preservation order shall have effect subject to the provisions of this paragraph.

18. The local planning authority by whom compensation is to be paid under section 279(1)(a) to statutory undertakers shall be the authority who referred the application for planning permission to the Secretary of State and the appropriate Minister, or from whose decision the appeal was made to them or who served the enforcement notice appealed against, as the case may be.

The Crown

19.—(1) Elsewhere than in a metropolitan county or a National Park the functions conferred by section 302 and Schedule 15 on the authority responsible for enforcing planning control shall, subject to sub-paragraph (3)—

(a) in the case of works on or a use of land which in the opinion of the district planning authority relates to a county matter, be exercised by the county planning authority;

(b) in any other case be exercised by the district planning authority.

(2) As respects an area in a National Park outside a metropolitan county those functions shall be exercised by the county planning authority.

(3) Every application made under subsection (3) of that section to an authority responsible for enforcing planning control shall be made to the district planning authority who, in the case of an application falling to be determined by the county planning authority, shall send it on to the latter.

(4) A county planning authority determining any such application shall give the district planning authority for the area in which the land to which the application relates is situated an opportunity to make recommendations to the county planning authority as to the manner in which the application should be determined and shall take any such recommendations into account.

(5) A county or district planning authority who have dealt with any such application shall notify the district or, as the case may be, the county planning authority of the terms of their determination or, in a case where the application has been referred to the Secretary of State, the date when it was so referred.

Miscellaneous

20.—(1) The local planning authority whom the Secretary of State is required to consult under section 100(3), 104(3) or 202(1) or serve with a notice of his proposals under section 100(4) or 104(4) shall be the county planning authority or the district planning authority, as he thinks appropriate, and references in sections 100(2), (3) and (4) and 104(2), (3) and (4) and 202 to the local planning authority shall be construed accordingly.

(2) In sections 96, 182 and 185 any reference to the local planning authority shall be construed as a reference to the county planning authority or the district planning authority, as the Secretary of State thinks appropriate.

(3) The power of a local planning authority to make agreements under section 106 may be exercised also, in relation to land in the area of a joint planning board, by the council of the county in which the land is situated; and references in that section to a local planning authority shall be construed accordingly. SCH. 1

(4) In paragraph 16 of Schedule 13 the reference to the local planning authority shall be construed—

(a) in relation to land in a National Park outside a metropolitan county, as a reference to the county planning authority; and

(b) in relation to land elsewhere, as a reference to the district planning authority.

21.—(1) Subject to sub-paragraph (2), the provisions of this Schedule do not apply in Greater London.

(2) Paragraph 5(3) of this Schedule applies in Greater London and paragraph 2(3) of Part I and of Part II of Schedule 2 shall apply as respects the temporary application of paragraph 7(1) of this Schedule in the metropolitan counties and in Greater London respectively.

SCHEDULE 2

Sections 28 and 54.

DEVELOPMENT PLANS: TRANSITIONAL PROVISIONS

PART I

THE METROPOLITAN COUNTIES

Continuation of structure plans,

local plans and old development plans

1.—(1) Subject to paragraphs 2 and 3—

(a) the structure plan,

(b) any local plan; and

(c) any old development plan,

which immediately before the commencement of this Act was in force in the area of a local planning authority in a metropolitan county (or in that and other areas) shall continue in force in respect of the area of that authority until a unitary development plan for that area becomes operative under Chapter I of Part II of this Act or, where parts of a unitary development plan become operative on different dates, until every part of it has become operative.

(2) A plan which continues in force by virtue of this paragraph shall, while it continues in force, be treated for the purposes of this Act, any other enactment relating to town and country planning, the Land Compensation Act 1961 and the Highways Act 1980 as being, or being comprised in, the development plan in respect of the area in question. 1961 c. 33. 1980 c. 66.

(3) In this paragraph "old development plan" means any plan which was in force in the area in question immediately before the commencement of this Act by virtue of Schedule 7 to the 1971 Act and paragraph 18 of Schedule 1 to the Local Government Act 1985. 1985 c. 51.

Revocation of structure plan

2.—(1) Where under Chapter I of Part II of this Act the Secretary of State approves all or any of Part I of a unitary development plan he may by order—

(a) wholly or partly revoke a structure plan continued in force by paragraph 1, either in its application to the whole of the area of a local planning authority or in its application to part of that area; and

SCH. 2

(b) make such consequential amendments to that plan as appear to him to be necessary or expedient.

(2) Before making an order under this paragraph the Secretary of State shall consult the local planning authority for the area to which the unitary development plan relates.

(3) Until the structure plan for an area in a metropolitan county ceases to be operative under paragraph 1 or this paragraph, paragraph 7(1) of Schedule 1 shall apply in that area with the omission of the words "in a non-metropolitan county".

Local plans until commencement of Chapter I of Part II

3.—(1) Until the coming into force of Chapter I of Part II of this Act in the area of a local planning authority in a metropolitan county section 30 and the provisions of Chapter II of that Part relating to the preparation, alteration, repeal or replacement of local plans by local planning authorities which are metropolitan district councils and section 54(5) shall apply in relation to that area, but subject to the following provisions of this paragraph.

(2) In respect of the matters referred to in sub-paragraph (1) the following provisions (which relate to county planning authorities) do not apply to metropolitan district councils, namely, sections 37, 38(4), 39(4) and (5)(c), 40(2)(c), 46(2) to (6), 47, 48(2) and 50(7).

(3) A metropolitan district council may at any time—

(a) make proposals for the preparation of a local plan or the alteration, repeal or replacement of a local plan adopted by them or adopted by the metropolitan county council and in force in the area of that authority on 1st April 1986;

(b) with the consent of the Secretary of State, make proposals for the alteration, repeal or replacement of a local plan approved by him.

(4) On the coming into force in any area of Chapter I of Part II of this Act, any local plan or proposal for the alteration, repeal or replacement of a local plan which—

(a) has been prepared by a metropolitan district council (or by such a council jointly with one or more other such councils); but

(b) has not been adopted or approved,

shall be treated as having been abandoned by that council or those councils.

(5) Paragraph 1 shall apply to plans which are prepared or altered in pursuance of this paragraph as it applies to those there mentioned.

Incorporation of current local plan in unitary development plan

4.—(1) A unitary development plan shall include any local plan which is in force in respect of the area in question at the time when the unitary development plan is prepared but subject to such alterations, if any, as may be specified in Part II of the unitary development plan.

(2) A unitary development plan shall as respects any such local plan indicate the extent, if any, to which it is subject to alteration in accordance with Part II of the unitary development plan.

(3) This paragraph shall not be construed as enabling any objections to be made to any part of a unitary development plan which consists of provisions of a local plan that are not subject to alterations as mentioned in sub-paragraph (1).

Publicity in connection with local plan

5. In determining the steps to be taken by a local planning authority or local planning authorities to secure the purposes of section 13(1)(a) to (c) or section 23(3)(a) to (c) in relation to proposals made in respect of a unitary development plan, the authority or authorities may under those provisions, and the Secretary of State may under section 13(6), take into account any steps taken by the authority or authorities to secure those purposes in relation to the same or similar proposals made in respect of a local plan.

Pending proposals by metropolitan county council

6. Where before 1st April 1986 the Secretary of State directed that any local plan or proposals for the alteration, repeal or replacement of a local plan which had been prepared by a metropolitan county council before 1st April 1986 but had not been adopted or approved should not have effect unless approved by him, he shall continue to consider the plan or the proposals and give his decision on them as if the plan or proposals had been prepared and submitted by the metropolitan district council whose area is affected by the plan or proposals or, where the areas of two or more such councils are affected, as if the plan or proposals had been a joint plan or joint proposals prepared by those councils.

PART II

GREATER LONDON

Continuation of Greater London Development Plan,

local plans and old development plans

1.—(1) Subject to paragraphs 2 and 3—

(a) the Greater London Development Plan,

(b) any local plan; and

(c) any old development plan,

which immediately before the commencement of this Act was in force in the area of a local planning authority in Greater London (or in that and other areas) shall continue in force in respect of the area of that authority until a unitary development plan for that area becomes operative under Chapter I of Part II of this Act or, where parts of a unitary development plan become operative on different dates, until every part of it has become operative.

(2) A plan which continues in force by virtue of this paragraph shall, while it continues in force, be treated for the purposes of this Act, any other enactment relating to town and country planning, the Land Compensation Act 1961 and the Highways Act 1980 as being, or being comprised in, the development plan in respect of the area in question. 1961 c. 33. 1980 c. 66.

(3) In this paragraph "old development plan" has the same meaning as in paragraph 1 of Part I of this Schedule.

Revocation of Greater London Development Plan

2.—(1) Where under Chapter I of Part II of this Act the Secretary of State approves all or any of Part I of a unitary development plan he may by order—

(a) wholly or partly revoke the Greater London Development Plan, either in its application to the whole of the area of a local planning authority or in its application to part of that area; and

(b) make such consequential amendments to that plan as appear to him to be necessary or expedient.

(2) Before making an order under this paragraph the Secretary of State shall consult the local planning authority for the area to which the unitary development plan relates.

SCH. 2 (3) Until the Greater London Development Plan ceases to be operative in an area under paragraph 1 or this paragraph, paragraph 7(1) of Schedule 1 shall apply in that area—

(a) with the omission of the words "in a non-metropolitan county"; and

(b) with the substitution for the reference to the structure plan of a reference to that Plan.

Surveys and local plans

3.—(1) Until the coming into force of Chapter I of Part II of this Act in the area of a local planning authority in Greater London, section 30 and paragraphs 4 to 16 of this Part of this Schedule and sections 49, 51, 52 and 53 (so far as those sections relate to the preparation, alteration, repeal or replacement of local plans by local planning authorities which are London borough councils) and section 54(5) shall apply in relation to that area, but subject to the following provisions of this paragraph.

(2) The matters to be examined or kept under review by a London borough council under section 30 shall be such of the matters mentioned in that section as were not examined or kept under review by the Greater London Council.

(3) In its application by virtue of this paragraph section 53(2)(f) shall have effect with the substitution for the references to section 39(2)(a) and section 39(5)(a) or 40(2)(a) of references to paragraph 8(1)(a) and (2) respectively.

(4) On the coming into force in any area of Chapter I of Part II of this Act, any local plan or proposal for the alteration, repeal or replacement of a local plan which—

(a) has been prepared by a London borough council or by such a council jointly with one or more other such councils; but

(b) has not been adopted or approved,

shall be treated as having been abandoned by that council or those councils.

(5) Paragraph 1 shall apply to plans which are prepared or altered in pursuance of this paragraph as it applies to those there mentioned.

4.—(1) A London borough council may at any time, if they think fit, prepare a local plan for the whole or any part of the borough (other than the whole or any part of a G.L.C. action area within the meaning of paragraph 5).

(2) Different local plans may be prepared for different purposes for the same area.

5.—(1) In this paragraph—

"action area" means any area indicated by the Greater London Development Plan as an area intended for comprehensive development, redevelopment or improvement as a whole which the Secretary of State has directed shall be treated as an action area, and

"G.L.C. action area" means an action area in whose case it was indicated in the Greater London Development Plan that it was for the Greater London Council, and not a London borough council, to prepare a local plan for that area.

(2) As soon as practicable in the case of any action area other than a G.L.C. action area—

(a) if it is wholly comprised within a London borough, the council of that borough shall prepare a local plan for the area, and

(b) if not, the council of every London borough in which any part of the action area falls shall prepare a local plan for that part, SCH. 2

but this sub-paragraph shall not be taken to require a council to do again anything which they have already done.

(3) Where a council are required by this paragraph to prepare a local plan, they shall take steps for the adoption of that plan.

6.—(1) Without prejudice to the previous provisions, a London borough council shall, if the Secretary of State gives them a direction in that behalf with respect to any area of Greater London, as soon as practicable prepare for that area a local plan of such a nature as may be specified in the direction, and take steps for the adoption of the plan.

(2) Before giving a direction to a council under this paragraph the Secretary of State shall consult the council with respect to it.

7.—(1) This paragraph shall apply with respect to any local plan prepared under Schedule 4 to the 1971 Act or this Schedule by a local planning authority and in this paragraph "the authority" means the authority preparing the local plan.

(2) The plan shall consist of a map and a written statement and shall—

(a) formulate in such detail as the authority think appropriate their proposals for the development and other use of land in the area for which the plan is prepared, or for any description of development or other use of such land (including in either case such measures as the authority think fit for the improvement of the physical environment and the management of traffic); and

(b) contain such matters as may be prescribed.

(3) The plan shall contain, or be accompanied by, such diagrams, illustrations and descriptive material as the authority think appropriate for the purpose of explaining or illustrating the proposals in the plan, or as may be prescribed; and any such diagrams, illustrations and descriptive material shall be treated as forming part of the plan.

(4) In formulating their proposals in the plan the authority shall—

(a) secure that the proposals conform generally to the Greater London Development Plan, and

(b) have regard to any information and any other considerations which appear to them to be relevant, or which may be prescribed, or which the Secretary of State may in any particular case direct them to take into account.

(5) Before giving a direction to the authority under this paragraph the Secretary of State shall consult the authority with respect to it.

8.—(1) Where a London borough council propose to prepare a local plan, the council shall take such steps as will in their opinion secure—

(a) that adequate publicity is given, in any London borough affected by the plan, to any relevant matter arising out of a survey under section 6 of the 1971 Act or section 30 of this Act (including any joint survey) and to the matters proposed to be included in the plan;

(b) that persons who may be expected to want an opportunity of making representations to the council with respect to those matters are made aware that they are entitled to such an opportunity; and

SCH. 2

(c) that such persons are given an adequate opportunity of making such representations;

and the council shall consider any representations made to them within the prescribed period.

(2) After preparing a local plan, the council shall before adopting it or submitting it for approval under paragraph 10, make copies of the plan available for inspection at their office and send a copy to the Secretary of State.

(3) Each copy of a plan made available for inspection as required by sub-paragraph (2) shall be accompanied by a statement of the time within which objections to the local plan may be made to the council who have prepared the plan; and the copy sent to the Secretary of State shall be accompanied by a statement containing particulars—

(a) of the steps which the council preparing the plan have taken to comply with sub-paragraph (1), and

(b) of the council's consultations with, and their consideration of the views of, other persons.

9.—(1) For the purpose of considering objections made to a local plan the local planning authority may and, in the case of objections so made in accordance with regulations, shall cause a local inquiry or other hearing to be held by a person appointed by the Secretary of State or, in such cases as may be prescribed, by the authority themselves, and—

1972 c. 70.

(a) subsections (2) and (3) of section 250 of the Local Government Act 1972 (power to summon and examine witnesses) shall apply to an inquiry held under this paragraph as they apply to an inquiry held under that section;

1971 c. 62.

(b) the Tribunals and Inquiries Act 1971 shall apply to a local inquiry or other hearing held under this paragraph as it applies to a statutory inquiry held by the Secretary of State, but as if in section 12(1) of that Act (statement of reasons for decisions) the reference to any decision taken by the Secretary of State were a reference to a decision taken by a local authority.

(2) Regulations made for the purposes of sub-paragraph (1) may—

(a) make provision with respect to the appointment and qualifications for appointment of persons to hold a local inquiry or other hearing under that sub-paragraph, including provision enabling the Secretary of State to direct a local planning authority to appoint a particular person, or one of a specified list or class of persons;

(b) make provision with respect to the remuneration and allowances of a person appointed for that purpose.

(3) The requirement for a local inquiry or other hearing to be held shall not apply if all persons who have made an objection have indicated in writing that they do not wish to appear.

10.—(1) After the expiry of the period given for making objections to a local plan or, if such objections have been duly made during that period, after considering the objections so made, the local planning authority may, subject to paragraph 11 and sub-paragraphs (2), (3) and (4), by resolution adopt the plan either as originally prepared or as modified so as to take account—

(a) of objections so made;

(b) of any other objections made to the plan;

(c) of any other considerations which appear to the authority to be material.

(2) Where— Sch. 2

(a) an objection to the plan has been made by the Minister of Agriculture, Fisheries and Food (in this paragraph referred to as "the Minister"); and

(b) the local planning authority do not propose to modify the plan to take account of that objection,

the authority—

(i) shall send the Secretary of State particulars of the Minister's objection, together with a statement of their reasons for not modifying the plan to take account of it; and

(ii) shall not adopt the plan unless the Secretary of State authorises them to do so.

(3) The local planning authority shall not adopt a local plan unless it conforms generally to the Greater London Development Plan.

(4) After copies of a local plan have been sent to the Secretary of State and before the plan has been adopted by the local planning authority, the Secretary of State may direct that the plan shall not have effect unless approved by him.

(5) Subject to sub-paragraph (6), where particulars of an objection to a local plan made by the Minister have been sent to the Secretary of State under sub-paragraph (2), it shall be the duty of the Secretary of State to give a direction under sub-paragraph (4).

(6) The Secretary of State need not give such a direction if he is satisfied that the Minister no longer objects to the plan.

(7) Where the Secretary of State gives a direction under sub-paragraph (4), the local planning authority shall submit the plan accordingly to him for his approval, and—

(a) the Secretary of State may, after considering the plan, either approve it (in whole or in part and with or without modifications or reservations) or reject it;

(b) in considering the plan, the Secretary of State may take into account any matters which he thinks are relevant, whether or not they were taken into account in the plan as submitted to him;

(c) subject to paragraph (d), where on taking the plan into consideration the Secretary of State does not determine then to reject it, he shall, before determining whether or not to approve it—

(i) consider any objections to the plan, so far as they are made in accordance with regulations;

(ii) give any persons whose objections so made are not withdrawn an opportunity of appearing before, and being heard by, a person appointed by him for the purpose; and

(iii) if a local inquiry or other hearing is held, also give the same opportunity to the authority and such other persons as he thinks fit;

(d) before deciding whether or not to approve the plan the Secretary of State shall not be obliged to consider any objections to it if objections to it have been considered by the authority, or to cause an inquiry or other hearing to be held into any objections to it if any such inquiry or hearing has already been held at the instance of the authority;

(e) without prejudice to paragraph (c), on considering the plan the Secretary of State may consult with, or consider the views of, any local planning authority or other persons, but shall not be under an obligation to consult with, or consider the views of, any other authority or persons or, except as provided by that paragraph, to give an opportunity for the making of any objections or other representations, or to cause any local inquiry or other hearing to be held; and

SCH. 2

(f) after the giving of the direction the authority shall have no further power or duty to hold a local inquiry or other hearing under paragraph 9.

(8) Where there is a conflict between any of the provisions of a local plan which has been adopted or approved under this paragraph or under section 14 of the 1971 Act and the provisions of the Greater London Development Plan, the provisions of the local plan shall be taken to prevail for all purposes.

11.—(1) If, on considering the statement submitted with, and the matters included in, a local plan (joint or other) prepared under Schedule 4 to the 1971 Act or under this Schedule and other information provided by the authority who prepared the plan (or as the case may be, the authorities who joined in its preparation), the Secretary of State is not satisfied that the purposes of paragraph 8(1)(a) to (c) have been adequately achieved by the steps taken in that behalf by the authority or authorities, he may within 21 days of the receipt of the statement direct that no further steps for the adoption of the plan be taken without such further action as he may specify having been taken in order better to achieve those purposes and his being satisfied that such action has been taken.

(2) A planning authority who are given directions by the Secretary of State under this paragraph shall—

(a) immediately withdraw copies of the local plan made available for inspection as required by paragraph 8; and

(b) in a case where objections to the plan have been made by any person, notify him that the Secretary of State has given such directions.

12.—(1) A local planning authority may at any time make proposals for the alteration, repeal or replacement of a relevant local plan and may at any time, with the consent of the Secretary of State, make proposals for the alteration, repeal or replacement of a local plan approved by him.

(2) Without prejudice to sub-paragraph (1), a local planning authority shall, if the Secretary of State gives them a direction in that behalf with respect to a relevant local plan or a local plan approved by him, as soon as practicable prepare proposals of a kind specified in the direction, being proposals for the alteration, repeal or replacement of the plan.

(3) In sub-paragraphs (1) and (2) "relevant local plan" means a local plan adopted by the authority or adopted by the Greater London Council and in force in respect of the area of the authority on 1st April 1986.

(4) The provisions of paragraphs 7(4) and (5), 8, 9 and 10 shall apply in relation to the making of proposals for the alteration, repeal or replacement of a local plan under this paragraph and to alterations to a local plan so proposed, as they apply in relation to the preparation of a local plan under this Schedule and to a local plan prepared under it.

Joint plans

13.—(1) The following provisions of this paragraph have effect where two or more local planning authorities prepare a local plan jointly.

(2) The local planning authorities shall jointly take such steps as will in their opinion secure—

(a) that adequate publicity is given in their areas to the matters proposed to be included in the plan;

(b) that persons who may be expected to want an opportunity of making representations to any of the authorities are made aware that they are entitled to an opportunity of doing so; and

(c) that such persons are given an adequate opportunity of making such representations.

(3) Sub-paragraph (1)(b) and (c) of paragraph 8 shall not apply in relation to joint local plans and the reference in sub-paragraph (3) of that paragraph to sub-paragraph (1) of that paragraph, and the reference in paragraph 11(1) to sub-paragraph (1)(a) to (c) of paragraph 8, shall both include a reference to sub-paragraph (2) of this paragraph.

(4) Each of the local planning authorities by whom a joint local plan has been prepared for any part of Greater London shall have the duty imposed by sub-paragraph (2) of paragraph 8 of making copies of the plan available for inspection, and objections to the plan may be made to any of those authorities, and the statement required by sub-paragraph (3) of that paragraph to accompany copies of the plan made available for inspection shall state that objections may be so made.

(5) In relation to joint proposals under paragraph 12(1) for the alteration, repeal or replacement of a local plan, the reference in paragraph 12(4) to paragraph 8 shall include a reference to this paragraph.

14. It shall fall to each of the local planning authorities by whom a joint local plan was prepared to adopt the plan under paragraph 10(1) and they may do so as respects any part of their area to which the plan relates but any modifications subject to which it is adopted must be agreed between all those authorities.

15. Where a local plan has been prepared jointly, the power of making proposals under paragraph 12(1) for the alteration, repeal or replacement of the plan may be exercised as respects their respective areas by any of the authorities by whom it was prepared and the Secretary of State may under paragraph 12(2) direct any of them to make such proposals as respects their respective areas.

16. The date appointed under section 53(5) for the coming into operation of a local plan prepared jointly by two or more local planning authorities or for the alteration, repeal or replacement of a local plan in pursuance of proposals so prepared shall be one jointly agreed by those authorities and be specified in their respective resolutions adopting the plan or proposals.

Incorporation of current local plan in unitary development plan

17.—(1) A unitary development plan shall include any local plan which is in force in respect of the area in question at the time when the unitary development plan is prepared but subject to such alterations, if any, as may be specified in Part II of the unitary development plan.

(2) A unitary development plan shall as respects any such local plan indicate the extent, if any, to which it is subject to alteration in accordance with Part II of the unitary development plan.

(3) This paragraph shall not be construed as enabling any objections to be made to any part of a unitary development plan which consists of provisions of a local plan that are not subject to alterations as mentioned in sub-paragraph (1).

Publicity in connection with local plan

18. In determining the steps to be taken by a local planning authority or local planning authorities to secure the purposes of section 13(1)(a) to (c) or section 23(3)(a) to (c) in relation to proposals made in respect of a unitary development plan, the authority or authorities may under those provisions, and the Secretary of State may under section 13(6), take into account any steps taken by the authority or authorities to secure those purposes in relation to the same or similar proposals made in respect of a local plan.

SCH. 2

PART III

OLD DEVELOPMENT PLANS

Preliminary

1. In this Part of this Schedule "old development plan" means a development plan to which paragraph 2 of Schedule 7 to the 1971 Act (continuation in force of development plans prepared before structure plans became operative) applied immediately before the commencement of this Act.

Continuation in force of old development plans

2. Any old development plan which immediately before the commencement of this Act was in force as respects any district shall, subject to the provisions of this Part of this Schedule, continue in force as respects that district and be treated for the purposes of this Act, any other enactment relating to town and country planning, the Land Compensation Act 1961 and the Highways Act 1980 as being comprised in the development plan for that district.

1961 c. 33.
1980 c. 66.

Other plans to prevail over old development plans

3. Subject to the following provisions of this Part of this Schedule, where by virtue of paragraph 2 the old development plan for any district is treated as being comprised in a development plan for that district—

(a) if there is a conflict between any of its provisions and those of the structure plan for that district, or, in the case of Greater London, the Greater London Development Plan the provisions of the structure plan or, as the case may be, that Plan shall be taken to prevail for the purposes of Parts III, V, VI, VII, VIII and IX of this Act and of the Planning (Listed Buildings and Conservation Areas) Act 1990 and the Planning (Hazardous Substances) Act 1990; and

1990 c. 9.
1990 c. 10.

(b) if there is a conflict between any of its provisions and those of a local plan, the provisions of the local plan shall be taken to prevail for those purposes.

Street authorisation maps

4. Where immediately before the commencement of this Act a street authorisation map prepared in pursuance of the Town and Country Planning (Development Plans) Regulations 1965 or the Town and Country Planning (Development Plans for Greater London) Regulations 1966 was treated for the purposes of the 1971 Act as having been adopted as a local plan for a district by a local planning authority, it shall continue to be so treated.

S.I. 1965/1453.
S.I. 1966/48.

Development plans for compensation purposes

5. Where there is no local plan in force in a district, then, for any of the purposes of the Land Compensation Act 1961—

(a) the development plan or current development plan shall as respects that district be taken as being whichever of the following plans gives rise to those assumptions as to the grant of planning permission which are more favourable to the owner of the land acquired, for that purpose, namely the structure plan or, as the case may be, the Greater London Development Plan, so far as applicable to the district, and any alterations to it, together with the Secretary of State's notice of approval of the plan and alterations, and the old development plan;

(b) land situated in an area defined in the current development plan as an area of comprehensive development shall be taken to be situated in whichever of the following areas leads to such assumptions as are mentioned in paragraph (a), namely any area wholly or partly within that district selected by the structure plan or, as the case may be, the Greater London Development Plan as an action area and the area so defined in the old development plan. SCH. 2

Discontinuance of old development plan on adoption of local plan

6. Subject to paragraph 8, on the adoption or approval of a local plan under section 43 or 45 or paragraph 10 of Part II of this Schedule so much of any old development plan as relates to the area to which the local plan relates shall cease to have effect.

7. The Secretary of State may by order direct that any of the provisions of the old development plan shall continue in force in relation to the area to which the local plan relates.

8. If the Secretary of State makes an order under paragraph 7, the provisions of the old development plan specified in the order shall continue in force to the extent so specified.

9. Subject to paragraph 10, the Secretary of State may by order wholly or partly revoke a development plan continued in force under this Schedule whether in its application to the whole of the area of a local planning authority or in its application to part of that area and make such consequential amendments to the plan as appear to him to be necessary or expedient.

10. Before making an order with respect to a development plan under paragraph 7 or 9, the Secretary of State shall consult with the local planning authority for the area to which the plan relates.

SCHEDULE 3

Sections 55, 107 and 114.

DEVELOPMENT NOT CONSTITUTING NEW DEVELOPMENT

PART I

DEVELOPMENT NOT RANKING FOR COMPENSATION UNDER S. 114

1. The carrying out of—

(a) the rebuilding, as often as occasion may require, of any building which was in existence on 1st July 1948, or of any building which was in existence before that date but was destroyed or demolished after 7th January 1937, including the making good of war damage sustained by any such building;

(b) the rebuilding, as often as occasion may require, of any building erected after 1st July 1948 which was in existence at a material date;

(c) the carrying out for the maintenance, improvement or other alteration of any building, of works which—

(i) affect only the interior of the building, or do not materially affect the external appearance of the building, and

(ii) are works for making good war damage,

so long as the cubic content of the original building is not substantially exceeded.

2. The use as two or more separate dwellinghouses of any building which at a material date was used as a single dwellinghouse.

SCH. 3

PART II

DEVELOPMENT RANKING FOR COMPENSATION UNDER S. 114

3. The enlargement, improvement or other alteration, as often as may be required, of any such building as is mentioned in paragraph 1(a) or (b), or any building substituted for such a building by the carrying out of any such operations as are mentioned in that paragraph, so long as the cubic content of the original building is not substantially increased or exceeded.

4.—(1) The carrying out, on land which was used for the purposes of agriculture or forestry at a material date, of any building or other operations required for the purposes of that use.

(2) Sub-paragraph (1) does not apply to operations for the erection, enlargement, improvement or alteration of dwellinghouses or of buildings used—

(a) for the purposes of market gardens, nursery grounds or timber yards, or

(b) for other purposes not connected with general farming operations or with the cultivation or felling of trees.

5. The winning and working, on land held or occupied with land used for the purposes of agriculture, of any minerals reasonably required for the purposes of that use, including—

(a) the fertilisation of the land so used, and

(b) the maintenance, improvement or alteration of buildings or works on the land which are occupied or used for those purposes.

6. In the case of a building or other land which—

S.I. 1948/955.

(a) at a material date was used for a purpose falling within any general class specified in the Town and Country Planning (Use Classes for Third Schedule Purposes) Order 1948, or

(b) having been unoccupied on and at all times since 1st July 1948, was last used (otherwise than before 7th January 1937) for any such purpose,

the use of that building or land for any other purpose falling within the same general class.

7. In the case of any building or other land which at a material date was in the occupation of a person by whom part only of it was used for a particular purpose, the use for that purpose of any additional part of the building or land not exceeding—

(a) one-tenth of the cubic content of the part of the building used for that purpose on 1st July 1948 or, if later, the date when the building began to be so used, or

(b) one-tenth of the area of the land so used on that date,

as the case may be.

8. The deposit of waste materials or refuse in connection with the working of minerals, on any land comprised in a site which at a material date was being used for that purpose, so far as may be reasonably required in connection with the working of those minerals.

PART III

SUPPLEMENTARY PROVISIONS

9. Where after 1st July 1948—

(a) any buildings or works have been erected or constructed, or any use of land has been instituted, and

(b) any condition imposed under Part III of this Act, limiting the period for which those buildings or works may be retained, or that use may be continued, has effect in relation to those buildings or works or that use,

this Schedule shall not operate except as respects the period specified in that condition.

10.—(1) Any reference in this Schedule to the cubic content of a building shall be construed as a reference to that content as ascertained by external measurement.

(2) For the purposes of paragraphs 1 and 3 the cubic content of a building is substantially increased or exceeded—

(a) in the case of a dwellinghouse, if it is increased or exceeded by more than one-tenth or 1,750 cubic feet, whichever is the greater; and

(b) in any other case, if it is increased or exceeded by more than one-tenth.

11. For the purposes of paragraph 3—

(a) the erection, on land within the curtilage of any such building as is mentioned in that paragraph, of an additional building to be used in connection with the original building shall be treated as the enlargement of the original building; and

(b) where any two or more buildings comprised in the same curtilage are used as one unit for the purposes of any institution or undertaking, the reference in that paragraph to the cubic content of the original building shall be construed as a reference to the aggregate cubic content of those buildings.

12.—(1) In this Schedule "at a material date" means at either—

(a) 1st July 1948; or

(b) the date by reference to which this Schedule falls to be applied in the particular case in question.

(2) Sub-paragraph (1)(b) shall not apply in relation to any buildings, works or use of land in respect of which, whether before or after the date mentioned in that sub-paragraph, an enforcement notice served before that date has become or becomes effective.

13.—(1) In relation to a building erected after 1st July 1948 which results from the carrying out of any such works as are described in paragraph 1, any reference in this Schedule to the original building is a reference to the building in relation to which those works were carried out and not to the building resulting from the carrying out of those works.

(2) This paragraph has effect subject to section 326(3).

SCH. 3

14.—(1) In the application of this Schedule for the purposes of any determination under section 138(1)—

(a) paragraph 3 shall be construed as not extending to works involving any increase in the cubic content of a building erected after 1st July 1948 (including any building resulting from the carrying out of such works as are described in paragraph 1); and

(b) paragraph 7 shall not apply to any such building.

(2) Sub-paragraph (1) applies also to the application of this Schedule for the purposes of any determination to which section 326(1) applies and for the purposes of that sub-paragraph, so far as applicable by virtue of this sub-paragraph to any determination of existing use value as defined in section 144(6)—

(a) references to this Schedule and to paragraphs 3 and 7 shall be construed as references to Schedule 3 to the 1947 Act and to the corresponding paragraphs of that Schedule; and

(b) that Schedule shall have effect as if it contained a paragraph corresponding to paragraph 13 of this Schedule.

Section 57(7).

SCHEDULE 4

SPECIAL PROVISIONS AS TO LAND USE IN 1948

1. Where on lst July 1948 land was being temporarily used for a purpose other than the purpose for which it was normally used, planning permission is not required for the resumption of the use of the land for the latter purpose before 6th December 1968.

2. Where on 1st July 1948 land was normally used for one purpose and was also used on occasions, whether at regular intervals or not, for another purpose, planning permission is not required in respect of the use of the land for that other purpose on similar occasions on or after 6th December 1968 if the land has been used for that other purpose on at least one similar occasion since 1st July 1948 and before the beginning of 1968.

3. Where land was unoccupied on 1st July 1948, but had before that date been occupied at some time on or after 7th January 1937, planning permission is not required in respect of any use of the land begun before 6th December 1968 for the purpose for which the land was last used before 1st July 1948.

4. Notwithstanding anything in paragraphs 1 to 3, the use of land as a caravan site shall not, by virtue of any of those paragraphs, be treated as a use for which planning permission is not required, unless the land was so used on one occasion at least during the period of two years ending with 9th March 1960.

Sections 72(5), 79(4), 97(5) and Schedule 9.

SCHEDULE 5

CONDITIONS RELATING TO MINERAL WORKING

PART I

CONDITIONS IMPOSED ON GRANT OF PERMISSION

Duration of development

1.—(1) Every planning permission for development consisting of the winning and working of minerals shall be subject to a condition as to the duration of the development.

(2) Except where a condition is specified under sub-paragraph (3), the condition in the case of planning permission granted or deemed to be granted after 22nd February 1982 is that the development must cease not later than the expiration of the period of 60 years beginning with the date of the permission.

(3) An authority granting planning permission after that date or directing after that date that planning permission shall be deemed to be granted may specify a longer or shorter period than 60 years, and if they do so, the condition is that the development must cease not later than the expiration of a period of the specified length beginning with the date of the permission.

(4) A longer or shorter period than 60 years may be prescribed for the purposes of sub-paragraphs (2) and (3).

(5) The condition in the case of planning permission granted or deemed to have been granted before 22nd February 1982 is that the development must cease not later than the expiration of the period of 60 years beginning with that date.

(6) A condition to which planning permission for development consisting of the winning and working of minerals is subject by virtue of this paragraph—

(a) is not to be regarded for the purposes of the planning Acts as a condition such as is mentioned in section 72(1)(b); but

(b) is to be regarded for the purposes of sections 78 and 79 as a condition imposed by a decision of the local planning authority, and may accordingly be the subject of an appeal under section 78.

Power to impose aftercare conditions

2.—(1) Where—

(a) planning permission for development consisting of the winning and working of minerals is granted, and

(b) the permission is subject to a condition requiring that after operations for the winning and working of minerals have been completed, the site shall be restored by the use of any or all of the following, namely, subsoil, topsoil and soil-making material,

it may be granted subject also to any such condition as the mineral planning authority think fit requiring that such steps shall be taken as may be necessary to bring land to the required standard for whichever of the following uses is specified in the condition, namely—

(i) use for agriculture;

(ii) use for forestry; or

(iii) use for amenity.

(2) In this Act—

(a) a condition such as is mentioned in paragraph (b) of sub-paragraph (1) is referred to as " a restoration condition"; and

(b) a condition requiring such steps to be taken as are mentioned in that sub-paragraph is referred to as "an aftercare condition".

(3) An aftercare condition may either—

(a) specify the steps to be taken; or

(b) require that the steps be taken in accordance with a scheme (in this Act referred to as an "aftercare scheme") approved by the mineral planning authority.

(4) A mineral planning authority may approve an aftercare scheme in the form in which it is submitted to them or may modify it and approve it as modified.

SCH. 5

(5) The steps that may be specified in an aftercare condition or an aftercare scheme may consist of planting, cultivating, fertilising, watering, draining or otherwise treating the land.

(6) Where a step is specified in a condition or a scheme, the period during which it is to be taken may also be specified, but no step may be required to be taken after the expiry of the aftercare period.

(7) In sub-paragraph (6) "the aftercare period" means a period of five years from compliance with the restoration condition or such other maximum period after compliance with that condition as may be prescribed; and in respect of any part of a site, the aftercare period shall commence on compliance with the restoration condition in respect of that part.

(8) The power to prescribe maximum periods conferred by sub-paragraph (7) includes power to prescribe maximum periods differing according to the use specified.

(9) In this paragraph "forestry" means the growing of a utilisable crop of timber.

Meaning of "required standard"

3.—(1) In a case where—

(a) the use specified in an aftercare condition is a use for agriculture; and

(b) the land was in use for agriculture at the time of the grant of the planning permission or had previously been used for that purpose and had not at the time of the grant been used for any authorised purpose since its use for agriculture ceased; and

(c) the Minister has notified the mineral planning authority of the physical characteristics of the land when it was last used for agriculture,

the land is brought to the required standard when its physical characteristics are restored, so far as it is practicable to do so, to what they were when it was last used for agriculture.

(2) In any other case where the use specified in an aftercare condition is a use for agriculture, the land is brought to the required standard when it is reasonably fit for that use.

(3) Where the use specified in an aftercare condition is a use for forestry, the land is brought to the required standard when it is reasonably fit for that use.

(4) Where the use specified in an aftercare condition is a use for amenity, the land is brought to the required standard when it is suitable for sustaining trees, shrubs or other plants.

(5) In this paragraph—

"authorised" means authorised by planning permission;

"forestry" has the same meaning as in paragraph 2; and

"the Minister" means—

(a) in relation to England, the Minister of Agriculture, Fisheries and Food; and

(b) in relation to Wales, the Secretary of State.

Consultations

4.—(1) Before imposing an aftercare condition, the mineral planning authority shall consult—

(a) the Minister, where they propose that the use specified in the condition shall be a use for agriculture; and

(b) the Forestry Commission, where they propose that the use so specified shall be a use for forestry, Sch. 5

as to whether it is appropriate to specify that use.

(2) Where after consultations required by sub-paragraph (1) the mineral planning authority are satisfied that the use that they ought to specify is a use for agriculture or for forestry, they shall consult—

(a) where it is for agriculture, the Minister; and

(b) where it is for forestry, the Forestry Commission,

with regard to whether the steps to be taken should be specified in the aftercare condition or in an aftercare scheme.

(3) The mineral planning authority shall also consult the Minister or, as the case may be, the Forestry Commission—

(a) as to the steps to be specified in an aftercare condition which specifies a use for agriculture or for forestry; and

(b) before approving an aftercare scheme submitted in accordance with an aftercare condition which specifies such a use.

(4) The mineral planning authority shall also, from time to time as they consider expedient, consult the Minister or the Commission, as the case may be, as to whether the steps specified in an aftercare condition or an aftercare scheme are being taken.

(5) In this paragraph "forestry" and "the Minister" have the same meanings as in paragraph 3.

Certificate of compliance

5. If, on the application of any person with an interest in land in respect of which an aftercare condition has been imposed, the mineral planning authority are satisfied that the condition has been complied with they shall issue a certificate to that effect.

Recovery of expenses of compliance

6. A person who has complied with an aftercare condition but who has not himself carried out any operations for the winning and working of minerals in, on or under the land shall be entitled, subject to any condition to the contrary contained in a contract which is enforceable against him by the person who last carried out such operations, to recover from that person any expenses reasonably incurred in complying with the aftercare condition.

Part II

Conditions imposed on Revocation or Modification of Permission

7. An order under section 97 may in relation to planning permission for development consisting of the winning and working of minerals, include such aftercare condition as the mineral planning authority think fit if—

(a) it also includes a restoration condition; or

(b) a restoration condition has previously been imposed in relation to the land by virtue of any provision of this Act.

8. Paragraphs 2(3) to (9) and 3 to 6 shall apply in relation to an aftercare condition so imposed as they apply in relation to such a condition imposed under paragraph 2.

SCHEDULE 6

Sections 79,175,195,208.

Determination of Certain Appeals by Person Appointed by Secretary of State

Determination of appeals by appointed person

1.—(1) The Secretary of State may by regulations prescribe classes of appeals under sections 78, 174, 195 and 208, which are to be determined by a person appointed by the Secretary of State for the purpose instead of by the Secretary of State.

(2) Those classes of appeals shall be so determined except in such classes of case—

(a) as may for the time being be prescribed, or

(b) as may be specified in directions given by the Secretary of State.

(3) Regulations made for the purpose of this paragraph may provide for the giving of publicity to any directions given by the Secretary of State under this paragraph.

(4) This paragraph shall not affect any provision in this Act or any instrument made under it that an appeal shall lie to, or a notice of appeal shall be served on, the Secretary of State.

(5) A person appointed under this paragraph is referred to in this Schedule as "an appointed person".

Powers and duties of appointed person

2.—(1) An appointed person shall have the same powers and duties—

(a) in relation to an appeal under section 78, as the Secretary of State has under subsections (1) and (4) of section 79;

(b) in relation to an appeal under section 174, as he has under sections 176(1), (2) and (5) and 177(1) to (4);

(c) in relation to an appeal under section 195, as he has under subsections (2) and (3) of that section and subsection (5) of section 196;

(d) in relation to an appeal under section 208, as he has under subsections (7) and (8) of that section.

(2) Sections 79(2), 175(3), 196(1) and 208(5) shall not apply to an appeal which falls to be determined by an appointed person, but before it is determined the Secretary of State shall ask the appellant and the local planning authority whether they wish to appear before and be heard by the appointed person.

(3) If both the parties express a wish not to appear and be heard the appeal may be determined without their being heard.

(4) If either of the parties expresses a wish to appear and be heard, the appointed person shall give them both an opportunity of doing so.

(5) Sub-paragraph (2) does not apply in the case of an appeal under section 78 if the appeal is referred to a Planning Inquiry Commission under section 101.

(6) Where an appeal has been determined by an appointed person, his decision shall be treated as that of the Secretary of State.

(7) Except as provided by Part XII, the validity of that decision shall not be questioned in any proceedings whatsoever.

(8) It shall not be a ground of application to the High Court under section 288, or of appeal to the High Court under section 289 or 290, that an appeal ought to have been determined by the Secretary of State and not by an appointed person, unless the appellant or the local planning authority challenge the appointed person's power to determine the appeal before his decision on the appeal is given.

(9) Where in any enactment (including this Act) there is a reference to the Secretary of State in a context relating or capable of relating to an appeal to which this Schedule applies or to anything done or authorised or required to be done by, to or before the Secretary of State on or in connection with any such appeal, then so far as the context permits it shall be construed, in relation to an appeal determined or falling to be determined by an appointed person, as a reference to him.

Determination of appeals by Secretary of State

3.—(1) The Secretary of State may, if he thinks fit, direct that an appeal which would otherwise fall to be determined by an appointed person shall instead be determined by the Secretary of State.

(2) Such a direction shall state the reasons for which it is given and shall be served on the person, if any, so appointed, the appellant, the local planning authority and any person who has made representations relating to the subject matter of the appeal which the authority are required to take into account under section 71(2)(a).

(3) Where in consequence of such a direction an appeal falls to be determined by the Secretary of State, the provisions of this Act which are relevant to the appeal shall, subject to the following provisions of this paragraph, apply to the appeal as if this Schedule had never applied to it.

(4) The Secretary of State shall give the appellant, the local planning authority and any person who has made any such representations as mentioned in sub-paragraph (2) an opportunity of appearing before and being heard by a person appointed by the Secretary of State for that purpose if—

(a) the reasons for the direction raise matters with respect to which any of those persons have not made representations; or

(b) in the case of the appellant or the local planning authority, either of them was not asked in pursuance of paragraph 2(2) whether they wished to appear before and be heard by the appointed person, or expressed no wish in answer to that question, or expressed a wish to appear and be heard, but was not given an opportunity of doing so.

(5) Sub-paragraph (4) does not apply in the case of an appeal under section 78 if the appeal is referred to a Planning Inquiry Commission under section 101.

(6) Except as provided by sub-paragraph (4), the Secretary of State need not give any person an opportunity of appearing before and being heard by a person appointed for the purpose, or of making fresh representations or making or withdrawing any representations already made.

(7) In determining the appeal the Secretary of State may take into account any report made to him by any person previously appointed to determine it.

4.—(1) The Secretary of State may by a further direction revoke a direction under paragraph 3 at any time before the determination of the appeal.

(2) Such a further direction shall state the reasons for which it is given and shall be served on the person, if any, previously appointed to determine the appeal, the appellant, the local planning authority and any person who has made representations relating to the subject matter of the appeal which the authority are required to take into account under section 71(2)(a).

(3) Where such a further direction has been given, the provisions of this Schedule relevant to the appeal shall apply, subject to sub-paragraph (4), as if no direction under paragraph 3 had been given.

SCH. 6

(4) Anything done by or on behalf of the Secretary of State in connection with the appeal which might have been done by the appointed person (including any arrangements made for the holding of a hearing or local inquiry) shall, unless that person directs otherwise, be treated as having been done by him.

Appointment of another person to determine appeal

5.—(1) At any time before the appointed person has determined the appeal the Secretary of State may—

(a) revoke his appointment; and

(b) appoint another person under paragraph 1 to determine the appeal instead.

(2) Where such a new appointment is made the consideration of the appeal or any inquiry or other hearing in connection with it shall be begun afresh.

(3) Nothing in sub-paragraph (2) shall require—

(a) the question referred to in paragraph 2(2) to be asked again with reference to the new appointed person if before his appointment it was asked with reference to the previous appointed person (any answers being treated as given with reference to the new appointed person); or

(b) any person to be given an opportunity of making fresh representations or modifying or withdrawing any representations already made.

Local inquiries and hearings

6.—(1) Whether or not the parties to an appeal have asked for an opportunity to appear and be heard, an appointed person—

(a) may hold a local inquiry in connection with the appeal; and

(b) shall do so if the Secretary of State so directs.

(2) Where an appointed person—

(a) holds a hearing by virtue of paragraph 2(4); or

(b) holds an inquiry by virtue of this paragraph,

an assessor may be appointed by the Secretary of State to sit with the appointed person at the hearing or inquiry to advise him on any matters arising, notwithstanding that the appointed person is to determine the appeal.

(3) Subject to sub-paragraph (4), the costs of any such hearing or inquiry shall be defrayed by the Secretary of State.

1972 c. 70.

(4) Subsections (2) to (5) of section 250 of the Local Government Act 1972 (local inquiries: evidence and costs) apply to an inquiry held under this paragraph with the following adaptations—

(a) with the substitution in subsection (4) (recovery of costs of holding the inquiry) for the references to the Minister causing the inquiry to be held of references to the Secretary of State; and

(b) with the substitution in subsection (5) (orders as to the costs of the parties) for the reference to the Minister causing the inquiry to be held of a reference to the appointed person or the Secretary of State.

(5) The appointed person or the Secretary of State has the same power to make orders under section 250(5) of that Act (orders with respect to costs of the parties) in relation to proceedings under this Schedule which do not give rise to an inquiry as he has in relation to such an inquiry.

Supplementary provisions SCH. 6

7. If before or during the determination of an appeal under section 78 which is to be or is being determined in accordance with paragraph 1, the Secretary of State forms the opinion mentioned in section 79(6), he may direct that the determination shall not be begun or proceeded with.

8.—(1) The Tribunals and Inquiries Act 1971 shall apply to a local inquiry or other hearing held in pursuance of this Schedule as it applies to a statutory inquiry held by the Secretary of State, but as if in section 12(1) of that Act (statement of reasons for decisions) the reference to any decision taken by the Secretary of State were a reference to a decision taken by an appointed person. 1971 c. 62.

(2) Where an appointed person is an officer of the Department of the Environment or the Welsh Office the functions of determining an appeal and doing anything in connection with it conferred on him by this Schedule shall be treated for the purposes of the Parliamentary Commissioner Act 1967— 1967 c. 13.

(a) if he was appointed by the Secretary of State for the time being having general responsibility in planning matters in relation to England, as functions of that Department; and

(b) if he was appointed by the Secretary of State for the time being having general responsibility in planning matters in relation to Wales, as functions of the Welsh Office.

SCHEDULE 7

Section 83.

SIMPLIFIED PLANNING ZONES

General

1.—(1) A simplified planning zone scheme shall consist of a map and a written statement, and such diagrams, illustrations and descriptive matter as the local planning authority think appropriate for explaining or illustrating the provisions of the scheme.

(2) A simplified planning zone scheme shall specify—

(a) the development or classes of development permitted by the scheme,

(b) the land in relation to which permission is granted, and

(c) any conditions, limitations or exceptions subject to which it is granted;

and shall contain such other matters as may be prescribed.

Notification of proposals to make or alter scheme

2. An authority who decide under section 83(2) to make or alter a simplified planning zone scheme shall—

(a) notify the Secretary of State of their decision as soon as practicable, and

(b) determine the date on which they will begin to prepare the scheme or the alterations.

Power of Secretary of State to direct making or alteration of scheme

3.—(1) If a person requests a local planning authority to make or alter a simplified planning zone scheme but the authority—

(a) refuse to do so, or

(b) do not within the period of three months from the date of the request decide to do so,

he may, subject to sub-paragraph (2), require them to refer the matter to the Secretary of State.

SCH. 7

(2) A person may not require the reference of the matter to the Secretary of State if—

(a) in the case of a request to make a scheme, a simplified planning zone scheme relating to the whole or part of the land specified in the request has been adopted or approved within the 12 months preceding his request;

(b) in the case of a request to alter the scheme, the scheme to which the request relates was adopted or approved, or any alteration to it has been adopted or approved, within that period.

(3) The Secretary of State shall, as soon as practicable after a matter is referred to him-

(a) send the authority a copy of any representations made to him by the applicant which have not been made to the authority, and

(b) notify the authority that if they wish to make any representations in the matter they should do so, in writing, within 28 days.

(4) After the Secretary of State has—

(a) considered the matter and any written representations made by the applicant or the authority, and

(b) carried out such consultations with such persons as he thinks fit,

he may give the authority a simplified planning zone direction.

(5) The Secretary of State shall notify the applicant and the authority of his decision and of his reasons for it.

4.—(1) A simplified planning zone direction is—

(a) if the request was for the making of a scheme, a direction to make a scheme which the Secretary of State considers appropriate; and

(b) if the request was for the alteration of a scheme, a direction to alter it in such manner as he considers appropriate.

(2) A direction under sub-paragraph (1)(a) or (b) may extend—

(a) to the land specified in the request to the authority,

(b) to any part of the land so specified, or

(c) to land which includes the whole or part of the land so specified;

and accordingly may direct that land shall be added to or excluded from an existing simplified planning zone.

Publicity and consultations: general

5.—(1) A local planning authority who propose to make or alter a simplified planning zone scheme shall proceed in accordance with this paragraph, unless paragraph 6 applies.

(2) They shall take such steps as will in their opinion secure—

(a) that adequate publicity for their proposals is given in the area to which the scheme relates,

(b) that persons who may be expected to wish to make representations about the proposals are made aware that they are entitled to do so, and

(c) that such persons are given an adequate opportunity of making such representations;

and they shall consider any representations made to them within the prescribed period.

(3) They shall then— Sch. 7

(a) prepare the proposed scheme or alterations,

(b) make copies of those documents available for inspection at their office, and

(c) send a copy of them to the Secretary of State.

(4) Each copy of the documents made available for inspection shall be accompanied by a statement of the time within which objections may be made.

(5) Before preparing the proposed scheme or alterations the local planning authority shall consult the Secretary of State having responsibility for highways as to the effect of their proposals on existing or future highways; and when they have prepared the proposed scheme or alterations they shall send him a copy.

Publicity and consultations: short procedure for certain alterations

6.—(1) Where a local planning authority propose to alter a simplified planning zone scheme and it appears to them that the issues involved are not of sufficient importance to warrant the procedure set out in paragraph 5, they may proceed instead in accordance with this paragraph.

(2) They shall prepare the proposed alterations and shall—

(a) make copies of them available for inspection at their office, and

(b) send a copy of them to the Secretary of State.

(3) Each copy of the documents made available for inspection shall be accompanied by a statement of the time within which representations or objections may be made.

(4) They shall then take such steps as may be prescribed for the purpose of—

(a) advertising the fact that the proposed alterations are available for inspection and the places and times at which, and the period during which, they may be inspected, and

(b) inviting the making of representations or objections in accordance with regulations;

and they shall consider any representations made to them within the prescribed period.

(5) The local planning authority shall send a copy of the proposed alterations to the Secretary of State having responsibility for highways.

Powers of Secretary of State to secure adequate publicity and consultations

7.—(1) The documents sent by the local planning authority to the Secretary of State under paragraph 5(3) shall be accompanied by a statement—

(a) of the steps which the authority have taken to comply with paragraph 5(2), and

(b) of the authority's consultations with other persons and their consideration of the views of those persons.

(2) The documents sent by the local planning authority to the Secretary of State under paragraph 6(2) shall be accompanied by a statement of the steps which the authority are taking to comply with paragraph 6(4).

(3) If, on considering the statement and the proposals and any other information provided by the local planning authority, the Secretary of State is not satisfied with the steps taken by the authority, he may, within 21 days of the receipt of the statement, direct the authority not to take further steps for the adoption of the proposals without—

(a) proceeding in accordance with paragraph 5 (if they have proceeded instead in accordance with paragraph 6), or

SCH. 7

(b) in any case, taking such further steps as he may specify,

and satisfying him that they have done so.

(4) A local planning authority who are given directions by the Secretary of State shall—

(a) immediately withdraw the copies of the documents made available for inspection as required by paragraph 5(3)(b) or 6(2)(a), and

(b) notify any person by whom objections to the proposals have been made to the authority that the Secretary of State has given such directions.

Objections: local inquiry or other hearing

8.—(1) The local planning authority may cause a local inquiry or other hearing to be held for the purpose of considering objections to their proposals for the making or alteration of a simplified planning zone scheme.

(2) They shall hold such a local inquiry or other hearing in the case of objections made in accordance with regulations unless all the persons who have made such objections have indicated in writing that they do not wish to appear.

(3) A local inquiry or other hearing shall be held by a person appointed by the Secretary of State or, in such cases as may be prescribed, by the authority themselves.

(4) Regulations may—

(a) make provision with respect to the appointment, and qualifications for appointment, of persons to hold a local inquiry or other hearing;

(b) include provision enabling the Secretary of State to direct a local planning authority to appoint a particular person, or one of a specified list or class of persons;

(c) make provision with respect to the remuneration and allowances of the person appointed.

1972 c. 70.

(5) Subsections (2) and (3) of section 250 of the Local Government Act 1972 (power to summon and examine witnesses) apply to an inquiry held under this paragraph.

1971 c. 62.

(6) The Tribunals and Inquiries Act 1971 applies to a local inquiry or other hearing held under this paragraph as it applies to a statutory inquiry held by the Secretary of State, with the substitution in section 12(1) (statement of reasons for decision) for the references to a decision taken by the Secretary of State of references to a decision taken by a local authority.

Adoption of proposals by local planning authority

9.—(1) The local planning authority shall consider any objections to proposals for the making or alteration of a simplified planning zone scheme which are duly made within the period given for making such objections and after that period has expired they may, subject to the following provisions of this paragraph and to paragraph 10, by resolution adopt the proposals.

(2) The authority may adopt the proposals as originally prepared or as modified so as to take account of—

(a) any such objections as are mentioned in sub-paragraph (1) or any other objections to the proposals, or

(b) any other considerations which appear to the authority to be material.

(3) If, before the proposals have been adopted by the local planning authority, it appears to the Secretary of State that they are unsatisfactory, he may direct the authority to consider modifying the proposals in such respects as are indicated in the direction.

(4) An authority to whom such a direction is given shall not adopt the proposals unless— SCH. 7

(a) they satisfy the Secretary of State that they have made the modifications necessary to conform with the direction, or

(b) the direction is withdrawn.

Calling in of proposals for approval by Secretary of State

10.—(1) Before the proposals have been adopted by the local planning authority the Secretary of State may direct that they shall be submitted to him for his approval.

(2) If the Secretary of State gives such a direction—

(a) the authority shall not take any further steps for the adoption of the proposals, and in particular shall not hold or proceed with a local inquiry or other hearing in respect of the proposals under paragraph 8; and

(b) the proposals shall not have effect unless approved by the Secretary of State and shall not require adoption by the authority.

Approval of proposals by Secretary of State

11.—(1) The Secretary of State may after considering proposals submitted to him under paragraph 10 either approve them, in whole or in part and with or without modifications, or reject them.

(2) In considering the proposals the Secretary of State may take into account any matters he thinks are relevant, whether or not they were taken into account in the proposals as submitted to him.

(3) Where on taking the proposals into consideration the Secretary of State does not determine then to reject them, he shall, before determining whether or not to approve them—

(a) consider any objections to them made in accordance with regulations,

(b) give any person who made such an objection which has not been withdrawn an opportunity of appearing before and being heard by a person appointed by him for the purpose, and

(c) if a local inquiry or other hearing is held, also give such an opportunity to the authority and such other persons as he thinks fit,

except so far as objections have already been considered, or a local inquiry or other hearing into the objections has already been held, by the authority.

(4) In considering the proposals the Secretary of State may consult with, or consider the views of, any local planning authority or any other person; but he need not do so, or give an opportunity for the making of representations or objections, or cause a local inquiry or other hearing to be held, except as provided by sub-paragraph (3).

Default powers

12.—(1) Where by virtue of any of the previous provisions of this Schedule—

(a) a simplified planning zone scheme or proposals for the alteration of such a scheme are required to be prepared, or

(b) steps are required to be taken for the adoption of any such scheme or proposals,

then, if the Secretary of State is satisfied, after holding a local inquiry or other hearing, that the local planning authority are not taking the steps necessary to enable them to prepare or adopt such a scheme or proposals within a reasonable period, he may make the scheme or the alterations, as he thinks fit.

SCH. 7

(2) Where under this paragraph anything which ought to have been done by a local planning authority is done by the Secretary of State, the previous provisions of this Schedule apply, so far as practicable, with any necessary modifications, in relation to the doing of that thing by the Secretary of State and the thing so done.

(3) Where the Secretary of State incurs expenses under this paragraph in connection with the doing of anything which should have been done by a local planning authority, so much of those expenses as may be certified by the Secretary of State to have been incurred in the performance of functions of that authority shall on demand be repaid by the authority to the Secretary of State.

Regulations and directions

13.—(1) Without prejudice to the previous provisions of this Schedule, the Secretary of State may make regulations with respect—

(a) to the form and content of simplified planning zone schemes, and

(b) to the procedure to be followed in connection with their preparation, withdrawal, adoption, submission, approval, making or alteration.

(2) Any such regulations may in particular—

(a) provide for the notice to be given of, or the publicity to be given to—

(i) matters included or proposed to be included in a simplified planning zone scheme, and

(ii) the adoption or approval of such a scheme, or of any alteration of it, or any other prescribed procedural step,

and for publicity to be given to the procedure to be followed in these respects;

(b) make provision with respect to the making and consideration of representations as to matters to be included in, or objections to, any such scheme or proposals for its alteration;

(c) without prejudice to paragraph (a), provide for notice to be given to particular persons of the adoption or approval of a simplified planning zone scheme, or an alteration to such a scheme, if they have objected to the proposals and have notified the local planning authority of their wish to receive notice, subject (if the regulations so provide) to the payment of a reasonable charge;

(d) require or authorise a local planning authority to consult with, or consider the views of, other persons before taking any prescribed procedural step;

(e) require a local planning authority, in such cases as may be prescribed or in such particular cases as the Secretary of State may direct, to provide persons making a request with copies of any document which has been made public for the purpose mentioned in paragraph 5(2) or has been made available for inspection under paragraph 5(3) or 6(2), subject (if the regulations so provide) to the payment of a reasonable charge;

(f) provide for the publication and inspection of a simplified planning zone scheme which has been adopted or approved, or any document adopted or approved altering such a scheme, and for copies of any such scheme or document to be made available on sale.

(3) Regulations under this paragraph may extend throughout England and Wales or to specified areas only and may make different provision for different cases.

(4) Subject to the previous provisions of this Schedule and to any regulations under this paragraph, the Secretary of State may give directions to any local planning authority or to local planning authorities generally—

(a) for formulating the procedure for the carrying out of their functions under this Schedule;

(b) for requiring them to give him such information as he may require for carrying out any of his functions under this Schedule. SCH. 7

SCHEDULE 8

Section 101(4).

PLANNING INQUIRY COMMISSIONS

PART I

CONSTITUTION AND PROCEDURE ON REFERENCES

Constitution of Commissions

1.—(1) A Planning Inquiry Commission shall consist of a chairman and not less than two nor more than four other members appointed by the Secretary of State.

(2) The Secretary of State may—

(a) pay to the members of any such commission such remuneration and allowances as he may with the consent of the Treasury determine, and

(b) provide for each such commission such officers or servants, and such accommodation, as appears to him expedient to provide for the purpose of assisting the commission in the discharge of their functions.

(3) The validity of any proceedings of any such commission shall not be affected by any vacancy among the members of the commission or by any defect in the appointment of any member.

(4) In relation to any matter affecting both England and Wales—

(a) the functions of the Secretary of State under sub-paragraph (1) shall be exercised by the Secretaries of State for the time being having general responsibility in planning matters in relation to England and in relation to Wales acting jointly, and

(b) his functions under sub-paragraph (2) shall be exercised by one of those Secretaries of State authorised by the other to act on behalf of both of them for the purposes of that sub-paragraph.

Reference to a Planning Inquiry Commission

2.—(1) Two or more of the matters mentioned in section 101(2) may be referred to the same commission if it appears to the responsible Minister or Ministers that they relate to proposals to carry out development for similar purposes on different sites.

(2) Where a matter referred to a commission under section 101 relates to a proposal to carry out development for any purpose at a particular site, the responsible Minister or Ministers may also refer to the commission the question whether development for that purpose should instead be carried out at an alternative site.

(3) On referring a matter to a commission, the responsible Minister or Ministers—

(a) shall state in the reference the reasons for the reference, and

(b) may draw the attention of the commission to any points which seem to him or them to be relevant to their inquiry.

SCH. 8

Functions of Planning Inquiry Commission on reference

3.—(1) A commission inquiring into a matter referred to them under section 101 shall—

(a) identify and investigate the considerations relevant to, or the technical or scientific aspects of, that matter which in their opinion are relevant to the question whether the proposed development should be permitted to be carried out, and

(b) assess the importance to be attached to those considerations or aspects.

(2) If—

(a) in the case of a matter mentioned in section 101(2)(a), (b) or (c), the applicant, or

(b) in any case, the local planning authority,

so wish, the commission shall give to each of them, and, in the case of an application or appeal mentioned in section 101(2)(a) or (b), also to any person who has made representations relating to the subject matter of the application or appeal which the authority are required to take into account under section 71(1) or (2), an opportunity of appearing before and being heard by one or more members of the commission.

(3) The commission shall then report to the responsible Minister or Ministers on the matter referred to them.

(4) A commission may, with the approval of the Secretary of State and at his expense, arrange for the carrying out (whether by the commission themselves or by others) of research of any kind appearing to them to be relevant to a matter referred to them for inquiry and report.

(5) In sub-paragraph (4) "the Secretary of State," in relation to any matter affecting both England and Wales, means—

(a) the Secretary of State for the time being having general responsibility in planning matters in relation to England, or

(b) the Secretary of State for the time being having responsibility in relation to Wales,

acting, by arrangements between the two of them, on behalf of both.

Procedure on reference to a Planning Inquiry Commission

4.—(1) A reference to a Planning Inquiry Commission of a proposal that development should be carried out by or on behalf of a government department may be made at any time.

(2) A reference of any other matter mentioned in section 101 may be made at any time before, but not after, the determination of the relevant application referred under section 77 or the relevant appeal under section 78 or, as the case may be, the giving of the relevant direction under section 90(1).

(3) The fact that an inquiry or other hearing has been held into a proposal by a person appointed by any Minister for the purpose shall not prevent a reference of the proposal to a Planning Inquiry Commission.

(4) Notice of the making of a reference to any such commission shall be published in the prescribed manner.

(5) A copy of the notice must be served on the local planning authority for the area in which it is proposed that the relevant development will be carried out, and—

(a) in the case of an application for planning permission referred under section 77 or an appeal under section 78, on the applicant and any person who has made representations relating to the subject matter of the application or appeal which the authority are required to take into account under section 71(1) or (2);

(b) in the case of a proposal that a direction should be given under section 90(1) with respect to any development, on the local authority or statutory undertakers applying for authorisation to carry out that development.

(6) Subject to the provisions of this paragraph and paragraph 5 and to any directions given to them by the responsible Minister or Ministers, a Planning Inquiry Commission shall have power to regulate their own procedure.

Local inquiries held by Planning Inquiry Commission

5.—(1) A Planning Inquiry Commission shall, for the purpose of complying with paragraph 3(2), hold a local inquiry; and they may hold such an inquiry, if they think it necessary for the proper discharge of their functions, notwithstanding that neither the applicant nor the local planning authority want an opportunity to appear and be heard.

(2) Where a Planning Inquiry Commission are to hold a local inquiry under sub-paragraph (1) in connection with a matter referred to them, and it appears to the responsible Minister or Ministers, in the case of some other matter falling to be determined by a Minister of the Crown and required or authorised by an enactment other than this paragraph to be the subject of a local inquiry, that the two matters are so far cognate that they should be considered together, he or, as the case may be, they may direct that the two inquiries be held concurrently or combined as one inquiry.

(3) An inquiry held by a commission under this paragraph shall be treated for the purposes of the Tribunals and Inquiries Act 1971 as one held by a Minister in pursuance of a duty imposed by a statutory provision. 1971 c. 62.

(4) Subsections (2) to (5) of section 250 of the Local Government Act 1972 (local inquiries: evidence and costs) shall apply in relation to an inquiry held under sub-paragraph (1) as they apply in relation to an inquiry caused to be held by a Minister under subsection (1) of that section, with the substitution for references to the Minister causing the inquiry to be held (other than the first reference in subsection (4)) of references to the responsible Minister or Ministers. 1972 c. 70.

PART II

MEANING OF "THE RESPONSIBLE MINISTER OR MINISTERS"

6. In relation to the matters specified in the first column of the Table below (which are matters mentioned in subsection (2)(a), (b), (c) or (d) of section 101 as matters which may be referred to a Planning Inquiry Commission under that section) "the responsible Minister or Ministers" for the purposes of that section and this Schedule—

(a) in the case of a matter affecting England only, are those specified opposite in the second column of the Table;

(b) in the case of a matter affecting Wales only, are those specified opposite in the third column of the Table; and

(c) in the case of a matter affecting both England and Wales, are those specified opposite in the fourth column of the Table.

7. Where an entry in the second, third or fourth columns of the Table specifies two or more Ministers, that entry shall be construed as referring to those Ministers acting jointly.

SCH. 8

TABLE

Referred matter	Affecting England only	Affecting Wales only	Affecting both England and Wales
1. Application for planning permission or appeal under section 78 relating to land to which section 266(1) applies.	The Secretary of State for the time being having general responsibility in planning matters in relation to England and the appropriate Minister (if different).	The Secretary of State for the time being having general responsibility in planning matters in relation to Wales and the appropriate Minister (if different).	The Secretaries of State for the time being having general responsibility in planning matters in relation to England and in relation to Wales and the appropriate Minister (if different).
2. Application for planning permission or appeal under section 78 relating to land to which section 266(1) does not apply.	The Secretary of State for the time being having general responsibility in planning matters in relation to England.	The Secretary of State for the time being having general responsibility in planning matters in relation to Wales.	The Secretaries of State for the time being having general responsibility in planning matters in relation to England and in relation to Wales.
3. Proposal that a government department should give a direction under section 90(1) or that development should be carried out by or on behalf of a government department.	The Secretary of State for the time being having general responsibility in planning matters in relation to England and the Minister (if different) in charge of the government department concerned.	The Secretary of State for the time being having general responsibility in planning matters in relation to Wales and the Minister (if different) in charge of the government department concerned.	The Secretaries of State for the time being having general responsibility in planning matters in relation to England and in relation to Wales and the Minister (if different) in charge of the government department concerned.

Section 102(8).

SCHEDULE 9

REQUIREMENTS RELATING TO DISCONTINUANCE OF MINERAL WORKING

Orders requiring discontinuance of mineral working

1.—(1) If, having regard to the development plan and to any other material considerations, it appears to a mineral planning authority that it is expedient in the interests of the proper planning of their area (including the interests of amenity)—

(a) that any use of land for development consisting of the winning and working of minerals in, on or under the land should be discontinued, or that any conditions should be imposed on the continuance of that use of land; or

(b) that any buildings or works on land so used should be altered or removed; or

(c) that any plant or machinery used for the winning and working of minerals should be altered or removed,

the mineral planning authority may by order require the discontinuance of that use, or impose such conditions as may be specified in the order on the continuance of it or, as the case may be, require such steps as may be so specified to be taken for the alteration or removal of the buildings or works or plant or machinery.

(2) Subject to sub-paragraph (3), subsections (2) to (7) of section 102 and section 103 apply to orders under this paragraph as they apply to orders under section 102.

(3) In their application by virtue of sub-paragraph (2) subsections (2) to (7) of section 102 and section 103 shall have effect as if references to the local planning authority were references to the mineral planning authority. SCH. 9

2.—(1) Where development consisting of the winning and working of minerals is being carried out in, on or under any land, the conditions which an order under paragraph 1 may impose include a restoration condition.

(2) If such an order—

(a) includes a restoration condition, or

(b) a restoration condition has previously been imposed in relation to the land by virtue of any provision of this Act,

the order may also include any such aftercare condition as the mineral planning authority think fit.

(3) Paragraphs 2(3) to (9) and 3 to 6 of Schedule 5 shall apply in relation to an aftercare condition imposed under this paragraph as they apply in relation to such a condition imposed under paragraph 2 of that Schedule, but with the substitution for sub-paragraphs (1) and (2) of paragraph 3 of that Schedule of sub-paragraphs (4) and (5) below.

(4) In a case where—

(a) the use specified in the aftercare condition is a use for agriculture;

(b) the land was in use for agriculture immediately before development consisting of the winning and working of minerals began to be carried out in, on or under it, or had previously been used for agriculture and had not been used for any authorised purpose since its use for agriculture ceased; and

(c) the Minister has notified the mineral planning authority of the physical characteristics of the land when it was last used for agriculture,

the land is brought to the required standard when its physical characteristics are restored, so far as it is practicable to do so, to what they were when it was last used for agriculture.

(5) In any other case where the use specified in the aftercare condition is a use for agriculture, the land is brought to the required standard when it is reasonably fit for that use.

Prohibition of resumption of mineral working

3.—(1) Where it appears to the mineral planning authority—

(a) that development consisting of the winning and working of minerals has been carried out in, on or under any land; but

(b) that it has permanently ceased,

the mineral planning authority may by order—

(i) prohibit the resumption of such development; and

(ii) impose, in relation to the site, any such requirement as is specified in sub-paragraph (3).

(2) The mineral planning authority may assume that development consisting of the winning and working of minerals has permanently ceased only when—

(a) no such development has been carried out to any substantial extent anywhere in, on or under the site of which the land forms part for a period of at least two years; and

(b) it appears to the mineral planning authority, on the evidence available to them at the time when they make the order, that resumption of such development in, on or under the land is unlikely.

SCH. 9

(3) The requirements mentioned in sub-paragraph (1) are—

(a) a requirement to alter or remove plant or machinery which was used for the purpose of the winning and working of minerals or for any purpose ancillary to that purpose;

(b) a requirement to take such steps as may be specified in the order, within such period as may be so specified, for the purpose of removing or alleviating any injury to amenity which has been caused by the winning and working of minerals, other than injury due to subsidence caused by underground mining operations;

(c) a requirement that any condition subject to which planning permission for development consisting of the winning and working of minerals was granted or which has been imposed by virtue of any provision of this Act shall be complied with; and

(d) a restoration condition.

(4) If—

(a) an order under this paragraph includes a restoration condition; or

(b) a restoration condition has previously been imposed in relation to the site by virtue of any provision of this Act,

the order under this paragraph may include any such aftercare condition as the mineral planning authority think fit.

(5) Paragraphs 2(3) to (9) and 3 to 6 of Schedule 5 apply in relation to an aftercare condition imposed under this paragraph as they apply to such a condition imposed under paragraph 2 of this Schedule.

4.—(1) An order under paragraph 3 shall not take effect unless it is confirmed by the Secretary of State, either without modification or subject to such modifications as he considers expedient.

(2) Where a mineral planning authority submit such an order to the Secretary of State for his confirmation under this paragraph, the authority shall serve notice of the order—

(a) on any person who is an owner or occupier of any of the land to which the order relates, and

(b) on any other person who in their opinion will be affected by it.

(3) The notice shall specify the period within which any person on whom the notice is served may require the Secretary of State to give him an opportunity of appearing before, and being heard by, a person appointed by the Secretary of State for that purpose.

(4) If within that period such a person so requires, before the Secretary of State confirms the order he shall give such an opportunity both to him and to the mineral planning authority.

(5) The period referred to in sub-paragraph (3) must not be less than 28 days from the service of the notice.

(6) Where an order under paragraph 3 has been confirmed by the Secretary of State, the mineral planning authority shall serve a copy of the order on every person who was entitled to be served with notice under sub-paragraph (2).

(7) When an order under paragraph 3 takes effect any planning permission for the development to which the order relates shall cease to have effect.

(8) Sub-paragraph (7) is without prejudice to the power of the mineral planning authority, on revoking the order, to make a further grant of planning permission for development consisting of the winning and working of minerals.

Orders after suspension of winning and working of minerals

5.—(1) Where it appears to the mineral planning authority—

(a) that development consisting of the winning and working of minerals has been carried out in, on or under any land; but

(b) that it has been temporarily suspended,

the mineral planning authority may by order require that steps shall be taken for the protection of the environment.

(2) An order under sub-paragraph (1) is in this Act referred to as a "suspension order".

(3) The mineral planning authority may assume that development consisting of the winning and working of minerals has been temporarily suspended only when—

(a) no such development has been carried out to any substantial extent anywhere in, on or under the site of which the land forms part for a period of at least 12 months; but

(b) it appears to the mineral planning authority, on the evidence available to them at the time when they make the order, that a resumption of such development in, on or under the land is likely.

(4) In this Act "steps for the protection of the environment" means steps for the purpose—

(a) of preserving the amenities of the area in which the land in, on or under which the development was carried out is situated during the period while operations for the winning and working of minerals in, on or under it are suspended;

(b) of protecting that area from damage during that period; or

(c) of preventing any deterioration in the condition of the land during that period.

(5) A suspension order shall specify a period, commencing with the date on which it is to take effect, within which any required step for the protection of the environment is to be taken and may specify different periods for the taking of different steps.

Supplementary suspension orders

6.—(1) At any time when a suspension order is in operation the mineral planning authority may by order direct—

(a) that steps for the protection of the environment shall be taken in addition to or in substitution for any of the steps which the suspension order or a previous order under this sub-paragraph specified as required to be taken; or

(b) that the suspension order or any order under this sub-paragraph shall cease to have effect.

(2) An order under sub-paragraph (1) is in this Act referred to as a "supplementary suspension order".

Confirmation and coming into operation of suspension orders

7.—(1) Subject to sub-paragraph (2), a suspension order or a supplementary suspension order shall not take effect unless it is confirmed by the Secretary of State, either without modification or subject to such modifications as he considers expedient.

SCH. 9

(2) A supplementary suspension order revoking a suspension order or a previous supplementary suspension order and not requiring that any fresh step shall be taken for the protection of the environment shall take effect without confirmation.

(3) Sub-paragraphs (2) to (5) of paragraph 4 shall have effect in relation to a suspension order or supplementary suspension order submitted to the Secretary of State for his confirmation as they have effect in relation to an order submitted to him for his confirmation under that paragraph.

(4) Where a suspension order or supplementary suspension order has been confirmed by the Secretary of State, the mineral planning authority shall serve a copy of the order on every person who was entitled to be served with notice of the order by virtue of sub-paragraph (3).

Registration of suspension orders as local land charges

8. A suspension order or a supplementary suspension order shall be a local land charge.

Review of suspension orders

9.—(1) It shall be the duty of a mineral planning authority—

(a) to undertake in accordance with the following provisions of this paragraph reviews of suspension orders and supplementary suspension orders which are in operation in their area; and

(b) to determine whether they should make in relation to any land to which a suspension order or supplementary suspension order applies—

(i) an order under paragraph 3; or

(ii) a supplementary suspension order.

(2) The first review of a suspension order shall be undertaken not more than five years from the date on which the order takes effect.

(3) Each subsequent review shall be undertaken not more than five years after the previous review.

(4) If a supplementary suspension order is in operation for any part of the area for which a suspension order is in operation, they shall be reviewed together.

(5) If a mineral planning authority have made a supplementary suspension order which requires the taking of steps for the protection of the environment in substitution for all the steps required to be taken by a previous suspension order or supplementary suspension order, the authority shall undertake reviews of the supplementary suspension order in accordance with sub-paragraphs (6) and (7).

(6) The first review shall be undertaken not more than five years from the date on which the order takes effect.

(7) Each subsequent review shall be undertaken not more than five years after the previous review.

(8) The duties to undertake reviews imposed by this paragraph are in addition to and not in substitution for the duties imposed by section 105.

Resumption of mineral working after suspension order

10.—(1) Subject to sub-paragraph (2), nothing in a suspension order or a supplementary suspension order shall prevent the recommencement of development consisting of the winning and working of minerals in, on or under the land in relation to which the order has effect.

(2) No person shall recommence such development without first giving the mineral planning authority notice of his intention to do so.

(3) A notice under sub-paragraph (2) shall specify the date on which the person giving the notice intends to recommence development consisting of the winning and working of minerals. SCH. 9

(4) The mineral planning authority shall revoke the order if development consisting of the winning and working of minerals has recommenced to a substantial extent in, on or under the land in relation to which the order has effect.

(5) If the authority do not revoke the order before the end of the period of two months from the date specified in the notice under sub-paragraph (2), the person who gave that notice may apply to the Secretary of State for the revocation of the order.

(6) Notice of an application under sub-paragraph (5) shall be given by the applicant to the mineral planning authority.

(7) If he is required to do so by the person who gave the notice or by the mineral planning authority, the Secretary of State shall, before deciding whether to revoke the order, give him and the mineral planning authority an opportunity of appearing before, and being heard by, a person appointed by the Secretary of State for the purpose.

(8) If the Secretary of State is satisfied that development consisting of the winning and working of minerals in, on or under the land has recommenced to a substantial extent, he shall revoke the order.

(9) If the Secretary of State revokes an order by virtue of sub-paragraph (8), he shall give notice of its revocation—

(a) to the person who applied to him for the revocation, and

(b) to the mineral planning authority.

Default powers of Secretary of State

11.—(1) If it appears to the Secretary of State to be expedient that any order under paragraph 1, 3, 5 or 6 should be made, he may himself make such an order.

(2) Such an order which is made by the Secretary of State shall have the same effect as if it had been made by the mineral planning authority and confirmed by the Secretary of State.

(3) The Secretary of State shall not make such an order without consulting the mineral planning authority.

(4) Where the Secretary of State proposes to make an order under paragraph 1 he shall serve a notice of the proposal on the mineral planning authority.

(5) The notice shall specify the period (which must not be less than 28 days from the date of its service) within which the authority may require an opportunity of appearing before and being heard by a person appointed by the Secretary of State for the purpose.

(6) If within that period the authority so require, before the Secretary of State makes the order he shall give the authority such an opportunity.

(7) The provisions of this Schedule and of any regulations made under this Act with respect to the procedure to be followed in connection with the submission by the mineral planning authority of any order to which sub-paragraph (1) applies, its confirmation by the Secretary of State and the service of copies of it as confirmed shall have effect, subject to any necessary modifications, in relation to any proposal by the Secretary of State to make such an order, its making by him and the service of copies of it.

Sections 111 and 114.

SCHEDULE 10

CONDITION TREATED AS APPLICABLE TO REBUILDING AND ALTERATIONS

1. Where the building to be rebuilt or altered is the original building, the amount of gross floor space in the building as rebuilt or altered which may be used for any purpose shall not exceed by more than ten per cent. the amount of gross floor space which was last used for that purpose in the original building.

2. Where the building to be rebuilt or altered is not the original building, the amount of gross floor space in the building as rebuilt or altered which may be used for any purpose shall not exceed the amount of gross floor space which was last used for that purpose in the building before the rebuilding or alteration.

3. In determining under this Schedule the purpose for which floor space was last used in any building, no account shall be taken of any use in respect of which an effective enforcement notice has been or could be served or, in the case of a use which has been discontinued, could have been served immediately before the discontinuance.

4.—(1) For the purposes of this Schedule gross floor space shall be ascertained by external measurement.

(2) Where different parts of a building are used for different purposes, floor space common to those purposes shall be apportioned rateably.

5. In relation to a building erected after 1st July 1948 which is a building resulting from the carrying out of any such works as are described in paragraph 1 of Schedule 3, any reference in this Schedule to the original building is a reference to the building in relation to which those works were carried out and not to the building resulting from the carrying out of those works.

Section 116.

SCHEDULE 11

COMPENSATION IN RESPECT OF CERTAIN ORDERS AFFECTING MINERAL WORKING

Power to modify compensation provisions

1.—(1) The Secretary of State may by regulations made with the consent of the Treasury direct that where mineral compensation requirements are satisfied sections 107, 115, 117, 279 and 280 shall have effect subject, in such cases as may be specified in the regulations, to such modifications (in this Schedule referred to as "mineral compensation modifications") as may be so specified.

(2) Any such regulations shall make provision as to circumstances in which compensation is not to be payable.

(3) Any such regulations shall make provision—

(a) for the modification of the basis on which any amount to be paid by way of compensation is to be assessed; or

(b) for the assessment of any such amount on a basis different from that on which it would otherwise have been assessed.

(4) Regulations made by virtue of sub-paragraph (3)(a) in relation to compensation where an order is made under section 97 or paragraph 1 of Schedule 9 shall provide that the amount of the compensation under section 107 or, as the case may be, section 115 shall be reduced—

(a) by the prescribed sum; or

(b) by a sum equal to the prescribed percentage of the appropriate sum.

(5) In sub-paragraph (4) "the appropriate sum" means the product of— SCH. 11

(a) the sum which represents the annual value of the right to win and work minerals at the site to which the order relates, and

(b) a multiplier which the Secretary of State considers appropriate having regard to the period at the expiry of which the minerals in, on or under that site might be expected to be exhausted if they continued to be extracted at the rate which has been assumed for the purpose of calculating the annual value of the right to win and work them.

(6) The prescribed percentage shall not be more than 10 per cent.

(7) The annual value of the right to win and work the minerals shall be calculated in the prescribed manner.

(8) Regulations under this paragraph—

(a) may make different provision for different cases; and

(b) may include such incidental or supplementary provisions as the Secretary of State considers expedient.

(9) No regulations under this paragraph shall have effect until approved by a resolution of each House of Parliament.

(10) Before making any such regulations the Secretary of State shall consult such persons or bodies of persons as appear to him to be representative—

(a) of persons carrying out mining operations;

(b) of owners of interests in land containing minerals; and

(c) of mineral planning authorities.

Circumstances in which mineral compensation modifications apply

2. Where—

(a) an order under section 97 modifies planning permission for development consisting of the winning and working of minerals, and

(b) mineral compensation requirements are satisfied in relation to the order in accordance with paragraph 4,

section 107 shall have effect subject to such mineral compensation modifications as may be prescribed under paragraph 1.

3. Where mineral compensation requirements are satisfied in relation to an order under paragraph 1, 3, 5 or 6 of Schedule 9, section 115 shall have effect subject to such mineral compensation modifications as may be prescribed under paragraph 1.

Mineral compensation requirements

4.—(1) Subject to sub-paragraph (3), mineral compensation requirements are satisfied in relation to such an order as is mentioned in paragraph 2 if—

(a) the order does not—

(i) impose any restriction on the winning and working of minerals; or

(ii) modify or replace any such restriction subject to which the planning permission was granted or which was imposed by a relevant order; and

(b) the mineral planning authority carried out special consultations about the making and terms of the order before they made it; and

(c) either—

SCH. 11

(i) the permission was granted not less than five years before the date of the order; or

(ii) the conditions specified in sub-paragraph (2) are satisfied.

(2) The conditions mentioned in sub-paragraph (1)(c)(ii) are—

(a) that the planning permission which the order modifies was granted before 22nd February 1982; and

(b) that the order—

(i) imposes an aftercare condition; and

(ii) does not impose any other condition.

(3) Where the mineral planning authority making the order under section 97 ("the subsequent order") have previously made a relevant order or orders, mineral compensation requirements are not satisfied in relation to the subsequent order unless it was made more than five years after the order previously made or the last such order.

5. Subject to paragraph 9, mineral compensation requirements are satisfied in relation to an order under paragraph 1 of Schedule 9 if—

(a) the order—

(i) imposes any conditions on the continuance of the use of land for the winning and working of minerals; or

(ii) requires that any buildings or works or plant or machinery used for the winning and working of minerals be altered or removed; and

(b) the conditions specified in paragraph 8 are satisfied.

6. Subject to paragraph 9, mineral compensation requirements are satisfied in relation to an order under paragraph 3 of Schedule 9 if the conditions specified in paragraph 8(a) and (c) are satisfied.

7. Mineral compensation requirements are satisfied in relation to an order under paragraph 5 or 6 of Schedule 9 if the conditions specified in paragraph 8(c) are satisfied.

8. The conditions mentioned in paragraphs 5(b), 6 and 7 are—

(a) that development consisting of the winning and working of minerals began not less than five years before the date of the order;

(b) that the order does not—

(i) impose any restriction on the winning and working of minerals; or

(ii) modify or replace any such restriction subject to which planning permission for development consisting of the winning and working of minerals was granted or which was imposed by a relevant order; and

(c) that the mineral planning authority carried out special consultations about the making and terms of the order before they made it.

9. Where the mineral planning authority—

(a) make—

(i) an order under paragraph 1 of Schedule 9 which imposes any such conditions or makes any such requirement as mentioned in paragraph 5(a) of this Schedule; or

(ii) an order under paragraph 3 of that Schedule; and

(b) have previously made a relevant order or orders,

mineral compensation requirements are not satisfied in relation to the order mentioned in paragraph (a) unless it was made more than five years after the order previously made or the last such order.

Restriction on the winning and working of minerals

10.—(1) In this Schedule "restriction on the winning and working of minerals" means—

(a) in relation to planning permission granted for development consisting of the winning and working of minerals, a condition subject to which the permission was granted and which made provision to which this paragraph applies; and

(b) in relation to an order under section 97 or paragraph 1 of Schedule 9, a term of the order which made such provision.

(2) This paragraph applies to—

(a) any provision—

(i) for the period before the expiration of which development consisting of the winning and working of minerals was to be begun;

(ii) for the size of the area to be used for the winning and working of minerals;

(iii) for the depth to which operations for the winning and working of minerals were to extend;

(iv) for the rate at which any particular mineral was to be extracted; or

(v) for the period at the expiry of which the winning and working of minerals was to cease; and

(b) any provision whose effect is in any way to restrict the total quantity of minerals to be extracted.

Relevant order

11. In this Schedule "relevant order", in relation to any land, means an order under section 97 or paragraph 1 or 3 of Schedule 9.

Special consultations

12.—(1) Any reference in this Schedule to a mineral planning authority carrying out special consultations about the making and terms of an order before they make it is a reference to their carrying out consultations—

(a) subject to sub-paragraph (2), with any person who has an interest—

(i) in the land to which the order will relate; or

(ii) in minerals in, on or under that land; and

(b) if the land to which the order will relate is in a non-metropolitan county, with the district council in whose area it is situated.

(2) The duty to consult imposed by sub-paragraph (1)(a) is only a duty to consult persons whom the mineral planning authority are able to trace by taking reasonable steps to do so.

Determination of claims

13. The references in section 118 to questions of disputed compensation under this Part of this Act include references to questions of disputed compensation under sections 107, 115, 117, 279 and 280 as modified by regulations under paragraph 1.

SCHEDULE 12

Section 119.

Unexpended Balance of Established Development Value

Derivation of unexpended balance from claims under Part VI of 1947 Act

1.—(1) In determining for the purposes of this Part whether land has an unexpended balance of established development value, regard shall be had to claims made, in pursuance of Part Vl of the 1947 Act, for payments under the scheme provided for by section 58 of that Act (that is to say, the scheme which, but for the provisions of section 2 of the Town and Country Planning Act 1953, would have fallen to be made under the said section 58, providing for payments in respect of interests in land depreciated in value by virtue of the provisions of the 1947 Act).

1953 c. 16.

(2) Where such a claim was made in respect of an interest in land, that claim shall for the purposes of this Part be taken to have been established in respect of that land under Part Vl of the 1947 Act if an amount was determined under that Part as being the development value of the interest to which the claim related, and payment in respect of that interest would not have been excluded—

(a) by section 63 of the 1947 Act (which excluded claims where the development value was small in proportion to the area, or to the restricted value, of the land); or

(b) by any of sections 82 to 85 of that Act (which related to certain land belonging to local authorities, development corporations and statutory undertakers, and to land held on charitable trusts); or

(c) by section 84 of that Act as applied by regulations under section 90 of that Act (which related to the National Coal Board).

(3) In this Part—

(a) "established claim" means a claim which by virtue of sub-paragraph (2) is to be taken to have been established as mentioned in that sub-paragraph, and references to the establishment of a claim shall be construed accordingly; and

(b) "the claim area", in relation to an established claim, means the land in respect of which the claim is by virtue of that sub-paragraph to be taken to have been established.

(4) References in this Part to the benefit of an established claim—

1953 c. 16.

(a) in relation to any time before the passing of the Town and Country Planning Act 1953, whether before or after the making of the claim, or before or after the establishment of it, shall be construed as references to the prospective right, under and subject to the provisions of the scheme referred to in sub-paragraph (1), to receive a payment in respect of the interest in land to which the claim related; and

(b) in relation to any time after the passing of that Act, shall be construed as references to such prospective right to the satisfaction of the claim as subsisted by virtue of section 2 of that Act immediately before lst January 1955 (the date of the commencement of the 1954 Act);

and references to part of the benefit of an established claim shall be construed accordingly.

(5) References in this Part to the amount of an established claim are references to the amount determined under Part Vl of the 1947 Act as being the development value of the interest in land to which the claim related.

(6) In this paragraph any reference to Part Vl of the 1947 Act includes a reference to the provisions of that Part as modified by Schedule 1 to the 1954 Act.

Original unexpended balance of established development value

2.—(1) In this Part "original unexpended balance of established development value", in relation to any land, means the unexpended balance of established development value which that land had immediately after the time when, in accordance with paragraph 4, the adjustment of claim holdings is deemed to have been completed.

(2) For the purposes of this Part land shall be taken to have had such a balance if, immediately after the time referred to in sub-paragraph (1)—

(a) there were subsisting one or more claim holdings whose area consisted of that land, or included that land together with other land; and

(b) there was not subsisting any claim holding whose area consisted of part only of that land, whether with or without other land.

(3) Where sub-paragraph (2) applies, there shall be attributed to the land referred to in that sub-paragraph—

(a) the value of any claim holding having an area consisting of that land; and

(b) such fraction of the value of any claim holding whose area included that land as attached to that land,

and the original unexpended balance of established development value of that land shall be taken to have been an amount equal to eight-sevenths of the amount or aggregate amount so attributed.

Claim holdings: their areas and values

3.—(1) Subject to this paragraph and to paragraph 4, in this Part—

(a) "claim holding" means the benefit of an established claim;

(b) references to the area of a claim holding are references to the land which, in relation to the established claim constituting that holding, is the claim area;

(c) references to the value of a claim holding are references to the amount of the established claim constituting that holding; and

(d) references to the fraction of the value of a claim holding which attached to a part of the area of the holding are references to so much of the amount of the established claim of which that holding represents the benefit or part of the benefit (in this paragraph referred to as "the relevant established claim") as was properly attributable to that part of the area of the holding.

(2) In the case of a claim holding where—

(a) the area of the holding is the same as the claim area of the relevant established claim; but

(b) the value of the claim holding is, by virtue of the adjustment of claim holdings, less than the amount of the relevant established claim,

the amount of any such fraction as is referred to in sub-paragraph (1)(d) shall be treated as reduced proportionately.

(3) In the case of a claim holding where—

(a) the area of the holding consists of part only of the claim area of the relevant established claim; and

(b) the value of the holding is, by virtue of the adjustment of claim holdings, less or greater than so much of the amount of the relevant established claim as was properly attributable to the area of the holding,

the amount of any such fraction as is referred to in sub-paragraph (1)(d) shall be treated as reduced, or (as the case may be) increased, proportionately.

SCH. 12

(4) For the purposes of this paragraph, the part of the amount of the relevant established claim which was properly attributable to any land forming part of the claim area shall be taken to have been so much of the amount of that claim as might reasonably be expected to have been attributed to that land if the authority determining that amount had been required to apportion it, in accordance with the same principles as applied to its determination, between that land and the residue of the claim area.

Adjustment of claim holdings: preliminary

4.—(1) Paragraphs 5 to 11 shall have effect with respect to the adjustment of claim holdings for the purposes of this Part.

(2) Any reference in this Part to the adjustment of claim holdings is a reference to the operation of those paragraphs.

(3) For the purposes of this Part the adjustment of claim holdings shall be deemed to have been completed on 1st January 1955.

(4) In paragraphs 5 to 11 "the time of completion" means the time when, in accordance with sub-paragraph (3), the adjustment of claim holdings is deemed to have been completed.

Adjustment of claim holdings pledged to Central Land Board as security for development charges

5.—(1) Where a claim holding was pledged to the Central Land Board in accordance with the special arrangements relating to owners of single house plots, that claim holding shall, subject to sub-paragraph (2), be deemed to have been extinguished as from the time when it was pledged to the Board.

(2) Where a claim holding (in this sub-paragraph referred to as "the original holding") was pledged as mentioned in sub-paragraph (1) but was so pledged by reference to a plot of land which did not extend to the whole of the area of the original holding, that sub-paragraph shall not apply, but there shall be deemed to have been substituted for the original holding, as from the time of the pledge, a claim holding with an area consisting of so much of the area of the original holding as was not comprised in that plot of land, and with a value equal to that fraction of the value of the original holding which then attached to so much of the area of the original holding as was not comprised in that plot.

(3) Without prejudice to sub-paragraphs (1) and (2), where a pledge to the Central Land Board comprised one or more claim holdings, and the unpaid balance of the development charge covered by the pledge, or (if more than one) the aggregate of the unpaid balances of the development charges so covered, was equal to or greater than the value of the claim holding, or the aggregate value of the claim holdings, as the case may be, the holding or holdings shall be deemed to have been extinguished as from the time of the pledge.

(4) Where a pledge to the Central Land Board comprised only a single claim holding with an area of which every part either consisted of, or formed part of, the land in respect of which some development charge covered by the pledge was determined, and sub-paragraph (3) does not apply, the value of that claim holding shall be deemed to have been reduced, as from the time of the pledge, by the unpaid balance of the development charge covered by the pledge, or (if more than one) by the aggregate of the unpaid balances of all the development charges covered by the pledge.

(5) Sub-paragraphs (6) to (9) shall have effect in the case of a pledge of one or more claim holdings to the Central Land Board to which neither sub-paragraph (3) nor (4) applies.

(6) Any claim holding comprised in the pledge with an area of which every part either consisted of, or formed part of, the land in respect of which some development charge covered by the pledge was determined shall be allocated to the development charge in question, or (if more than one) to those development charges collectively.

(7) Any claim holding comprised in the pledge with an area part of which did, and part of which did not, consist of, or form part of, such land as is mentioned in sub-paragraph (6) shall be treated as if, at the time of the pledge, the claim holding (in this sub-paragraph referred to as "the parent holding") had been divided into two separate claim holdings, that is to say—

(a) a claim holding with an area consisting of so much of the area of the parent holding as consisted of, or formed part of, such land as is mentioned in sub-paragraph (6), and with a value equal to that fraction of the value of the parent holding which then attached to that part of the area of the parent holding; and

(b) a claim holding with an area consisting of the residue of the area of the parent holding, and with a value equal to that fraction of the value of the parent holding which then attached to the residue of the area of the parent holding,

and the claim holding referred to in paragraph (a) shall be allocated to the development charge in question, or (if more than one) to those development charges collectively.

(8) Sub-paragraph (3) or (4) shall then apply in relation to each claim holding (if any) allocated in accordance with sub-paragraph (6) or sub-paragraph (7) to any development charge, or to any development charges collectively, as if the pledge had comprised only that claim holding and had covered only that development charge or those development charges.

(9) If, after the application of the previous provisions of this paragraph, there remains outstanding any claim holding not allocated in accordance with those provisions, or any claim holding which (having been so allocated) is deemed to have been reduced in value but not extinguished, an amount equal to the aggregate of—

(a) the unpaid balance of any development charge covered by the pledge to which no claim holding was so allocated; and

(b) the amount (if any) by which the value of any claim holding so allocated which is deemed to have been extinguished falls short of the unpaid balance of the development charge, or the aggregate of the unpaid balances of the development charges, to which it was so allocated,

shall be treated as having been deducted from the value of the claim holding so remaining outstanding, or (if more than one) as having been deducted rateably from the respective values of those claim holdings, and the value of any such holding shall be deemed to have been reduced accordingly as from the time of the pledge.

6.—(1) In paragraph 5 and this paragraph references to the pledging of a claim holding to the Central Land Board are references to any transaction by which—

(a) the holder of the claim holding mortgaged it to the Central Land Board as security, or part of the security, for one or more development charges determined, or thereafter to be determined, by the Board; or

(b) the holder and the Central Land Board agreed that a development charge determined by the Board should be set off against any payment which might thereafter become payable to the holder by reference to that holding; or

SCH. 12

(c) the Central Land Board refrained from determining a development charge, which would otherwise have fallen to be determined by them, in consideration of a mortgage of the holding, with or without other claim holdings.

(2) All pledges of claim holdings to the Central Land Board made by the same person, whether or not made at the same time, other than any pledge to which paragraph 5(1) applies, shall for the purposes of paragraph 5 and this paragraph be treated collectively as a single pledge made at the time when the last of those pledges was made.

(3) Where a development charge covered by a pledge to the Central Land Board was determined in respect of land consisting of, or forming part of, the area of a claim holding—

(a) which was not comprised in the pledge; but

(b) whose holder immediately before the time of completion was the person who would, apart from the pledge, have been liable to pay the unpaid balance of the development charge,

then, for the purposes of paragraph 5 and this paragraph, that claim holding shall be deemed to have been comprised in the pledge.

(4) In paragraph 5 and this paragraph references to the determination of a development charge in respect of any land are references to a determination of the Central Land Board that the charge was payable in respect of the carrying out of operations in, on, over or under that land, or in respect of the use of that land.

(5) For the purposes of paragraph 5 and this paragraph the amount of a development charge—

(a) in a case where the Central Land Board determined that amount as a single capital payment, shall be taken to have been the amount of that payment; and

(b) in a case where the Board determined that amount otherwise than as a single capital payment, shall be taken to have been the amount of the single capital payment which would have been payable if the Board had determined the amount as such a payment;

and references in those paragraphs to the unpaid balance of a development charge are references to the amount of the charge, if no sum was actually paid to the Board on account of the charge, or if any sum was so paid, are references to the amount of the charge reduced by the amount or aggregate amount of the sum or sums so paid, other than any sum paid by way of interest.

(6) In relation to the pledging of a claim holding to the Central Land Board, references in paragraph 5 and this paragraph to a development charge covered by the pledge are references to a development charge the payment of which was secured, or partly secured, by the pledge, or, as the case may be, which was agreed to be set off against any payment which might become payable by reference to that claim holding.

(7) References in paragraph 5 and this paragraph to a mortgage of a claim holding do not include a mortgage which was subsequently discharged.

Adjustment by reference to payments in respect of war-damaged land

7.—(1) This paragraph shall have effect where a payment under the scheme has become, or becomes payable in respect of an interest in land, and a claim holding related (or would, apart from this paragraph, have related) to the same interest in the whole or part of that land, with or without any other land.

(2) In this paragraph—

"the scheme" means the scheme made under section 59 of the 1947 Act,

"the date of the scheme" means 12th December 1949,

"payment under the scheme" means a payment which has become, or becomes, payable by virtue of the scheme, SCH. 12

and in relation to any payment under the scheme—

(a) references to the payment area are references to the land in respect of which the payment became or becomes payable, and

(b) references to the amount of the payment shall be construed as references to the principal amount of it, excluding any interest payable on it in accordance with section 65(3) of the 1947 Act.

(3) If the payment area is identical with the area of the claim holding, then—

(a) in the case of a payment of an amount equal to the value of the claim holding, the claim holding shall be deemed to have been extinguished as from the date of the scheme;

(b) in the case of a payment of an amount less than the value of the claim holding, the value of the claim holding shall be deemed to have been reduced, as from the date of the scheme, by the amount of the payment.

(4) If the payment area forms part of the area of the claim holding, the holding (in this sub-paragraph referred to as "the parent holding") shall be treated, as from the date of the scheme, as having been divided into two claim holdings, that is to say—

(a) a claim holding with an area consisting of that part of the area of the parent holding which constituted the payment area, and with a value equal to that fraction of the value of the parent holding which attached to that part of the area of the parent holding; and

(b) a claim holding with an area consisting of the residue of the area of the parent holding, and with a value equal to that fraction of the value of the parent holding which attached to the residue of the area of the parent holding;

and sub-paragraph (3) shall have effect in relation to the claim holding referred to in paragraph (a) as if it were the parent holding.

(5) If the payment area includes the area of the claim holding together with other land, sub-paragraph (3) shall apply as if—

(a) the payment area had been identical with the area of the claim holding; but

(b) the amount of the payment had been so much of the actual amount of it, as might reasonably be expected to have been attributed to the area of the claim holding if, under the scheme, the authority determining the amount of the payment had been required (in accordance with the same principles as applied to the determination of that amount) to apportion it between the area of the claim holding and the rest of the payment area.

(6) If the payment area includes part of the area of the claim holding together with other land not comprised in the area of the claim holding—

(a) sub-paragraph (4) shall apply as if the part of the payment area comprised in the area of the claim holding had been the whole of the payment area; and

(b) sub-paragraph (5) shall apply as if the part of the area of the claim holding comprised in the payment area had been the whole of the area of the claim holding.

SCH. 12

Adjustment in cases of partial disposition of claim holdings

8.—(1) This paragraph shall have effect where, by virtue of a disposition of part of the benefit of an established claim, not being a mortgage made otherwise than by way of assignment (in this paragraph referred to as "the relevant disposition"), different persons became entitled to different parts of the benefit of that established claim.

(2) As from the date of the relevant disposition, each of those different parts shall be treated as having constituted a separate claim holding.

(3) The area and value of any such separate claim holding at any time after the relevant disposition shall be taken to have been such as may, in the requisite manner, be or have been determined to be just and appropriate in all the circumstances.

(4) In sub-paragraph (3) the reference to determination in the requisite manner of the area and value of a claim holding is a reference to the determination of it on the occasion of an apportionment affecting that holding which fell or falls to be made for any of the purposes of the 1954 Act, Part VI of the 1962 Act or Schedule 5 to that Act, Part VII of the 1971 Act or this Part of this Act, being a determination made—

(a) by the authority making that apportionment; or

(b) where, under the 1954 Act, Part VI of the 1962 Act, Part VII of the 1971 Act or this Part that authority's findings were or are referred to the Lands Tribunal, by that Tribunal,

having regard in particular to the principles mentioned in sub-paragraphs (5) to (8).

(5) The aggregate of the values of all claim holdings representing parts of the benefit of the same established claim must not exceed the amount of the established claim.

(6) Subject to sub-paragraph (5), where a claim holding representing part only of the benefit of an established claim was pledged to the Central Land Board, otherwise than as mentioned in paragraph 5(1), and by virtue of paragraph 5 the value of that claim holding is deemed to have been reduced by reference to an amount due by way of development charge, the value of that holding at the time of the pledge is not to be taken to have been less than the amount credited for the purposes of the pledge by reference to the holding.

(7) In the case of the claim holding representing the part of the benefit of an established claim which was the subject of the relevant disposition, if it was not a claim holding to which sub-paragraph (8) applies—

(a) the area of that claim holding is to be taken to be the claim area of that established claim, less the area of any claim holding to which that sub-paragraph applies which represents part of the benefit of the same established claim; and

(b) the value of the claim holding immediately after the relevant disposition is, subject to sub-paragraphs (5) and (6), to be taken to have been that part of the amount of the established claim to which the holder purported to become entitled under the terms of the relevant disposition.

(8) Where any person who was entitled to a claim holding representing part only of the benefit of an established claim—

(a) at any time while so entitled was also entitled to the interest in land to which the established claim related in so far as that interest subsisted in part only of the claim area; and

(b) became entitled to both that holding and that interest in such circumstances that the authority making the apportionment in question or the Lands Tribunal, as the case may be, were or are satisfied that the holding and the interest were intended to relate to one another,

the area of that claim holding is to be taken to be that part of the claim area, and the value of the holding immediately after the relevant disposition (however that or any other disposition affecting the holding was expressed, but subject to sub-paragraphs (5) to (7)) is to be taken to have been an amount equal to so much of the amount of the established claim as might reasonably be expected to have been attributed to that part of the claim area if the authority determining the amount of that established claim had been required to apportion it, in accordance with the same principles as applied to its determination, between that part and the residue of the claim area.

(9) Paragraph 6 shall apply for the purposes of this paragraph as it applies for the purposes of paragraph 5.

Adjustment in respect of payments under Part I of 1954 Act

9.—(1) This paragraph shall have effect where, by virtue of Part I of the 1954 Act, a payment became or becomes payable in respect of a claim holding.

(2) Subject to the following provisions of this paragraph, if either—

(a) the principal amount of the payment was or is not less than the value of the claim holding; or

(b) the payment (whatever its amount) became or becomes payable under Case D (that is to say, by virtue of section 8 of the 1954 Act, which related to cases where a claim holding had been disposed of for valuable consideration),

the claim holding shall be deemed to have been extinguished; and if the principal amount of the payment (not being a payment under Case D) was or is less than the value of the claim holding, the value of that holding shall be deemed to have been reduced by the principal amount of the payment.

(3) Sub-paragraph (2) shall apply where two or more payments under Part I of the 1954 Act were or are payable in respect of the same claim holding, with the substitution, for references to the principal amount of the payment, of references to the aggregate of the principal amounts of the payments.

(4) Where one or more relevant acts or events have occurred in relation to a claim holding (in this paragraph referred to as "the parent holding") and any such act or event did not extend to the whole of the area of the parent holding, then, for the purposes of sub-paragraphs (1) to (3) and paragraph 10 and of the relevant provisions—

(a) the parent holding shall be treated as having been divided immediately before the time of completion, into as many separate claim holdings, with such areas, as may be necessary to ensure that, in the case of each holding, either any relevant act or event extending to the area of that holding extended to the whole of it or no relevant act or event extended to the area of that holding;

(b) the value of each of the separate holdings respectively shall be taken to have been that fraction of the value of the parent holding which then attached to the part of the area of the parent holding constituting the area of the separate holding; and

(c) the portion of the amount of any payment under Part I of the 1954 Act which, by the authority determining that amount, was or is apportioned to the area of any of the separate claim holdings shall be taken to have been a payment payable under that Part in respect of that claim holding.

SCH. 12

(5) In this paragraph—

"relevant act or event", in relation to a claim holding, means an act or event by which, in accordance with the provisions of Part I of the 1954 Act, one or more payments became or become payable in respect of that claim holding, and

"the relevant provisions" means sections 119 to 136 and paragraphs 1 to 4, 12 to 14, 16 and 18 to 20.

(6) For the purposes of this paragraph—

(a) a payment shall be treated as having become payable notwithstanding that the right to receive the payment was extinguished by section 14(2) of the 1954 Act (which enabled the Central Land Board to set off payments against liabilities in respect of development charges);

(b) any reduction of the principal amount of a payment by virtue of that subsection shall be disregarded; and

(c) where in accordance with subsection (3) of section 14 or subsection (6) of section 58 of the 1954 Act (which provided for cases of failure to apply for a payment within the appropriate period) an amount was determined as being the principal amount of a payment to which a person would have been entitled as mentioned in those subsections respectively, that payment shall be treated as if it had become due and as if the principal amount of it had been the amount so determined.

(7) Where in accordance with sub-paragraphs (1) to (6) a claim holding is deemed to have been extinguished or the value of a claim holding is deemed to have been reduced, the extinguishment or reduction, as the case may be, shall be deemed to have had effect immediately before the time of completion.

(8) References in this paragraph to the value of a claim holding are references to the value of it immediately before the time of completion.

Adjustment in respect of compensation under

Part V of 1954 Act

10.—(1) Where compensation under Part V of the 1954 Act became or becomes payable by reference to a claim holding, then (subject to the following provisions of this paragraph) for the purposes of this Part—

(a) if the principal amount of the compensation was or is equal to the value of the claim holding at the time of completion (ascertained apart from this paragraph) the claim holding shall be deemed to have been extinguished immediately before that time;

(b) if the principal amount of the compensation was or is less than the value of the claim holding at that time (ascertained apart from this paragraph) the value of the claim holding shall be deemed to have been reduced immediately before that time by the principal amount of the compensation.

(2) Where—

(a) compensation became or becomes payable as mentioned in sub-paragraph (1), and

(b) at any time an amount became or becomes recoverable in respect of it under section 29 of the 1954 Act, as applied by section 46 of that Act, or under section 159 of the 1971 Act as applied by Schedule 24 to that

Act to compensation under Part V of the 1954 Act, or under section 133 of this Act as applied by virtue of Schedule 3 to the Planning (Consequential Provisions) Act 1990 to such compensation, 1990 c. 11.

then, for the purposes of this Part, sub-paragraph (1) shall have effect as from that time as if the principal amount of that compensation had been reduced by a sum equal to seven-eighths of the amount which so became or becomes recoverable.

(3) Where, in the case of a claim holding (in this sub-paragraph referred to as "the parent holding"), compensation under Part V of the 1954 Act became or becomes payable in respect of depreciation of the value of an interest in land by one or more planning decisions or orders, and any such decision or order did not extend to the whole of the area of the parent holding, then for the purposes of sub-paragraphs (1) and (2) and for the purposes of the relevant provisions (within the meaning of paragraph 9(5))—

(a) the parent holding shall be treated as having been divided immediately before the time of completion into as many separate claim holdings, with such areas, as may be necessary to ensure that, in the case of each holding, either any such decision or order extending to the area of that holding extended to the whole of it or no such decision or order extended to the area of that holding;

(b) the value of each of the separate holdings respectively shall be taken to have been that fraction of the value of the parent holding which then attached to the part of the area of the parent holding constituting the area of the separate holding; and

(c) the portion of the amount of any such compensation which, by the authority determining that amount, was or is apportioned to the area of any of the separate claim holdings shall be taken to have been compensation payable under Part V of the 1954 Act in respect of that claim holding.

Adjustment of claim holdings: supplementary provisions

11.—(1) Where in accordance with any of paragraphs 5 to 10 a part of the benefit of an established claim constituted a separate claim holding, the interest in land to which that claim holding related—

(a) if the established claim related to the fee simple of the claim area, shall be taken to have been the fee simple of the area of the claim holding;

(b) if the established claim related to a leasehold interest, shall be taken to have been that leasehold interest in so far as it subsisted in the area of the claim holding.

(2) Where in accordance with any of those paragraphs a claim holding (in this sub-paragraph referred to as "the parent holding") is to be treated as divided into two or more claim holdings, a person who was the holder of one of those holdings shall be treated as having been the holder of it at any time when he was the holder of the parent holding.

(3) In paragraphs 5 to 10 and this paragraph expressions used in the relevant provisions (within the meaning of paragraph 9(5)) have the same meanings as in those provisions.

(4) In paragraphs 5 to 10 and this paragraph "the holder", in relation to a claim holding, means—

(a) the person for the time being entitled to the holding, or

(b) in the case of a holding subject to a mortgage made otherwise than by way of assignment, the person who would for the time being have been entitled to the holding if it had not been mortgaged.

SCH. 12

General provision for continuance of original unexpended balance

12. Where in accordance with paragraph 2 land had an original unexpended balance of established development value, then, subject to the following provisions of this Schedule (except for paragraphs 15 and 17) and to sections 120 to 136, that land shall be taken—

(a) to have continued to have that balance until the commencement of this Act; and

(b) to continue to have that balance at all times after that commencement.

Reduction or extinguishment of balance in consequence of compensation

13.—(1) Where at any time compensation becomes payable under this Part, or became payable under Part II of the 1954 Act or Part VI of the 1962 Act or Part VII of the 1971 Act, in respect of depreciation of the value of an interest in land by a planning decision, then, for the purpose of determining whether that land or any part of it has or had an unexpended balance of established development value at any subsequent time—

(a) the amount of the compensation shall be deducted from the original unexpended balance of established development value of that land, and

(b) the original unexpended balance of that land or that part of it shall be treated as having been reduced or extinguished accordingly immediately before that subsequent time.

(2) Where an amount has become recoverable under section 133 in respect of the compensation specified in a compensation notice, except where, and to the extent that, payment of that amount has been remitted under section 134, for the purpose of determining any question as to the unexpended balance of established development value of any land at any subsequent time, so much (if any) of that compensation as is attributable to that land shall be treated as not having become payable, and accordingly (notwithstanding anything in sub-paragraph (1)) shall not be deducted from that balance.

Reduction or extinguishment of balance on initiation of new development

14.—(1) Where in accordance with paragraph 2 land had an original unexpended balance of established development value, and at any time on or after 1st July 1948 (whether before or after the commencement of this Act) any new development of that land is or was initiated, then (subject to the following provisions of this paragraph) for the purpose of determining whether that land or any part of it has or had an unexpended balance of established development value at any subsequent time—

(a) if the development relates or related only to that land, the value of that development (ascertained, with reference to that subsequent time, in accordance with the provisions of paragraph 15); or

(b) if the development relates or related to that land together with other land, so much of the value of that development (so ascertained) as is or was attributable to that land,

shall be deducted from the original unexpended balance of established development value of that land, and the original unexpended balance of that land or that part of it shall be treated as having been reduced or extinguished accordingly immediately before that subsequent time.

(2) Sub-paragraph (1) shall not apply to any land if, in respect of any interest in it, a payment has become or becomes payable under section 59 of the 1947 Act (which provided for payments in respect of certain war-damaged land).

(3) For the purposes of sub-paragraph (1) no account shall be taken of any development initiated before lst January 1955, if—

(a) a development charge under Part VII of the 1947 Act was determined to be payable in respect of it, or would have fallen to be so determined but for any exemption conferred by regulations under that Part of that Act, or by any provisions of Part VIII of that Act; or

(b) in a certificate issued under section 58 of the 1954 Act (which related to monopoly value of licensed premises) it was certified that a development charge could have been determined to be payable in respect of that development if the circumstances referred to in sub-paragraph (l)(a) or (b) of that section had not existed.

Calculation of value of previous development of land

15.—(1) Where for the purposes of paragraph 14 the value of any development initiated before a time referred to in that paragraph has to be ascertained with reference to that time, the value of the development shall be calculated in accordance with the provisions of this paragraph.

(2) Subject to the following provisions of this paragraph, the value shall be calculated by reference to prices current at the time in question—

(a) as if the development had not been initiated, but the land had remained in the state in which it was immediately before the development was initiated; and

(b) on the assumption that (apart from the provisions of Part III of this Act, the provisions of Part III of the 1971 Act, the provisions of Part III of the 1962 Act or the provisions of the 1947 Act, as the case may be) the development could at that time lawfully be carried out,

and shall be taken to be the difference between—

(i) the value which in those circumstances the land would have had at that time if planning permission for that development had been granted unconditionally immediately before that time, and

(ii) the value which in those circumstances the land would have had at that time if planning permission for that development had been applied for and refused immediately before that time and it could be assumed that planning permission for that development, and any other new development of that land, would be refused on any subsequent application.

(3) If the development involved the clearing of any land, the reference in sub-paragraph (2)(a) to the state of the land immediately before the development shall be construed as a reference to the state of the land immediately after the clearing of it but before the carrying out of any other operations.

(4) If the development was initiated in pursuance of planning permission granted subject to conditions, sub-paragraph (2) shall apply as if the reference to the granting of permission unconditionally were a reference to the granting of permission subject to the same conditions.

(5) If the permission referred to in sub-paragraph (4) was granted subject to conditions which consisted of, or included, a requirement expressed by reference to a specified period, the reference in that sub-paragraph to the same conditions shall be construed, in relation to the condition imposing that requirement, as a reference to a condition imposing the same requirement in respect of a period of the same duration beginning at the time in question.

(6) In the application of this paragraph to development initiated, but not completed, before the time in question, references to permission for that development shall be construed as references to permission for so much of that development as had been carried out before that time.

SCH. 12

Reduction or extinguishment of balance on acquisition under compulsory powers

16.—(1) Where in the case of—

(a) a compulsory acquisition to which this paragraph applies; or

(b) a sale of an interest in land by agreement in circumstances corresponding to such an acquisition,

any of the land in which the interest acquired or sold subsists or subsisted has or had an unexpended balance of established development value immediately before the relevant date (in this paragraph referred to as "the relevant balance") this paragraph shall have effect for the purpose of determining whether that land or any part of it has or had an unexpended balance of established development value at any subsequent time.

(2) This paragraph applies—

(a) to every compulsory acquisition of an interest in land in pursuance of a notice to treat served on or after 30th October 1958, whether before or after the commencement of this Act; and

(b) to every compulsory acquisition of an interest in land, in pursuance of a notice to treat served on or after 1st January 1955 but before 30th October 1958, by an authority possessing compulsory purchase powers, being at that time a government department or local or public authority within the meaning of the Acquisition of Land (Assessment of Compensation) Act 1919, or a person or body of persons to whom that Act applied as it applied to such a department or authority.

1919 c. 57.

(3) Unless, immediately after the acquisition or sale, there is or was outstanding some interest (other than an excepted interest) in the land to which some person other than the acquiring authority is or was entitled, the original unexpended balance of established development value of that land shall be treated as having been extinguished immediately before the subsequent time referred to in sub-paragraph (1).

(4) If, immediately after the acquisition or sale, there is or was such an outstanding interest (other than an excepted interest) as is mentioned in sub-paragraph (3), there shall be deducted from that original balance an amount equal to any part of the relevant balance which is or was not attributable to any such outstanding interest, and the original unexpended balance of established development value of the land or the part of it in question shall be treated as having been reduced or extinguished accordingly immediately before that subsequent time.

(5) For the purposes of this paragraph any question as to the portion of the relevant balance which is or was attributable to an interest in land—

(a) in relation to a compulsory acquisition to which this paragraph applies, shall be determined in accordance with paragraph 17; and

(b) in relation to a sale of an interest in land by agreement in circumstances corresponding to such an acquisition, shall be determined in accordance with the provisions of that paragraph as those provisions would apply if the sale had been a compulsory acquisition in pursuance of a notice to treat served on the relevant date.

(6) Any reference in this paragraph or in paragraph 18 to a sale of an interest in land by agreement in circumstances corresponding to a compulsory acquisition to which this paragraph applies is a reference to a sale of it—

(a) to an authority possessing compulsory purchase powers, in pursuance of a contract made on or after 30th October 1958, whether before or after the commencement of this Act; or

(b) to such an authority possessing compulsory purchase powers as is mentioned in sub-paragraph (2)(b), in pursuance of a contract made on or after 1st January 1955 but before 30th October 1958.

(7) In this paragraph— SCH. 12

(a) "the relevant date" means the date of service of the notice to treat or the date of the contract in pursuance of which the interest was sold, as the case may be, and

(b) "excepted interest" means the interest of any such person as is mentioned in section 20(1) of the Compulsory Purchase Act 1965 (which relates to persons having no greater interest than as tenant for a year or from year to year). 1965 c. 56.

Apportionment of unexpended balance of established development value

17.—(1) Where, in the case of a compulsory acquisition to which paragraph 16 applies, any area of the relevant land which, immediately before the relevant date, has an unexpended balance of established development value does not satisfy the following conditions, namely—

(a) that all the interests (other than excepted interests) subsisting in the area in question subsist in the whole of that area; and

(b) that any rentcharge charged on that area is charged on the whole of it,

that area shall be treated as divided into as many separate areas as may be requisite to ensure that each of those separate areas satisfies those conditions.

(2) Any area of the relevant land which has an unexpended balance of established development value and which complies with the conditions mentioned in sub-paragraph (1) is in this paragraph referred to, in relation to the interests subsisting in it, as "the relevant area", and the following provisions of this paragraph shall have effect separately in relation to each relevant area.

(3) There shall be calculated the amount referable to the relevant area of the rent which might reasonably be expected to be reserved if the relevant land were to be let on terms prohibiting the carrying out of any new development but permitting the carrying out of any other development; and the amount so calculated is in this paragraph referred to as "the existing use rent".

(4) If, in the case of an interest in fee simple which is subject to a rentcharge, or in the case of a tenancy, so much of the rent reserved under the rentcharge or tenancy as is referable to the relevant area exceeds the existing use rent, there shall be calculated the capital value of the right to receive, for the period of the remainder of the term of the rentcharge or tenancy, an annual payment equal to the excess; and any amount so calculated in the case of any interest is in this paragraph referred to as "the rental liability" of that interest.

(5) Where the interest in fee simple is subject to more than one rentcharge, then, for the purposes of sub-paragraph (4), in relation to any period included in the term of two or more of those rentcharges, those two or more rentcharges shall be treated as a single rentcharge charged on the relevant area for the duration of that period, with a rent reserved thereunder of an amount equal to the aggregate of so much of their respective rents as is referable to the relevant area.

(6) In the case of any interest in reversion—

(a) there shall be calculated the capital value, as at the time immediately before the relevant date, of the right to receive a sum equal to the unexpended balance of established development value of the relevant area at that time, but payable at the end of the tenancy upon the termination of which the interest in question is immediately expectant; and the amount so calculated in the case of any interest is in this paragraph referred to as "the reversionary development value" of that interest;

SCH. 12

(b) if so much of the rent reserved under that tenancy as is referable to the relevant area exceeds the existing use rent, there shall also be calculated the capital value as at the said time of the right to receive, for the period of the remainder of the term of that tenancy, an annual payment equal to the excess;

and any amount so determined in the case of any interest is in this paragraph referred to as "the rental increment" of that interest.

(7) Where two or more interests (other than excepted interests) subsist in the relevant area, the portion of the unexpended balance of established development value of the relevant area attributable to each of those interests respectively shall be taken to be—

(a) in the case of the interest in fee simple, an amount equal to the reversionary development value of that interest, less the amount (if any) by which any rental liability of that interest exceeds any rental increment of it;

(b) in the case of a tenancy in reversion, an amount equal to the reversionary development value of that tenancy, less the aggregate of—

(i) the reversionary development value of the interest in reversion immediately expectant upon the termination of that tenancy; and

(ii) the amount (if any) by which any rental liability of that tenancy exceeds any rental increment of it;

(c) in the case of a tenancy other than a tenancy in reversion, the remainder (if any) of the said balance after the deduction of the aggregate of—

(i) the reversionary development value of the interest in reversion immediately expectant upon the termination of that tenancy; and

(ii) any rental liability of that tenancy.

(8) In relation to any compulsory acquisition to which paragraph 16 applies, where the relevant date was a date before the commencement of this Act, the previous provisions of this paragraph shall have effect with the necessary modifications.

(9) In this paragraph—

(a) "the relevant land", in relation to a compulsory acquisition to which paragraph 16 applies, means the land in which the interest acquired subsisted or subsists;

(b) "tenancy" does not include an excepted interest;

(c) any reference to an interest or tenancy in reversion does not include an interest or tenancy in reversion immediately expectant upon the termination of an excepted interest;

(d) "the relevant date" and "excepted interest" have the same meanings as in paragraph 16; and

(e) other expressions have the same meanings as in the relevant provisions (within the meaning of paragraph 9(5)).

Reduction or extinguishment of balance in consequence of severance or injurious affection

18.—(1) Where in connection with—

(a) a compulsory acquisition to which paragraph 16 applies; or

(b) a sale of an interest in land by agreement in circumstances corresponding to such an acquisition,

compensation is or was payable, or an amount is or was included in the purchase price, in respect of an interest in land other than the relevant land (in this paragraph referred to as "the interest affected"), for damage sustained by reason that the relevant land is or was severed from other land held with it, or that any other land (whether held with the relevant land or not) is or was injuriously affected, then (subject to the following provisions of this paragraph) for the purpose of determining whether that other land or any part of it has or had an unexpended balance of established development value at any subsequent time—

(i) there shall be deducted from the original unexpended balance of established development value of that other land an amount calculated in accordance with the following provisions of this paragraph, and

(ii) the original unexpended balance of that land, or of the part of it in question, as the case may be, shall be treated as having been reduced or extinguished accordingly immediately before that subsequent time.

(2) In the case of an acquisition or sale in pursuance of a notice to treat served, or contract made, on or after 30th October 1958, the amount to be deducted, as mentioned in sub-paragraph (1), shall be the amount (if any) by which the compensation payable, or the amount included in the purchase price, as so mentioned exceeds or exceeded the compensation which would have been so payable, or the amount which would have been so included, if the extent of the damage sustained in respect of the other land in question had fallen to be ascertained on the assumption that planning permission would not be granted for any new development of that land, but would be granted for any development of it other than new development.

(3) Sub-paragraphs (4) to (6) shall have effect with respect to any such acquisition or sale as is mentioned in sub-paragraph (1), being an acquisition or sale in pursuance of a notice to treat served, or contract made, before 30th October 1958.

(4) No such deduction as is mentioned in sub-paragraph (1) shall be made in the case of such an acquisition or sale as is mentioned in sub-paragraph (3) unless—

(a) where it was a compulsory acquisition, an amount was paid by way of compensation as mentioned in sub-paragraph (1);

(b) the amount which was so paid, or, in the case of a sale by agreement, was included in the purchase price as mentioned in sub-paragraph (1), ("the sum paid for severance or injurious affection") exceeded the loss of immediate value of the interest affected; and

(c) where it was a sale by agreement, the other land in question was held with the relevant land.

(5) Subject to sub-paragraph (4), the amount to be deducted as mentioned in sub-paragraph (1), in the case of such an acquisition or sale as is mentioned in sub-paragraph (3), shall be the amount by which the sum paid for severance or injurious affection exceeded the loss of immediate value of the interest affected.

(6) This sub-paragraph shall have effect, in the case of such an acquisition or sale as is mentioned in sub-paragraph (3), where so much (if any) of the sum paid for severance or injurious affection as was attributable to the loss of immediate value of the interest affected was less than the depreciation in restricted value of that interest, that is to say—

(a) the amount of the difference shall be ascertained; and

(b) for the purpose of determining whether, at any time after the acquisition or sale, the land in which the interest affected subsisted or any part of it had or has an unexpended balance of established development value (whether or not that land or any part of it would apart from this sub-paragraph have had an original unexpended balance of established development value) a claim holding with an area consisting of that land and a value equal to seven-eighths of the amount of the difference shall be deemed to have subsisted immediately after the time when the adjustment of claim holdings was completed.

SCH. 12

(7) In this paragraph—

"the loss of immediate value" means the amount (if any) by which the difference in the value of the interest affected, immediately before and immediately after the acquisition or sale, exceeded the loss of development value;

"the loss of development value" means the amount (if any) by which the value of the interest affected immediately before the acquisition or sale, if calculated on the assumption that, until such time as the land in which that interest subsisted might reasonably be expected to become ripe for new development, no use whatever could be made of that land, would have exceeded the value of that interest immediately after the acquisition or sale if calculated on the like assumption;

"the depreciation in restricted value" means the amount (if any) by which the value of the interest affected, immediately after the acquisition or sale, would have been less than the value of that interest immediately before the acquisition or sale, if both values were calculated on the assumption that planning permission would not be granted for any new development of that land, but would be granted for any development of it other than new development;

"the relevant land", in relation to an acquisition or sale, means the land in which the interest acquired or sold subsisted.

Supplementary provisions as to deductions from original balance

19.—(1) Where, immediately after the time when the adjustment of claim holdings was completed, any land taken as a whole had an original unexpended balance of established development value, and at any later time (whether before or after the commencement of this Act) an act or event occurs or has occurred in relation to part of that land such that, in accordance with any of the provisions of section 119 and paragraphs 1 to 4, 12 to 14, 16 and 18, an amount is required to be deducted from the original unexpended balance of that part of that land for the purpose of determining whether it has or had an unexpended balance of established development value at any subsequent time, then (without prejudice to the operation of any of those provisions with respect to any part of the land taken separately) the land taken as a whole shall be treated as not having (or as not having had) any such balance at that subsequent time.

(2) Where in accordance with those provisions an amount is required to be deducted from the original unexpended balance of established development value of any land, there shall be attributed to the various parts of that land so much of that amount as might reasonably be expected to have been attributed to it if the authority determining the amount had been required to apportion it between those parts in accordance with the same principles as applied to its determination.

(3) Where two or more acts or events occur or have occurred in relation to the same land (whether before or after the commencement of this Act) such that, in accordance with those provisions, an amount is required to be deducted from the original unexpended balance of established development value of that land or any part of it, those provisions shall apply cumulatively, and the requisite deduction from the original unexpended balance of established development value of that land shall be made by reference to each of those acts or events.

Provision of information relating to unexpended balance

20.—(1) Subject to this paragraph, the Secretary of State shall, on application being made to him by any person, and may if he thinks fit without any such application, issue a certificate in the prescribed form with respect to any land stating whether any of that land had an original unexpended balance of established development value, and, if so—

(a) giving a general statement of what was taken by the Central Land Board, for the purposes of Part VI of the 1947 Act, to be the state of that land on 1st July 1948; and

(b) specifying (subject to any outstanding claims under Part I or Part V of the 1954 Act) the amount of that original balance.

(2) Any such certificate issued with respect to any land may, if the Secretary of State thinks fit, contain additional information with respect to acts or events in consequence of which, in accordance with any of the provisions of section 119 and paragraphs 1 to 4, 12 to 14, 16 and 18, an amount is required to be deducted from the original unexpended balance of established development value of any of that land.

(3) Where, at any time on or after 1st January 1955 (whether before or after the commencement of this Act), a notice to treat has been served with a view to the compulsory acquisition of an interest in land by an authority possessing compulsory purchase powers, that authority may apply to the Secretary of State for, and shall be entitled to the issue of, a certificate showing the unexpended balance of established development value (if any) of any of that land immediately before the service of that notice.

(4) Where the issue of a certificate under this paragraph with respect to any land involves a new apportionment, or, in the case of a certificate under sub-paragraph (3), involves the calculation of a deduction from the original unexpended balance of established development value by virtue of paragraph 14, then—

(a) except in the case of a certificate under sub-paragraph (3), or of a certificate which the Secretary of State proposes to issue without any application being made for it, the certificate shall not be issued otherwise than on the application of a person who is for the time being entitled to an interest in that land;

(b) before issuing the certificate, the Secretary of State shall give notice in writing to any person entitled to an interest in land appearing to him to be an interest which will be substantially affected by the apportionment or calculation, giving particulars of the proposed apportionment or calculation, and stating that objections or other representations with respect to it may be made to the Secretary of State within the period of 30 days from the date of the notice; and

(c) the certificate shall not be issued before the end of that period, and if within that period an objection to the proposed apportionment or calculation has been made by any person to whom notice has been given under paragraph (b), or by any other person who establishes that he is entitled to an interest in land which is substantially affected by the apportionment or calculation, and that objection has not been withdrawn, sub-paragraph (5) shall have effect.

(5) Where by virtue of sub-paragraph (4)(c) this sub-paragraph is to have effect, then—

(a) if within a further period of 30 days the person by whom any such objection was made requires the dispute to be referred to the Lands Tribunal, the dispute shall be so referred, and the certificate shall not be issued until either the Tribunal has decided the matter or the reference to the Tribunal has been withdrawn;

(b) the certificate may be issued before the end of the said further period if every such objection has been withdrawn;

(c) the certificate shall be issued at the end of that further period, notwithstanding that every such objection has not been withdrawn, if no requirement has within that period been made under paragraph (a).

SCH. 12

(6) Where, on a reference to the Lands Tribunal under this paragraph, it is shown that a new apportionment relates partly to the same matters as a previous apportionment, and is consistent with that previous apportionment in so far as it relates to those matters, the Tribunal shall not vary the new appointment in such a way as to be inconsistent with the previous apportionment in so far as it relates to those matters.

(7) A certificate under sub-paragraph (3) shall be conclusive evidence of the unexpended balance shown in it; and a certificate under sub-paragraph (1) shall be sufficient proof of any facts stated in it unless the contrary is shown.

(8) An application for a certificate under this paragraph shall be made in such form and manner as may be prescribed, and shall be accompanied by sufficient particulars (including a map if necessary) to enable the land to be identified, and, where a new apportionment will be involved, particulars of the nature of the applicant's interest, and such information as to the nature of any other interest in the land, and as to the name and address of the person entitled to that other interest, as may be known to the applicant.

(9) On any application under sub-paragraph (1) the applicant shall pay in the prescribed manner a fee of 25 pence, and, if the application involves a new apportionment, the certificate shall not be issued until the applicant has paid in the prescribed manner a further fee of 75 pence.

(10) In this paragraph "new apportionment" means an apportionment which relates wholly or partly to any matter to which no previous apportionment related.

Section 149.

SCHEDULE 13

BLIGHTED LAND

Land allocated for public authority functions in development plans etc.

1. Land indicated in a structure plan in force for the district in which it is situated either—

(a) as land which may be required for the purposes—

(i) of the functions of a government department, local authority or statutory undertakers, or of the British Coal Corporation, or

(ii) of the establishment or running by a public telecommunications operator of a telecommunication system, or

(b) as land which may be included in an action area.

Notes

(1) In this paragraph the reference to a structure plan in force includes a reference to—

(a) proposals for the alteration or repeal and replacement of a structure plan which have been submitted to the Secretary of State under section 32;

(b) modifications proposed to be made by the Secretary of State in any such plan or proposals, being modifications of which he has given notice in accordance with regulations under Part II.

(2) Note (1) shall cease to apply when the copies of the proposals made available for inspection have been withdrawn under section 33(9) or 34 (but section 34(2) shall not invalidate any blight notice served by virtue of Note (1) before the withdrawal of copies of the proposals).

(3) Note (1) shall also cease to apply when—

(a) the relevant proposals become operative (whether in their original form or with modifications), or

(b) the Secretary of State decides to reject the proposals and notice of the decision has been given by advertisement. SCH. 13

(4) In Note (1) references to anything done under any provision include reference to anything done under that provision as it applies by virtue of section 51.

(5) This paragraph does not apply to land situated in a district for which a local plan is in force, where that plan—

(a) allocates any land in the district for the purposes of such functions as are mentioned in this paragraph; or

(b) defines any land in the district as the site of proposed development for the purposes of any such functions.

(6) This paragraph does not apply to land within paragraph 5 or 6.

(7) In the application of this paragraph to Greater London the reference to a structure plan shall be construed as a reference to the Greater London Development Plan and all references to alteration and repeal and replacement shall be omitted.

2. Land which—

(a) is allocated for the purposes of any such functions as are mentioned in paragraph 1(a)(i) or (ii) by a local plan in force for the district, or

(b) is land defined in such a plan as the site of proposed development for the purposes of any such functions.

Notes

(1) In this paragraph the reference to a local plan in force includes a reference to—

(a) a local plan of which copies have been made available for inspection under section 39(5);

(b) proposals for the alteration or repeal and replacement of a local plan of which copies have been made available for inspection under section 39(5) or 40(2);

(c) modifications proposed to be made by the local planning authority or the Secretary of State in any such plan or proposals as are mentioned in paragraph (a) or (b), being modifications of which notice has been given by the authority or the Secretary of State in accordance with regulations under Part II.

(2) Note (1) shall cease to apply when the copies of the plan or proposals made available for inspection have been withdrawn under section 41(4).

(3) Note (1) shall also cease to apply when—

(a) the relevant plan or proposals become operative (whether in their original form or with modifications), or

(b) the Secretary of State decides to reject, or the local planning authority decide to abandon, the plan or proposals and notice of the decision has been given by advertisement.

(4) In Note (1) references to anything done under any provision include references to anything done under that provision as it applies by virtue of section 51.

(5) In the application of this paragraph to Greater London—

(a) in Note (1) for the reference in paragraph (a) to section 39(5) there shall be substituted a reference to paragraph 8(2) of Part II of Schedule 2 and for the reference in paragraph (b) to that section there shall be substituted a reference to that paragraph as applied by paragraph 12 of that Part;

SCH. 13

(b) in Note (2) for the reference to section 41(4) there shall be substituted a reference to paragraph 11(2) of that Part.

3. Land indicated in a unitary development plan in force for the district in which it is situated—

(a) as land which may be required for the purpose of any such functions as are mentioned in paragraph 1(a)(i) or (ii), or

(b) as land which may be included in an action area.

Notes

(1) In this paragraph the reference to a unitary development plan includes references to—

(a) a unitary development plan of which copies have been made available for inspection under section 13(3);

(b) proposals for the alteration or replacement of a unitary development plan of which copies have been made available for inspection under that provision as applied by section 21(2) or under section 22;

(c) modifications proposed to be made by the local planning authority or the Secretary of State to any such plan or proposals as are mentioned in paragraph (a) or (b), being modifications of which notice has been given in accordance with regulations under Chapter I of Part II.

(2) Note (1) shall cease to apply when the copies of the plan or proposals made available for inspection have been withdrawn under section 13(7) or 14(2) (but section 14(4) shall not invalidate any blight notice served by virtue of Note (1) before the withdrawal of copies of the plan or proposals).

(3) Note (1) shall also cease to apply when—

(a) the relevant plan or proposals become operative (whether in their original form or with modifications), or

(b) the Secretary of State decides to reject, or the local planning authority decide to withdraw, the plan or proposals and notice of the decision has been given by advertisement.

(4) In Note (1) references to anything done under any provision include references to anything done under that provision as it applies by virtue of section 25(2).

4. Land which by a unitary development plan is allocated for the purposes, or defined as the site, of proposed development for any such functions as are mentioned in paragraph 1(a)(i) or (ii).

Notes

(1) In this paragraph the reference to a unitary development plan includes references to—

(a) a unitary development plan of which copies have been made available for inspection under section 13(3):

(b) proposals for the alteration or replacement of a unitary development plan of which copies have been made available for inspection under that provision as applied by section 21(2) or under section 22;

(c) modifications proposed to be made by the local planning authority or the Secretary of State to any such plan or proposals as are mentioned in paragraph (a) or (b), being modifications of which notice has been given in accordance with regulations under Chapter I of Part II.

(2) Note (1) shall cease to apply when the copies of the plan or proposals made available for inspection have been withdrawn under section 13(7) or 14(2) (but section 14(4) shall not invalidate any blight notice served by virtue of Note (1) before the withdrawal of copies of the plan or proposals). SCH. 13

(3) Note (1) shall also cease to apply when—

(a) the relevant plan or proposals become operative (whether in their original form or with modifications), or

(b) the Secretary of State decides to reject, or the local planning authority decide to withdraw, the plan or proposals and notice of the decision has been given by advertisement.

(4) In Note (1) references to anything done under any provision include references to anything done under that provision as it applies by virtue of section 25(2).

5. Land indicated in a plan (other than a development plan) approved by a resolution passed by a local planning authority for the purpose of the exercise of their powers under Part III as land which may be required for the purposes of any functions of a government department, local authority or statutory undertakers.

6. Land in respect of which a local planning authority—

(a) have resolved to take action to safeguard it for development for the purposes of any such functions as are mentioned in paragraph 5, or

(b) have been directed by the Secretary of State to restrict the grant of planning permission in order to safeguard it for such development.

New towns and urban development areas

7. Land within an area described as the site of a proposed new town in the draft of an order in respect of which a notice has been published under paragraph 2 of Schedule 1 to the New Towns Act 1981. 1981 c. 64

Note

Land shall cease to be within this paragraph when—

(a) the order comes into operation (whether in the form of the draft or with modifications), or

(b) the Secretary of State decides not to make the order.

8. Land within an area designated as the site of a proposed new town by an order which has come into operation under section 1 of the New Towns Act 1981.

9. Land which is—

(a) within an area intended to be designated as an urban development area by an order which has been made under section 134 of the Local Government, Planning and Land Act 1980 but has not come into effect; or 1980 c. 65.

(b) within an area which has been so designated by an order under that section which has come into effect.

Clearance and renewal areas

10. Land within an area declared to be a clearance area by a resolution under section 289 of the Housing Act 1985. 1985 c. 68.

SCH. 13

11. Land which—

1985 c. 68.

(a) is surrounded by or adjoining an area declared to be a clearance area by a resolution under section 289 of the Housing Act 1985, and

(b) is land which a local authority have determined to purchase under section 290 of that Act.

1989 c. 42.

12. Land indicated by information published in pursuance of section 92 of the Local Government and Housing Act 1989 as land which a local authority propose to acquire in exercise of their powers under Part VII of that Act (renewal areas).

Highways

13. Land indicated in a development plan (otherwise than by being dealt with in a manner mentioned in paragraphs 1, 2, 3 and 4) as—

(a) land on which a highway is proposed to be constructed, or

(b) land to be included in a highway as proposed to be improved or altered.

1980 c. 66.
1959 c. 25.
1971 c. 41.

14. Land on or adjacent to the line of a highway proposed to be constructed, improved or altered, as indicated in an order or scheme which has come into operation under Part II of the Highways Act 1980 (or under the corresponding provisions of Part II of the Highways Act 1959 or section 1 of the Highways Act 1971), being land in relation to which a power of compulsory acquisition conferred by any of the provisions of Part XII of that Act of 1980 (including a power compulsorily to acquire any right by virtue of section 250) may become exercisable, as being land required for purposes of construction, improvement or alteration as indicated in the order or scheme.

Notes

(1) In this paragraph the reference to an order or scheme which has come into operation includes a reference to an order or scheme which has been submitted for confirmation to, or been prepared in draft by, the Minister of Transport or the Secretary of State under Part II of that Act of 1980 and in respect of which a notice has been published under paragraph 1, 2 or 10 of Schedule 1 to that Act.

(2) Note (1) shall cease to apply when—

(a) the relevant order or scheme comes into operation (whether in its original form or with modifications), or

(b) the Secretary of State decides not to confirm or make the order or scheme.

(3) In this paragraph the reference to land required for purposes of construction, improvement or alteration as indicated in an order or scheme includes a reference to land required for the purposes of section 246(1) of the Highways Act 1980.

15. Land shown on plans approved by a resolution of a local highway authority as land comprised in the site of a highway as proposed to be constructed, improved or altered by that authority.

16. Land on which the Secretary of State proposes to provide a trunk road or a special road and has given to the local planning authority written notice of his intention to provide the road, together with maps or plans sufficient to identify the proposed route of the road.

17. Land shown on plans approved by a resolution of a local highway authority as land proposed to be acquired by them for the purposes of section 246(1) of the Highways Act 1980. SCH. 13 1980 c. 66

18. Land shown in a written notice given by the Secretary of State to the local planning authority as land proposed to be acquired by him for the purposes of section 246(1) of the Highways Act 1980 in connection with a trunk road or special road which he proposes to provide.

New streets

19. Land which—

(a) either—

(i) is within the outer lines prescribed by an order under section 188 of the Highways Act 1980 (orders prescribing minimum width of new streets) or section 159 of the Highways Act 1959 (which is the predecessor of that section); or 1959 c. 25.

(ii) has a frontage to a highway declared to be a new street by an order under section 30 of the Public Health Act 1925 and lies within the minimum width of the street prescribed by any byelaws or local Act applicable by virtue of the order; and 1925 c. 71.

(b) is, or is part of—

(i) a dwelling erected before, or under construction on, the date on which the order is made; or

(ii) the curtilage of any such dwelling.

Note

This paragraph does not include any land in which the appropriate authority have previously acquired an interest either in pursuance of a blight notice served by virtue of this paragraph or by agreement in circumstances such that they could have been required to acquire it in pursuance of such a notice.

General improvement areas

20. Land indicated by information published in pursuance of section 257 of the Housing Act 1985 as land which a local authority propose to acquire in the exercise of their powers under the provisions of Part VIII of that Act relating to general improvement areas. 1985 c. 68.

Compulsory purchase

21. Land authorised by a special enactment to be compulsorily acquired, or land falling within the limits of deviation within which powers of compulsory acquisition conferred by a special enactment are exercisable.

22. Land in respect of which—

(a) a compulsory purchase order is in force; or

(b) there is in force a compulsory purchase order providing for the acquisition of a right or rights over that land;

and the appropriate authority have power to serve, but have not served, notice to treat in respect of the land or, as the case may be, the right or rights.

Notes

(1) This paragraph applies also to land in respect of which—

(a) a compulsory purchase order has been submitted for confirmation to, or been prepared in draft by, a Minister, and

SCH. 13

1981 c. 67.

(b) a notice has been published under paragraph 3(1)(a) of Schedule 1 to the Acquisition of Land Act 1981 or under any corresponding enactment applicable to it.

(2) Note (1) shall cease to apply when—

(a) the relevant compulsory purchase order comes into force (whether in its original form or with modifications); or

(b) the Minister concerned decides not to confirm or make the order.

Section 259.

SCHEDULE 14

PROCEDURE FOR FOOTPATHS AND BRIDLEWAYS ORDERS

PART I

CONFIRMATION OF ORDERS

1.—(1) Before an order under section 257 or 258 is submitted to the Secretary of State for confirmation or confirmed as an unopposed order, the authority by whom the order was made shall give notice in the prescribed form—

(a) stating the general effect of the order and that it has been made and is about to be submitted for confirmation or to be confirmed as an unopposed order;

(b) naming a place in the area in which the land to which the order relates is situated where a copy of the order may be inspected free of charge and copies of it may be obtained at a reasonable charge at all reasonable hours; and

(c) specifying the time (which must not be less than 28 days from the date of the first publication of the notice) within which, and the manner in which, representations or objections with respect to the order may be made.

(2) Subject to sub-paragraphs (6) and (7), the notice to be given under sub-paragraph (1) shall be given—

(a) by publication in at least one local newspaper circulating in the area in which the land to which the order relates is situated; and

(b) by serving a similar notice on—

(i) every owner, occupier and lessee (except tenants for a month or a period less than a month and statutory tenants within the meaning of the Rent Act 1977) of any of that land; and

1977 c. 42.

(ii) every council, the council of every rural parish and the parish meeting of every rural parish not having a separate council, being a council or parish whose area includes any of that land; and

(iii) any statutory undertakers to whom there belongs, or by whom there is used, for the purposes of their undertaking, any apparatus under, in, on, over, along or across that land; and

(iv) every person on whom notice is required to be served in pursuance of sub-paragraph (4); and

(v) such other persons as may be prescribed in relation to the area in which that land is situated or as the authority may consider appropriate; and

(c) by causing a copy of the notice to be displayed in a prominent position—

(i) at the ends of so much of any footpath or bridleway as is to be stopped up, diverted or extinguished by the order;

(ii) at council offices in the locality of the land to which the order relates; and

(iii) at such other places as the authority may consider appropriate.

(3) In sub-paragraph (2)— SCH. 14

"council" means a county council, a district council, a London borough council or a joint authority established by Part IV of the Local Government Act 1985; 1985 c. 51.

"council offices" means offices or buildings acquired or provided by a council or by the council of a parish or community or the parish meeting of a parish not having a separate parish council.

(4) Any person may, on payment of such reasonable charge as the authority may consider appropriate, require an authority to give him notice of all such orders under section 257 or 258 as are made by the authority during a specified period, are of a specified description and relate to land comprised in a specified area.

(5) In sub-paragraph (4) "specified" means specified in the requirement.

(6) Except where an owner, occupier or lessee is a local authority or statutory undertaker, the Secretary of State may in any particular case direct that it shall not be necessary to comply with sub-paragraph (2)(b)(i).

(7) If the Secretary of State gives a direction under sub-paragraph (6) in the case of any land, then—

(a) in addition to publication the notice shall be addressed to "the owners and any occupiers" of the land (describing it); and

(b) a copy or copies of the notice shall be affixed to some conspicuous object or objects on the land.

(8) Sub-paragraph (2)(b) and (c) and, where applicable, sub-paragraph (7) shall be complied with not less than 28 days before the expiry of the time specified in the notice.

(9) A notice required to be served by sub-paragraph (2)(b)(i), (ii), (iii) or (v) shall be accompanied by a copy of the order.

(10) A notice required to be displayed by sub-paragraph (2)(c)(i) at the ends of so much of any way as is affected by the order shall be accompanied by a plan showing the general effect of the order so far as it relates to that way.

2. If no representations or objections are duly made, or if any so made are withdrawn, the authority by whom the order was made may, instead of submitting the order to the Secretary of State, themselves confirm the order (but without any modification).

3.—(1) This paragraph applies where any representation or objection which has been duly made is not withdrawn.

(2) If the objection is made by a local authority the Secretary of State shall, before confirming the order, cause a local inquiry to be held.

(3) If the representation or objection is made by a person other than a local authority the Secretary of State shall, before confirming the order, either—

(a) cause a local inquiry to be held; or

(b) give any person by whom any representation or objection has been duly made and not withdrawn an opportunity of being heard by a person appointed by the Secretary of State for the purpose.

(4) After considering the report of the person appointed under sub-paragraph (2) or (3) to hold the inquiry or hear representations or objections, the Secretary of State may confirm the order, with or without modifications.

SCH. 14

(5) In the case of an order under section 257, if objection is made by statutory undertakers on the ground that the order provides for the creation of a public right of way over land covered by works used for the purpose of their undertaking, or over the curtilage of such land, and the objection is not withdrawn, the order shall be subject to special parliamentary procedure.

(6) Notwithstanding anything in the previous provisions of this paragraph, the Secretary of State shall not confirm an order so as to affect land not affected by the order as submitted to him, except after—

(a) giving such notice as appears to him requisite of his proposal so to modify the order, specifying the time (which must not be less than 28 days from the date of the first publication of the notice) within which, and the manner in which, representations or objections with respect to the proposal may be made;

(b) holding a local inquiry or giving any person by whom any representation or objection has been duly made and not withdrawn an opportunity of being heard by a person appointed by the Secretary of State for the purpose; and

(c) considering the report of the person appointed to hold the inquiry or, as the case may be, to hear representations or objections.

(7) In the case of an order under section 257, if objection is made by statutory undertakers on the ground that the order as modified would provide for the creation of a public right of way over land covered by works used for the purposes of their undertaking or over the curtilage of such land, and the objection is not withdrawn, the order shall be subject to special parliamentary procedure.

4.—(1) A decision of the Secretary of State under paragraph 3 shall, except in such classes of case as may for the time being be prescribed or as may be specified in directions given by the Secretary of State, be made by a person appointed by the Secretary of State for the purpose instead of by the Secretary of State.

(2) A decision made by a person so appointed shall be treated as a decision of the Secretary of State.

(3) The Secretary of State may, if he thinks fit, direct that a decision which, by virtue of sub-paragraph (1) and apart from this sub-paragraph, falls to be made by a person appointed by the Secretary of State shall instead be made by the Secretary of State.

(4) A direction under sub-paragraph (3) shall—

(a) state the reasons for which it is given; and

(b) be served on the person, if any, so appointed, the authority and any person by whom a representation or objection has been duly made and not withdrawn.

(5) Where the Secretary of State has appointed a person to make a decision under paragraph 3 the Secretary of State may, at any time before the making of the decision, appoint another person to make it instead of the person first appointed to make it.

(6) Where by virtue of sub-paragraph (3) or (5) a particular decision falls to be made by the Secretary of State or any other person instead of the person first appointed to make it, anything done by or in relation to the latter shall be treated as having been done by or in relation to the former.

(7) Regulations under this Act may provide for the giving of publicity to any directions given by the Secretary of State under this paragraph.

5.—(1) The Secretary of State shall not confirm an order under section 257 which extinguishes a right of way over land under, in, on, over, along or across which there is any apparatus belonging to or used by statutory undertakers for the purposes of their undertaking, unless the undertakers have consented to the confirmation of the order. SCH. 14

(2) Any such consent may be given subject to the condition that there are included in the order such provisions for the protection of the undertakers as they may reasonably require.

(3) The consent of statutory undertakers to any such order shall not be unreasonably withheld.

(4) Any question arising under this paragraph whether the withholding of consent is unreasonable, or whether any requirement is reasonable, shall be determined by whichever Minister is the appropriate Minister in relation to the statutory undertakers concerned.

6. Regulations under this Act may, subject to this Part of this Schedule, make such provision as the Secretary of State thinks expedient as to the procedure on the making, submission and confirmation of orders under sections 257 and 258.

PART II

PUBLICITY FOR ORDERS AFTER CONFIRMATION

7.—(1) As soon as possible after an order under section 257 or 258 has been confirmed by the Secretary of State or confirmed as an unopposed order, the authority by whom the order was made—

(a) shall publish, in the manner required by paragraph 1(2)(a), a notice in the prescribed form—

(i) describing the general effect of the order,

(ii) stating that it has been confirmed, and

(iii) naming a place in the area in which the land to which the order relates is situated where a copy of the order as confirmed may be inspected free of charge and copies of it may be obtained at a reasonable charge at all reasonable hours;

(b) shall serve a similar notice on any persons on whom notices were required to be served under paragraph 1(2)(b) or (7); and

(c) shall cause similar notices to be displayed in a similar manner as the notices required to be displayed under paragraph 1(2)(c).

(2) No such notice or copy need be served on a person unless he has sent to the authority a request in that behalf, specifying an address for service.

(3) A notice required to be served by sub-paragraph (1)(b) on—

(a) a person on whom notice was required to be served by paragraph 1(2)(b)(i), (ii) or (iii); or

(b) in the case of an order which has been confirmed with modifications, a person on whom notice was required to be served by paragraph 1(2)(b)(v),

shall be accompanied by a copy of the order as confirmed.

(4) As soon as possible after a decision not to confirm an order under section 257 or 258, the authority by whom the order was made shall give notice of the decision by serving a copy of it on any persons on whom notices were required to be served under paragraph 1(2)(b) or (7).

SCH. 14

8. Where an order under section 257 or 258 has come into force otherwise than—

(a) on the date on which it was confirmed by the Secretary of State or confirmed as an unopposed order; or

(b) at the expiration of a specified period beginning with that date,

then as soon as possible after it has come into force the authority by whom it was made shall give notice of its coming into force by publication in at least one local newspaper circulating in the area in which the land to which the order relates is situated.

Section 302(5).

SCHEDULE 15

ENFORCEMENT AS RESPECTS WAR-TIME BREACHES BY THE CROWN OF PLANNING CONTROL

Preliminary

1. In this Schedule an application under section 302(3) and a determination given on such an application are referred to respectively as "a compliance determination application" and "a compliance determination".

Making of compliance determination applications

2.—(1) A compliance determination application may be made with respect to any land—

(a) by the owner or occupier of the land, or

(b) by any person who proves that he has or intends to acquire an interest in the land which will be affected by a compliance determination or that he has borne any of the cost of carrying out works on the land during the war period.

(2) In the case of land owned or occupied by or on behalf of the Crown, or leased to, or to a person acting on behalf of, the Crown, or land with respect to which it is proved that there is held, or intended to be acquired, by or on behalf of the Crown an interest in the land which will be affected as mentioned in sub-paragraph (1) or that any of the cost there mentioned has been borne by the Crown, a compliance determination application may be made by any person acting on behalf of the Crown.

3. A compliance determination application shall be accompanied by such plans and other information as are necessary to enable the application to be determined.

4.—(1) The authority to whom a compliance determination application is made shall within 14 days from the receipt of the application publish notice of it in one or more local newspapers circulating in the area in which the land is situated and serve notice of it on any person appearing to the authority to be specially affected by the application.

(2) The authority shall take into consideration any representations made to them in connection with the application within 14 days from the publication of the notice.

Determination of applications

5.—(1) Where a compliance determination application is made to an authority the authority shall determine whether the works or use in question fail to comply with any planning control which the authority are responsible for enforcing and, if so, shall specify the control in question.

(2) Where the authority determine that works or a use fail so to comply they shall further determine whether having regard to all relevant circumstances the works or use shall, notwithstanding the failure, be deemed so to comply, either unconditionally or subject to such conditions as to the time for which the works or use may be continued, the carrying out of alterations, or other matters, as the authority think expedient.

Appeals against compliance determinations or failure to make such determinations

6.—(1) Where the applicant is aggrieved by a compliance determination, or where a person by whom representations have been made as mentioned in paragraph 4 is aggrieved by such a determination, he may appeal to the Secretary of State.

(2) The applicant may also appeal if he is aggrieved by the failure of the authority to determine the application within two months from the last day on which representations under paragraph 4 may be made and has served notice on the authority that he appeals to the Secretary of State.

(3) An appeal under this paragraph must be made within the period of 28 days after the applicant has notice of the determination or, in the case of an appeal under sub-paragraph (2), after the applicant has served notice on the authority of the appeal, or within such extended period as the Secretary of State may allow.

7.—(1) On such an appeal the Secretary of State may give, in substitution for the determination, if any, given by the authority, such determination as appears to him to be proper having regard to all relevant circumstances, or, if he is satisfied that the applicant was not a person entitled to make the application, may decide that the application is not to be entertained.

(2) At any stage of the proceedings on such an appeal to him the Secretary of State may, and shall if so directed by the High Court, state in the form of a special case for the opinion of the High Court any question of law arising in connection with the appeal.

8. Subject to paragraph 9 and to any determination or decision of the Secretary of State on an appeal under paragraph 7, any compliance determination shall be final and any such failure to give a determination as mentioned in paragraph 6(2) shall be taken on the service of the notice there mentioned as a final refusal by the authority to entertain the application, and any determination or decision of the Secretary of State on an appeal under paragraph 7 shall be final.

Fresh applications where alteration in circumstances

9. Where a compliance determination has been given that works on land or a use of land shall not be deemed to comply with planning control or shall be deemed to comply with it subject to conditions, then if a person entitled to make a compliance determination application with respect to the land satisfies the authority or on appeal the Secretary of State that there has been a material change of circumstances since the previous application was determined, he may make a subsequent application and on such an application the authority or on appeal the Secretary of State may substitute for the compliance determination such determination as appears proper having regard to all relevant circumstances.

References of application to Secretary of State

10.—(1) If it appears to the Secretary of State that it is expedient, having regard to considerations affecting the public interest (whether generally or in the locality concerned), that any compliance determination application to an authority or any class or description of such applications, should instead of being

SCH. 15 determined by the authority be referred to him for decision, he may give directions to the authority requiring that application, or applications of that class or description, to be so referred.

(2) This Schedule shall apply to any such reference as if it were an appeal under paragraph 6(2) following failure of the authority to entertain the application.

Information

11. The Secretary of State may give directions to any authority responsible for enforcing planning control requiring them to furnish him with such information with respect to compliance determination applications received by them as he considers necessary or expedient in connection with the exercise of his functions under this Schedule.

Opportunity for hearing

12. On any compliance determination application or any appeal under this Schedule the applicant or, in the case of an application referred to the Secretary of State for decision or an appeal to the Secretary of State, the applicant or the authority responsible for enforcing the planning control in question, may require the authority by whom the application is to be determined or, as the case may be, the Secretary of State to give him or them an opportunity before the application or appeal is determined of appearing before and being heard by a person appointed by the authority or, as the case may be, the Secretary of State for the purpose.

Notice of proposed enforcement

13.—(1) This paragraph applies where before the relevant date any person proposes to take steps for enforcing a planning control in the case of such works or such a use as mentioned in subsection (1) of section 302.

(2) Subject to sub-paragraph (4), unless a compliance determination application has been made in relation to the land which has not been finally determined, that person shall serve on every owner and occupier of the land not less than 28 days' notice of the proposal, and if within that period any person makes such an application in relation to the land and within seven days of making it serves on the person proposing to take steps as aforesaid notice that the application has been made, no steps for enforcing the control shall be taken until the final determination of the application.

(3) If such an application has been made which has not been finally determined, no such steps shall be taken until the final determination of it.

(4) No notice shall be required under sub-paragraph (2) if steps for enforcing a planning control in the case of any works on land are begun within 28 days of the final determination of a compliance determination application in relation to the land.

(5) For the purpose of this paragraph a compliance determination application shall be treated as having been finally determined notwithstanding that a subsequent application may be made under paragraph 9.

Power of entry

14.—(1) At any time before the relevant date any officer of an authority responsible for enforcing planning control shall, on producing, if so required, some duly authenticated document showing his authority to act for the purposes of this paragraph, have a right, subject to the provisions of this paragraph, to enter any premises at all reasonable hours—

Sch. 15

(a) for the purpose of ascertaining whether there are on the premises any works carried out during the war period which do not comply with planning control, or whether a use of the premises continues which was begun during that period and does not comply with it;

(b) where a compliance determination application has been made to the authority, for the purpose of obtaining any information required by the authority for the exercise of their functions under section 302 and this Schedule in relation to the application.

(2) Admission to any premises which are occupied shall not be demanded as of right unless 24 hours' notice of the intended entry has been served on the occupier.

(3) Any person who wilfully obstructs any officer of an authority acting in the exercise of his powers under this section shall be liable on summary conviction to a fine not exceeding level 1 on the standard scale.

(4) If any person who in compliance with this paragraph is admitted into a factory, workshop or workplace, discloses to any person any information obtained by him in it with regard to any manufacturing process or trade secret, he shall, unless such disclosure was made in the performance of his duty, be liable on summary conviction to a fine not exceeding level 3 on the standard scale or to imprisonment for a term not exceeding three months.

Service of notices

15.—(1) Any notice or other document required or authorised to be served under this Schedule may be served on any person either by delivering it to him, or by leaving it at his proper address or by post.

(2) Any such document required or authorised to be served upon an incorporated company or body shall be duly served if it is served upon the secretary or clerk of the company or body.

(3) For the purposes of this paragraph and of section 7 of the Interpretation Act 1978, the proper address of any person upon whom any such document is to be served is— 1978 c. 30.

(a) in the case of the secretary or clerk of any incorporated company or body, that of the registered or principal office of the company or body, and

(b) in any other case, the last known address of the person to be served.

(4) If it is not practicable after reasonable enquiry to ascertain the name or address of an owner or occupier of land on whom any such document is to be served, the document may be served by addressing it to him by the description of "owner" or "occupier" of the premises (describing them) to which it relates, and by delivering it to some person on the premises or, if there is no person on the premises to whom it can be delivered, by affixing it, or a copy of it, to some conspicuous part of the premises.

Supplementary provisions

16. Parts XIV and XV do not apply to section 302 and this Schedule.

SCHEDULE 16

Sections 314 to 319.

Provisions of the Planning Acts referred to in Sections 314 to 319

Part I

Section 1(1), (2), (3) and (5).

Section 2.

Section 9.

SCH. 16

Section 55.

Section 57.

Section 59.

Section 60 except subsection (4).

Sections 61 to 64.

Section 69(1), (2) and (5).

Section 70.

Section 72(1) to (4).

Section 74.

Section 75.

Section 77 with the omission in subsection (4) of the reference to sections 65(2) and (9), 66 and 67.

Sections 78 and 79(1) to (5) with the omission in subsection (4) of section 79 of the reference to sections 66 and 67.

Section 90(1), (3) and (4).

Sections 96 to 98 except subsection (5) of section 97.

Section 100.

Sections 102 to 104 except subsection (8) of section 102.

Section 106.

Section 107.

Section 108.

Sections 114 and 115.

Sections 117 and 118.

Section 137 except subsections (6) and (7).

Section 138.

Section 139(1) to (4).

Sections 140 and 141.

Sections 143 and 144.

Section 148.

Section 175(5).

Sections 178 to 182.

Section 185.

Section 186(6) and (7).

Section 188.

Section 189.

Section 190 (in so far as it applies to orders under section 102).

Sections 198 to 200.

Sections 202 and 203.

Section 205.

Section 208(10).

Section 209(6). SCH. 16

Section 210.

Section 211(4).

Sections 215 to 224.

Section 227.

Sections 229 to 233.

Sections 235 to 247.

Sections 251 and 252.

Sections 254 to 256.

Section 260.

Section 263.

Section 265(1) and (4).

Sections 266 to 272.

Sections 274 to 278.

Section 279 except subsection (4).

Section 280 except subsections (6) and (8)(b).

Sections 281 to 283.

Section 284(1) except paragraphs (e) and (f).

Section 285 except subsections (5) and (6).

Section 287.

Section 289.

Section 292 with the omission in subsection (2) of the references to section 288.

Section 293(1) to (3).

Section 294(1).

Section 296(1) (the reference in paragraph (c) to Part III not being construed as referring to sections 65 to 68), and (2) to (4).

Section 297.

Sections 305 and 306.

Section 314.

Section 315.

Section 316(1) to (4).

Section 318 except subsections (2)(a), (4) and (5).

Section 324(1), (3) and (5) to (9).

Section 325.

Section 330.

Section 334.

Paragraphs 13 and 20(3) of Schedule 1.

Schedule 3.

Paragraphs 1 to 3 of Schedule 4.

SCH. 16

Schedule 17.

Any other provisions of the planning Acts in so far as they apply, or have effect for the purposes of, any of the provisions specified above.

PART II

Sections 30 to 49.

Section 50(5).

Section 51.

Sections 53 and 54.

Section 56(2) to (6) with the omission in subsection (3) of the references to sections 85, 86(6) and 87(4).

Section 65(2) to (8) except subsection (2)(a) and the reference to it in subsection (7).

Section 68(1) and (2) with the omission in subsection (1) of the references to section 66 or 67.

Section 69(3) and (4).

Section 79(6) and (7).

Sections 91 to 93.

Section 94(1)(a) and (2) to (6).

Section 95.

Section 99.

Section 101.

Section 137(6) and (7).

Section 142.

Section 157(1) and (2).

Sections 162 and 163.

Section 166.

Sections 172 to 174.

Section 175(1) to (4) and (6).

Sections 176 and 177.

Sections 183 and 184.

Section 186(1) to (5).

Section 187.

Sections 191 to 196.

Section 208(9).

Section 226.

Section 228(1), (3), (4) and (7).

Sections 248, 249 and 250.

Section 253.

Section 257.

Section 258(1).

Section 259.

Section 261.

Section 264(1) to (6).

Section 273.

Section 279(4).

Section 280(6) and (8)(b).

Section 304.

Section 307.

Section 331.

Paragraphs 3 to 12 of Part II of Schedule 2, Part III of Schedule 2, Schedules 6 and 14.

PART III

Sections 80 and 81.

Sections 109 to 113.

Sections 119 to 136.

Section 298.

Sections 308 to 310.

Section 312(2).

Section 318(4) and (5).

Section 324(4).

Sections 327 and 328.

Paragraphs 1 to 16 and 18 to 20 of Schedule 12.

Any other provisions of the planning Acts in so far as they apply, or have effect for the purposes of, any of the provisions specified above.

PART IV

Section 197.

Section 201.

Sections 206 and 207.

Section 208(1) to (9).

Section 209(1) to (5).

Section 210(1) to (3).

Section 324(2).

PART V

Section 55.

Section 57.

Sections 59 to 64.

Section 69 except subsections (3) and (4).

Section 70.

SCH. 16 Section 71(3) and (4).

Section 72.

Sections 74 and 75.

Sections 77 to 79.

Sections 82 to 87.

Section 90(1), (3) and (4).

Sections 97 and 98.

Sections 102 and 103.

Section 106.

Sections 172 to 181.

Sections 183 and 184.

Section 186(1) to (5).

Sections 187 to 196.

Sections 198 to 200.

Section 209(6).

Section 210.

Section 211(4).

Sections 215 to 222.

Sections 224 and 225.

Paragraphs 13 and 14 of Schedule 1.

Schedule 4.

Paragraphs 7 and 8 of Schedule 5.

Paragraphs 1 to 10 of Schedule 9.

PART VI

Section 60(4).

Section 65 except subsections (2)(b) and (3) to (9).

Sections 66 and 67.

Section 68 in so far as it relates to the provisions of sections 65 to 67 mentioned in this Part of this Schedule.

Section 71(1) and (2).

Sections 149 to 151.

Section 153(1) to (7).

Sections 154 to 156.

Section 161(1) in so far as it relates to provisions mentioned in this Part of this Schedule.

Section 164.

Sections 168 to 171.

Section 284 except subsection (1)(a) to (d).

Section 285(5) and (6).

Section 288. SCH. 16

Sections 290 and 291.

Section 292(2).

Section 296(1) (construed as if the reference to Part III were a reference only to sections 65 to 68) and (5).

Section 318(2) except paragraph (b).

In Schedule 12, paragraph 16 (except sub-paragraphs (2)(b) and (6)(b)), paragraph 17, and paragraph 18 (construed as if in paragraph 16 the said sub-paragraphs were omitted).

In Schedule 13, paragraphs 1 to 4, 12 to 16 and 20 to 22.

Any other provisions of this Act in so far as they apply, or have effect for the purpose of, any of the provisions specified above.

SCHEDULE 17

Section 333(6).

ENACTMENTS EXEMPTED FROM SECTION 333(6)

1. Section 107 of the Public Health Act 1936. 1936 c. 49.

2. The following provisions of the Highways Act 1980— 1980 c. 66.

section 73(1) to (3), (6) and (9) to (11)

section 74 (except subsection (6))

sections 188, 193 and 196

section 200(2) and (4)

section 241

section 261(5) and, so far as it relates to it, section 261(6)

section 307(5) and (7)

Schedule 9.

3. The following further provisions of the Highways Act 1980—

(a) sections 187 and 200(1) so far as applicable for the purposes of section 188 of that Act;

(b) section 247(6) so far as applicable for the purposes of section 241 of that Act;

(c) in section 307—

(i) subsections (1) to (3) so far as applicable for the purposes of section 73 of that Act;

(ii) subsections (1), (3) and (6) so far as applicable for the purposes of section 74 of that Act;

(iii) subsections (1) and (3) so far as applicable for the purposes of sections 193 and 200(2) of that Act;

(d) section 311 so far as applicable for the purposes of section 74 of that Act.

4. Section 279 of the Highways Act 1980 so far as the purposes in question are the purposes of the exercise by a county council or metropolitan district council in relation to roads maintained by that council of their powers under section 73(1) to (3), (6) and (9) to (11) or section 241 of that Act.

SCH. 17

5. Any enactment making such provision as might by virtue of any Act of Parliament have been made in relation to the area to which the order applies by means of a byelaw, order or regulation not requiring confirmation by Parliament.

6. Any enactment which has been previously excluded or modified by a development order, and any enactment having substantially the same effect as any such enactment.

TABLE OF DERIVATIONS

Notes:

1. The following abbreviations are used in this Table:—

1946 c. 35 =	The Building Restrictions (War-Time Contraventions) Act 1946
1951 c. 60 =	The Mineral Workings Act 1951
1953 c. 49 =	The Historic Buildings and Ancient Monuments Act 1953
1958 c. 69 =	The Opencast Coal Act 1958
1969 c. 22 =	The Redundant Churches and Other Religious Buildings Act 1969
1969 c. 48. =	The Post Office Act 1969
1971 c. 78 =	The Town and Country Planning Act 1971
1972 c. 5 =	The Local Employment Act 1972
1972 c. 42 =	The Town and Country Planning (Amendment) Act 1972
1972 c. 70 =	The Local Government Act 1972
1973 c. 26 =	The Land Compensation Act 1973
1973 c. 37 =	The Water Act 1973
1973 c. 41 =	The Fair Trading Act 1973
1974 c. 7 =	The Local Government Act 1974
1974 c. 32 =	The Town and Country Amenities Act 1974
1974 c. 36 =	The Mines (Working Facilities and Support) Act 1974
1975 c. 24 =	The House of Commons Disqualification Act 1975
1975 c. 10 =	The Statute Law (Repeals) Act 1975
1975 c. 71 =	The Housing (Consequential Provisions) Act 1975
1975 c. 76 =	The Local Land Charges Act 1975
1977 c. 29 =	The Town and Country Planning (Amendment) Act 1977
1977 c. 38 =	The Administration of Justice Act 1977
1977 c. 40 =	The Control of Office Development Act 1977
1977 c. 45 =	The Criminal Law Act 1977
1977 SI/293 =	The Local Authorities Etc. (Miscellaneous Provisions) Order 1977
1978 c. 30 =	The Interpretation Act 1978
1979 c. 46 =	The Ancient Monuments and Archaeological Areas Act 1979
1980 c. 43 =	The Magistrates' Courts Act 1980
1980 c. 65 =	The Local Government, Planning and Land Act 1980
1980 c. 66 =	The Highways Act 1980
1981 c. 36 =	The Town and Country Planning (Minerals) Act 1981
1981 c. 38 =	The British Telecommunications Act 1981
1981 c. 41 =	The Local Government and Planning (Amendment) Act 1981

1981 c. 43 =	The Disabled Persons Act 1981
1981 c. 54 =	The Supreme Court Act 1981
1981 c. 64 =	The New Towns Act 1981
1981 c. 66 =	The Compulsory Purchase (Vesting Declarations) Act 1981
1981 c. 67 =	The Acquisition of Land Act 1981
1981 c. 69 =	The Wildlife and Countryside Act 1981
1982 c. 16 =	The Civil Aviation Act 1982
1982 c. 21 =	The Planning Inquiries (Attendance of Public) Act 1982
1982 c. 30 =	The Local Government (Miscellaneous Provisions) Act 1982
1982 c. 48 =	The Criminal Justice Act 1982
1982 c. 52 =	The Industrial Development Act 1982
1982 SI/86 =	The Town and Country Planning (Minerals) Act 1981 (Commencement No 1) Order 1982
1983 c. 47 =	The National Heritage Act 1983
1984 c. 10 =	The Town and Country Planning Act 1984
1984 c. 12 =	The Telecommunications Act 1984
1984 c. 32 =	The London Regional Transport Act
1985 c. 9 =	The Companies (Consequential Provisions) Act 1985
1985 c. 19 =	The Town and Country Planning (Compensation) Act 1985
1985 c. 51 =	The Local Government Act 1985
1985 c. 52 =	The Town and Country Planning (Amendment) Act 1985
1985 c. 71 =	The Housing (Consequential Provisions) Act 1985
1986 c. 31 =	The Airports Act 1986
1986 c. 63 =	The Housing and Planning Act 1986
1986 c. 44 =	The Gas Act 1986
1986 SI/452 =	The Local Government Reorganisation (Miscellaneous Provision) (No 4) Order 1986
1987 c. 3 =	The Coal Industry Act 1987
1988 c. 4 =	The Norfolk and Suffolk Broads Act 1988
1988 c. 40 =	The Education Reform Act 1988
1988 c. 50 =	The Housing Act 1988
1989 c. 15 =	The Water Act 1989
1989 c. 29 =	The Electricity Act 1989
1989 c. 34 =	The Law of Property (Miscellaneous Provisions) Act 1989
1989 c. 42 =	The Local Government and Housing Act 1989
1989 c. 43 =	The Statute Law (Repeals) Act 1989
1990 SI/465 =	The Town and Country Planning (Blight Provisions) Order 1990
1990 SI/776 =	The Local Government Finance (Repeals, Savings and Consequential Amendments) Order 1990

2. The Table does not show the effect of transfer of functions orders.

3. The letter R followed by a number indicates that the provision gives effect to the Recommendation bearing that number in the Law Commission's Report on the Consolidation of Certain Enactments relating to Town and Country Planning (Cmnd.958).

4. The entry "drafting" indicates a provision of a mechanical or editorial nature only affecting the arrangement of the consolidation.

Provision	*Derivation*
1(1)	1971 c.78 s.1(1)(a), (2A); 1985 c.51 s.3(1); 1986 c.63, Sch.11 para. 14.
(2)	1971 c.78 s.1(1)(b), (c); 1985 c.51 s.3(1).
(3)	1972 c.70 s.182(2); 1985 c. 51 s.3(5).
(4)	1971 c.78 s.1(2B); 1985 c. 51 s.3(3).
(5)(a)	1971 c.78 s.1(6); 1972 c.70 Sch.16 para. 43(b); 1988 c.4 s.2(5), Sch.3 para. 8.
(b)	1971 c.78 s.1(1).
(c)	1972 s.182(2).
2(1),(2)	1971 c.78 s.1(2); 1972 c.70 s.182(1).
(3)	1971 c.78 s.1(4).
(4), (5)	1971 c.78 Sch.1 paras. 1, 2 .
(6)	1971 c.78 Sch.1 para. 3; 1972 c.70 Sch.16 paras. 49,52; 1972 s.272(2).
(7)	1971 c.78 s.1(6); 1972 c.70 s.182(2) Sch.16 para. 43(b); 1988 c.4 Sch. 3 para. 8.
3 (1)	1985 c.51 s.5(1), drafting.
(2) to (4)	1985 c.51 s.5(2) to (4).
4(1)	1972 c.70 s.182(4); 1985 c. 51 s.7(1), Sch.3 para. 3(1).
(2)	1972 c. 70 s.182(5); 1985 c. 51 Sch.3 para. 3(1); R 1.
(3)	1972 c. 70 s.182(6).
(4)	1985 c. 51 s.7(1), Sch.3 para. 2(2) (part).
5(1)	1971 c.78 ss.212(10), 280(10)(b); 1984 c.10 s.6(5); 1988 c.4 Sch.3 paras. 21, 23, 32, 48; R 2.
(2),(3)	1971 c.78 ss.273A, 280(10)(a); 1972 c.70 Sch 16 para 10(5); 1988 c.4 Sch.3 paras. 7, 23, 28.
6(1)	1980 c.65 Sch.32 para. 5(7).
(2)	1980 c.65 Sch.32 para. 15(2)(b)(i).
(3)	1980 c.65 Sch.32 para. 20(1).
(4)	1980 c.65 Sch.32 para. 25(1)(c).
(5)	1980 c.65 Sch.32 para. 25(2).

Provision	*Derivation*
7(1) to (4)	1980 c.65 s. 149(1) to (4).
(5)	1980 c.65 s.149(11).
8(1)	1988 c.50 s.67(1).
(2)	1988 c.50 s.67(3).
9	1971 c.78 s.1(5)
10	1985 c.51 s.4(1), Sch.3 para. 2(2)(part).
11	1985 c.51 Sch.1 para. 1.
12(1)	1985 c.51 Sch.1 para. 2(1).
(2) to (4)	1985 c.51 Sch.1 para. 2(2).
(5) to (9)	1985 c.51 Sch.1 para. 2(3) to (7).
13(1), (2)	1985 c.51 Sch.1 para. 3(1).
(3), (4)	1985 c.51 Sch.1 para. 3(2).
(5) to (7)	1985 c.51 Sch.1 para. 3(3) to (5).
14	1985 c.51 Sch.1 para. 4.
15	1985 c.51 Sch.1 para. 5.
16(1) to (3)	1985 c.51 Sch.1 para. 6(1).
(4), (5)	1985 c.51 Sch.1 para. 6(2), (3).
17(1)	1985 c.51 para. 6A; 1986 c.63 Sch. 10 Pt. II para. 2.
(2)	1985 c.51 para. 6A; 1986 c.63 Sch. 10 Pt. II para. 2.
18(1), (2)	1985 c.51 Sch.1 para. 7(1).
(3), (4)	1985 c.51 Sch.1 para. 7(2), (3).
19	1985 c.51 Sch.1 para. 8.
20	1985 c.51 Sch.1 para. 9.
21(1)	1985 c.51 Sch.1 para. 10(1).
(2)	1985 c.51 Sch.1 para. 10(2); 1986 c.63 Sch.10 Pt.II para. 3.
(3)	1985 c.51 Sch.1 para. 10(3).
22	1985 c.51 Sch. 1 para. 10A; 1986 c.63 Sch. 10 Pt. II para. 4.
23(1)	1985 c.51 Sch.1 para. 12(1), and (7) (part).
(2)	1985 c.51 Sch.1 para. 12(3).
(3), (4)	1985 c.51 Sch.1 para. 12(2).
(5), (6)	1985 c.51 Sch.1 para. 12(4).
(7), (8)	1985 c.51 Sch.1 para. 12(5), (6).
(9)	1985 c.51 Sch.1 para. 12(7)(a); 1986 c.63 Sch.11 para. 26.
(10)	1985 c.51 Sch.1 para. 12(7)(b),(7A); 1986 c.63 Sch.11 para. 26.
(11)	1985 c.51 Sch.1 para. 12(8).
24	1985 c.51 Sch.1 para. 11.
25	1985 c.51 Sch. 1 para. 13.

Provision	*Derivation*
26(1)	1985 c.51 Sch.1 para. 14(1).
(2)	1985 c.51 Sch.1 para. 14(1); R 3.
(3), (4)	1985 c.51 Sch.1 para. 14(2), (3).
27	1985 c.51 Sch.1 para. 15.
28(1),(2)	1985 c.51 s.4(1), Sch. 3, para 2(2)(part).
(3)	1985 c.51 s.4(2), Sch.1 para. 18(1),20(2)(part) drafting.
(4)	1985 c.51 s.103(1)(part).
29	Drafting.
30(1)	1971 c.78 s.6(1)(part), (2).
(2)	1971 c.78 s.6(3).
(3)	1971 c.78 s.6(5)(part).
(4)	1971 c.78 s.6(4).
31(1)	Drafting.
(2)	1971 c.78 s.7(1A); 1980 c.65 s.89, Sch.14 para. 2(a).
(3)	1971 c.78 s.7(6); 1980 c.65 s.89, Sch.14 para. 2(c).
(4)	1971 c.78 s.7(4); 1982 c.30. Sch 6 para 7.
(5)	1971 c.78 s.7(7)(part).
32(1), (2)	1971 c.78 s.10(1); 1980 c.65 Sch.14 para. 5.
(3) to (7)	1971 c.78 s.10(2) to (6); 1980 c.65 Sch.14 para. 5.
33(1),(2)	1971 c.78 ss.8(1),10(7); 1980 c.65 Sch.14 para. 3(a).
(3),(4)	1971 c.78 s.8(2); 1980 c.65 Sch.14 para. 3(b).
(5)	1971 c.78 s.8(3).
(6), (7)	1971 c.78 s.8(4).
(8) to (10)	1971 c.78 s.8(5) to (7).
34(1)	1971 c.78 s.10B(1); 1972 c.42 s.2; R 4.
(2)	1971 c.78 s.10B(1); 1972 c.42 s.2; R 4.
(3)	1971 c.78 s.10B(2); 1972 c.42 s.2; R 4.
(4), (5)	1971 c.78 s.10B(3); 1972 c.42 s.2; R 4.
35(1)	1971 c.78 ss.9(1),10(7).
(2)	1971 c.78 s.9(2).
(3)	1971 c.78 s.9(3); 1972 c.42 s.3(1).
(4)	1978 c.78 s.10(8)
(5)	1971 c.78 s.9(4); 1972 c.42 s.3(1).
(6), (7)	1971 c.78 s.9(5); 1972 c.42 s.3(1).
(8) to (10)	1971 c.78 s.9(6) to (8); 1972 c.42 s.3(1).
36(1) to (3)	1971 c.78 s.11(1) to (3); 1986 c.63 Sch.10.
(4) to (5)	1971 c.78 s.11(5); 1986 c.63 Sch.10.

Provision	*Derivation*
(6), (7)	1971 c.78 s.11(6),(7); 1986 c.63 Sch.10.
37	1971 c.78 s.11A; 1986 c.63 Sch. 10 Pt. I.
38	1971 c.78 s.11B; 1986 c.63 Sch. 10 Pt. I.
39(1)	1971 c.78 s.12(1); 1986 c.63 Sch.10.
(2), (3)	1971 c.78 s.12(2); 1986 c.63 Sch.10.
(4) to (6)	1971 c.78 s.12(3) to (5); 1986 c.63 Sch.10.
40(1) to (3)	1971 c.78 s.12A(1) to (3); 1986 c.63 Sch.10 Pt. I.
(4), (5)	1971 c.78 s.12A(4); 1986 c.63 Sch. 10 Pt. I.
41	1971 c.78 s.12B; 1986 c.63 Sch. 10 Pt. I.
42	1971 c.78 s.13; 1986 c.63 Sch. 10 Pt. I.
43	1971 c.78 s.14; 1986 c.63 Sch. 10 Pt. I.
44	1971 c.78 s.14A; 1986 c.63 Sch. 10 Pt. I.
45	1971 c.78 s.14B; 1986 c.63 Sch. 10 Pt. I.
46(1)	1971 c.78 s.11(4); 1986 c.63 Sch. 10 Pt. I.
(2) to (6)	1971 c.78 s.15; 1986 c.63 Sch. 10 Pt. I.
47(1), (2)	1971 c.78 s.15A(1); 1986 c.63 Sch.10.
(3) to (6)	1971 c.78 s.15A(2) to (5); 1986 c.63 Sch.10.
48	1971 c.78 s.15B; 1986 c.63 Sch. 10 Pt. I.
49	1971 c.78 s.16; 1980 c.66 Sch.24 para. 20(a).
50(1)	1972 c.70 Sch.16 para. 9(1); 1980 c.65 Sch.14 para. 17.
(2)	1972 c.70 Sch.16 paras. 8(3),9(2).
(3)	1972 c.70 Sch.16 paras. 8(2),9(2); 1971 c.78 s.10(7); 1982 c.30 Sch.6 para. 7(a).
(4)	1972 c.70 Sch.16 paras. 8(4), 9; R 5.
(5)	1971 c.78 s.10B(1); 1972 (c.42) s.2.
(6)	1972 c.70 Sch.16 para. 10; 1986 c.63 Sch.11 para. 23.
(7)	1972 c.70 Sch.16 para. 11; 1986 c.63 Sch.11 para. 23.
(8)	1972 c.70 Sch.16 para. 12; 1986 c.63 Sch.11 para. 23.
(9)	1972 c.70 Sch.16 para. 13; R 6.
51(1)	1971 c.78 s.17(1); 1972 c.70 Sch.16 paras.4, 52.
(2), (3)	1971 c.78 s.17(2), (3).
(4)	1971 c.78 s.17(4), (5).
52(1), (2)	1980 c.65 Sch.32 para. 23(1), (2).
(3)	1980 c.65 Sch.32 para. 23(4).
53(1)(2)	1971 c.78 s.18(1), 1986 c.63 Sch.11 para. 15; 1972 c.70 Sch.16 paras.5, 52.
(3) to (5)	1971 c.78 s.18(2) to (4).
54(1)	1971 c.78 s.20(1); 1980 c.66 Sch.24 para. 20.

Provision	*Derivation*
(2) to (5)	1971 c.78 s.20(3) to (5).
55(1)	1971 c.78 s.22(1).
(2)	1971 c.78 s.22(2); 1986 c.63 Sch. 11 para. 1.
(3)	1971 c.78 s.22(3).
(4)	1971 c.78 s.22(3A); 1981 c.36 s.1(1).
(5)	1971 c.78 s.22(4).
(6)	1971 c.78 s.22(5).
56(1)	1971 c.78 s.290(5).
(2), (3)	1971 c.78 ss. 24C(4), 24D(6), 24E(4), 43(1), 44(1); 1980 c.65 Sch.32 para. 26(1A); 1986 c.63 ss.25(1), 54 (2).
(4)	1971 c.78 s.43(2).
(5)	1971 c.78 s.43(3) (part).
(6)	1971 c.78 s.43(3) (part).
57(1)	1971 c.78 s.23(1).
(2)	1971 c.78 s.23(5).
(3)	1971 c.78 s.23(8) (part).
(4)	1971 c.78 s.23(9); 1982 c.30 s.47(1), Sch. 6 para. 7.
(5)	1971 c.78 s.23(6), (8) (part).
(6)	1971 c.78 s.23(10).
(7)	1971 c.78 s.23(1).
58	1971 c.78 ss.24(1), (2), 24A(2), 40; 1980 c.65 Sch.32 para. 17.
59(1)	1971 c.78 s.24(1).
(2)	1971 c.78 s.24(2).
(3)	1971 c.78 s.24(3) (part); 1986 c.63 Sch. 11 para. 2.
60(1)	1971 c.78 s.24(4).
(2), (3)	1971 c.78 s.24(5).
(4)	1971 c.78 s.24(6).
61(1)	1971 c.78 s.24(3)(a); 1986 c.63 Sch. 11 para. 2.
(2)	1971 c.78 s.24(7).
(3)	1971 c.78 s.24(8); 1980 c.66 Sch. 24 para. 20(c).
62	1971 c.78 s.25
63(1), (2)	1971 c.78 s.32(1).
(3)	1971 c.78 s.32(2)(part).
(4)	1971 c.78 s.32(3).
(5)	1971 c.78 s.32(2).
64(1)	1971 c.78 s.53(1) (part), (2)(part); 1980 c.65 Sch. 32 para. 18(3); 1986 c.63 Sch. 6 Pt II para. 3.
(2)	1971 c.78 s.53(1) (part).

Provision	Derivation
(3)	1971 c.78 s.53(2).
65(1) to (4)	1971 c.78 s.26(1) to (4).
(5), (6)	1971 c.78 s.26(5).
(7), (8)	1971 c.78 s.26(6).
(9)	1971 c.78 s.26(7).
66(1)	1971 c.78 s.27(1)(a), (b), (c), (d); 1980 c.65 Sch. 15 para. 2.
(2), (3)	1971 c.78 s.27(2).
(4), (5)	1971 c.78 s.27(3).
(6)	1971 c.78 s.27(4).
(7)	1971 c.78 s.27(7); 1978 c.30 s.17; 1980 c.65 Sch. 15 para. 3.
67(1)	Drafting.
(2)	1971 c.78 s.27(1A); 1981 c.36 s.4(2).
(3)	1971 c.78 s.27(1), (part)(1A); 1981 c.36 s.4(1).
(4)	1971 c.78 s.27(1B); 1981 c.36 s.4(2).
(5), (6)	1971 c.78 s.27(2) (part).
(7)	1971 c.78 s.27(2A); 1981 c.36 s.4(4).
(8), (9)	1971 c.78 s.27(2B); 1981 c.36 s.4(4).
(10)	1971 c.78 s.27(2C); 1981 c.36 s.4(4).
(11)	1971 c.78 s.27(2) to (4); drafting; R 7.
68(1)	1971 c.78 ss.26(8)(part), 27(5)(part).
(2)	1971 c.78 s.26(8) (part), s.27(5) (part); 1982 c.48 ss.38, 46.
(3)	1971 c.78 ss.26(9), 27(6) (part).
(4)	1971 c.78 s.27(6) (part).
69(1)	1971 c.78 s.34(1) (part).
(2)	1971 c.78 s.34(1) (part); 1986 c.63 Sch. 6, Pt II para. 1.
(3)	1971 c.78 s.34(2) (part).
(4)	1971 c.78 s.34(2) (part).
(5)	1971 c.78 s.34(3).
70(1)	1971 c.78 s.29(1) (part); 1986 c.63 Sch. 11 Pt I para. 16.
(2)	1971 c.78 s.29(1) (part).
(3)	1971 c.78 s.29(1) (part), drafting.
71(1)	1971 c.78 s.29(2).
(2)	1971 c.78 s.29(3); R 7.
(3)	1971 c.78 s.29(5).
(4)	1971 c.78 s.29(6).
72(1)	1971 c.78 s.30(1).
(2)	1971 c.78 s.30(2).

Provision	*Derivation*
(3)	1971 c.78 s.30(3) (part).
(4)	1971 c.78 s.30(3)(part); 1981 c.36 Sch.1 para. 1.
(5)	Drafting; 1971 c.78 s.30(2)(part); 1981 c.36 Sch.1 para. 1.
73(1)	1971 c.78 s.31A(1); 1986 c.63 Sch.11 para. 4.
(2)	1971 c.78 s.31A(3); 1986 c.63 Sch.11 para. 4.
(3)	1971 c.78 s.31A(2); 1986 c.63 Sch.11 para. 4.
(4)	1971 c.78 S.31A(4); 1986 c.63 Sch.11 para. 4.
74(1)	1971 c.78. s.31(1) (part); 1972 c.70 Sch. 16 para. 22; 1980 c.65 Sch. 15 para. 4(1).
(2)	1971 c.78 s.31(1) (part).
75(1)	1971 c.78 s.33(1).
(2), (3)	1971 c.78 s.33(2).
76(1)	1971 c.78 ss.29A(1) (part), 29B(1) (part); 1981 c.43 s.3; 1988 c.40 Sch.12 para. 70.
(2)	1971 c.78 ss.29A(1) (part), (2); 29B(1) (part); 1981 c.43 s.3; 1986 c.63 Sch.11 para. 3, Sch. 12 Pt. III.
(3)	1971 c.78 s.29B(1A); 1988 c.40 Sch.12 para. 70.
77(1) to (3)	1971 c.78 s.35(1) to (3).
(4)	1971 c.78 s.35(4)(part); 1981 c.36 Sch.1 para. 2; 1986 c.63 Sch.11 para. 17.
(5), (6)	1971 c.78 s.35(5).
(7)	1971 c.78 s.35(6).
78(1)	1971 c.78 s.36(1); 1980 c.65 Sch. 15 para. 4(2).
(2)	1971 c.78 s.37 (part); 1980 c.65 Sch. 15 para. 4(3).
(3)	1971 c.78 s.36(2) (part).
(4)	1971 c.78 ss.36(2) (part), 37 (part).
(5)	1971 c.78 s.37 (part); R 8(a), (c), (d).
79(1)	1971 c.78 ss.36(3), 37.
(2), (3)	1971 c.78 s.36(4).
(4)	1971 c.78 s.36(5); 1981 c.36 Sch. 1 para. 3; 1986 c.63 Sch.11 para. 17.
(5)	1971 c.78 s.36(6).
(6)	1971 c.78 s.36(7); 1986 c.63 Sch. 11 para. 18.
(7)	1971 c.78 s.36(8).
80(1), (2)	1971 c.78 s.38(1), (2).
(3)	1971 c.78 s.38(4).
(4)	1971 c.78 s.38(3).
81(1), (2)	1971 c.78 s.39(1).
(3), (4)	1971 c.78 s.39(2), (3).

Provision	*Derivation*
82	1971 c.78 s.24A(1) to (3); 1986 c.63 s.25(1).
83(1)	1971 c.78 s.24A(4)(a); 1986 c.63 s.25(1).
(2)	1971 c.78 s.24A(4)(b); 1971 c.78 Sch.8A para. 2(1); 1986 c.63 s.25(1).
(3)	1971 c.78 s.24A(5); 1986 c.63 s.25(1).
84(1), (2)	1971 c.78 s.24B(1); 1986 c.63 s.25(1).
(3), (4)	1971 c.78 s.24B(2) (part); 1986 c.63 s.25(1).
85	1971 c.78 s.24C(1), (2); 1986 c.63 s.25(1).
86(1) to (5)	1971 c.78 s.24D(1) to (5); 1986 c.63 s.25(1).
(6)	1971 c.78 s.24D(6) (part); 1986 c.63 s.25(1).
87(1)	1971 c.78 s.24E(1); 1986 c.63 s.25(1); 1988 c.4 Sch.3 para. 10.
(2), (3)	1971 c.78 s.24E(2), (3); 1986 c.63 s.25(1).
(4)	1971 c.78 s.24E(4) (part); 1986 c.63 s.25(1).
88(1)	1980 c.65 Sch.32 paras. 5(4)(a), 17(1).
(2)	1980 c.65 Sch.32 paras. 11(3), 17(2).
(3) to (6)	1980 c.65 Sch.32 para. 17(3) to (6).
(7)	1980 c.65 Sch.32 para. 25(1)(a), (b).
(8)	1980 c.65 Sch.32 para. 25(2).
(9), (10)	1980 c.65 Sch.32 para. 17(7), (8).
89(1)	1980 c.65 Sch.32 para. 21; 1986 c.63 s.54(1).
(2)	1980 c.65 Sch.32 para. 22(1); 1986 c.63 s.54(1).
90(1)	1971 c.78 s.40(1)
(2)	1989 c.29 Sch. 8 para. 7(1).
(3)	1971 c.78 s.40(2); 1989 c.29 Sch. 8 para. 7(3).
(4)	1971 c.78 s.40(3)
(5)	1989 c.29 Sch. 8 para. 7(4).
91(1), (2)	1971 c.78 s.41(1).
(3)	1971 c.78 s.41(2).
(4)	1971 c.78 s.41(3); 1980 c.65 Sch.32 para. 18(2); 1981 c.36 s.6; 1986 c.63 Sch.6 Pt II para. 2.
92	1971 c.78 s.42
93	1971 c.78 s.43(4) to (7); 1989 c.29 Sch. 8 para 7(3).
94(1)	1971 c.78 ss.44(1), 24C(3); 1980 c.65 Sch. 32 para. 22(2); 1986 c.63 ss.25, 54(1).
(2), (3)	1971 c.78 s.44(2).
(4)	1971 c.78 s.44(3)(a).
(5), (6)	1971 c.78 s.44(6).
95(1), (2)	1971 c.78 s.44(3)(b).
(3)	1971 c.78 s.44(4).

Provision	*Derivation*
(4), (5)	1971 c.78 s.44(5).
96(1), (2)	1971 c.78 s.276(5); 1981 c.41 Sch. para. 24.
(3)	1971 c.78 s.276(5) (part); 1981 c.41 Sch. para. 24.
97(1), (2)	1971 c.78 s.45(1).
(3)	1971 c.78 s.45(4) (part).
(4)	1971 c.78 s.45(4) (proviso).
(5)	1971 c.78 s.45(5); 1981 c.36 s.8.
98(1)	1971 c.78 s.45(2) (part).
(2) to (5)	1971 c.78 s.45(3).
(6)	1971 c.78 s.45(2) (part).
99(1)	1971 c.78 s.46(1); 1974 c.7 Sch.6 para. 25(3), Sch.8.
(2)	1971 c.78 s.46(1)(part), (2)(part).
(3)	1971 c.78 s.46(3); 1974 c.7 Sch.8.
(4)	1971 c.78 s.46(2)(a)(part).
(5)	1971 c.78 s.46(2)(b)(part).
(6) to (8)	1971 c.78 s.46(4) to (6).
100(1) to (3)	1971 c.78 s.276(1); 1974 c.7 Sch. 6 para. 25(12), Sch. 8.
(4) to (6)	1971 c.78 s.276(4).
(7)	1971 c.78 s.276(2), (3).
(8)	1971 c.78 s.45(5); R 9.
101(1)	1971 c.78 ss.47(1), 48(1) (part).
(2)	1971 c.78 s.48(1).
(3)	1971 c.78 s.48(2).
(4)	1971 c.78 s.48(8); drafting.
(5)	1971 c.78 s.47(6) (part).
102(1)	1971 c.78 s.51(1).
(2), (3)	1971 c.78 s.51(2).
(4)	1971 c.78 s.51(3) (part).
(5)	1971 c.78 s.51(3) (part) and s.32(3).
(6)	1971 c.78 s.51(8).
(7)	1971 c.78 s.51(9).
(8)	1971 c.78 s.51(1A); 1981 c.36 s.9; drafting.
103(1)	1971 c.78 s.51(4).
(2)	1971 c.78 s.51(5).
(3) to (6)	1971 c.78 s.51(6).
(7)	1971 c.78 s.51(7).
(8)	1971 c.78 s.51(9).

Provision	*Derivation*
104(1)	1971 c.78 s.276(1) (part), (2) (part).
(2), (3)	1971 c.78 s.276(1) (part).
(4) to (7)	1971 c.78 s.276(4) (part).
(8)	1971 c.78 s.276(2),(3).
105(1)	1971 c.78 s.264A(1); 1981 c.36 s.3.
(2)	1971 c.78 s.264A(2); 1981 c.36 s.3.
106(1)	1971 c.78 s.52(1) (part).
(2)	1971 c.78 s.52(1) (part).
(3), (4)	1971 c.78 s.52(2), (3).
107(1)	1971 c.78 s.164(1); 1974 c.7, Sch. 6 para. 25(11), Sch. 8; 1981 c.36 ss.12, 34, Sch. 1 para. 4.
(2) to (5)	1971 c.78 s.164(2) to (5).
108(1)	1971 c.78 s.165(1),(2) (part).
(2)	1971 c.78 s.165(1A).
(3)	1971 c.78 s.165(3); 1985 c.19 s.1(1).
109(1)	1971 c.78 s.166(1).
(2)	1971 c.78 ss.165(2) (part), 166(2).
(3), (4)	1971 c.78 ss.156(2),(3), 166(3).
(5)	1971 c.78 s.166(4).
(6)	1971 c.78 ss.165(2), 166(6).
110(1)	1971 c.78 s.166(5).
(2)	1971 c.78 ss.158(4) (part), 166(5); 1972 c.70 s. 179(3).
(3)	1971 c.78 ss.158(4) (part), 165(2) (part), 166(5).
(4)	1971 c.78 ss.158(5), 166(5).
(5)	1971 c.78 ss.158(6), 166(5).
111(1)	1971 c.78 ss.159(1), 168(1).
(2)	1971 c.78 ss.159(2), 168(1).
(3)	1971 c.78 ss.159(3), 168(1).
(4)	1971 c.78 ss.165(2), 168(1),(proviso).
(5)	1971 c.78 s.168(4).
112(1)	1971 c.78 ss.160(1), 168(1).
(2), (3)	1971 c.78 ss.160(2), 168(1).
(4)	1971 c.78 ss.160(3), 168(1).
(5)	1971 c.78 ss.160(4), 168(1).
(6)	1971 c.78 ss.160(5)(a), 168(1).
(7)	1971 c.78 ss.160(5)(a) (part), 168(1).
(8)	1971 c.78 ss.160(5)(b), 168(1).
(9), (10)	1971 c.78 ss.160(6), 168(1).

Provision	Derivation
(11)	1971 c.78 s.168(2).
(12)	1971 c.78 s.168(3).
(13)	1971 c.78 s.168(3),(proviso).
113	1971 c.78 ss. 165(2), 167.
114(1) to (3)	1971 c.78 s.169(1) to (3).
(4), (5)	1971 c.78 s.169(4) (part).
(6)	1971 c.78 s.169(6),(6A); 1985 c.19 s.1(2).
(7), (8)	1971 c.78 s.169(7),(8).
115(1)	1971 c.78 s.170(1); 1981 c.36 s.34, Sch. 1 para. 5.
(2)	1971 c.78 s.170(2); 1981 c.36 s.14.
(3), (4)	1971 c.78 s.170(3),(4).
(5)	1971 c.78 ss.170(1)(part), 170A (part); 1981 c.36 s.15, Sch. 1 para. 5; R 10.
(6)	1971 c.78 ss.170(1), 170A (part); 1981 c.36 s.15; R 10.
116	Drafting.
117(1)	1971 c.78 s.178(1).
(2)	1971 c.78 s.178(2); 1981 c.36 Sch. 1 para. 6.
(3)	1971 c.78 s.178(3).
118(1)	1971 c.78 s.179(1) (part).
(2)	1971 c.78 s.179(2) (part).
119(1)	1971 c.78 s.134(1), (2).
(2)	Drafting.
(3)	1971 c.78 s.134(3).
(4)	1971 c.78 s.134(4); 1972 c.70 Sch. 16 para. 33.
120	1971 c.78 s.146.
121(1)	1971 c.78 s.147(1).
(2), (3)	1971 c.78 s.147(2).
(4)	1971 c.78 s.147(3).
(5)	1971 c.78 s.147(4) (part).
(6)	1971 c.78 s.147(4),(proviso); 1973 c.37 Sch. 8 para. 94.
(7)	1971 c.78 s.147(5).
(8)	1971 c.78 s.147(6).
122(1)	1971 c.78 s.148(1).
(2)	1971 c.78 s.148(1),(proviso).
(3)	1971 c.78 s.148(2).
(4)	1971 c.78 s.148(3).
123(1),(2)	1971 c.78 s.149(1),(2); 1987 c.3 s.1.
(3), (4)	1971 c.78 s.149(3); 1987 c.3 s.1.

Provision	*Derivation*
(5)	1971 c.78 s.149(4): 1987 c.3 s.1.
124	1971 c.78 s.150.
125	1971 c.78 s.152.
126	1971 c.78 s.153.
127(1),(2)	1971 c.78 s.154(1),(2)(part).
(3)	1971 c.78 s.154(2),(proviso).
(4)	1971 c.78 s.154(3).
(5), (6)	1971 c.78 s.154(4).
(7), (8)	1971 c.78 s.154(5).
128	1971 c.78 s.155.
129	1971 c.78 s.156.
130	1971 c.78 s.157.
131	1971 c.78 s.158(1) to (3).
132(1),(2)	1971 c.78 s.158(4); 1972 c.70 s. 179(3), Sch. 30.
(3)	1971 c.78 s.158(5); 1975 c.76 Sch. 1.
(4)	1971 c.78 s.158(6).
133	1971 c.78 s.159.
134(1)	1971 c.78 s.160(1).
(2),(3)	1971 c.78 s.160(2).
(4),(5)	1971 c.78 s.160(3),(4).
(6) to (8)	1971 c.78 s.160(5).
(9),(10)	1971 c.78 s.160(6).
135	1971 c.78 s.162; R 11.
136(1)	1971 c.78 s.163(1) (part).
(2)	1971 c.78 s.163(1),(proviso).
(3)	1971 c.78 s.163(2).
137(1)(a)	1971 c.78 s.180(1), (part).
(b)	1971 c.78 s.188(1), (part).
(c)	1971 c.78 s.189(1), (part).
(2)(a)	1971 c.78 ss.180(1)(part),(7), 188(1)(part),(2)(part); 1972 c.70 s. 179(3), Sch.30.
(b)	1971 c.78 s.189(1)(part),(2)(part); 1972 c.70 s. 179(3), Sch.30.
(3)	1971 c.78 ss.180(1)(part), 188(1)(part).
(4)	1971 c.78 s.189(1)(part).
(5)	1971 c.78 s.180(4); 1986 c.63 Sch.12 Pt.III.
(6)	1971 c.78 s.180(5); R 12.
(7)	1971 c.78 s.180(6); R 12, R 41.
(8)	1971 c.78 s.189(5).

Provision	Derivation
138(1)	1971 c.78 ss.180(2) (part), 188(2) (part), 189(2) (part).
(2)	1971 c.78 ss.180(2) (part), 188(3) (part), 189(3) (part), 198(3) (part).
139(1)	1971 c.78 ss.181(1) (part), 188(2) (part), 189(2) (part); 1986 c.63 Sch.11 para. 5(1)(a).
(2)	1971 c.78 s.181(1) (part), s.188(2) (part); s.189(2) (part).
(3)	1971 c.78 s.181(2), s.188(2) (part) s.189(2) (part).
(4)	1971 c.78 s.181(3), s.188(2) (part); s.189(2) (part), 1986 c.63 Sch. 11 para. 5(1)(b).
(5)	1971 c.78 s.208.
140(1)	1971 c.78 ss.182(1), 188(2) (part), 189(2) (part).
(2)	1971 c.78 s.182(2), s.188(2) (part), s.189(2) (part); 1972 c.70 Sch. 16 paras. 37, 52.
(3),(4)	1971 c.78 s.182(3), s.188(2) (part), s.189(2) (part).
(5)	1971 c.78 s.182(4), s.188(2) (part), s. 189(2) (part).
141(1)	1971 c.78 ss.183(1), 188(2) (part), 189(2) (part), (3) (part); R 13(a).
(2)	1971 c.78 ss.183(2), 188(2) (part), (3) (part), 189(2) (part), (3) (part).
(3) to (5)	1971 c.78 s.183(3) to (5), s.188(2) (part), s.189(2) (part).
142(1)	1971 c.78 ss.184(1), 188(2) (part), 189(2) (part); 1986 c.63 Sch. 11 para. 6(a); R 13(b).
(2)	1971 c.78 s.184(2).
(3)	1971 c.78 s.184(3); 1986 c.63 Sch. 11 para. 6(b).
143(1)	1971 c.78 ss.186(1), 188(2) (part), 189(2) (part).
(2),(3)	1971 c.78 ss.186(2),(3), 188(2) (part), 189(2) (part).
(4)	1971 c.78 ss.186(3A), 188(2) (part), 189(2) (part); 1986 c.63 Sch.11 para. 7(1).
(5),(6)	1971 c.78 ss.186(4), 188(2) (part), 189(2) (part).
(7)	1971 c.78 ss.186(5), 188(2) (part), 189(2) (part).
(8)	1971 c.78 s.208.
144(1)	1971 c.78 ss.187(1), 188(2) (part), 189(2) (part).
(2)	1971 c.78 s.187(2), s.188(2) (part), s.189(2) (part).
(3),(4)	1971 c.78 ss.187(3), 188(2) (part), 189(2) (part).
(5),(6)	1971 c.78 ss.187(4),(5), 188(2) (part), 189(2) (part).
(7)	1971 c.78 s.189(4).
145(1),(2)	1973 c.26 s.53(1), (5).
(3),(4)	1973 c.26 s.53(3),(4); 1981 c. 66 Sch. 3 para. 1.
(5)	1973 c.26 s.53(2)
(6)	1973 c.26 s.53(1),(2).

Provision	*Derivation*
(7)	1973 c.26 s.53(6).
146(1),(2)	1973 c.26 s.54(1).
(3)	1973 c.26 s.54(2).
(4),(5)	1973 c.26 s.54(3).
(6),(7)	1973 c.26 s.54(4),(5).
(8),(9)	1973 c.26 s.54(6).
(10),(11)	1973 c.26 s.54(7),(8).
147(1)	1973 c.26 s.84(2).
(2)	1973 c.26 s.87(1).
148(1)	1971 c.78 ss.181(4), 186(6), 191A; 1984 c.12 Sch. 4 para. 53(5).
(2)	R 13(c).
149(1)	1971 c.78 s.192(1) (part), drafting.
(2)	1971 c.78 s.192(3),(4)(part),(5)(part).
(3)	1971 c.78 s.192(4) (part); 190 SI/465.
(4)	1971 c.78 s.192(4) (part), (5) (part).
(5)	1971 c.78 s.192(6); 1973 c.26 s.82(2).
150(1)	1971 c.78 s.193(1); 1973 c.26 s.77.
(2),(3)	1971 c.78 s.193(2).
(4)	1971 c.78 s.193(4)
151(1),(2)	1971 c.78 s.194(1)
(3)	1971 c.78 s.194(5) (part).
(4)	1971 c.78 s.194(2); 1980 c.65 Sch.15 paras. 18,19; 1985 c.51 Sch.1 para. 16(2).
(5)	1971 c.78 s.194(4); 1973 c.26 s.75(3)(a).
(6)	1971 c.78 s.194(3).
(7)	1973 c.26 s.76(2).
(8)	1971 c.78 s.194(6); 1973 c.26 s.75(3)(b).
152(1)	1973 c.26 ss.68(6)(part), 69(3); 1985 c.51 Sch. 1 para. 17(4).
(2)	1973 c.26 s.68(6)(part).
153(1),(2)	1971 c.78 s.195(1).
(3) to (7)	1971 c.78 s.195(2) to (6).
(8)	1973 c.26 s.68(6) (part).
154(1),(2)	1971 c.78 s.196(1).
(3)	1971 c.78 s.196(2).
(4),(5)	1971 c.78 s.196(3).
(6)	1971 c.78 s.196(4).
155	1971 c.78 s.199.

Provision	*Derivation*
156(1),(2)	1971 c.78 s.198(1).
(3),(4)	1971 c.78 s.198(2),(3).
157(1),(2)	1971 c.78 s.197; 1981 c.67 Sch.4 para. 1; 1985 c.71 Sch.2 para. 22.
(3),(4)	1973 c.26 s.81(6),(7)(part).
158(1),(2)	1973 c.26 s.79(1).
(3)	1973 c.26 s.79(2).
159(1)	1973 c.26 s.80(1).
(2),(3)	1973 c.26 s.80(2).
(4) to (8)	1973 c.26 s.80(3) to (7).
160(1) to (5)	1973 c.26 s.81(1) to (5).
(6)	1973 c.26 s.81(7).
161(1)	1971 c.78 s.200; 1973 c.26 s.81(8); R 14.
(2)	1973 c.26 s.78(1).
(3) to (4)	1973 c.26 s.78(2).
(5)	1973 c.26 s.78(3).
162(1)	1971 c.78 s.201(1); 1973 c.26 s.77(1),(2).
(2),(3)	1971 c.78 s.201(2).
(4)	1971 c.78 s.201(3).
(5)	1971 c.78 s.201(6).
163(1)	1971 c.78 s.201(4); 1973 c.26 s.78(4).
(2)	1971 c.78 s.201(5); 1973 c.26 s.78(4).
164	1971 c.78 s.204.
165(1),(2)	1973 c.26 s.72(4); 1980 c.65 s.147(4).
(3)	1973 c.26 s.72(5); 1980 c.65 s.147(5); 1981 c.64 Sch.12 para. 11.
166(1)	1971 c.78 s.202(1),(2) (part).
(2)	1971 c.78 s.202(2) (part).
167	1971 c.78 s.208.
168	1971 c.78 s.203.
169(1) to (3)	1971 c.78 s.205; 1984 c.12 Sch.4 para. 53(6).
(4)	1973 c.26 s.72(3) (part); 1980 c.65 s.147(3) (part).
(5)	1973 c.26 s.76(3) (part).
170(1)	1971 c.78 s.206(1).
(2)	1971 c.78 s.206(2); 1985 c.51 Sch.1 para 17(6) (part).
(3)	1973 c.26 s.68(10) (part); 1985 c.51 Sch.1 para. 17(6) (part).
(4)	1973 c.26 s.71(3).
(5)	1973 c.26 s.72(3) (part); 1980 c.65 s.147(3) (part).

Provision	*Derivation*
(6)	1973 c.26 s.73(3); 1985 c.71 Sch.2 para. 24(8).
(7)	1973 c.26 s.76(3) (part); 1980 c.66 Sch.24 para. 23.
(8)	1973 c.26 s.70(3).
(9)	1971 c.78 s.206(3).
(10)	1971 c.78 s.206(4); 1980 c.66 Sch.24 para. 20.
(11),(12)	1971 c.78 s.206(5),(6).
171	1971 c.78 s.207; 1973 c.26 ss.82(5), 87(1); 1990 SI/465.
172(1) to (4)	1971 c.78 s.87(1) to (4); 1981 c.41 Sch. para. 1.
(5)	1971 c.78 s.87(13).
(6)	1971 c.78 s.87(5).
(7)	1971 c.78 s.87(14).
(8)	1971 c.78 s.87(15).
173(1)	1971 c.78 s.87(6).
(2)	1971 c.78 s.87(7).
(3)	1971 c.78 s.87(9).
(4)	1971 c.78 s.87(10).
(5)	1971 c.78 s.87(8).
(6)	1971 c.78 s.87(11).
(7)	1971 c.78 s.87(12).
(8)	1971 c.78 s.87(16).
174(1)	1971 c.78 s.88(1); 1981 c.41 Sch. para. 1; 1984 c.10 s.4(2).
(2) to (4)	1971 c.78 s.88(2) to (4), (5)(a).
(5)	1971 c.78 s.88(9).
(6)	1984 c.10 s.4(2).
175(1)	1971 c.78 s.88(5)(b) to (e).
(2)	1971 c.78 s.88(5)(d).
(3)	1971 c.78 s.88(7).
(4)	1971 c.78 s.88(10).
(5)	1971 c.78 s.110(2).
(6)	1971 c.78 s.88(11).
176(1),(2)	1971 c.78 s.88A(1),(2); 1981 c.41 Sch.para. 1.
(3)	1971 c.78 s.88(6); 1981 c.41 Sch.para. 1.
(4)	1971 c.78 s.88(8); 1981 c.41 Sch.para. 1.
(5)	1971 c.78 s.88A(3); 1981 c.41 Sch.para. 1.
177(1)	1971 c.78 s.88B(1); 1981 c.41 Sch para 1.
(2)	1971 c.78 s.88B(2).
(3)	1971 c.78 s.88B(2); R 15.

Provision	Derivation
(4)	1971 c.78 s.88B(2).
(5) to (8)	1971 c.78 s.88B(3).
178(1),(2)	1971 c.78 s.91(1),(2); 1981 c.41 Sch.para. 4.
(3)	1971 c.78 s.91(3),(4); 1974 c.7 Sch.8.
(4)	1971 c.78 s.91(3).
(5)	1971 c.78 s.91(5).
(6)	1971 c.78 s.111.
(7)	1971 c.78 ss.89(6),90(10),91(1); drafting.
179(1)	1971 c.78 s.89(1); 1981 c.41 Sch.para. 2(1).
(2)	1971 c.78 s.89(1); 1980 c.43 s.32(2); 1982 c.48 ss.46,74.
(3)	1971 c.78 s.89(2).
(4)	1971 c.78 s.89(3).
(5)	1971 c.78 s.89(4); 1986 c.63 Sch.11 para. 13.
(6)	1971 c.78 s.89(5).
(7), (8)	1971 c.78 s.89(5); 1980 c.43 s.32(2); 1982 c.48 ss.46,74; 1986 c.63 Sch.11 para. 13.
180(1)	1971 c.78 s.92(1); 1981 c.41 Sch.para. 5
(2),(3)	1971 c.78 s.92(2),(3).
181(1)	1971 c.78 s.93(1); 1981 c.41 Sch.para. 7(1).
(2) to (4)	1971 c.78 s.93(2) to (4).
(5)	1971 c.78 s.93(5); 1981 c.41 Sch.para. 7(2); 1982 c.48 s.46.
182(1) to (3)	1971 c.78 s.276(5A); 1981 c.41 Sch.para. 24.
(4)	1971 c.78 s.276(5B)(part); 1981 c.41 Sch.para. 24; R 16.
183(1),(2)	1971 c.78 s.90(1); 1981 c.41 Sch.para. 3; 1977 c.29 s.1.
(3) to (5)	1971 c.78 s.90(2); 1977 c.29 s.1.
(6)	1971 c.78 s.90(5)(part); 1977 c.29 s.1.
(7)	1971 c.78 s.90(6)(part); 1977 c.29 s.1.
184(1)	1971 c.78 s.90(1)(part); 1977 c.29 s.1.
(2),(3)	1971 c.78 s.90(3); 1977 c.29 s.1.
(4),(5)	1971 c.78 s.90(4); 1977 c.29 s.1.
(6)	1971 c.78 s.90(5)(part); 1977 c.29 s.1.
(7)	1971 c.78 s.90(6)(part); 1977 c.29 s.1.
(8)	1971 c.78 s.90(9); 1977 c.29 s.1.
185	1971 c.78 s.276(5); 1981 c.41 Sch.para. 24.
186(1) to (5)	1971 c.78 s.177; 1977 c.29 s.2.
(6),(7)	1971 c.78 s.179.
187(1)	1971 c.78 s.90(7).
(2)	1971 c.78 s.90(7); 1986 c.63 Sch.11 para. 13

Provision	Derivation
(3)	1971 c.78 s.90(8).
188(1)	1971 c.78 s.92A(1); 1981 c.41 Sch.para. 6; 1985 c.51 s.3(4).
(2)	1971 c.78 s.92A(3); 1981 c.41 Sch.para. 6; 1985 c.51 Sch.17.
(3)	1971 c.78 s.92A(4); 1981 c.41 Sch.para. 6.
189(1) to (3)	1971 c.78 s.108(1) to (3); 1981 c.36 s.11.
(4),(5)	1971 c.78 s.108(6),(7); 1981 c.36 s.11.
190(1)	1971 c.78 s.108(4)(part); 1981 c.36 s.11.
(2)	1971 c.78 s.108(4)(part),(5)(part); 1981 c.36 s.11.
(3)	1971 c.78 s.108(4) (part); 1981 c.36 s.11.
(4)	1971 c.78 s.111; R 17.
(5)	1971 c.78 s.108(4)(part); 1981 c.36 s.11.
191	1971 c.78 s.94(1)
192(1) to (3)	1971 c.78 s.94(2).
(4)	1971 c.78 s.94(7); 1981 c.41 Sch.para. 8.
(5)	1971 c.78 s.95(1)(part).
(6)	1971 c.78 Sch.14 para. 6(part).
193(1)	1971 c.78 s.94(6); 1971 c.78 Sch.14 para. 1.
(2),(3)	1971 c.78 Sch.14 para. 3(1).
(4)	1971 c.78 Sch.14 para. 3(2); R 18.
(5)	1971 c.78 Sch.14 para. 3(2)(part); 1982 c.48 ss.46,74.
(6)	1971 c.78 s.94(8).
(7)	1971 c.78 s.94(8)(part); 1980 c.43 s.32;1982 c.48 ss.46,74.
194(1)	1971 c.78 ss.94(4), 95(1) (part).
(2)	1971 c.78 s.94(3).
(3)	1971 c.78 Sch.14 para. 4(a),(b).
(4)	1971 c.78 Sch.14 para. 4(c).
(5),(6)	1971 c.78 Sch.14 para. 2.
195(1)	1971 c.78 ss.94(5),95(2).
(2)	1971 c.78 s.95(2).
(3)	1971 c.78 s.95(2)(b).
(4)	1971 c.78 s.94(8); Sch.14 para 3(1).
(5)	R 8(a).
(6)	1971 c.78 s.95(7).
196(1)	1971 c.78 s.95(4).
(2)	1971 c.78 Sch.14 para. 5.
(3)	1971 c.78 s.95(5).
(4)	1971 c.78 Sch.14 para. 6(part).

Provision	*Derivation*
(5)	1971 c.78 s.95(3).
(6),(7)	1971 c.78 s.95(6).
197	1971 c.78 s.59.
198(1)	1971 c.78 s.60(1); 1980 c.65 Sch.15 para. 13(1)(a), (2).
(2)	1971 c.78 s.60(1)
(3)	1971 c.78 s.60(1); 1974 c.32 s.10(1).
(4)	1971 c.78 ss.60(2), 191(1).
(5)	1971 c.78 s.60(3).
(6)	1971 c.78 s.60(6); 1974 c.32 s.10(2)(a).
(7)	1971 c.78 s.60(10); 1986 c.63 Sch.12 Pt II.
199(1)	1971 c.78 s.60(4); 1980 c.65 Sch.15 para. 13(1)(c).
(2)	1971 c.78 s.60(5).
(3)	1971 c.78 s.60(5); 1980 c.65 Sch.15 para. 13(1)(d), (2), Sch.34 Pt X.
200(1)	1971 c.78 s.60(7).
(2)	1971 c.78 s.60(7); 1978 c.30 s.17(2)(a).
(3)	1971 c.78 s.60(8); 1978 c.30 s.17(2)(a).
(4)	1971 c.78 s.60(7),(9); 1978 c.30 s.17(2)(a).
201(1)	1971 c.78 s.61(1).
(2)	1971 c.78 s.61(2); 1980 c.65 Sch.15 para. 14, Sch.34 Pt X.
202(1),(2)	1971 c.78 s.276(1),(2)(c); 1974 c.7 s.35, Sch.6 para. 25(12).
(3)	1971 c.78 s.276(3).
203	1971 c.78 s.174.
204(1)(a)	1971 c.78 s.175(1).
(b)	1971 c.78 s.175(2); 1978 c.30 s.17(2)(a).
(2) to (4)	1971 c.78 s.175(2) to (4).
205	1971 c.78 s.179.
206(1),(2)	1971 c.78 s.62(1); 1974 c.32 s.10(2)(b); 1985 c.52 s.1(2).
(3)	1971 c.78 s.62(1A);1985 c.51 s.1(3).
(4)	1971 c.78 s.62(2).
(5)	1971 c.78 s.62(3)(part).
207(1),(2)	1971 c.78 s.103(1).
(3),(4)	1971 c.78 s.103(2).
(5)	1971 c.78 s.62(3)(part).
208(1),(2)	1971 c.78 s.103(3); 1981 c.41 Sch. para. 12.
(3)	1971 c.78 s.103(3A); 1981 c.41 Sch. para. 12.
(4)	1971 c.78 s.103(3B); 1981 c.41 Sch. para. 12.
(5)	1971 c.78 s.103(3C); 1981 c.41 Sch. para. 12.

Provision	*Derivation*
(6)	1971 c.78 s.103(3D); 1981 c.41 Sch. para. 12.
(7)	1971 c.78 s.103(3E); 1981 c.41 Sch. para. 12.
(8)	1971 c.78 s.103(3F); 1981 c.41 Sch. para. 12.
(9)	1971 c.78 s.103(4).
(10)	1971 c.78 s.110(2).
209(1)	1971 c.78 ss.103(5), 91(1); 1981 c.41 Sch. para. 4(a); 1972 c.70 Sch.16 paras. 29, 52.
(2)	1971 c.78 ss.103(5), 91(2); 1981 c.41 Sch. para. 4(b) (i), (ii).
(3), (4)	1971 c.78 ss.91(3),(4), 103(5); 1974 c.7 Sch.8.
(5)	1971 c.78 ss.91(5), 103(5).
(6)	1971 c.78 s.111.
210(1)	1971 c.78 s.102(1); 1974 c.32 s.10(3).
(2)	1971 c.78 s.102(1); 1974 c.32 s.10(3); 1980 c.43 ss.32(9), 143(1).
(3)	1971 c.78 s.102(1)(b); 1974 c.32 s.10(3).
(4)	1971 c.78 s.102(2); 1974 c.32 s.10(4); 1982 (c.48) s.46(1).
(5)	1971 c.78 s.102(3), 1974 c.32 s.10(5).
211(1) to (3)	1971 c.78 s.61A(1) to (3); 1974 c.32 s.8.
(4)	1971 c.78 s.102(4); 1974 c.32 s.10(6).
212(1)	1971 c.78 s.61A(4); 1974 c.32 s.8.
(2), (3)	1971 c.78 s.61A(5); 1974 c.32 s.8.
(4)	1971 c.78 s.61A(6); 1974 c.32 s.8.
213(1),(2)	1971 c.78 s.61A(8); 1974 c.32 s.8.
(3)	1971 c.78 s.61A(9); 1974 c.32 s.8.
214	1971 c.78 s.61A(7); 1974 c. 32 s. 8.
215(1),(2)	1971 c.78 s.65(1),(2); 1986 c.63 s.46.
(3),(4)	1971 c.78 s.65(3); 1986 c.63 s.46.
216(1)	1971 c.78 s.104(1); 1981 c.41 Sch. para. 13.
(2)	1971 c.78 s.104(2); 1981 c.41 Sch. para. 13; 1982 c.48 ss.38, 46
(3)	1971 c.78 s.104(3); 1981 c.41 Sch. para. 13.
(4)	1971 c.78 s.104(4)(5); 1981 c.41 Sch. para. 13.
(5)	1971 c.78 s.104(6); 1981 c.41 Sch. para 13.
(6)	1971 c.78 s.104(7); 1981 c.41 Sch. para. 13; 1986 c.63 s.49(1), Sch.11 para. 13.
(7)	1971 c.78 s.104(8); 1981 c.41 Sch. para. 13.
217(1)	1971 c.78 s.105(1); 1986 c.63 s.49, Sch.11 para. 20.
(2) to (5)	1971 c.78 s.105(2) to (5).
(6)	1971 c.78 s.110(2).

Provision	*Derivation*
218	1971 c.78 s.106; 1981 c.41 Sch. para. 14.
219(1)	1971 c.78 s.107(1); 1981 c.41 Sch. para. 15.
(2)	1971 c.78 s.107(2); 1981 c.41 Sch. para. 15.
(3) to (5)	1971 c.78 s.107(3).
(6)	1971 c.78 s.111.
220(1),(2)	1971 c.78 s.63(1),(2).
(3)	1971 c.78 ss.63(2)(c), 191(1).
(4)	1971 c.78 s.63(7).
(5)	1971 c.78 s.63(7); R 19.
221(1)	1971 c.78 s.63(3); 1974 c.32 s.3(1); 1986 c.63 s.45.
(2)	1971 c.78 s.63(3A); 1986 c.63 s.45.
(3),(4)	1971 c.78 s.63(3B); 1986 c.63 s.45.
(5)	1971 c.78 s.63(4).
(6)	1971 c.78 s.63(5).
(7) to (9)	1971 c.78 s.63(6).
222	1971 c.78 s.64.
223(1)	1971 c.78 s.176.
(2)	1971 c.78 s.179(1); 1981 c.36 s.17.
(3)	1971 c.78 s.179(2).
224(1),(2)	1971 c.78 s.109(1).
(3)	1971 c.78 s.109(2); 1981 c.41 Sch. para 16; 1982 c.48 s.46; 1986 c.63 s.49(1), Sch.11 para. 13.
(4),(5)	1971 c.78 s.109(3).
225(1)	1971 c.78 s.109A(1),(6); 1982 c.30 s.36(a).
(2)	1971 c.78 s.109A(2); 1982 c.30 s.36(a).
(3)	1971 c.78 s.109A(3),(6); 1982 c.30 s.36(a).
(4),(5)	1971 c.78 s.109A(4),(5).
226(1) to (4)	1971 c.78 s.112(1)(1A) to (1C); 1980 c.65 s.91(1).
(5)	1971 c.78 s.112(2).
(6)	1971 c.78 s.112(3); 1972 c.70 s. 179(3), Sch. 30.
(7)	1971 c.78 s.112(4); 1981 c.67 Sch. 6 Pt. I; 1981 c.67 Sch. 4 para. 1.
(8)	1971 c.78 s.112(5); 1972 c.70 s. 179(3), Sch. 30.
227(1)	1971 c.78 s.119(1)(a); 1972 c.70 s. 179(3), Sch. 30.
(2)	1971 c.78 s.119(3).
228(1)	1971 c.78 s.113(1); 1980 c.65 s.122(2).
(2)	1980 c.65 s.122(1).
(3)	1971 c.78 s.113(2).

Provision	*Derivation*
(4)	1971 c.78 s.113(2) (proviso); 1981 c.67 Sch. 4 para. 1.
(5),(6)	1980 c.65 s.122(3).
(7)	1971 c.78 s.113(3); 1981 c.67 Sch. 4 para. 1, Sch. 6 Pt. I.
229(1)	1971 c.78 s.121(1).
(2)	1971 c.78 s.121(1); 1980 c.65 Sch. 34 Pt. XIII.
(3)	1971 c.78 s.121(2); 1981 c.67 Sch. 4, para. 21(6).
(4) to (6)	1971 c.78 s.121(4) to (6).
230	1971 c.78 s.120.
231(1)	1971 c.78 s.276(6)(a); 1972 c.70 s. 179.
(2)	1971 c.78 s.276(6)(b).
(3)	1971 c.78 s.276(7).
232(1)	1971 c.78 s.122(1).
(2) to (4)	1971 c.78 s.122(2)(2A)(2B); 1980 c.65 Sch. 23 para. 10.
(5),(6)	1971 c.78 s.122(4),(5); 1972 c.70 s.272(2).
233(1) to (4)	1971 c.78 s.123(1),(2),(2A); 1980 c.65 Sch. 23 para. 11,Sch. 34, Part XIII.
(5) to (7)	1971 c.78 s.123(7).
(8)	1971 c.78 s.123(9); 1972 c.70 s.272(2).
234	1980 c.65 s.122(6).
235(1)	1971 c.78 s.124(1), (5).
(2)	1971 c.78 s.124(2).
(3)	1971 c.78 s.124(1), (5).
(4)	1971 c.78 s.124(6); 1974 c.7 s.35, Sch. 6 para. 25(9).
(5)	1971 c.78 s.124(6) (proviso), (7).
(6)	1971 c.78 s.124(8); 1972 c.5 Sch. 3; 1982 c.52 s.19(1), Sch. 2 para. 7(2).
236(1)	1971 c.78 s.118(1).
(2)	1971 c.78 s.118(2); 1984 c.12 Sch. 4 para. 53(3).
(3) to (5)	1971 c.78 s.118(3) to (5).
237(1),(2)	1971 c.78 s.127(1),(2).
(3)	1971 c.78 s.127(1) (proviso); 1984 c.12 Sch. 4 para. 53(4).
(4)	1971 c.78 s.127(3).
(5),(6)	1971 c.78 s.127(4).
(7)	1971 c.78 s.127(5).
238(1),(2)	1971 c.78 s.128(1) (part).
(3),(4)	1971 c.78 s.128(2).
(5)	1971 c.78 s.128(3).
(6)	1971 c.78 s.128(7) (part).

Provision	*Derivation*
239(1),(2)	1971 c.78 s.128(4).
(3)	1971 c.78 s.128(7) (part).
240(1),(2)	1971 c.78 s.128(5), (6).
(3)	1971 c.78 s.128(8), (1) (part).
241	1971 c.78 s.129.
242	1971 c.78 s.130; 1973 c.26 Sch. 3; 1978 c.30 s.17(2)(a); 1989 c.42 Sch.11 para 19.
243(1)	1971 c.78 s.131(1).
(2),(3)	1971 c.78 s.131(2)
(4)	1971 c.78 s.131(3).
244(1)	1980 c.65 s.119(1); 1982 c.30 s.35(a).
(2)	1980 c.65 s.119(2); 1982 c.30 s.35(b).
(3)	1980 c.65 s.119(3); 1982 c.30 s.35(c)
(4)	1980 c.65 s.119(4); 1982 c.30 s.35(d).
245(1)	1971 c.78 s.132(1); 1981 c.67 Sch. 4 para. 21(7)(a).
(2)	1971 c.78 s.132(2); 1981 c.67 Sch. 4 para. 21(7)(b).
(3)	1971 c.78 s.132(3); 1981 c.67 Sch. 4 para. 21(7)(c).
(4)	1971 c.78 s.132(4).
246	1971 c.78 s.133.
247(1)	1971 c.78 s.209(1); 1980 c.65 Sch. 32 para. 18(4).
(2)	1971 c.78 s.209(2)(part).
(3)	1971 c.78 s.209(2); 1972 c.70 Sch. 16 para. 39; 1980 c.66 Sch. 24 para. 20; 1985 c.51 Sch. 4 para. 50(a), Sch. 17.
(4)	1971 c.78 s.209(3).
(5)	1971 c.78 s.209(4).
(6)	1971 c.78 s.209(5); 1981 c.67 Sch. 4 para. 21(8).
248(1),(2)	1971 c.78 s.211(1).
(3)	1971 c.78 s.211(2); R 20.
249(1)	1971 c.78 s.212(1); 1974 c.7 Sch. 8.
(2)	1971 c.78 s.212(2); 1972 c.70 Sch.16 paras. 41(1),(2),52.
(3)	1971 c.78 s.212(3); 1972 c.70 Sch.16 paras.41(1),(3),52.
(4)	1971 c.78 s.212(3).
(5)	1971 c.78 s.212(4).
(6)	1971 c.78 s.212(8).
(7)	1971 c.78 s.212(8A); 1982 c.30 Sch.5 para. 2.
(8)	1971 c.78 s.212(2),(8); 1972 c.70 Sch.16 paras. 41(1),(5),52.
(9)	1971 c.78 s.212(9).
250(1),(2)	1971 c.75 s.212(5); 1972 c.70 Sch.16 paras.41(4),52.

Provision	*Derivation*
(3)	1971 c.78 s.212(6); 1972 c.70 Sch.16 paras.41(4),52.
(4) to (7)	1971 c.78 ss.212(7), 178, 179; 1972 c.70 Sch.16 paras.41(4),52.
251(1)	1971 c.78 s.214(1)(a).
(2)	1971 c.78 s.214(2).
(3)	1971 c.78 s.214(3); 1988 c.4 Sch.3 para. 22.
252(1)	1971 c.78 s.215(1).
(2)	1971 c.78 s.215(2)(a), (7A)(part); 1986 c.44 Sch.7 para. 2(2)(c); 1989 c.15 Sch.25 para 42(1).
(3)	1971 c.78 s.215(2)(b).
(4),(5)	1971 c.78 s.215(3).
(6)	1971 c.78 s.215(4).
(7)	R 21.
(8)	1971 c.78 s.215(5).
(9)	1971 c.78 s.215(6).
(10),(11)	1971 c.78 s.215(7).
(12)	1971 c.78 s.215(7A) (part),(8); 1972 c. 70 s.179(3); 1985 c.51 Sch.14 para. 48(a), Sch.17; 1988 c.40 Sch.13; 1988 c.50 Sch.17 para. 18; 1989 c.15 Sch.25 para 42(1); 1989 c.29 Sch.16 para 2(5)(b).
253(1)	1971 c.78 s.216(1)
(2)	1971 c.78 s.216(2); 1987 c.3 Sch.1 para. 19.
(3)	1971 c.78 s.216(3).
(4)	1971 c.78 s.216(4); 1972 c.70 Sch.30; 1985 c.51, Sch.4 para. 50(b); 1988 c.40 Sch.12 para 40.
(5)	1971 c.78 s.216(5).
254(1)	1971 c.78 s.218(1); R 22.
(2)	1971 c.78 s.218(2); 1981 c.67 Sch.4 para. 1, Sch.6 Pt.I.
255	1971 c.78 s.219.
256(1),(2)	1971 c.78 s.220(1); 1984 c.12 Sch.4 para. 53(7).
(3),(4)	1971 c.78 s.220(2); 1984 c.12 Sch.4 para. 53(7).
(5)	1971 c.78 s.220(6); 1984 c.12 Sch.4 para. 53(7).
(6)	1971 c.78 s.220(7); 1984 c.12 Sch.4 para. 53(7).
257(1) to (3)	1971 c.78 s.210(1) to (3).
(4)	1971 c.78 s.210(4); 1972 c.70 Sch.16 para. 40.
258(1)	1971 c.78 s.214(1).
(2)	1971 c.78 s.214(2).
(3)	1971 c.78 s.214(3); 1988 c.4 Sch.3 para. 22.
259	1971 c.78 s.217.
260(1)	1971 c.78 s.220(3)(part),(4);1984 c.12 Sch.4 para. 53(7).

Provision	*Derivation*
(2)	1971 c.78 s.220(4)(part); 1984 c.12 Sch.4 para. 53(7), drafting.
(3)	1971 c.78 s.220(3)(a); 1984 c.12 Sch.4 para 53(7).
(4)	1971 c.78 s.220(3)(b); 1984 c.12 Sch.4 para. 53(7).
(5)	1971 c.78 s.220(3)(c); 1984 c.12 Sch.4 para. 53(7).
(6)	1971 c.78 s.220(3)(d); 1984 c.12 Sch.4 para. 53(7).
(7)	1971 c.78 s.220 (3)(e); 1984 c.12 Sch.4 para. 53(7).
(8)	1971 c.78 s.220(5); 1984 c.12 Sch.4 para. 53(7).
(9)	1971 c.78 s.220(6),(7); 1984 c.12 Sch.4 para. 53(7).
261(1)	1951 c.60 s.32(1); 1971 c.78 s.221(1), (3).
(2)	1951 c.60 s.32(1); 1971 c.78 s.221(1),(3).
(3)	1951 c.60 s.32(2); 1971 c.78 s.221(1),(3).
(4)	1951 c.60 s.32(3); 1971 c.78 s.221(2),(3).
(5)	1958 c.69 s.13(5) 1986 c.63 Sch.8 para. 4.
262(1)	1971 c.78 s.290(1); 1986 c.31 Sch.2 para. 1(1); 1986 c.44 Sch.9; 1989 c.15 Sch.25 para. 42(3); 1989 c.29 Sch.18.
(2)	1971 c.78 s.290(1); 1986 c.31 Sch.2 para. 1(1).
(3) to (5)	1969 c.48 Sch.4 para. 93(1)(xxxiii), (4)(ii); 1980 c.65 Sch.33 para. 12; 1981 c.38 Sch.3 para. 10(2)(c); 1982 c.16 Sch.2 paras.4, 5(c); 1986 c.44 Sch.7 para. 2(1); 1986 c.63 Sch.7 para. 9; 1989 c.15 Sch.25 para. 1(2).
(6), (7)	1989 c.29 Sch.16 paras. 1(1)(xxii), (xxiv), (xxv), 2(2)(c), (4)(c).
263(1),(2)	1971 c.78 s.222.
(3), (4)	1969 c. 48 Sch.4 para. 93(4); 1982 c.16 Sch.2 para 5, Sch.13 Part III para. 1.
264(1)	1971 c.78 s.223(1).
(2)	1971 c.78 s.223(1)(part), (2)(part); 1969 c.48 Sch.4 para. 89(1).
(3)	1971 c.78 s.223(2)(a).
(4)	1971 c.78 s.223(2)(b); 1984 c.32 Sch.6 para. 9; 1986 c.44; Sch.7 para. 12; 1986 c.31 Sch.4 para. 1; 1989 c.15 Sch.25 para. 42(2).
(5), (6)	1971 c.78 s.223(3).
(7)	1969 c.48 Sch.4 para. 89(2).
(8)	1982 c.16 Sch.2 para. 6(1).
265(1)	1971 c.78 s.224(1); 1986 c.31 Sch. 2 para. 1(2), Sch.6; 1936 c.44 Sch.7 para 2(1); 1989 c.15 Sch.27.
(2)	1986 c.44 Sch.7 para. 2(9); 1989 c.29 Sch.16 para. 3(1)(d).
(3)	1989 c.15 Sch.25 para. 1(9),(10).
(4)	1971 c.78 s.224(2).

Provision	*Derivation*
266(1)	1971 c.78 s.225(1); 1981 c.41 Sch. para. 17.
(2)	1971 c.78 s.225(2).
(3)	1971 c.78 s.225(3).
(4)	1971 c.78 s.225(5).
(5)	1982 c.16 Sch.2 para. 6(2).
267	1971 c.78 s.225(4).
268(1)	1971 c.78 s.226(1).
(2)	1971 c.78 s.226(1).
(3)	1971 c.78 ss.40(3), 226(2).
269	1971 c.78 s.227; R 23.
270	1971 c.78 s.228; R 23; R 24.
271(1), (2)	1971 c.78 s.230(1).
(3)	1971 c.78 s.230(2).
(4)	1971 c.78 s.230(3).
(5)	1971 c.78 s.230(4).
(6)	1971 c.78 s.230(5).
(7)	1971 c.78 s.230(6).
(8)	1971 c.78 s.230(1)(part).
272(1)	1971 c.78 s.230(1),(7); 1984 c.12 Sch.4 para. 53(9).
(2)	1971 c.78 s.230(1),(7); 1984 c.12 Sch.4 para. 53(9).
(3)	1971 c.78 s.230(2),(7); 1984 c.12 Sch.4 para. 53(9).
(4)	1971 c.78 s.230(3),(7); 1984 c.12 Sch.4 para. 53(9).
(5)	1971 c.78 s.230(4),(7); 1984 c.12 Sch.4 para. 53(9).
(6)	1971 c.78 s.230(5),(7); 1984 c.12 Sch.4 para. 53(9).
(7)	1971 c.78 s.230(6), (7); 1984 c.12 Sch.4 para. 53(9).
(8)	1971 c.78 s.230(1)(part),(7); 1984 c.12 Sch.4 para. 53(9).
273(1) to (6)	1971 c.78 s.232(1) to (6).
(7),(8)	1971 c.78 s.232(7); 1984 c.12 s.109, Sch.4 para. 53(10).
274	1971 c.78 ss.231, 230(7); 1984 c.12 Sch. 4 para. 53(9)
275	1971 c.78 s.233.
276(1), (2)	1971 c.78 s.234(1).
(3)	1971 c.78 s.234(2).
277(1), (2)	1971 c.78 s.235(1),(2).
(3),(4)	1971 c.78 s.235(3).
(5)	1971 c.78 s.235(4).
(6)	1971 c.78 s.235(5).
(7)	1971 c.78 s.235(6).

Provision	*Derivation*
(8)	1971 c.78 s.235(7).
278(1) to (5)	1971 c.78 s.236(1) to (5).
(6),(7)	1971 c.78 s.236(6).
(8),(9)	1971 c.78 s.236(7).
(10)	1971 c.78 s.236(8).
(11)	1971 c.78 s.236(2) proviso.
279(1)	1971 c.78 s.237(1).
(2)	1971 c.78 s.237(2).
(3)	1971 c.78 ss.230(7), 237(2); 1984 c.12 Sch.4 para. 53(9).
(4)	1971 c.78 s.237(3).
(5),(6)	1971 c.78 s.237(4).
(7)	1971 c.78 s.237(5); 1986 c.63 Sch.12 Pt.III.
280(1)	1971 c.78 ss.238(1), 230(7); 1981 c.36 Sch.1 para. 7; 1984 c.12 Sch.4 para. 53(9).
(2), (3)	1971 c.78 s.238(2); 1984 c.12, Sch.4 para. 53(9).
(4), (5)	1971 c.78 s.238(3); 1984 c.12 Sch.4 para. 53(9).
(6)	1971 c.78 s.238(4).
(7)	1971 c.78 s.238(5).
(8)	1971 c.78 s.238(6); 1981 c.67 Sch.4 para. 21(9).
281(1),(2)	1971 c.78 s.239(1).
(3)	1971 c.78 s.239(2).
(4)	1971 c.78 s.239(3).
282	1971 c.78 s.240.
283	1971 c.78 s.241.
284(1)	1971 c.78 s.242(1); 1985 c.51 Sch.1 para. 16(3); 1986 c.63 Sch.6 Pt.II para. 4.
(2)	1971 c.78 s.242(2); 1981 c.36 Sch.1 para. 8
(3)	1971 c.78 s.242(3); 1982 c.30 Sch.6 para. 7(b).
(4)	1971 c.78 s.242(4).
285(1)	1971 c.78 s.243(1); 1981 c.41 Sch.para. 18(1).
(2)	1971 c.78 s.243(2); 1981 c.41 Sch.para. 18(2).
(3)	1971 c.78 s.243(3).
(4)	1971 c.78 s.243(4).
(5),(6)	1971 c.78 s.243(5).
286(1)	1972 c.70 Sch.16 paras.51(1),54(6).
(2)	1972 c.70 Sch.16 para. 51(2); 1981 c.41 Sch.para. 28(d)
287(1)	1971 c.78 s.244(1),(6); 1985 c.51 Sch.1 para. 16(4).
(2)	1971 c.78 s.244(2).

Provision	*Derivation*
(3)	1971 c.78 s.244(3) to (7); 1986 c.63 Sch.6 Pt.II para. 5.
(4)	1971 c.78 s.244(1) (part).
(5)	1971 c.78 s.244(1),(3) to (7); 1986 c.63 Sch.6 Pt.II para. 5; R 25(a).
(6)	1971 c.78 s.244(7)(a); 1986 c.63 Sch.6 Pt.II para. 5.
288(1)	1971 c.78 s.245(1).
(2)	1971 c.78 s.245(2).
(3)	1971 c.78 s.245(1)(2); R 25(b).
(4)	1971 c.78 s.245(3)
(5),(6)	1971 c.78 s.245(4).
(7)	1971 c.78 s.245(5).
(8)	1971 c.78 s.245(6).
(9)	1971 c.78 s.245(7).
(10)	1971 c.78 s.245(7); 1972 c.70 Sch.16 para. 46; R 26.
289(1)	1971 c.78 s.246(1); 1981 c.41 Sch. para. 19.
(2)	1971 c.78 s.246(1A); 1981 c.41 Sch. para. 19.
(3)	1971 c.78 s.246(2).
(4)	1971 c.78 s.246(2); 1981 c.54 Sch.5.
(5)	1971 c.78 s.246(3).
(6)	1971 c.78 s.246(4); 1977 c.38 Sch.5 Pt.IV.
(7)	1971 c.78 s.246(5).
290	1971 c.78 s.247; R 8(b).
291	1971 c.78 s.248.
292	1971 c.78 s.249.
293(1) to (3)	1971 c.78 ss.266(7), 268(4); 1984 c.10 s.6(1), (2)
(4)	1984 c.10 s.4(1).
294(1)	1971 c.78 s.266(3); 1981 c.41 Sch. para 20(b).
(2)	1984 c.10 s.3(1).
(3)	1984 c.10 s.3(2).
(4)	1984 c.10 s.3(3).
(5)	1984 c.10 s.3(4).
(6), (7)	1984 c.10 s.3(5).
295(1), (2)	1984 c.10 s.3(6).
(3), (4)	1984 c.10 s.3(7).
(5),(6)	1984 c.10 s.3(8).
296(1)	1971 c.78 s.266(1); 1985 c.51 Sch.1 para. 16(6).
(2)	1971 c.78 s.266(2); 1981 c.36 Sch.1 para. 9; 1981 c.41 Sch. para. 20(a).

Provision	*Derivation*
(3), (4)	1971 c.78 s.266(5).
(5)	1971 c.78 s.266(6).
297(1), (2)	1971 c.78 s.267(1).
(3)	1971 c.78 s.267(2).
(4)	1971 c.78 s.267(3).
298	1971 c.78 s.268.
299(1) to (5)	1984 c.10 s.1(1) to (5).
(6)	1984 c.10 s.1(7).
(7)	1984 c.10 s.1(6)(part).
300(1)	1984 c.10 s.2(1).
(2)	1984 c.10. s.2(2).
(3), (4)	1984 c.10 s.2(3).
(5)	1984 c.10 s.2(4).
(6), (7)	1984 c.10 s.2(5).
301(1) to (4)	1984 c.10 s.5(1) to (4).
(5)	1984 c.10 s.5(6).
302(1), (2)	1946 c.35 ss.1(2), 7(6).
(3)	1946 c.35 s.2(1) to (3).
(4)	1946 c.35 s.4(1).
(5)	Drafting
(6)	1946 c.35 ss.1(2), (3), (5), 2(1), 4(1), 7(1), (6); 1989 c.43 Sch 2 para. 11.
(7)	1946 c.35 s.7(3).
(8)	1946 c.35 s.7(6).
303 (1)	1980 c.65 s.87(1).
(2)	1980 c.65 s.87(2)(a).
(3)	1980 c.65 s.87(3).
(4)	1980 c.65 s.87(4).
(5)	1980 c.65 s.87(6).
304	1971 c.78 s.253.
305	1971 c.78 s.254.
306(1)	1971 c.78 s.255(1); 1980 c.66 Sch.24 para. 20(g)
(2)	1971 c.78 s.255(2); 1985 c.51 Sch.1 para. 16(5); R 27(a) and (b).
(3)	1971 c.78 s.255(3).
(4)	1971 c.78 s.255(4).
(5)	1971 c.78 s.255(5).
307	1971 c.78 s.256; 1972 c.70 s. 179(3), Sch.30; 1980 c.65 Sch.15 para. 22.

Provision	Derivation
308(1),(2)	1971 c.78 s.257(1),(2).
(3) to (6)	1971 c.78 s.257(3) to (6).
309(1) to (5)	1971 c.78 s.258(1) to (5).
(6),(7)	1971 c.78 s.258(6).
310	1971 c.78 s.259.
311	1971 c.78 s.260.
312(1)	1971 c.78 s.261(1).
(2)	1971 c.78 s.261(4).
313	1971 c.78 s.262; 1980 c.65 s.87(7).
314	1971 c.78 s.263(1); 1972 c. 70 Sch. 29 Pt. I para 3(b).
315(1)	1971 c.78 s.264(1).
(2)	1971 c.78 s.264(2)
(3)	1971 c.78 s.264(1) to (3).
(4)	1971 c.78 s.264(4); 1987 c.3 Sch.1 para. 19.
(5)	1971 c.78 s.264(4).
316(1)	1971 c.78 s.270(1).
(2)	1971 c.78 s.270(2); 1981 c.41 Sch. para. 21.
(3)	1971 c.78 s.270 (3).
(4)	1971 c.78 s.272.
(5)	1980 c.65 s.149(5); 1988 c.50 s.67(5).
317(1), (2)	1971 c.78 s.273(1); 1974 S.I./692 art.2(1), 5(3), Sch.1 Pt.I; 1987 c.3 s.1, Sch.1 para. 19.
(3)	1971 c.78 s.273(2).
318(1)	1971 c.78 s.274(1); 1981 c.41 Sch. para. 23; 1981 c.67 Sch.4 para. 1.
(2)	1971 c.78 s.274(2).
(3)	1971 c.78 s.274(3).
(4)	1971 c.78 s.274(4).
(5)	1971 c.78 s.274(4).
(6)	1971 c.78 s.274(5).
319(1)	1971 c.78 s.269(1), (3); 1980 c.65 Sch.15 para. 23(1); 1981 c.36 s.18; 1984 c.10 s.6(3).
(2)	1971 c.78 s.269(2); 1972 c.70 s. 179(3); 1982 c.30 s.36(b).
(3)	1971 c.78 s.269(3); 1972 c.70 s. 179(3).
(4)	1971 c.78 s.269(1), (3).
(5)	1971 c.78 s.269(4).
320(1)	1971 c.78 s.282(1).
(2)	1971 c.78 s.282(2); 1986 c.63 Sch.11 para. 8(1).
321(1)	1982 c.21 s.1(5).

Provision	*Derivation*
(2)	1982 c.21 s.1(1).
(3)	1982 c.21 s.1(2),(3).
(4)	1982 c.21 s.1(4).
322	1971 c.78 s.282A; 1986 c.63 Sch.11 para. 9(1).
323	1971 c.78 s.282B; 1986 c.63 Sch.11 para. 10.
324(1)	1971 c.78 s.280(1); 1981 c.41 Sch.para. 25; 1985 c.51 Sch.1 para. 16(7).
(2)	1971 c.78 s.280(4).
(3)	1971 c.78 s.280(4A); 1982 c.30 s.36(c).
(4)	1971 c.78 s.280(5).
(5)	1971 c.78 s.280(6).
(6)	1971 c.78 s.280(7).
(7)	1971 c.78 s.280(8).
(8)	1971 c.78 s.280(9).
(9)	1971 c.78 s.280(10); 1985 c.51 Sch.2 para. 1(16).
325(1)	1971 c.78 s.281(1)
(2)	1971 c.78 s.281(2); 1982 c.48 s.46.
(3) to (5)	1971 c.78 s.281(3).
(6)	1971 c.78 s.281(4).
(7)	1971 c.78 s.281(5).
(8)	1971 c.78 s.281(6)(a).
(9)	1971 c.78 s.281(6)(b).
326(1)	1971 c.78 s.278(1).
(2)	1971 c.78 s.278(2).
(3)	1971 c.78 s.278(4).
(4)	1971 c.78 s.278(5).
327(1)	1971 c.78 s.279(1).
(2)	1971 c.78 s.279(2)(a).
(3)	1971 c.78 s.279(2)(b).
(4)	1971 c.78 s.279(3).
(5)	1971 c.78 ss.279(4); 258(5).
328(1)	1971 c.78 s.275(1).
(2)	1971 c.78 s.275(1).
329	1971 c.78 s.283.
330(1)	1971 c.78 s.284(1); 1977 c.29 s.3(1),(2); 1981 c.41 Sch. para. 26.
(2)	1971 c.78 s.284(1A); 1977 c.29 s.3(1),(3).
(3)	1971 c.78 s.284(1)(part); 1977 c.29 s.3(1),(2); 1981 c.41 Sch. para. 26.

Provision	*Derivation*
(4)	1971 c.78 s.284(2); 1977 c.29 s.3(4); 1982 c.48 ss.38, 46.
(5)	1971 c.78 s.284(3); 1977 c.29 s.3(5); 1982 c.48 s.74.
331	1971 c.78 s.285.
332	1971 c.78 s.286.
333(1)	1971 c.78 s.287(1).
(2), (3)	1971 c.78 s.287(2).
(4)	1971 c.78 s.287(4); 1985 c.51 s.103(1); 1986 c.63 Sch.6 Pt.II para. 6(a), Sch.9 para. 5(2)(a), Sch.12 Pt.III.
(5)	1971 c.78 s.287(5); 1985 c.51 s.103(2); 1986 c.63 Sch.6 Pt.II para. 6(b), Sch.9 para. 5(2)(b), Sch.12 Pt.III.
(6)	1971 c.78 s.287(6).
(7)	1971 c.78 s.287(3).
334	1971 c.78 s.288.
335	1971 c.78 s.289.
336(1)	1971 c.78 ss. 264(1A), 290(1); 1972 c.70 s. 179(3), Sch.30; 1977 S.I./293 art.4(4); 1980 c.65 Sch.32 para. 18(5); 1980 c.66 Sch.24 para. 20(h); 1981 c.36 s.1(2), Sch.1 para. 11; 1985 c.51 Sch.1 para. 16(8), Sch.17; 1986 c.63 Sch.6 Pt.II para. 7, Sch.7 Pt.I para. 7, Sch.12 Pt.III; 1988 c.4 Sch.3 para. 25; 1989 c.15 Sch.25 paras.1(11)(ii), 42(3), 1990 SI/776 Sch.3 para. 15; R 28.
(2), (3)	1971 c.78 s.290(2).
(4)	1971 c.78 s.290(3).
(5)	1971 c.78 s.290(4).
(6)	1971 c.78 s.290(5)(part).
(7)	1971 c.78 s.290(6); 1989 c. 34 s.2.
(8)	1971 c.78 s.290(7).
(9)	1971 c.78 s.290(8).
(10)	1971 c.78 ss.40(4) 181(5), 182(5), 280(10)(c), 284(4); 1988 c.4 Sch.3 paras. 11,19,20,23,24,25.
337	—
Sch. 1 para. 1	1972 c.70 Sch. 16 paras. 32, 32A; 1980 c.65 s.86(4), Sch. 34 Pt X; 1981 c.36 s.2(1), Sch para 12.
para. 2	1972 c.70 s.183(1).
para. 3	1972 c.70 Sch. 16 para. 15; 1980 c.65 s.86(1), Sch. 34 Pt X.
para. 4	1972 c.70 Sch. 16 para. 16.
para. 5(1)	1972 c.70 Sch. 16 para. 17; 1980 c.66 Sch. 24 para. 22; 1986 c.63 Sch. 11 para. 2(2).
(2),(3)	1980 c.65 s.150.
para. 6	1972 c.70 Sch. 16 para. 18.
para. 7	1972 c.70 Sch. 16 para. 19; 1980 c.65 s.86(2),(3); 1986 c.63 Sch. 11 para. 23(3); R 29.

Provision	*Derivation*
para. 8	1972 c.70 Sch. 16 para. 20; 1986 SI/452.
para. 9(1)	1971 c.78 s.24A(6); 1986 c.63 s.25(1).
(2)	1971 c.78 Sch.8A para. 5(6); 1986 c.63 s.25(2).
(3)	1971 c.78 Sch.8A para. 6(6); 1986 c.63 s.25(2).
para. 10	1972 c.70 Sch. 16 para. 23.
para. 11	1972 c.70 Sch. 16 para. 24; 1981 c.36 s.2(4)(c); 1981 c.41 Sch. para. 28(a).
para. 12	1972 c.70 Sch. 16 para. 29; 1978 c.30 s.17(2)(a); 1981 c.41 Sch. para. 28(b).
para. 13	1971 c.78 s.60(1A); 1972 c.70 Sch. 16 para. 27; 1980 c.65 Sch.15 para 13; R 2.
para. 14	1971 c.78 ss.61A(3),(7), 65(4), 109A; 1972 c.70 Sch. 16 para. 25 (part); 1980 c.65 Sch. 34 Pt X; 1986 c.63 s.46.
para. 15	1972 c.70 Sch. 16 para. 26.
para. 16	1972 c.70 Sch. 16 paras. 34, 38.
para. 17	1972 c.70 Sch. 16 para. 35.
para. 18	1972 c.70 Sch. 16 para. 36.
para. 19	1972 c.70 Sch. 16 para. 54(1) to (5); 1985 c.51 s.3(5), Sch. 3 para. 4.
para. 20	1972 c.70 Sch. 16 paras. 45,47 (part); 1971 c.78 s.52(4).
para. 21	1972 c.70 Sch. 16 para. 52.
Sch. 2 Pt.I para. 1	1985 c.51 Sch. 1 para. 18 (part), drafting.
para. 2	1985 c.51 Sch. 1 para. 19; 1971 c.78 Sch. 4 para. 5.
para. 3(1)	1971 c.78 Sch.23 Pt.I; 1985 c.51 Sch. 1 para. 20(1), (2); 1986 c.63 Sch. 11 para. 27(1), (2).
(2)	1985 c.51 Sch. 1 para. 20(2A); 1986 c.63 Sch. 11 para. 27(1), (3).
(3)	1985 c.51 Sch. 1 para. 20(3A); 1986 c.63 Sch. 11 para. 27(1), (4) (part).
(4)	1985 c.51 Sch. 1 para. 20(4).
(5)	R 30.
para. 4(1),(2)	1985 c.51 Sch. 1 para. 21(1)
(3)	1985 c.51 Sch. 1 para. 21(2)
para. 5	1985 c.51 Sch. 1 para. 22
para. 6	1985 c.51 Sch. 1 para. 23(3)
Sch. 2 Pt. II, para. 1	1971 c.78 Sch.4 para. 5(1); 1985 c.51 Sch. 1 para. 18.
para. 2	1985 c.51 Sch. 1 para. 19
para. 3(1)	1971 c. 78 Sch. 4 para. 7, Sch. 23 Pt.I; 1985 c.51 Sch. 1 para. 20(1), (2); 1986 c.63 Sch. 11 para. 27(1), (2)

Provision	Derivation
(2)	1971 c.78 Sch. 4 para. 2; 1972 c.42 Sch. 1; 1985 c.51 Sch.1 para. 20(2).
(3)	1971 c.78 Sch. 4 para. 5(1); 1985 c.51 Sch. 1 para. 20, drafting.
(4)	1981 c.51 Sch. 1 para. 20(4).
(5)	R 30.
para. 4(1)	1971 c.78 Sch. 4 para. 8(3); 1972 c.42 Sch. 1
(2)	1971 c.78 Sch. 4 para. 8(5); 1972 c.42 Sch. 1
para. 5(1)	1971 c.78 Sch. 4 paras. 5(3), 8(1); 1972 c.42 Sch. 1
(2)	1971 c.78 Sch. 4 para. 9(1)(b); 1972 c.42 Sch. 1
(3)	1971 c.78 Sch. 4 para. 9(3); 1972 c.42 Sch. 1
para. 6	1971 c.78 Sch. 4 para. 10; 1972 c.42 Sch. 1
para. 7(1)	1971 c.78 Sch. 4 para. 11(1); 1972 c.42 Sch. 1; 1972 c.70 Sch. 30
(2)	1971 c.78 Sch. 4 para. 11(2); 1972 c.42 Sch. 1; 1980 c.65 Sch. 14 para. 13(1)
(3)	1971 c.78 Sch. 4 para. 11(3); 1972 c.42 Sch. 1; 1980 c.65 Sch. 14 para. 13(1)
(4),(5)	1971 c.78 Sch. 4 para. 11(4),(5); 1972 c.42 Sch. 1
para. 8(1)	1971 c.78 Sch. 4 para. 12(1); 1972 c.42 Sch. 1
(2)	1971 c.78 Sch. 4 para. 12(2)(part); 1972 c.42 Sch. 1; 1980 c.65 Sch. 14 para. 13(1)
(3)	1971 c.78 Sch. 4 para. 12(3); 1972 c.42 Sch. 1; 1980 c.65 Sch. 14 para. 13(1)
para. 9(1)	1971 c.78 s.13(1); 1972 c.70 s.272(2)
(2)	1971 c.78 s.13(2)
(3)	1971 c.78 s.13(3); 1980 c.65 Sch. 14 para. 9
para. 10	1971 c.78 s.14 Sch.4 para. 14; 1980 c.65 Sch. 14 para. 10.
para. 11(1)	1971 c.78 Sch. 4 para. 14(2); 1972 c.42 Sch. 1; 1972 c.70 Sch. 30
(2)	1971 c.78 Sch. 4 para. 14(3); 1972 c.42 Sch. 1
para. 12(1),(2)	1971 c.78 s.15(1),(2)
(3)	1985 c.51 Sch. 1 para. 20(3); 1986 c.63 Sch. 11 para. 27(4)
(4)	1971 c.78 s.15(3), Sch. 4 para. 16(1); 1972 c.42 s.3(3), Sch. 1; 1972 c.70 Sch. 30.
para. 13(1)	1972 c.70 Sch. 16 para. 10(1); 1986 c.63 Sch. 12 Pt. III
(2)	1972 c.70 Sch. 16 para. 10(2) (as it applies in London); 1986 c.63 Sch. 12 Pt. III
(3)	1972 c.70 Sch. 16 para. 14(3)
(4),(5)	1972 c.70 Sch. 16 para. 14(5),(6)
para. 14	1972 c.70 Sch. 16 para. 11(1) (as it applies in London).

Provision	*Derivation*
para. 15	1972 c.70 Sch. 16 para. 12; 1986 c.63 Sch. 12 Pt. III
para. 16	1972 c.70 Sch. 16 para. 13; R 6.
para. 17(1),(2)	1985 c.51 Sch. 1 para. 21(1)
(3)	1985 c.51 Sch. 1 para. 21(2)
para. 18	1985 c.51 Sch. 1 para. 22
Sch. 2 Pt. III, para. 1	Drafting
para. 2	1971 c.78 Sch. 7 para. 2; 1980 c.66 Sch. 24 para. 20(j)
para. 3	1971 c.78 Sch. 4 para 5, Sch. 7 para. 3; 1980 c.65 Sch. 14 para. 14
para. 4	1971 c.78 Sch. 7 para. 4.
para. 5	1971 c.78 Sch. 7 para. 5
para. 6	1971 c.78 Sch. 7 para. 5A; 1980 c.65 Sch. 14 para. 15(1)
para. 7	1971 c.78 Sch. 7 para. 5B; 1980 c.65 Sch. 14 para. 15(1)
para. 8	1971 c.78 Sch. 7 para. 5C; 1980 c.65 Sch. 14 para. 15(1)
para. 9	1971 c.78 Sch. 7 para. 6
para. 10	1971 c.78 Sch. 7 para. 7; 1980 c.65 Sch. 14 para. 15(2); 1985 c.51 Sch. 17
Sch. 3 para. 1	1971 c.78 Sch. 8 para. 1 (part)
para. 2	1971 c.78 Sch. 8 para. 2.
para. 3	1971 c.78 Sch. 8 para. 3 (part)
para. 4 to 8	1971 c.78 Sch. 8 paras. 4 to 8.
para. 9	1971 c.78 Sch. 8 para. 10.
para. 10(1)	1971 c.78 Sch. 8 para. 9.
(2)	1971 c.78 Sch. 8 paras. 1 (part), 3 (part).
paras. 11 to 13	1971 c.78 Sch. 8 paras. 11 to 13.
para. 14(1)	1971 c.78 s.180(3).
(2)	1971 c.78 s.278(2), (3).
Sch. 4 paras. 1 to 3	1971 c.78 s.23(2) to (4).
para. 4	1971 c.78 s.23(7).
Sch. 5 para. 1	1971 c.78 s.44A; 1981 c.36 s.7; 1982 SI/86.
para. 2	1971 c.78 s.30A(1) to (8), (19) (part); 1981 c.36 s.5.
para. 3	1971 c.78 s.30A(9) to (12), (19); 1981 c.36 s.5.
para. 4	1971 c.78 s.30A(13) to (16), (19); 1981 c.36 s.5.
para. 5	1971 c.78 s.30A(17); 1981 c.36 s.5.
para. 6	1971 c.78 s.30A(18); 1981 c.36 s.5.
para. 7	1971 c.78 s.45(6); 1981 c.36 s.8.
para. 8	1971 c.78 s.45(7); 1981 c.36 s.8.

Provision	*Derivation*
Sch. 6 para. 1	1971 c.78 Sch. 9 para. 1.
para. 2	1971 c.78 Sch. 9 para. 2; 1981 c.41 Sch. para. 27.
para. 3	1971 c.78 Sch. 9 para. 3.
para. 4	1971 c.78 Sch. 9 para. 3A; 1986 c.63 Sch. 11 para. 11.
para. 5	1971 c.78 Sch. 9 para. 4.
para. 6	1971 c.78 Sch. 9 para. 5; 1972 c.70 s.272(2); 1986 c.63 Sch. 11 paras. 8(2), 9(2), 12.
para. 7	1971 c.78 Sch.9 para. 6.
para. 8	1971 c.78 Sch. 9 para. 7.
Sch. 7 para. 1	1971 c.78 Sch.8A para. 1; 1986 c.63 s.25(2).
para. 2	1971 c.78 Sch.8A para. 2(2); 1986 c.63 s.25(2).
para. 3,4	1971 c.78 Sch.8A paras. 3,4; 1986 c.63 s.25(2).
para. 5	1971 c.78 Sch.8A para. 5(1) to (5); 1986 c.63 s.25(2).
para. 6	1971 c.78 Sch.8A para. 6(1) to (5); 1986 c.63 s.25(2).
paras. 7 to 12	1971 c.78 Sch.8A paras. 7 to 12; 1986 c.63 s.25(2).
para. 13(1),(2)	1971 c.78 Sch.8A para. 13(1),(2); 1986 c.63 s.25(2); R 31.
(3)	1971 c.78 Sch.8A para. 13(3); 1978 c.30 Sch.1; 1986 c.63 s.25(2).
(4)	1971 c.78 Sch.8A para. 13(4); 1986 c.63 s.25(2).
Sch. 8 para. 1	1971 c.78 s.47(2) to (4),(6).
para. 2	1971 c.78 s.48(3) to (5).
para. 3.	1971 c.78 s.48(6),(7).
para. 4.	1971 c.78 s.49(1),(2),(7).
para. 5	1971 c.78 s.49(3) to (6); 1972 c.70 s.272(2).
para. 6.	1971 c.78 Sch.10 para. 1.
para. 7.	1971 c.78 Sch.10 para. 2.
Sch. 9 para. 1	1971 c.78 s.51(1) to (1C),(2) to (9); 1981 c.36 s.9.
para. 2	1971 c.78 s.51(1D) to (1H); 1981 c.36 s.9.
para. 3	1971 c.78 s.51A(1) to (7); 1981 c.36 s.10.
para. 4	1971 c.78 s.51A(8) to (11); 1981 c.36 s.10.
para. 5	1971 c.78 s.51B(1) to (4); 1981 c.36 s.10.
para. 6	1971 c.78 s.51B(5); 1981 c.36 s.10.
para. 7	1971 c.78 s.51C; 1981 c.36 s.10.
para. 8	1971 c.78 s.51D; 1981 c.36 s.10.
para. 9	1971 c.78 s.51E; 1981 c.36 s.10.
para. 10	1971 c.78 s.51F; 1981 c.36 s.10.
para. 11	1971 c.78 s.276(1) to (4); 1974 c.7 Sch. 6 para. 25(12), Sch. 8; 1981 c.36 Sch. 1 para. 10; R 9.
Sch. 10	1971 c.78 Sch. 18.

Provision	*Derivation*
Sch. 11 para. 1	1971 c.78 s.178A; 1981 c.36 s.16; 1981 c.36 Sch. 1 paras. 4 to 6.
para. 2	1971 c.78 s.164A(1); 1981 c.36 s.13.
para. 3	1971 c.78 s.170B(1); 1981 c.36 s.15.
para. 4	1971 c.78 s.164A(2)(b) to (4); 1981 c.36 s.13; 1982 SI/86.
para. 5	1971 c.78 s.170B(2); 1981 c.36 s.15.
para. 6	1971 c.78 s.170B(3); 1981 c.36 s.15.
para. 7	1971 c.78 s.170B(4); 1981 c.36 s.15.
para. 8	1971 c.78 s.170B(5); 1981 c.36 s.15.
para. 9	1971 c.78 s.170B(6); 1981 c.36 s.15.
para. 10	1971 c.78 s.178C(1),(2); 1981 c.36 s.16.
para. 11	1971 c.78 s.178C(3); 1981 c.36 s.16.
para. 12	1971 c.78 s.178B; 1981 c.36 s.16.
para. 13	1971 c.78 s.179(1) (part); 1981 c.36 s.17.
Sch. 12 para. 1	1971 c.78 s.135.
para. 2	1971 c.78 s.136.
para. 3	1971 c.78 s.137.
para. 4	1971 c.78 s.138, Sch. 15 para. 29 (part).
para. 5	1971 c.78 Sch. 15 paras. 2 to 5.
para. 6	1971 c.78 Sch. 15 para. 1.
para. 7	1971 c.78 Sch. 15 paras. 6 to 10.
para. 8	1971 c.78 Sch. 15 paras. 11 to 16.
para. 9	1971 c.78 Sch. 15 paras. 17 to 22.
para. 10	1971 c.78 Sch. 15 paras. 23 to 25.
para. 11	1971 c.78 Sch. 15 paras. 26 to 28, 29 (part).
para. 12	1971 c.78 s.139.
para. 13	1971 c.78 ss.140, 161.
para. 14	1971 c.78 s.141.
para. 15	1971 c.78 Sch. 16.
para. 16	1971 c.78 s.142.
para. 17	1971 c.78 Sch. 17.
para. 18	1971 c.78 s.143.
para. 19	1971 c.78 s.144.
para. 20	1971 c.78 s.145.
Sch. 13 para. 1	1971 c.78 s.192(1)(a); 1984 c.12 Sch.4 para. 53(6); 1987 c.3 Sch.1 para. 19.
Notes (1)	1973 c.26 s.68(1); R 32(a).
(2)	1973 c.26 s.68(4); R 32(a).

Provision	Derivation
(3)	1973 c.26 s.68(5) (part).
(4)	1973 c.26 s.68(7) (part).
(5)	1971 c.78 s.192(2).
(6)	1973 c.26 s.71(2).
(7)	1971 c.78 Sch. 4 para. 5; 1973 c.26 s.68(8); 1985 c.51, Sch. 1 para. 20(2).
para. 2	1971 c.78 s.192(1)(b).
Notes (1)	1973 c.26 s.68(2), (9); R 32(b).
(2)	1973 c.26 s.68(4) (part); R 32(b).
(3)	1973 c.26 s.68(5) (part)(9).
(4)	1973 c.26 s.68(7) (part).
(5)	1973 c.26 s.68(8).
para. 3	1971 c.78 s.192(1)(bb); 1985 c.51 Sch.1 para. 16(1).
Notes (1)	1985 c.51 Sch.1 para. 17(1) (part); R 32(c).
(2)	1985 c.51 Sch.1 para. 17(2) (part).
(3)	1985 c.51 Sch.1 para. 17(3) (part).
(4)	1985 c.51 Sch.1 para. 17(5) (part).
para. 4	1971 c.78 s.192(1)(bc); 1985 c.51 Sch.1 para. 16(1).
Notes (1)	1985 c.51 Sch.1 para. 17(1) (part); R 32(c).
(2)	1985 c.51 Sch.1 para. 17(2) (part).
(3)	1985 c.51 Sch.1 para. 17(3) (part).
(4)	1985 c.51 Sch.1 para. 17(5) (part).
para. 5	1973 c.26 s.71(1)(a).
para. 6	1973 c.26 s.71(1)(b).
para. 7	1973 c.26 s.72(1)(a); 1981 c.64 Sch.12 para. 11.
Note	1973 c.26 s.72(2).
para. 8	1973 c.26 s.72(1)(b); 1981 c.64 Sch.12 para. 11.
para. 9	1980 c.65 s.147(1).
Note	1980 c.65 s.147(2).
para. 10	1973 c.26 s.73(1)(a); 1985 c.71 Sch.2 para. 24(8).
para. 11	1973 c.26 s.73(1)(b); 1985 c.71 Sch.2 para. 24(8).
para. 12	1971 c.78 s.192(1)(ha); 1989 c.42 Sch.11 para. 20.
para. 13	1971 c.78 s.192(1)(c).
para. 14	1971 c.78 s.192(1)(d); 1980 c.66 Sch.24 para. 20.
Notes (1)	1973 c.26 s.69(1)(a); 1980 c.66 Sch.24 para. 23.
(2)	1973 c.26 s.69(2).
(3)	1973 c.26 s.74(1); 1980 c.66 Sch.24 para. 23.
para. 15	1971 c.78 s.192(1)(e).

Provision	*Derivation*
para. 16	1971 c.78 s.192(1)(f).
para. 17	1973 c.26 s.74(2)(a); 1980 c.66 Sch.24 para. 23.
para. 18	1973 c.26 s.74(2)(b).
para. 19	1973 c.26 s.76(1); 1980 c.66 Sch.24 para. 23.
Note	1973 c.26 s.76(4).
para. 20	1971 c.78 s.192(1)(h); 1985 c.71 Sch.2 para. 22.
para. 21	1971 c.78 s.192(1)(i).
para. 22	1971 c.78 s.192(1)(g), (j); 1973 c.26 s.75(1),(2).
Notes (1)	1973 c.26 s.70(1); 1978 c.30 s.17(2)(a).
(2)	1973 c.26 s.70(2).
Sch. 14 para 1	1971 c.78 Sch.20 para 1; 1981 c.69 Sch.16 para. 1; 1985 c.51 Sch.14 para. 48.
para 2	1971 c.78 Sch.20 para. 2.
para 3	1971 c.78 Sch.20 para. 3.
para 4	1971 c.78 Sch.20 para. 3A; 1981 c.69 Sch.16 paras. 2,10.
para 5	1971 c.78 Sch.20 para. 4.
para 6	1971 c.78 Sch.20 para 5.
para 7	1971 c.78 Sch.20 para. 6; 1981 c.69 Sch.16 paras. 3, 10; R 33.
para 8	1971 c.78 Sch.20 para. 7, 1981 c.69 Sch.16 paras. 4,10.
Sch. 15 para. 1	Drafting
para 2	1946 c.35 s.2(4),(5).
para. 3	1946 c.35 s.2(6).
para. 4	1946 c.35 s.2(7) (part).
para. 5	1946 c.35 s.2(2),(3).
para. 6	1946 c.35 s.2(8) (part), (7) (part).
para. 7	1946 c.35 s.2(8) (part).
para. 8	1946 c.35 s.2(9) (part).
para. 9	1946 c.35 s.2(9) proviso.
para. 10	1946 c.35 s.2(10).
para. 11	1946 c.35 s.2(11).
para. 12	1946 c.35 s.2(12).
para. 13	1946 c.35 s.3(1),(7).

Provision	*Derivation*
para. 14	1946 c.35 s.5.
para. 15	1946 c.35 s.6.
para. 16	Drafting.
Sch. 16	1971 c.78 Sch. 21.
Sch. 17	1971 c.78 Sch. 22; 1980 c.66 Sch.24 para. 20(k),(l),(m); 1985 c.51 Sch.4 para. 50.

PRINTED IN THE UNITED KINGDOM BY PAUL FREEMAN
Controller and Chief Executive of Her Majesty's Stationery Office
and Queen's Printer of Acts of Parliament